AF149336

THE MORMON HANDCART MIGRATION

THE MORMON
HANDCART
MIGRATION

"Tounge nor pen can never tell the sorrow"

CANDY MOULTON

UNIVERSITY OF OKLAHOMA PRESS : NORMAN

Publication of this book is made possible through
the generosity of Edith Kinney Gaylord.

LIBRARY OF CONGRESS CATALOGING-IN-PUBLICATION DATA

Names: Moulton, Candy Vyvey, 1955– author.
Title: The Mormon handcart migration : "tounge nor pen can never tell the sorrow" /
    Candy Moulton.
Description: Norman : University of Oklahoma Press, [2019] | Includes bibliographical
    references and index.
Identifiers: LCCN 2018040073 | ISBN 978-0-8061-6261-4 (hardcover : alk. paper)
Subjects: LCSH: Mormon handcart companies. | Mormon pioneers. | James G. Willie
    Emigrating Company. | Edward Martin Emigrating Company. | Church of Jesus Christ
    of Latter-day Saints—History—19th century. | Mormon Church—History—
    19th century.
Classification: LCC BX8611 .M68 2019 | DDC 289.3/7809034—dc23
LC record available at https://lccn.loc.gov/2018040073

The paper in this book meets the guidelines for permanence and durability of the Committee
on Production Guidelines for Book Longevity of the Council on Library Resources, Inc. ∞

Copyright © 2019 by Candy Moulton. Published by the University of Oklahoma Press, Norman,
Publishing Division of the University. Manufactured in the U.S.A.

All rights reserved. No part of this publication may be reproduced, stored in a retrieval system,
or transmitted, in any form or by any means, electronic, mechanical, photocopying, recording,
or otherwise—except as permitted under Section 107 or 108 of the United States Copyright
Act—without the prior written permission of the University of Oklahoma Press. To request
permission to reproduce selections from this book, write to Permissions, University of Oklahoma Press, 2800 Venture Drive, Norman, OK 73069, or email rights.oupress@ou.edu.

1 2 3 4 5 6 7 8 9 10

To my granddaughters,
Macy Marie Shockley and Aspen Grace Shockley

CONTENTS

ILLUSTRATIONS

PREFACE

Sarah Elizabeth Moulton, eldest child of Thomas Moulton, left Northamptonshire, England, in April 1856 with her father, stepmother, and seven brothers and sisters to immigrate to America. These converts to the Church of Jesus Christ of Latter-day Saints had made the decision to follow their faith to the place that they called Zion: Great Salt Lake City. The Moultons were poor people. With such a large family, they had not been able to join earlier groups of converts that traveled by ship to America and then took wagons across the plains. The year of their exodus, however, was seminal for the church in its movement of people. Instead of organizing large wagon trains, church president Brigham Young had decreed that the travelers would haul their own possessions, pushing and pulling two-wheeled carts across the plains. This use of handcarts uniquely defined the Mormon migration.

Thousands had already forged a well-defined trail from Winter Quarters to Great Salt Lake by 1856, when the first handcart pioneers set off across the plains. The earliest Mormon parties traveling to what would become Utah went overland in 1846 from Nauvoo, Illinois, to the Missouri River, where they established their Winter Quarters on the west bank, at the location of present-day Florence, Nebraska. They pushed on into the West the following year, ultimately arriving in the Great Salt Lake Valley by July 24, 1847. They called the community that they built Great Salt Lake City, Deseret, or Zion; I use those terms, as well as Utah Territory or Utah, for the same geographical region. Although Wyoming had not yet achieved territorial status, let alone statehood, when this handcart migration occurred, I use that state name as well to make it easier for readers to understand the geography of the trail. I include ages for travelers throughout when possible, but sometimes there are discrepancies: some accounts give one age while the exceptional Mormon Pioneer Overland Trail database for the Mormon travelers has a different age. In most cases, I use the trails database information. In quoting from overland journals, diaries, letters, and other documents, I have retained most of the original spelling and punctuation, inserting editorial changes only when they seemed necessary for understanding by modern readers. Emphasis by underscoring or italics in quoted text comes from the original document, as do a few instances of words crossed out.

The handcart treks began in the spring of 1856 when Edmund Ellsworth and members of the First Company crossed the Atlantic on the *Enoch Train* and *Samuel Curling*, which sailed from Liverpool on March 23 and April 19, respectively. Daniel D. McArthur's Second Company also sailed on April 19, packed onto the *Samuel Curling* along with the members of the Third Company, Welsh emigrants led by Edward Bunker. The Moultons were part of the Fourth Company, led by James Grey Willie, which crossed the sea on the ship *Thornton*.

Sarah Elizabeth Moulton did not realize when she wrote a letter from Florence in August 1856 that other people would be traveling behind them on the trail. But a Fifth Company also set out in 1856, led by Captain Edward Martin. A number of Mormon wagon companies traveled the trail in 1856 too. The late-starting groups found themselves in desperate situations in October and November as winter snow and cold weather blanketed the trail. Five more handcart companies would travel the plains from 1857 to 1860.

I am indebted to many people for support of this book, most particularly Will Bagley, Terry Del Bene, Bob Clark, Byron Price, and Chuck Rankin, who encouraged me to undertake the journey on paper, as I had already done in a wagon and with a handcart. Chuck particularly had a role in shaping this manuscript, and I sincerely thank him.

I owe special thanks to Donny Marincic and my dear, dear friend, wagonmaster Ben Kern for sharing rough, cold, hot, windy, rainy wagon rides. If Ben had not taken me on the trail, I never would have known the story to write.

I am particularly grateful to the historians who have recorded this story through the years and most of all to the people who traveled the trail and left behind their journals, letters, diaries, reminiscences, and autobiographies. I could not have prepared the manuscript without the incredible collections of the Church History Library and Archives in Salt Lake City, Utah, and sources available through Brigham Young University in Provo, Utah. I am indebted to the early readers of this manuscript, who provided valuable comments that helped me improve the text.

I have been fortunate in my years of writing to travel all of the major overland emigration trails by wagon train. I was introduced to a slower mode of travel in 1990 when I rode a wagon on the Bridger Trail across Wyoming. Subsequently I have ridden in wagons and walked many miles along the Oregon Trail (1993), Mormon Pioneer National Historic Trail (1997), California Trail (1999), Bozeman Trail (2001), Cherokee

Trail South Branch (2002 and 2003), and Overland Trail (2006 and 2007). These many, many days on the trail, living in a tent, sleeping on the ground or in a wagon, dealing with all kinds of weather conditions and the temperaments of diverse travelers, gave me an understanding and appreciation for the journey of the Mormon handcart pioneers of 1856–60. I know how physically demanding this form of travel can be. Even with all my experience, however, I simply cannot fathom the challenges that my children's ancestors endured.

In 1997 I had the opportunity to travel the Mormon Trail from Winter Quarters to Salt Lake City as part of the Mormon Trail Sesquicentennial Wagon Train. I was reporting on the trail and the wagon train for the *Casper Star-Tribune*. To separate myself from the participants I wore jeans and a cowboy hat rather than a prairie dress and bonnet. I walked many miles, some of them in company with the travelers pushing and pulling handcarts, and rode in the wagon for even more miles.

I am not a member of the Church of Jesus Christ of Latter-day Saints, so I expected that I could easily travel with the wagon train, write the history, and record the adventures of the people during the commemorative event while remaining emotionally unattached to the story. However, the family of my husband, Steve, had traveled the trail in 1856 (his great-grandfather, Charles, was the youngest child of Thomas and Sarah Moulton, born on the *Thornton* after they sailed from Liverpool). That made the journey as personal for me as it was for everyone else involved, including Steve and our children, Shawn and Erin Marie, who had the opportunity to spend a few days on the trail that summer too. This book is for them, for the very extended Moulton family, and especially for my granddaughters, Macy Marie Shockley and Aspen Grace Shockley. Not one word would have been possible without Steve's incredible support and love.

Encampment, Wyoming, Summer 2018

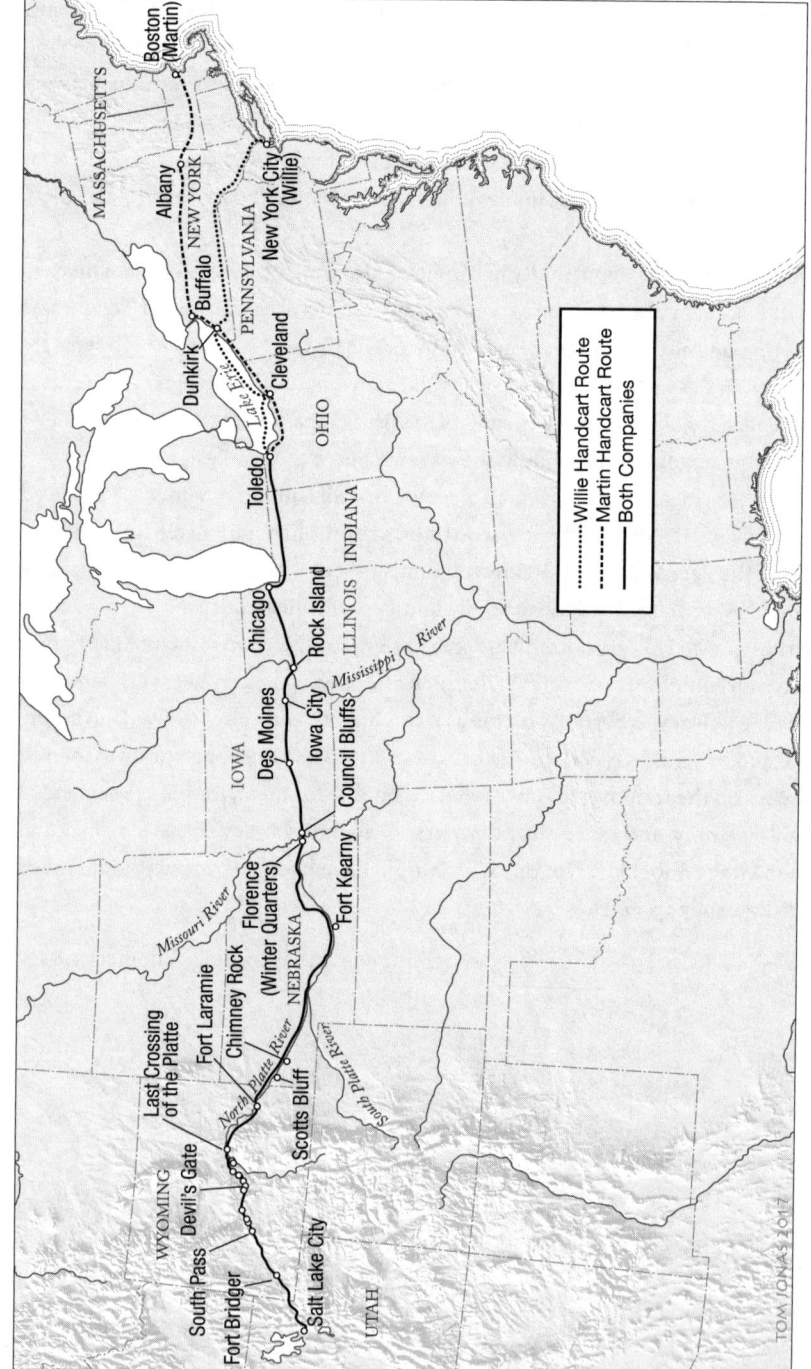

Handcart travel routes from Boston and New York to Salt Lake City.

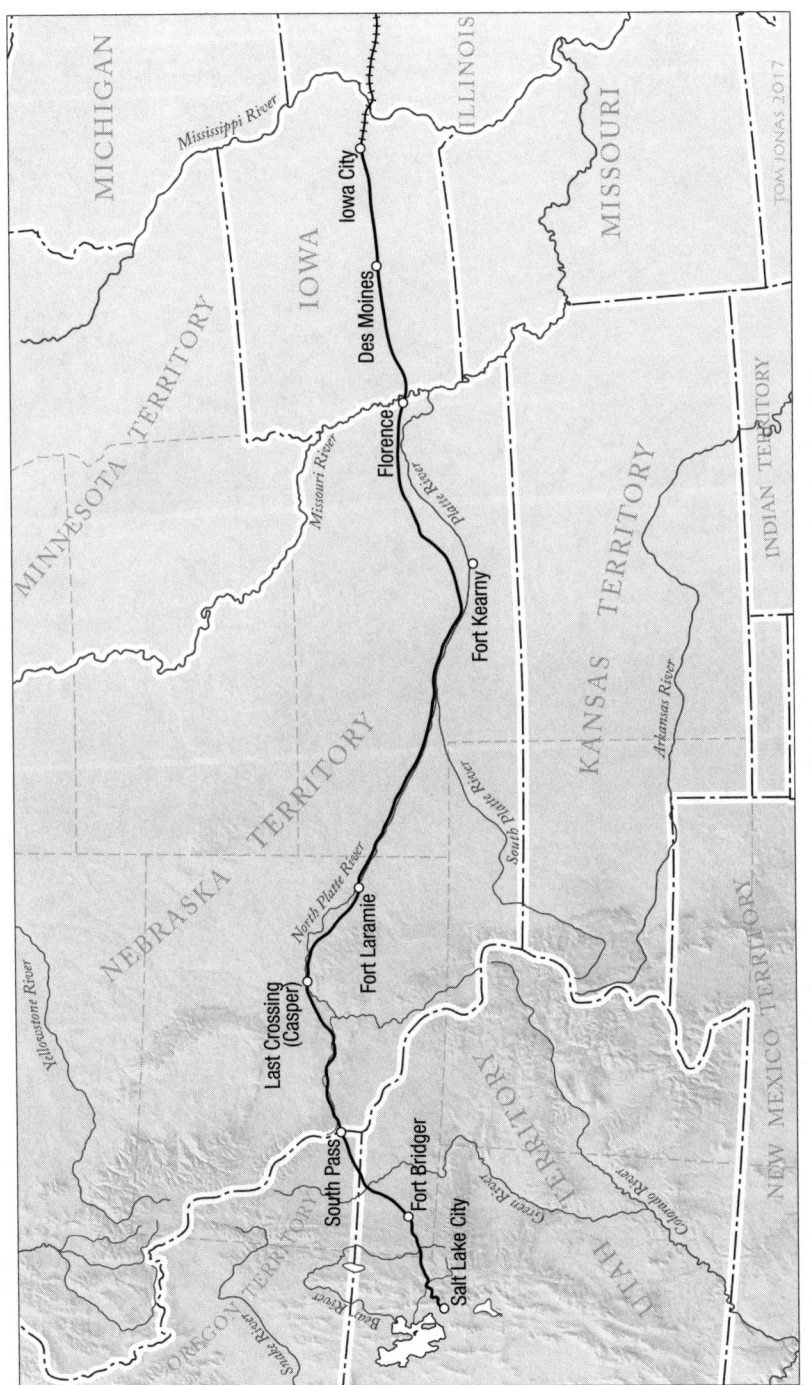

The handcart company route from Iowa City, Iowa, to Salt Lake City, Utah.

THE MORMON HANDCART MIGRATION

A detailed account would melt a heart of Stone.

— Daniel Tyler

FLORENCE, NEBRASKA, APRIL 19, 1997

Today was cold and a steady rain fell as we loaded the wagons and handcarts to begin our journey to Great Salt Lake. There is a feeling of camaraderie and anticipation of the coming journey. Everyone has new clothes. It is obvious that many women spent the winter laboring over their sewing machines! The children are eager to get on the road, and so are the teams. We have horses and mules pulling the wagons. And there is a group of people who also have handcarts that they will push and pull themselves. They look strong and healthy. Their carts are piled high with tents, bedding, personal possessions, food, and water. I've been on overland trails before; many of these people have not. I wonder how they will fare.

— Candy Moulton

WINTER QUARTERS, AUGUST 13, 1856

I feel it a great blessing that I am so far on my way to Zion.... I never had my health so well in my life before I walked about three hundred miles and pulled the hand cart all the way [from Iowa City] and we walked sometimes 20 & 17 miles a day and I never had a blister on my foot & cannot think to tell you my feelings when I was coursing along the road but I often think of the prophet Brighams words about the weak becoming strong ... some of the saints as they call themselves are going to stay here for they do not feel as though they could go through this year because it is so late. ... we are going to start for the plains to morrow—and there is not any more going this year so the brethren say.

— Sarah Moulton

GEORGE ROWLEY COMPANY, 1859

There were lots of dreadful things happened that I won't talk about because I'm sure those poor people would not like them talked about. I think we were not so badly off as the people who came in the cold weather. The man who built this house told me that he had seen men, women and children frozen to death while they were sitting up-right. We met a few wagons on their way to and from California and these companies certainly were strange sights to them. They often pitied us and gave us food. Yes, I crossed the plains with a handcart once but I am thankful I have never had to again. I couldn't do it. One such experience is quite enough.

— Sarah Beesley

CHAPTER 1

CALLING THE FAITHFUL

It must be done wisely, prudently, and judiciously.
MORMON, DECEMBER 1, 1855

The Church of Jesus Christ of Latter-day Saints was barely out of infancy when Heber C. Kimball, Orson Hyde, Willard Richards, and four others crossed the Atlantic in 1837 to spread the message of their faith to Europeans. Brigham Young later joined those three men.[1] All four would be leaders in the church for decades to come. They began spreading the idea that the church had a mission not only to share its gospel in America, where it was born, but also to take it around the world. Their message of the "gathering," a "sign of one's faithfulness," came from church teachings.[2] These included the 1831 commandment that they should "look to the poor and needy, and administer to their relief that they shall not suffer."[3]

The first shipload of foreign converts left Liverpool, England, for New York on June 6, 1840. Sailing on the ship *Britannia* were two hundred English men, women, and children. Due to the high cost of the crossing, half of that first group of immigrants made it only as far as Buffalo, New York, and Kirtland, Ohio. The other half went on to Nauvoo, Illinois, where the saints were then gathering to build a powerful city and construct a temple as one hallmark of their faith. The next year more converts from Herefordshire and neighboring areas of England sailed to America on the *Sheffield*. Others followed these early groups, setting sail for such American ports as New York, Philadelphia, and Boston before eventually migrating to Nauvoo.[4]

The English migration was initially organized by several LDS missionaries, including Parley P. Pratt, Hyrum Clark, and Reuben Hedlock. From 1840 to 1846 the main objective of the immigration was building up Nauvoo. "Joseph Smith and the Twelve Apostles, constantly exhorted the immigrating Saints who had capital, to establish manufactories in that city," James Linforth wrote in his guide to the trail, published in 1855.[5]

Overland travel, in fact mass exodus, is a hallmark of the Mormons. The church has been on the move since its earliest years. The faithful traveled west out of Palmyra,

New York, where Joseph Smith had started the church, to Kirtland, Ohio, and then to Missouri.

Near Far West and other Missouri communities, the Mormons built towns, cleared ground, and began farming. This was an important early developmental period for the Church of Jesus Christ of Latter-day Saints. The Mormons dedicated the site for a church temple and laid the cornerstone. From this area the Quorum of the Twelve Apostles—the church leadership—first departed to begin missionary work in Europe. As the church became more organized, it came into conflict with non-Mormon Missourians. Differences in religious, political, and economic views led to problems when the state militia arrested and jailed Joseph Smith and other church leaders. An attack on Mormons at Haun's Mill resulted in the death of seventeen church members and injuries to even more. Prior to the attack Missouri governor Lilburn Boggs issued his infamous Order 44, calling for removal of the Mormons from Missouri or their extermination.[6]

Facing such hostility, the church abandoned Missouri in the winter and spring of 1838 and 1839 to establish a new home in Nauvoo, Illinois. Church members called it the City Beautiful. It would serve as the primary enclave for the church for the next few years until additional conflicts in 1844 resulted in Joseph Smith and his brother Hyram again being jailed in Carthage, Illinois, where they lost their lives in an attack on the jail.

After Smith's death on June 27, 1844, came a period of reorganization. Brigham Young emerged to lead the church as its new president. Anti-Mormon sentiment intensified as work continued to build a temple in Nauvoo, so church leaders decided upon another relocation. In the winter of 1846 they began abandoning Nauvoo, this time headed much farther west. They broke a trail from Nauvoo to the Missouri River where they stopped in the area that would become known as Kanesville (now Council Bluffs, Iowa).

Lands west of the Missouri were Indian country. Young raised a regiment—the Mormon Battalion—to support Colonel Stephen Watts Kearny as he took American troops west to Santa Fe in the opening moves of the Mexican-American War. Young thus obtained permission for his followers to move onto land across the Missouri River in Omaha and Otoe Indian country, where the Mormon families and men who did not travel with the Mormon Battalion could spend the winter of 1846–47. This place, initially known as Winter Quarters, became the community of Florence, Nebraska, now a part of the Omaha metro area. The families built rough cabins but were unprepared for the cold winter weather and lack of sanitary conditions. Dysentery, malnutrition, and "black leg" (scurvy) killed most of the 600 who are buried on a hillside above the Missouri River at Winter Quarters.

In the spring of 1847 the vanguard of the Mormon migration (143 men, 3 women, and 2 children) set off across the plains from this Missouri River community. While some left the company and others joined as they traveled west, this group forged the path that would become the Mormon Pioneer National Historic Trail, today a nationally recognized historic trail. Although the members of this early party traveled fairly rapidly, they made some improvements to the road and established services for the families who would follow. Their route took them west from Florence to the Elkhorn River, where a ferry was eventually established. From there they crossed the Loup River and traveled north of the Platte River.

Fort Kearny did not exist when the first Mormon wagon train crossed Nebraska. But this post, which opened later that year on the south side of the river, became an important supply point for non-Mormon travelers. For the most part the Mormon immigrants remained on the north side of the Platte River, but Fort Kearny became a marker for them. Where the Platte River separates into south and north branches in western Nebraska, the Mormons followed the north branch through the sandy soil past such landmarks as Chimney Rock and Scotts Bluff, stopping long enough to examine prehistoric fossils and plant corn that later travelers could harvest.

Another trading post served those who traveled a few days by wagon west of Scotts Bluff. Started as a fur trade post, Fort William became known as Fort John then was replaced by Fort Laramie, which became a military installation in 1849. For many travelers this post was essential for rest and resupply, but Mormon trains usually avoided the fort, whose sutlers seldom had provisions.

When the members of the Pioneer Company reached the site of present Casper, Wyoming, in 1847, they found no services at all but forded the North Platte River for a final time. Beyond this last crossing of the river, the Mormons took the route used by travelers headed to Oregon (and after 1849 by those going to California's gold fields). Key landmarks were Red Buttes, just west of the North Platte Crossing; Avenue of Rocks, also called the Devil's Backbone; Willow Springs, a routine camping area; and Independence Rock, where many trail-era travelers carved or painted their names on the granite monolith. The Mormons then followed the Sweetwater River, crossing and recrossing the stream several times as they traveled past Devil's Gate, then Split Rock, and on to South Pass, where they bridged the Continental Divide.

In what was then Oregon Country, they went past Pacific Springs, traveled west to cross the Green River, and turned southwest to Fort Bridger, a trading post established in 1842 by former mountain men Jim Bridger and Louis Vasquez to serve the trail traffic. The Pioneer Company obtained information from Bridger when they encountered him not far west of South Pass. Travelers on all the trails traded at Fort Bridger. By

1853 the Mormons had gained ownership of Bridger's post, no doubt recognizing its importance as a supply center along the trails west.

From Fort Bridger the Pioneer Company moved across the Wasatch Mountain range, traversing Big Mountain and Little Mountain before descending to the Great Salt Lake Valley through what became known as Emigration Canyon. They arrived in late July 1847.

The Mormons settled the area and began building Great Salt Lake City. On December 23, 1847, the Quorum of Twelve, who had returned to Winter Quarters, issued a general epistle to the saints in England, Scotland, Ireland, and Wales, seeking to reinvigorate the European missions. They had been put on hiatus in 1846 when the saints in America began fleeing Nauvoo. Now the church needed foreign immigration to build its fledgling economy in Utah. "Emigrate as speedily as possible to this vicinity," the dispatch said. "Come immediately and prepare to go West—bringing with you all kinds of choice seeds, of grain, vegetables, fruit, shrubbery, trees, and vines."[7]

Because the American saints had so few resources in their new home in the Great Basin, the immigrants were also called to bring tools, spinning wheels, looms, and equipment such as corn shellers, grain threshers, and cleaners. The document warned that the immigrants would "pass through a savage country, and their safety depends on good fire arms and plenty of ammunition;—and then they may have their teams run off in open daylight, as we have had, unless they shall watch closely and continually" (5). "The long-wished for time of gathering has come," elder Orson Spencer wrote in a set of special instructions issued on February 1, 1848 (5).

Three weeks later, on February 20, 1848, after a two-year hiatus, English immigration began again. A group of 120 immigrants (most of them adults) along with three returning missionaries—Franklin D. Richards, Cyrus H. Wheelock, and Andrew Cahoon—sailed on the *Carnatic* to New York. Orson Pratt, one of the Twelve Apostles, was appointed that April to travel from Winter Quarters to England, where he would take charge of church affairs (6).

More missionaries went to Europe in 1849. John Taylor spread the LDS message in France and Germany, Lorenzo Snow went to Switzerland and Italy, Erastus Snow and Peter Hansen worked in Denmark, and John Forsgren served in Sweden.[8] By that time Liverpool was the headquarters for Mormon proselytizing in England; Copenhagen played a similar role in Scandinavia.

The Fifth General Epistle of the Presidency of the Church, issued April 7, 1851, appeared in the church newspaper *Millennial Star* (published in Liverpool) beginning in July and also in the first issue of *Skandinaviens Stjerne* (Scandinavian Star), published in October. The epistle outlined preparations being made by the Utah residents in anticipation of the arrival of Scandinavian immigrants, urging them to bring "choice seeds, hedges for fencing, lath and shingle nails, glass, wire, raw cotton, yarn, machinery, and other 'domestics.'"[9]

To aid the overland migration and now the trans-Atlantic movements, William Clayton wrote *The Latter-day Saints Emigrants' Guide*, published in 1848 in St. Louis. Another guide, *Route from Liverpool to Great Salt Lake Valley Illustrated* by James Linforth, was published in England in 1855. Engravings by Frederick Piercy lavishly illustrated Linforth's guide, which also served as a general history of the early immigration from England to the United States.[10]

The Mormon migration, highly organized in regard to detailed instructions on transportation, outfitting, lodging, and supplies needed, nevertheless encouraged converts to look out for themselves. In the early 1840s it was very hard for many European converts to save adequate money to pay the fees to cross the ocean and then travel to Nauvoo. Indeed, the number of people making the journey across the ocean and then overland to Utah was limited before 1852. The costs increased when the saints relocated from Nauvoo to Great Salt Lake City, because it was a longer distance to the end of their trail. The Nauvoo saints, however, pledged to work until all the American saints who wanted to move west were gathered. This covenant was later extended to the foreign saints, particularly the British (few had resources of their own, because most of them were from the poorer classes).

During the Church General Conference in October 1849, Heber C. Kimball introduced a measure to raise a fund to assist converts. With unanimous approval, the church allocated $5,000 to create the Perpetual Emigrating Fund Company (PEF). Initial support for the fund came in various forms: California gold, livestock teams, and even wheat. The goal was to loan money to pay transportation costs to help converts reach Utah. Once there, they would repay the loan, so the fund would continue into perpetuity. The PEF stemmed from the "covenant" of 1846: when the Mormons abandoned Nauvoo, they pledged then never to desert "the poor who are worthy."[11]

The PEF was first used to help Mormons still living along the Missouri River in their move to Zion, but after 1852 it was used to assist foreign members. "The few thousands we send out by our agent at this time is like a grain of mustard seed in the earth; we send it forth into the world and among the Saints, a good soil, and we expect it will grow and flourish, and spread abroad in a few years so that it will cover England, cast its shadow in Europe and in the process of time compass the whole earth," the fund's letter of instruction noted.[12]

Three fundamental concepts guided use of the fund and those it would help. First were people who already had relatives in Utah who provided some funding aid; second were those with skills in construction, stonemasonry, and other trades that would help build up Utah; and third were individuals who had been converted to the Mormon faith at least ten years earlier and who were too poor to migrate without aid.[13]

Thirty-one wagons of primarily English immigrants led by Abraham O. Smoot were the first foreign arrivals in Utah under the Perpetual Emigrating Fund. They were known as the Poor Company. When they arrived in Salt Lake City late in the afternoon on Friday, September 3, 1852, they were greeted by citizens on horseback and in carriages, including members of the First Presidency of the Church and the Twelve Apostles. According to Linford's guide, when these immigrants reached the area where the Mormon Temple would be built, the sound of nine rounds of artillery "made the everlasting hills to shake their sides with joy." Brigham Young greeted the travelers, giving them advice about growing crops, building homes, and finding work.[14]

In 1853 the PEF supported the travels of 2,312 people from England to Zion. They were followed by 3,167 travelers in 1854, with one-third of them receiving PEF assistance.[15] By 1854 church leaders recognized that Mormon missionary success in Ireland, Scotland, Denmark, and Sweden as well as in England made it necessary to enlarge the PEF.[16] While those who could contribute to the fund were asked to do so, people who wanted to follow their faith were urged to save every possible penny with the goal of migrating.

Economic challenges, combined with crop failures and famines in Sweden and Ireland and compounded by political unrest and religious persecution in certain areas, led some people living in the British Isles and Europe to seek change. Some wanted to escape poverty, while others wanted class equality. Their desires—and opportunities—to move grew more powerful as the actual methods of migration improved. For example, there were more sailing ships, and steamships later reduced the transit time.

The call to immigrate to America touched the hearts of Mormon converts in the British Isles and Europe. The numbers grew to 4,225 people making their way to Zion in 1855, with 1,161 of them using resources of the PEF. People pledged to repay to the PEF the funds advanced to them. Margaret Dening, for example, agreed to repay $9.91 received for provisions for her trip from Florence to Great Salt Lake City.[17] Most of the PEF resources expended on behalf of foreign converts went to immigrants from the British mission. Cash loans were available in the early 1850s, but by early 1855 the fund was more than $100,000 in debt and was clearly inadequate to provide loans for paying the full costs of wagon passage to Utah.[18]

With such funds in decline, Brigham Young wrote to Franklin D. Richards, president of the European Mission, in September 1855:

I have been thinking how we should operate another year. We cannot afford to purchase wagons and teams as in times past. I am consequently thrown back upon my old plan—to make hand-carts, and let the emigration foot it, and draw upon them [the handcarts] the necessary supplies, having a cow or two for every ten. They can come just as quick, if not quicker, and much cheaper—can start earlier and escape the prevailing sickness which annually lays so many of our brethren in the dust. A great majority of them walk now, even with the teams which are provided.[19]

The *Mormon*, an LDS newspaper published in New York by John Taylor, reported in 1855 that the "experiment" of traveling by hand-drawn carts needed to be "judiciously arranged, wisely and prudently conducted, and sufficiently guarded against contingencies by the contiguity of ox or other trains which, in case of trouble, would be sufficiently near to render timely assistance."[20] This New York publication was not often read by European or British converts, and the church agents in Britain, including Franklin D. Richards, were not nearly as cautious as New York agent John Taylor. Instead, they strongly urged all who could undertake the journey to do so, regardless of age or physical ability.

Young laid out the plan for these handcart migrants in precise detail. "They will need only 90 days' rations from the time of their leaving the Missouri River, and as the settlements extend up the Platte, not that much. The carts can be made without a particle of iron, with wheels hooped, made strong and light, and one, or if the family be large, two of them will bring all that they will need upon the plains."

I think the emigration had better come the northern route from New York, or Philadelphia, or Boston, direct to Iowa City.... Their passage [by train] through to Iowa City will not cost more than 8 or 9 dollars, and they will only have to be supplied with money for provisions and a few cows, which should be of the very best quality.... Of course you will perceive the necessity of dispensing with all wooden chests, extra freight, luggage, etc. They should only bring a change of clothing.

Although he recommended rations for ninety days, Young perhaps too optimistically believed that the travelers with their carts could make the journey in seventy days, moving from twenty to thirty miles each day "with all ease, and no danger of giving out, but will continue to get stronger and stronger; the little ones and sick, if there are any, can be carried on the carts, but there will be none sick in a little time after they get started. There will have to be some few tents."[21]

Young told Richards: "In your elections of the Saints who shall be aided by the Fund, those who have proven themselves by long continuance in the Church shall be helped first, whether they can raise any means of their own or not; . . . if they have not a sixpence in the world." He instructed Richards not to allow new converts to be included in the emigration because their "chief aim and intention may be to get to America."[22] He wanted to be sure that the most faithful and dedicated saints had the first chance to travel to America with the help of the PEF and the new handcart scheme, not people who simply sought better economic opportunities, which he knew was a driving factor for immigration at the time.

Richards himself noted that the possibility of using handcarts to cross the plains instead of wagons pulled by ox teams "has been under consideration for several years. The plan is novel, and, when we allow our imaginations to wander into the future and paint the scenes that will transpire on the prairies next summer, they partake largely of the romantic. The plan is the device of inspiration, and the Lord will own and bless it."[23]

Mormon leaders increasingly allowed optimism to overrule the possibility of failure. In a report to John Taylor, who by then served as president of the church mission in New York, several experienced Mormon travelers, including Asa Calkin, J. Lavander, J. S. Scofield, Williams Allen, H. Bowley, Conrad Klineman, and C. Christianson, gave advice on the use of handcarts for traveling across the plains. Their article was published in the *Mormon* on December 1, 1855: "We have had some experience in crossing the plains, and on foot. Yet we are aware that there is a wide difference between walking across the plains by the side of a team and wagon and drawing the wagon yourself; that is as yet an untried experiment." Still, they joined the general optimism:

> We are of the unanimous opinion that it can be done with much less expense, and comparatively little increase of toil and hardship, than with ox teams, and that with a judicious selection of a pioneer hand-cart company, and careful and proper management . . . the ice, as it were, will be broken, and a way opened through which thousands of our brethren, who are not able to furnish themselves with an outfit under the present system of emigration; but who could nevertheless very readily fit themselves out for this mode, as well as a great portion of our Perpetual Fund emigration will hereafter move on to the Valley.[24]

Taylor added that proper management of the handcart migration would be a key to its success.

One idea was that four people (two men and two women) could draw each cart. Into each of the small vehicles they could load 435 pounds of goods, including up to 240 pounds of flour, 50 pounds of bacon, and 30 pounds of other food and fruit, along with "perhaps an infant or two." For supplies they also would have a tent weighing 20 pounds, bedding and clothing weighing 60 pounds (15 pounds per person not counting the children), 15 pounds of cooking utensils, a gun and ammunition weighing 10 pounds, and various other items also weighing 10 pounds.

Young expected to provide support for the handcarts. He decreed that there would be a wagon drawn by three yoke of oxen for every fifty people and on average a cow for milking for every ten people. Additional teams and wagons might be advisable. Even with this wagon support, however, the experienced trail travelers said that the west-bound train of handcart pioneers would need to be met with supplies sent from the Salt Lake Valley. Resupply was to occur in central Wyoming "at the last crossing of the Platte, or at farthest, at Devil's Gate."

Calkin, Lavander, and their co-signers outlined in their recommendations to Taylor how the handcarts were to be constructed. They should be "sufficiently narrow to run within the tracks of common wagons, to avoid the ruts." They described the carts precisely:

> The hub should be six inches long and five inches in diameter, with two and one and a quarter inch boxes; the wheel at least four and a half feet across, the rim of good hickory, bent, not more than one and an eighth inch deep and seven eighths or 1" wide.... The axle-tree should be hickory, two by three or three and a half inches; the bed about fifty-four by thirty-two inches, of quarter inch stuff, with three bows to support the cover, as low as possible, to avoid gathering wind.

The authors of the recommendations gave considerable thought to the rim of the wheels, noting that a broad, thin rim, which would easily move through mud or sand, might split. But it would be difficult to negotiate wheels with a heavier rim over rough country or through the sandy soils of western Nebraska. As a result they suggested a rim as narrow as practicable to create the least amount of resistance. The handcarts would weigh about sixty pounds. Many of these recommendations and suggestions were not implemented, particularly in the first year of the handcart migration.

The article containing these recommendations laid out the justification for relying on individual power to pull handcarts as a way to aid church members in migrating. Brigham Young needed to build up Utah, which would require an influx of a labor force and any possible capital. He recognized that his desire for population growth would be hindered without continued immigrant arrivals. He also knew the lack of financial resources of the European converts meant that many of them would likely be "detained for years from accomplishing a journey which is to them of the first importance, if they have to fit out in the ordinary manner." For those willing to pay the price of physical labor, this mode of transportation not only would speed immigration but would also sit better with proud people who found it "very painful" to rely on the aid of others. These "high-minded, sensitive" yet poor people could "aid themselves by their own right arm." By depending on their own resources they would be "delivered from the humiliation of obligation."

John Taylor in New York believed in testing the use of handcarts, though he warned that "it must be done wisely, prudently, and judiciously, and be under the strictest regulations." Rather than expecting converts to make their own carts, Taylor recommended that experienced builders should construct the conveyances instead. "They must be made of well-seasoned, tough timber . . . otherwise they will give way on the plains." Richards in England and Brigham Young in Utah, however, were not advocating the same degree of planning, preparation, and caution espoused by Taylor and those working with him in New York.

The article in the *Mormon* conceded that people would want to take more of their personal possessions:

> if persons . . . should want other things taken, and have the means, they can either unite together and purchase an ox-team, or hire their luggage carried. . . . We do not wish to cramp men. . . . We say to all Saints, go, if [you] can take clothing, merchandize, machinery, tools, books, scientific apparatus, music instruments, gold, silver, precious stones, or anything valuable, beautiful and useful for science, literature, the arts, or to ornament Zion, and can furnish teams to haul it—take it along; but if you have these things, and not means, dispose of them; you cannot take them with this company.

The authors of the article attempted to warn people that a trip across America would be difficult, noting that "there is nothing very pleasing nor inviting about this journey; but we think, after all, it is better to go there among friends, poor, than to endure the buffetings of a cold, heartless world, in poverty."

John Taylor, the Mormon agent in New York, was anxious. He would shoulder much of the responsibility for putting in place the organization that would aid the converts and worried whether "everything shall be conducted properly, with due care and safety, as far as may be practicable, for the comfort of those who may be going by hand-carts. It is a new project, and will require our greatest attention and vigilance."[25]

Joining Taylor in preliminary planning were Orson Spencer in St. Louis and Franklin D. Richards, then the superintendent of emigration based in Liverpool, England. Spencer's death in October 1855 created a void in the organization. Richards appointed Spencer's older brother Daniel, still in England on a mission, to step into a supporting role. Taylor also recruited Andrew Cunningham, just back in America from a mission in England, sending him to Council Bluffs, Iowa, to take charge of emigration preparations there along with James McGaw, who served as chief outfitter.

While Cunningham was familiar with the English immigrants who would be traveling to America in the spring of 1856, McGaw had his own skills. He had led a wagon train over the trail in 1852 and assisted with the European immigrants during the 1855 migration season, welcoming them in New Orleans before sending them north to St. Louis.

To prepare for the year's traveling companies, Taylor made preliminary arrangements for a camping area at Iowa City and negotiated for ferry service, storage, and other accommodations at the site of the old Winter Quarters, in what was by then the settlement of Florence, Nebraska. He again urged that the handcarts be stoutly built of the "best of seasoned timber." He admitted that he did not know how many travelers would be on the trail that year (not having been informed by Richards in England, who was arranging passage) and therefore could not make "any correct estimate as to the number that would be required." Although unaware of the number of travelers, Taylor ordered one hundred handcarts at a cost of $20 each from the Espenschied Wagon Factory in St. Louis. "They are a very neat article, well finished, ironed, and painted," he noted.[26]

To hedge against having more travelers than carts, Daniel Spencer, who had arrived in Iowa City in the spring of 1856, ordered another one hundred carts to be built by the Iowa City Plow Factory "in a more primitive style, and without iron" under direction of George D. Grant. He expected these carts to cost just $10 each. Despite Taylor's recommendation that all carts be built by experienced carpenters, some were constructed even more economically by the immigrants themselves under stewardship of Mormon wheelwright Chauncey Webb.[27] The two hundred professionally constructed carts would be adequate for about a thousand travelers, based on Brigham Young's premise that each cart would serve five people.

Daniel Spencer, who took over the financial affairs of the people traveling under the PEF, was also appointed superintendent of the immigration to the West by Taylor. At age sixty-two, Spencer was an experienced manager. He had lived in Nauvoo and led one of the earliest wagon trains to Great Salt Lake City in 1847. He became a stake president in Salt Lake City but was Richards's counselor in 1856 before being sent to Iowa City.

From the beginning, Taylor intended for the travelers to be almost constantly on the move, with only a day or two of delay at outfitting points. He believed that this continual motion would reduce sickness (cholera and other diseases were thought to spread when people camped too long in a single location) and prevent unnecessary delay so that the travelers could arrive in Utah with time to prepare for winter. Decreasing delays also would reduce expense and make supplies hold out for the journey. "I feel deeply solicitous for the welfare of the travelling Saints, and more especially am I anxious that everything shall be conducted properly, with the care and safety, and as far as may be practicable, for the comfort of those who may be going by hand-carts."[28]

FACING "RIDICULE AND SCORN"

Membership in the Church of Jesus Christ of Latter-day Saints was difficult for some in England. Both the Anglican and Catholic churches frowned upon one of the Mormon tenets of the time: the practice of plural marriage. This led to disparagement of the Mormon missionaries as well as those in England who embraced the faith. Members of the LDS Church also faced persecution in England for other reasons, of course, just as they did in America.

Family disapproval was one consequence. For Ebenezer Crouch's parents, William and Elizabeth, the act of joining the church "brought down upon their heads the ridicule and scorn of their very religious parents, and [they] were looked upon as being a disgrace to their families." Crouch's father had a successful mercantile business in Protestant England, but "as soon as it became known that he had joined the hated and despised people known as the Mormons, a great change was soon apparent. His old patrons withdrew their patronage and did all they could to injure his business." This forced Crouch to close his store "at a great loss, which left him very reduced in circumstances."[29] Crouch would seek a more friendly community in Great Salt Lake City.

A history written by descendants of George Harrison also recalled the persecution his family endured in England after they converted to Mormonism. "They became very unpopular with some of their friends, but were willing to stand the jibes and persecutions for the sake of what they felt was the truth." The Harrisons attended church three times each Sunday. He was overjoyed when the missionaries visited after services, "because mother would always set a large mince pie in the oven for when we arrived home. Oh, it was good after the walk and the long meeting."[30] The Harrisons joined the handcart migration to Utah with the Fifth Company in 1856.

Henry Moyle, whose father was a leader in the newly organized Mormon congregation in Plymouth, England, recalled the conflicts they endured at the first meetings. As the saints gathered one night in fall 1852 in the upstairs room of an Odd Fellows Hall, a group of men Moyle identified as Methodist ministers came to the hall "to Disturb & try to brak up the meeting. My Brother James who had been ordained deacon had charge at the lower door & when the meen came, James told them it was a privet meeting that night." The leader of the encroaching group objected and said he would go in. An alarm spread to the Mormons in their meeting, who "met the mob at the top of the stairways." Moyle's father "struck the leeder between the eyes with his fist and landed him 8 feet down the stairs & knocked two or three more as best he could, at the same time Dunn who was a soldier in uniform took off his large balt [belt] which had a brass buckle on the end of it and comenced to cut [and] lash them with it and it was not long till the rebles was glad to leave with some loss of thair blood."[31]

The following year the talk within the family centered on helping James Moyle migrate to America. He was a stonecutter by trade. Knowing of Brigham Young's desire for tradesmen who could help with the work of building Great Salt Lake City, the family believed that James could assist with work in Utah. That might be the leverage they needed for all of them to immigrate eventually. They hoped that James would earn enough money to contribute to the PEF so they could join him in Utah.[32] James was eighteen when he traveled to America in 1854 as part of the Darwin Richardson Company, composed of three hundred people who used forty wagons for their overland crossing from Westport, Missouri, to Utah. Sending James to America indeed paved the way for the family, which followed him to Utah with a handcart brigade in 1856.

Langley Allgood Bailey also was eighteen when his family prepared to leave England. He later recalled that his parents were "anxious that we gather to Zion. They did not like the company we were in [in England.]" To prepare for their departure, "Father engaged an auctioneer to sell our furniture, a Saint, by the name of Machire, a member of the church; the town crier, was engaged, went all over the town with bell in hand ringing—O yes, O yes—Brother and Sister Bailey are leaving for Zion. Come one, come all, and buy their goods. . . . I felt a little ashamed, I wanted father to stop him. Mother said no, he is not ashamed to let people know that we with him are Latter-day Saints."[33] The Baileys also emigrated by handcart in 1856.

Not all Mormons faced such issues. As Henry Hobbs prepared to leave England in 1859 with what would become the Eighth Handcart Company, his English neighbors provided aid. The items he received included a pair of stockings and a pot of preserves from one woman and additional stockings from other women, plus a cotton handkerchief, a cap, a pair of trousers, a can of eggs, a bed quilt, some money, and even a small bottle of brandy. He recommended that any traveler should have "good flour, potatoes, salt, preserves, a good cooked ham, plenty of eggs, lemons, a good cheese, some good coffee, currants, plums, ink, spices, porter, port wine, . . . preserved fish, . . . a few sweet biscuits." He further suggested "good tins to hold your water & a barrel to hold your provisions. Some good bags to hold your rations; baking powder; lard;

suit; good thick shoes; carpet slippers & warm clothing; plenty of soap & don't forget towels, a lamp & candles; a rolling pin, board, knives, forks, spoons, a little sugar, consecrated oil, shoe brushes, pepper, cream of tarter or ginger, cayenne pepper, some pickled cabbage."[34]

Twenty-one-year-old English convert and missionary Mark H. Forscutt was actively spreading the word about the Church of Jesus Christ of Latter-day Saints in his home country by 1855. Throughout the fall and winter he met with church members, encouraging them to migrate to America and instructing them about their "duty and privileges." Over the course of that winter he came to know the family of Thomas Moulton of Irchester. Forscutt was in Wellingborough, England, on Friday, February 15, 1856, when Brother Sheffields "invited me to fetch down Sister Sarah Moulton and take tea with them as this is my last day in Wellingbone which I accordingly did and we enjoyed ourselves very much[.] Bro Sheffields had made me a new pair of boots of which I was very much in want and which I am to send him the money for as soon as I can. After tea we went over to Irchester supped & slept at Sarah's Father's . . . Bro T. Moulton's."[35]

The following day Forscutt ate breakfast with the Thomas Moulton family, "after which I started for Eynesbur[y] accompanied a mile or two on the road by Sister Sarah when I affectionately parted with her and pray the Lord to bless her with every needful blessing to prepare her for everything that awaits her and preserve her in purity holiness and virtue that she may arrive in Zion in safety and I pray that he will also hasten the time when I shall be gathered home." After parting, he wrote, "I felt somewhat dull as I knew I had then left a company of Saints that had and did still love me even as themselves and did not expect to see them any more in these lands[;] having a heavy load I arrived at Eynesburg very tired."[36]

By the time Mark Forscutt took tea with nineteen-year-old Sarah Elizabeth Moulton in February 1856, the Moulton family had already decided to immigrate to America. Mother Sarah Denton Moulton had been saving money for years, placing coins taken from her husband's pay as a butcher into a fruit jar in anticipation of following her faith to America. As excited as she was, she must also have been fearful.[37] Not only would the family leave its familiar home, but Sarah also would have the responsibility of caring for her youngsters on an ocean journey and then an overland trek across two-thirds of the North American continent. She desired to make the trip in part because her sisters had already immigrated. Older sister Mary Denton left England and settled in Nauvoo, Illinois, in 1844, while Eliza Denton Cussley sailed to America in 1855 on the *Siddons* with her husband, Samuel Cussley. The Cussleys traveled as ordinary passengers, in a second-class cabin, departing from Liverpool on February 27, 1855, and reaching Philadelphia on April 20, 1855.[38]

As the years and then months of anticipation came down to weeks, Sarah Denton Moulton faced a challenge that could affect their plans to immigrate: the youngest girls in the family contracted smallpox.[39] Mark Forscutt, who obviously stayed in contact with the Moultons after his visit at their home in February 1856, recorded in his journal on April 9 that one of the elder Moulton women, quite likely mother Sarah, also had the disease. He "received a letter from Wellingbore stating that the Saints were some better but Bro. J. Fenks of Irchester and Sister Chapman & child of Wellingbore were dead and I pray God to restore Sis Moulton who is now down with the small pox."[40]

Just three weeks later the Moulton family was in Liverpool, preparing to board the *Thornton*, along with other members of the company led by James Grey Willie. To conceal the smallpox sores, which likely were scabbed over by that time, the young girls wore gloves that their mother had made. There is no account of either Sarah Denton or Sarah Elizabeth wearing similar gloves, although perhaps they also wore them to conceal pox marks. On May 2, 1856, Forscutt noted, "Sis Moulton, Bro Clayton & inlaws are better." Forscutt was not in Liverpool that day to see the saints that he had counseled during the winter board the *Thornton* and prepare to leave England forever. The day after the ship sailed from Liverpool, carrying the Moultons and other immigrants toward America, Forscutt went to Rockland and Thompson, where he "gave out a hymn," sang a prayer, and addressed an audience of church members on what he called the first principles of the gospel. "Great confusion" made it difficult to conduct the meeting, when "several rotten eggs were thrown at us and also a few stones. Several old tin kettles, pans &c were kicked about the road."[41]

The Mormons discontinued the gathering, found a place to spend the night, and then reassembled. But dissenters interrupted this second session as well. "We separated amid a volley of rotten eggs, stones, and sods to celebrate our departure." In this last flurry of missiles a stone hit Forscutt in the leg and one man told him, "'I should think you will not come here again seeing the people will not receive you[,'] to which I answered that when the wolves roared the sheep were right. He said it did almost seem as though we were the persecuted few and he could not but admire our courage" (179/204–5).

Subsequent meetings drew opposition even as they continued to attract converts. The missionaries still faced persecution. On May 12, 1856, Forscutt was again in Rockland, where he observed

a printed paper stuck up in the town to prejudice the people against us in which the church of Jesus Christ is called a system of irreligion, deception, seduction, incest, adultery, rapine, Secret assassination, torture, and the word of crimes concealed under a religious mask as they are in reality practiced in the Salt Lake Valley Settlements.—On the same bill is advertised the 'Female life among the Mormons' as it is added. Wives Mothers & daughters bought & sold in large letters. The subtle progress of the spiritual wife abominations of the Latter Day Saints throughout the British dominions demands that you and every one of you male and female relations should seriously read the truthful exposures this important work contained. (181/247–48)

These attacks referred to the Mormon practice of polygamy, which had started under Joseph Smith's leadership and was growing in popularity among the Saints with Brigham Young as president of the church. Like other faithful members of the church, Forscutt ignored such claims. He spent the morning of June 18, "in fasting & prayer before the Lord as this is the last day of my 21st year being 22 to morrow morning." He prayed for the "holy spirit to guide me throughout the coming year and my future life" (190/267).

Forscutt had been a good worker for the Mormon Church in England. On his twenty-second birthday, on June 19, 1856, he wrote that during the previous year he had "added to the church by baptism & rebaptism 32 members conformed 21 ordained 12 blessed 6 children.... I have also traveled during the year over 3000 miles, 2700 of which I have walked" (191–92/268 and 271). Such was the perseverance and determination of many converts in England, some of whom made their way to America.

CHAPTER 2

CASTING LOTS WITH GOD

Gathering from England to new homes in the American West meant a long ocean voyage that posed its own challenges. By one means or another, converts in the British Isles, Scandinavia, and other European locales gathered in Liverpool, England, where they were assigned to various seagoing vessels.

John William Southwell's parting from his family at the age of twenty-three reflects a scene undoubtedly played out across England by many handcart pioneers. According to Southwell, the night before traveling from Nottingham (where his sisters lived) to Liverpool the saints held a farewell meeting with recitations, songs, and speeches. Early the next morning they filled the train station to overflowing, singing a few lines of a hymn before exchanging their final goodbyes. Southwell's two sisters clung to him, begging a blessing from God "upon the brother with whom they so reluctantly separated." Southwell himself found that leaving "dear old mother . . . is heart rending in the extreme . . . [an] 'agony of spirit.'" After exchanging tearful goodbyes, the travelers gave a tremendous cheer. Then the whistle engine blew a long blast, signaling their departure to Liverpool.[1]

Church records show that 4,326 members departed from England in 1856, including 3,318 in the ships that carried members of the handcart companies.[2] Of these, around 1,948 actually traveled with the handcarts from Florence to Great Salt Lake City. More than half of them (512 and 641, respectively) were in the Willie and Martin Companies. During the period from 1852 to 1887 about 73,000 people followed their Mormon faith from Europe and the British Isles to Utah, including around 26,000 who were assisted by the Perpetual Emigrating Fund.

"In the year 1856 all of our possessions were sold for cash and this money turned over to the Church Emigration Fund," recalled twelve-year-old John Oborn, a member of the Fourth Handcart Company. He was traveling with his parents, Joseph and Maria Stradling Oborn of Wellington, England. "Father, mother and I said goodbye to Sister Eliza and Brother Henry and other relatives and friends and took a last farewell look about the old home, realizing we would never again see that always-to-be-remembered 'Home, Sweet Home.' We had now cast our lot with the Saints of God and were on our way westward, little realizing and never fearing the terrible hardships between us and the valleys of Utah."[3]

In April 1856, two years after his brother left for America, Henry Moyle and his family departed from Plymouth in Devonshire, where his father had been a leading member of the Church of Jesus Christ of Latter-day Saints. They took an Irish sternwheel packet to Liverpool, which was a "very cheep conveyance, & afford us the Privelege of takeing in the sights along the coast around landsend, [and] also the old town of Dublin, Irland." Leaving their home city on the steamer, they waved hats and handkerchiefs "to the saints & friends who whare thare to see us off, we sang the old hymn 'Oh Babylon, oh Babylon.' We bith [bid] the farewell, we are going to the mountains of Ephriam to Dwell."[4] Their route took them south and then west, around the Cornish peninsula, and north to Dublin before heading east to Liverpool.

As the converts reached the wharf in Liverpool, they piled their large quantities of luggage on the ground near the ship. In some cases the amount that they had hauled to Liverpool exceeded what they would be allowed to take on board. Furious unpacking and repacking took place before boxes, bags, crates, and trunks holding the allowed amounts were hoisted aboard. The remainder was left on the dock, no doubt soon to be taken by needy folks in the city. Once the goods were on board, the people quickly followed. Joseph Beecroft, prior to his departure on the *Horizon* in late May 1856, wrote: "It is a truly wonderful sight to see so many on ship board of all ages, sizes, complexions, and shapes. Some appear quite respectable while others appear to be quite poor. One is a poor cripple, another walks with crutches." Some of the immigrants were in fine physical shape, "very stout, straight young men, likely to build up Zion," according to Beecroft, but others "are repulsive in appearance."[5] This is some evidence that Mormon leaders did not discriminate against or discourage the ill or infirm by asking whether they had the physical ability to *walk* hundreds of miles across the American plains and prairie to reach Utah.

From the earliest days of Mormon immigration, the church arranged travel to minimize the time spent in Liverpool. The goal was to avoid the costs associated with lodging and meals while families waited for ships to arrive or depart. Most immigrants therefore reached the city one day, loaded their belongings and boarded the ship that they were assigned to, and then departed the following day. That policy created crowded scenes at the docks before every Mormon sailing vessel embarked. The wharves along the River Mersey bustled with activity as hundreds of families milled about in their last few hours on English soil.

One such ship was the *Enoch Train*, commanded by Captain Henry P. Rich when it sailed from Liverpool on March 23, 1856. It carried the first shipload of handcart immigrants bound for America that season under the Perpetual Emigrating Fund. Most but not all people on the ship were bound to travel with handcarts once they reached America, though their stories came to be intertwined. Fifteen-year-old Emily Hodgetts was aboard with her mother, her sister Maria (who was seventeen), and three other girls for whom her mother had paid passage. Before their ship could depart, however, Emily's father came on board. "We all hid," she said, but the patriarch located the family and convinced her mother to return with him to their home, along with two other girls and a boy. But Emily and her sister Maria remained on board to set off on their own to America, along with four blue chests filled with a variety of goods.[6]

Whether father Hodgett's efforts to keep his wife in England were lasting is unclear. Archer Walters observed: "I guess he has shut the gate, but as soon as she sees it open, she will be out. This only strengthens her faith in this work."[7]

That spring a multitude of Mormon converts gathered in Liverpool to make final preparations and board a variety of vessels headed to America. Departures occurred every few weeks. The *Thornton* with 764 people (of which 484 were PEF immigrants) sailed from Bramley-Moore docks, port of Liverpool, on May 4, 1856. Whether at home or bound for America, life went on. Two days after settling her family in the upper between deck area of the *Thornton* and setting sail, Sarah Moulton gave birth to a son, Charles Alma, at three o'clock in the morning.[8] Just days earlier Jennet McNeil had delivered a son, Charles Thornton.[9] On May 21 Hannah Bayliss had a stillborn daughter. She was reported as doing well despite the infant's burial at sea within six hours of the delivery.[10]

With the trip begun, celebrations were in order. On May 13 the *Thornton* had fair winds and the people were "all called up on deck and had another good meeting on which occasion we got the sacrament and some good instructions," recalled Archibald McPhail. That evening "the captain invited all the Saints to come on deck which we all did to see some sky rockets set off which had a very fine appearance."[11]

Edward Martin had charge of 856 immigrants who sailed on May 25, 1856, from Liverpool on the three-mast clipper ship *Horizon*. Of these, 625 traveled under the PEF. Among them were Samuel Pucell and his family. An early convert to the church, Pucell had given the first sixpence to the Mormon elders upon their first arrival in England in 1837.[12] The English, Scottish, and Welsh passengers on the *Horizon* were "old men with their grandchildren" and "very aged men and women some in spectacles. . . . We have quite a number who go with crutches of both sexes. One is a very crooked legged cripple who . . . appears to be a little bit deficient in intellect."[13] It is difficult to imagine what the Mormon elders said to encourage such travelers to undertake a journey that would involve walking almost 1,300 miles after enduring a weeks-long ocean crossing.

Franklin D. Richards met with the converts on the *Horizon* before they sailed, telling them that he had been in England for years to "sow the seeds of life" and that the pilgrims "were the crop that were being harvested." Joseph Beecroft said Richards told them that "we were going under peculiar circumstances to the valleys of the mountains." Richards encouraged the *Horizon* travelers: "If we would carry out our religion, there should not a soul be lost, nor anyone come to much harm . . . blessed from now to our journey's end and that the angels should be with us to guard the ship and us."[14]

Rain poured down as the tugboat *Great Conquest* pushed the *Horizon* from the dock in Liverpool. Josiah Rogerson recalled that the church members took a parting glance and soothed their hearts with the song Mormon elder Cyrus H. Wheelock had composed for them to sing on their departure:

> Our gallant ship is underway to bear me out to sea.
> And yonder floats the steamer gay that says she waits to me.
> The seamen dip their ready oars as ebbing waves oft tell.
> To bear me swiftly from the shore, my native land, farewell.[15]

All was not placid on board, however. Some of the crew objected to orders given by the mate. "I was up on deck in time to witness a little—not very civil 'jaw' between the first mate and one or two of the crew," twenty-nine-year-old John Jaques wrote to Franklin Richards on May 29, 1856. "The mate paced the deck, flourishing a Colt's revolver, and swearing and threatening grandly." Jaques abhorred the mate's threats with what he called a mortal weapon. "My maxim is to keep them still till wanted, and when necessary, use them, and over with it. That seems to me most consistent with 'Mormonism.'"[16]

Heber Robert McBride, who turned thirteen on May 13, just as the *Horizon* set sail for America, recalled inspection of the ship and its passengers:

> When we got out on the river and cast anchor, the government officers and doctor came on board and everything had to be inspected by the officers and the people by the doctors. And after all things had been restored to order and the officers left, then the sailors and the ship officers got into a quarrel and began to fight. This almost frightened some of the emigrants to death, but the first mate ran into the cabin and came out facing the men that was after him with a pistol in each hand [which] caused them to stop very quick. He told them the first man that moved he would shoot him down. He stood there and kept them back till

a signal of distress was sent up and it was hardly any time before boats came alongside with policemen and all the crew was put in irons and taken to shore.[17]

The incident, according to Jaques, stemmed from the mate's complaint that the recalcitrant crewmembers were "blacklegs" who "came on board to plunder the passengers and the rest of the crew." For their part the sailors called the mate a drunk. The captain replaced the unruly crewmembers, but the fracas delayed the *Horizon*'s departure.[18]

For two days the *Horizon* traversed the calmer waters in the channel between Great Britain and Ireland. As it moved farther into open waters, however, the ship began heaving and tossing on the waves. Samuel Openshaw noted that many passengers felt the effects of the moving vessel and became violently seasick. The Openshaw family had taken plenty of good provisions, but the food did little for his mother, who remained in her bed vomiting, unable to eat.[19]

Accustomed only to land-based travel, the immigrants could not cope with the constant motion of the ship's rocking caused by the wind and the waves of the open ocean. On May 27 Beecroft complained of feeling "very queer." His wife took him breakfast in bed, where he lay watching his fellow travelers.

> Some were eating like farmers, others were vomiting like drunken men. Some emptying slop pails, others running with boilers and kettles. Some lay in bed sick, others sat and leaned against ought they could find while on deck. The Saints, men, women, and children, lay on deck one against another like pigs. Some could manage to walk about, but staggered like drunken men, while husbands had to paddle and otherwise carry their wives to the privy and other places.[20]

Jaques, also on the *Horizon*, recalled that "seasickness changed our countenances to a pitiful, pallid hue.... A soberer company of passengers than we were that day, you would scarcely wish to see. Such a worshiping of buckets and tins, and unmentionable pans, I shall not attempt to describe." Jaques himself "paid the most devoted attention to the slop-pail about every half hour." While he heaved, his young daughter Flora "passed through it all with scarcely a serious look, having been all the time as lively as usual."[21]

Travelers on the *Samuel Curling* earlier in 1856 also had rough weather shortly after departing from Liverpool. "It blew a hurricane," John Rowe Moyle later wrote. "The water came in upon us so that our beds were wet for several days." Twelve-year-old Henry Moyle agreed. "It blew a huracane & the lightening & thunder was fierce & terrible which tore & carried away the main canvas & the waves roled very high & at times came over the Deck & great streems of water came Poreing down the tophatch, and the storm so fierce & terable, that most of the Pasingers thought that we would go to the bottom of the sea."[22]

A month into the journey, on June 5, Samuel Openshaw's mother was feeling better as those on the *Horizon* watched "several great fish play in the water." But all was not well: the "potatoes began to sprit and spoil," Openshaw wrote, adding "we carried them all on deck to dry."[23] It is unclear whether this effort salvaged the potatoes.

The *Horizon* had heavy side winds on Friday, June 6, again sending Openshaw and his mother to their bunks with seasickness. The following day, however, he helped prepare "our puddings for a Sunday's dinner" (they did not cook on Sunday, spending the day in church meetings). As the stout wind filled the *Horizon*'s sails, they "passed a vessel on our left as quick as a man running passes one that is walking."[24] The gale "blew so strong that it tore one sail right up from the bottom to top," Joseph Beecroft recalled. "For fear of something worse all of the crew was ordered to work to fold up some [sails] and to reef [fold] others, which gave us a grand opportunity to see the activity of sailors in climbing the ropes and their daring in going to the top gallant and amidst all the wind and wet to perch at the end of the sail yards."[25]

For all those who sailed in 1856, the routine was similar. The people organized on shipboard into companies, with captains over each group of men. The organization was similar to the system that they would use on the trail west. Regular prayer meetings were held on deck, usually both morning and night, with longer services on Sundays.

Once the ships were sailing on the open ocean, the weather began to take a toll. High winds caused rough waters with big waves that resulted in widespread seasickness. When there was no wind at all, the ships barely made headway. The great majority of the immigrants had spent their lives in areas with neighbors close by, but no one was accustomed to the shoulder-to-shoulder confines aboard ship. Being on deck gave people an opportunity to breathe the fresh sea air. With hundreds crowded onto each of the ships, however, it was impossible for the travelers to escape for long from the dank air of the middle and lower decks. Nor did they expect to see such vast expanses. On the open ocean, away from land, the horizon seemingly stretched forever, curving away. People had no markers to know whether they made any progress at all as the ships sliced through foamy water. Few could have anticipated how bright the sun would be when reflected off ocean water; nor did they expect the night to be so dark. For the first time in their lives, many saw the glittering of millions of stars overhead—the broad ribbon of the Milky Way and the constellations, which many may have heard of but had never clearly seen before.

On June 3, 1856, Beecroft had a meal of meat and pudding and then rested for a while before attending an evening meeting. Afterward he "went on deck and beheld the new moon and stars of the first magnitude, all was still and beautiful, the air serene and clear with scarcely a cloud to be seen . . . the broad ocean lay stretched out on all sides, smooth and unruffled."[26]

Many of the travelers came from rural areas or farms where they worked the land. Others had abandoned small homes in cities. Now the peaty smell of soil and the odors of coal smoke and general refuse had given way to the tang of salt ever present from the spray of the water. And nothing seemed solid. They struggled to develop sea legs. Even when no wind filled the sails, the ships were in constant motion. Captain Daniel Jones, a returning missionary who managed the saints traveling on the *Samuel Curling* in 1856, described how the ship, "a mammoth of her species, with her 700 passengers and luggage, crew, and withal 2,000 tons of iron [in] her bowels, rocked like a crow's nest on a lone sapling in the gale."[27]

While choppy waters often tossed the *Samuel Curling* to and fro, the wind was favorable. At times the ship ran fourteen miles an hour. Even so, the passengers were all sick. General disarray prevailed in the ship's hold. Patrick Twiss Bermingham wrote on June 25, 1856, "Between the decks was a horrid mess, as the ship was rolling perpetually."[28] The mess probably involved scattered clothing and goods that had not been secured well enough and had fallen to the deck. The horridness no doubt derived from filth as people retched from seasickness.

Despite the difficulties, the illness, and generally crowded conditions, immigrants attempted to develop normal routines. Each day of activity on the *Horizon* in 1856 started at five in the morning "by the sound of the cornet" and ended at ten at night when a similar bugle call swept through the vessel.[29] The fiddler Joseph Beecroft noted that one evening the horn sounded for bed "to the tune of 'Cottage in a Wood'" and the following day the saints were roused at 6 A.M. "to the tune of 'The Girl I Left Behind Me.'" Beecroft generally followed his morning ritual: "I got up, washed, shaved, dressed, carried my water to fire for breakfast, attended prayer meeting."[30]

During the days some played musical instruments, women sewed, and children made a playground below decks in an area near one of the ship portholes. "In looking down the gangway or passage on either side of our berths it looks like a long bazaar," Beecroft wrote. "Some are eating, some preparing food, some reading, others passing to . . . and fro, one making a bed. It is one continued scene of bustle from morn to night."[31] Likening the atmosphere to a bazaar, John Jaques observed: "We want by the stalls and gingerbread to give our deck the appearance of an English country fair." Writing to Franklin Richards, he added that the ship had none of the "drunkenness, quarreling, profanity, and obscenity which generally characterize such assemblies." Still, he said, "I will admit that we do not appear in holiday attire exactly."[32]

Each passenger had more space on the lower deck than was allowed on the upper deck. Because the warm air rose, the lower deck space, although dark and gloomy, was cooler. Berths for two passengers, Jaques said, were "about six feet long by four feet four inches wide, lined up like horses mangers, two in height, with about two feet underneath the lowest."[33] One evening a crash disrupted the serene night when some of the beds on the *Horizon* collapsed. Repairs were made while the ship "continued to rock like a cradle and the boards made awful cracks and creaks." Then there was "another big crash followed by a shout of 'Get up! Get up!'" Beecroft peered from his bunk toward the berth of a fellow traveler, "filled with boards and bed from the berth over." Before all settled down, a dozen people were aroused. Most of them then spent the night in the beds that they made on the floor.[34]

Children made the best of it all, as they always seem to do. John Linford described daily life on the *Thornton* in 1856: "The children run about and play at cat after the mouse or any other things they please."[35] The children on the *Horizon* played with marbles and skipped ropes, while older boys helped tug on the ropes with the sailors.

It was not all play, however. Trying to maintain some degree of routine life, William Woodward held a school session aboard the *Samuel Curling.* "The boys were assembled [and] held on the lower deck in the forward part of the ship. The instructions were spelling, mental arithmetic, & questions in geography & history. I called the boys together by the request of Brother [Dan] Jones. I have taught the boys several times since we left Liverpool."[36]

"TELL ME IF JOHN POWELL'S TEAKETTLE IS BOILING"

Those who were not ill had to eat. The task of preparing food for hundreds with only limited cooking areas quickly became a challenge and a source of conflict. "Cooking for 800 hungry people at one galley is not a trifling affair," John Jaques wrote in late May 1856, when he traveled on the *Horizon*, "especially when each family or person has a private pot or dish. Too many pots at the fire seems as bad as too many irons in it."[37]

Henry Hamilton worked his way across the Atlantic as a passenger cook on the *Horizon*. On his first day, poor ventilation made the galley very smoky when he started a fire. Then the captain remedied the problem by poking a hole in the top of the galley to allow the smoke to dissipate. Basic foods included gruel, and sometimes potatoes for breakfast, plus beef and pork for other meals, but salt for seasoning was in short supply.[38]

Just how hot the cook stoves actually were is questionable. John Powell put his name on the family teakettle, filled it with water, and took it to the passenger cook stove that the immigrants used to prepare their own meals. As his daughter Mary later recalled,

From time to time, all day long, I was sent to ask the cook, "Will you please tell me if John Powell's teakettle is boiling?" Toward late afternoon, I met a couple of Scotsmen who laughed uproariously at my questions. I ran back, and told father that he would have to fetch it himself. It took until five o'clock to get that cup of tea for mother. After this experience, father made arrangements with the captain's cook to boil the water on his stove. We were now able to get mother's cup of tea on short notice.

Powell, whose family had sold their feather beds, bedsteads, bedding, and other furniture before leaving Wales, "paid the colored man, the captain's cook, to prepare our food," Mary said. But the family ate little due to seasickness.[39]

John Oborn sailed on the *Thornton* with his parents and later claimed that his family had use of the stove just one hour each week. The struggle for access to cooking facilities was common. Too many people were crammed into tight spaces, and public areas were inadequate. The Oborn family diet consisted largely of "bean biscuit soaked overnight," he recalled. The biscuits were so hard that even with that soaking they were still dry in the center in the morning.[40]

Sharing a stove, cramped quarters, and monotonous travel wore on the immigrants, who grumbled most about the cooking conditions and food. "Ten gallons of water for every 100 persons, but none did we get," complained Archer Walters, a passenger on the *Enoch Train*. "My children dissatisfied with habituals. Some could eat one thing and some another. Could not please all, but expect they will get better as they get used to it." Just a week later Walters's wife was "very poorly," which he attributed to the difference in diet and "cooking so badly managed. Having only the ship allowance. No preserves, butter, cheese, ham."[41]

Elizabeth White Steward, who did not travel with the handcarts once on land but was with the company on the ship, recalled weekly prayer meetings as well as singing and dancing at other times during the crossing. For food they had "hard sailor's biscuits made of very coarse flour, so hard we could scarcely break them, salt pork and beef, rice and split peas." Water was rationed and "was very poor," no doubt warm and brackish.[42]

Some passengers brought extra rations. When he started out John Southwell had "a fine boiled ham, a fine cheddar cheese and several laoves [*sic*] of old English plum cake and a good size plum pudding."[43] James and Elizabeth Bleak felt prepared for their crossing when they wrote in a letter home from Liverpool on May 23, 1856, just before the *Horizon* sailed, that they had fifteen pounds of Indian meal, ten pounds of flour, four quarter loaves, cheese, raisins, and spice.[44]

Jaques, who served as the historian for Martin's Company on the *Horizon*, traveled with elders Jesse W. Haven and George P. Waugh; John Thompson, who served as a steward; cooks Henry Hamilton and Joseph Jackson; and F. C. Robinson, sergeant of the guard. The men used their spare clothing to create beds. They bought a pound of molasses, a pound of marine soap, some round lamp wick, six one-penny packets of violet powder, six one-penny boxes of wax lights, and six red herrings.[45] On the crossing they would have beef and pork, peas, biscuits, flour, oatmeal, rice, and tea as well as salt, mustard, pepper, sugar, and vinegar.

Beecroft seemed to have a good supply of food. He wrote of eating boiled beef, potatoes, rice, biscuits, and preserves as well as pork and bread and a cold meal of hash. One day "we baked a [l]arge parkin [soft cake made of molasses and oatmeal] and two cakes and got tea a little after five." They seem to have had a relatively steady supply of food, including a meal of boiled beef and pudding on June 21. Nonetheless, Beecroft's wife, Sarah, "buttoned or fastened the top . . . of her gown, a thing she has not been able to do for many years," indicating that she had lost weight on their journey.[46]

Henry Hobbs wrote of having pork, flour, biscuits, oatmeal, beef, rice, peas, potatoes, sugar, tea, salt, mustard, pepper, and vinegar as he set off on the *William Tapscott* in 1859. "Our water we receive every morning. 3 quarts of water daily is allowed to each adult."[47]

Sometimes careful preparations were not enough. One day Mary Powell and other children watched as two old men "set their table and lay out their lunch, in careful, painstaking fashion. They asked the blessing on the food. Just then a large wave came up and threw the dishes right and left. Everybody laughed, even the two old men."[48]

Taking tea was a common occurrence, but not always in the style that Beecroft reported. "Our ward sat down to a grand tea drinking. Tables were made of boxes set in rows and reached the entire length of the ward." The tea "was put in the copper in the cook house and was brought down in large cans and turned into our cans and pots. The cooks took in our bread and baked it the first. We had a good tea. Aftersward there was a social party. The Saints recited and sang and kept up the interest of the meeting till past 9 o'clock."[49]

In mid-May 1856, when contrary winds delayed the *Thornton*, the passengers voted to ration water. "It was deemed advisable that a lesser quantity of water be served out and a vote was taken which was unanimous that 2 quarts instead of 3 qts. [per day] be the quantity for each adult until we get into warm weather," James Grey Willie reported. They also agreed to cook only twice a day, with passengers coming on deck from 10 A.M. to 1 P.M. The following Tuesday was "set apart for fasting and prayer before the Lord."[50] These were the first lessons for the travelers. They would not be their last.

"SHIP ROLLED AND BOXES RATTLED"

The landlubbers had differing opinions of the ocean crossing. Some disliked every minute, finding the journey tedious. Many spent days in their berths, too ill to move. At times the passengers were "sent sprawling across the deck or thrown down, which very near brought about broken legs," Andrew Smith recalled from his trip on the *Thornton*.[51] "Ship rolled and boxes rattled," Archer Walters noted in his journal. "Bottles upset. Bedsteads broke down and cooking did not please all for the sauce pans upset. Some were [scalded] and some fell and hurt themselves." It was, as he said, "a thing to try the patience."[52] But thirteen-year-old Heber McBride found the 1856 ocean crossing on the *Horizon* exciting: "I was in my element all the time and the harder the wind did blow the better I enjoyed myself."[53]

Special moments broke the tedium, such as sperm whales blowing and playing around the ships or porpoises racing along behind.[54] "The water seems all alive with them," Walters noted.[55]

Mary Powell grew to love the ocean. "Each afternoon I watched the sun sink like a ball of fire beneath the waves. Next morning it rose again out of the water." When she leaned far over the deck banister to watch the ship "plowing the waves and cutting the water," she must have felt the spray of salty water and seen droplets that turned into rainbow colors as they reflected in the sun.[56]

"When we reached deep water," John Southwell of the Fifth Company said, "the first deep water tribe made their appearance. The captain said they were a large school of dolphins. Their backs of gold were showing above the surface of the sea green water."[57]

Even more thrilling was the sight of what one traveler described as "a large man-eating shark." The monster quickly turned, but a huge wave brought it to the surface. Anticipating this action, the mate fired his rifle, striking the shark. An old sailor instantly launched his harpoon. The metal flashed as it struck the shark, which made a few terrific lunges. But the harpoon, attached to the ship with a strong rope, held. The creature was subdued after a furious struggle. The sailors now used a block and tackle to hoist the shark aboard. When it came to rest on the deck, "a line was laid along his carcass and he proved to measure 30 feet long. Proof was not taken of his weight, but the old whaler judged him to weigh 2,500 pounds," Southwell recalled. The hunt did not end there. Soon the old whaler and other crewmembers cut up the carcass and deposited the pieces in a large barrel in the hold of the ship. Later they added chemicals to extract the oil. "A large drove of porpoises were next seen," Southwell wrote. "They resembled a band of horses on the run. This attitude gave me the name of the seahorse. It was a wonderful sight. It seemed to fill a space of half a mile square."[58]

"By way of the first sunset on the sea, I cannot find language to explain its beauties, it was magnificent," Southwell said. "The next morning, after breakfast, there was a great surprise in store for us. The lookout had sighted a huge whale ahead. This thrilling call brought all hands to the deck. At that moment, the skies were filled with a thousand rainbows, caused by the whale spouting the water with the spray in the sun in such a way that it resembled the effect spoken of. The sights on the waters were endless and sublime."[59]

Henry Hobbs, sailing on the *William Tapscott* in 1859, wrote of sitting on the poop deck on Sunday, April 24. He was awestruck at the sight of "the furious waves of the ocean rolling up into mountains & then lashing themselves one over the other.... At one time it has the appearance of hills covered with snow & the wind drifting it about from one place to the other. At other times it is like the clouds of heaven. At times there are valleys to be seen & then in an instant they will swell into hills."[60]

While some people saw beauty, others gagged and vomited, rolling in wretched misery in their sea sickness. Still others celebrated: on the *Horizon* a newlywed couple took tea along with company leader Edward Martin and his counselors. Once they had completed their repast, the party moved to the deck, where they danced and frolicked in celebration to the sounds of Beecroft playing his fiddle and someone shaking a tambourine.

Marriages on board were sometimes numerous. Fourteen couples, eight of them from Denmark and another six from England, married in a single ceremony in April 1859 as the Eighth Handcart Company crossed the ocean. Hans Olson Magleby recorded the fact in his journal and just a week later wrote of his own feelings for fellow passenger Gjertrude Marie Christiansen Roe (twenty-one): "In the evening I revealed some of my feelings for [Marie] which I understood were with joy received," he happily noted, "and we made a covenant with each other to bless her, and I pressed the first kiss upon her cheek."[61]

Close confinement led Magleby, who had turned twenty-four on April 14, and Marie to a rapid courtship, but the decision to make their relationship more permanent was soon made for them. On May 7 Magleby was called "to the president Nassling for the English and Guld for the Scandinavians to explain if it was my intention to love and to marry Marg [Marie].... Marg was also called forth and the same questions put to her, and as it was with her and with my will, it became settled that we were to get married the next day." Magleby spent the early morning of May 8 "fasting and preparing for the coming celebration." At mid-morning he and Marie were married along with four other couples, including the Norwegians Christian Haagensen, twenty-nine, and Karen Petra, twenty-eight. "The meeting opened and Nassling gave a long and instructive sermon in English, which I understood in part," Magleby wrote. "After this he performed the marriage ordinance for us, after we promised that we would love each other, be true to each other, and so forth. . . . We had great joy this day."[62]

Regular worship services were a part of the routine on all of the ships. The Mormons on the *Samuel Curling* in 1856 had prayer meetings twice daily. In the morning the men went on deck early, allowing the women time to dress before the morning prayer meeting. "At dusk the bugle called all hands to prayer again, by wards, and it pleased me much to see," wrote Dan Jones to Franklin Richards. "Seven hundred Saints on their way to Zion, pent up in so small a space, all bow the knee, and, with their hearty Amen, lift their hearts in aspirations of praise to him who deserves our all."[63]

Even so the crossing was challenging. Chicken pox broke out among the children on the *Samuel Curling* and spread through the ship despite efforts to check its progress, in which the doctor of the ship and Captain Samuel Curling were said to have distinguished themselves. Some on the ship "devoted all our time to nourish the sick, especially the old, and the mothers of infants, by preserves, soups, sago, arrowroot, and all the well assorted stock [that Richards had] furnished for the company," Jones said.[64] Children on the *Horizon* fell ill with measles. The *Enoch Train* became lice infested before reaching Boston, leading the Mormons to appoint a special "Louse Committee."[65]

One day in 1856 a seven-year-old boy on the *Horizon* saw a line running from one bulkhead to another that was swinging in the breeze. Seeing it as a plaything, the boy "grabbed the rope and it swung him over the bulwark of the ship," wrote one observer. "The act was seen immediately and a boat lowered, manned by two expert swimmers. But it was too late and the poor boy was swallowed by the heavy, rolling waves."[66]

As the ships neared Newfoundland, the weather changed. The travelers found themselves sailing in perpetual fogs and heavy mists. Passengers crossing the cold waters of the northern Atlantic on the *Thornton* saw "some very large icebergs towering up in the sky like huge mountains," wrote George Cunningham, who was fifteen when he made the trip. "The cold was very intense for several days before we passed them," he added.[67]

Samuel Openshaw, on the *Thornton*, wrote, "the man on lookout at the bow of the vessel kept up a continual beating night and day on something like an old brass drum which sounded very unmusical to my ear. We were told that this was done to warn the men of fishing crafts to keep out of the way, there being danger of them being run down by large vessels." The crew on the *Horizon* also kept sounding the ship's horn as they sailed through heavy fog near Newfoundland, to avoid striking a fishing boat. They also took measurements of water depth, making sure to avoid the shoreline. In dense fog on June 19 Openshaw saw several flocks of wild ducks close by the vessel and some fishing boats. In the afternoon they pulled out of the fog and soon had clear sailing.[68]

Passing near the fishing boats allowed some passengers to make a few trades. In one instance fishermen in their little boat approached the *Horizon* and traded some codfish for nails, giving the passengers something fresh to eat.[69]

Newfoundland could also mean rough seas and other dangers. As the *William Tapscott* skirted Newfoundland in 1859, the water was filled with icebergs, though the ship remained "in full sail." The seas were rolling, with a large wave sweeping across the deck every few minutes, drenching the travelers. "We were [feeling] very poorly from the severe rocking of the ship all night," Hobbs said. "A considerable deal of water came through the portholes & sent things swimming. Lots of tins tumbled about & made a tremendous roar."[70]

It was a "terrible day and night," Mark Lindsey wrote. "It seem as though everything was going down. Carried off the sails and [one] of the bulwarks was [damaged]." The "fog bell," he said, "is going night and day."[71] Hans P. Freece, who later left the church, hoped for divine intervention. "On board the ship we were under command of certain priests of the Melchizedek Order," he wrote to his son. "We believed that they would perform miracles. One day a storm came up and the waves threatened to sink the ship. I was sure that the elders would still the sea, but they huddled together, frightened like the rest of us."[72]

The *Horizon* passengers had been blessed by Richards and been assured the angels would watch over them and protect them. But Eliza Pear's child died on June 1, 1856, and an old woman who had died in the morning was launched into the deep through the porthole without ceremony.[73]

Deaths among the company aboard the *Thornton* included the Danish child Thomas Peterson, age eight, who fell through a hatchway and fractured his skull; three-year-old Margaret Kay, who died of fever; ten-year-old Mary Lark, whose death was attributed to consumption; ten-year-old Rasmine Rasmussen of Jutland, Denmark, who died of "inflammation of the brain"; and nine-month-old Jane James of Pindin Branch, Worcestershire, who "died of the thrush in the mouth."[74] Mary Ann James later wrote of her baby sister's death: "Death claimed our little Jane and we were obliged to place the precious bundle in a watery grave. Mother's heart strings were torn, but the brave little mother that she was felt not to murmur against the will of him who gave."[75] Some adults did not survive the passage to America either, including Rachel Curtis, seventy-five, whose death was attributed to old age.[76]

Sharing his opinions on sailing the ocean in a letter to Franklin Richards, written July 23, 1856, and published in the *Millennial Star* on August 30, 1856, John Jaques wrote that "sea life is to me dull and fusty life." He liked "the beginning and end of a sea voyage better than any other part of it" but admitted that he could "sit for hours on the forecastle, and watch our noble vessel dashing through the briny waves, and lashing them into an innumerable variety of fantastic forms of spray and foam." However, the constant motion irked him. "Who can possibly like to be continually rocked about, as though he were having a child's ride in an English swing boat? Who has any taste for a dizzy head at every breeze? Who admires treading on a platform that seems the plaything of an everlasting earthquake?" Sailing vessels seemed "behind the times" to Jaques because they relied on nature for power. "The idea of waiting, day after day, on the idle wind is bad enough, but the reality is much worse. It makes one feel like getting out and pushing behind." Then the wind will rise, forcing the ship through the waters "like a mad thing."[77]

Most of all there was monotony. When the seas were calm, the women spent their time reading, sewing, or walking on the deck. They listened to the sailors singing as the men pumped water from the ship's hold.[78] The women sewed tents that they would use when crossing the plains, and the passengers signed receipts for their passage to America, pledging to repay the costs of their passage to the PEF, plus the standard 10 percent annual interest rate.[79]

When Englishman Henry Hobbs sailed on the *William Tapscott* in 1859, one experienced overland traveler told the passengers that the ocean crossing was the "easiest part of our journey and they should make the most of it for when they had hold of the handcart & in the mud & cetera we would find out."[80]

That same year one of the Mormon leaders, Hans P. Freece, "found it necessary to knock down one of the brethren because he insisted that the priest [mission president] had falsely taken from him some of his emigration funds." Freece added: "The priest would take our money and buy our tickets and provide for our food, and I heard many complaints to the effect that they were defrauding the believing followers." The accuser abandoned the party when the ship docked in New York, but Freece said that no action was taken against the elder. "For a Mormon priest to strike a brother was permissible," Freece wrote, "because he did it with authority from God."[81]

Time and again high winds disrupted the routine work, forcing people below decks as the sailors trimmed the canvas in their efforts to ride out rough weather. But when the boxes that had been lashed broke away from their fastenings, they rolled and bounced all over the ship. Children and adults fell, sometimes getting just bumps and bruises but at other times being truly hurt. In one such storm Patrick Twiss Bermingham got no rest because he was "obliged to hold the children, one under each arm, to prevent them from being thrown out of bed." This particularly violent storm carried two of the sails away as the Mormons gathered in the middle hatch to pray for "calmer weather and a more prosperous voyage."[82]

Parents christened their new babies in some manner related to their ocean journey. One boy born on the ship *Samuel Curling* was named Dan Curling Dee: his first name from Daniel Jones, the church elder in charge of the traveling saints on that ship, and his middle name from the captain of the ship (which was also the ship's name). A girl born on that ship was named Claudia Curling Reynolds, again for the ship and her captain.

The son of Thomas and Jennet McNeil of Scotland was named Charles Thornton, for the ship *Thornton* and the captain, Charles Collins. Thomas and Sarah Denton Moulton also named their son Charles for the ship's captain. He was born on May 6, 1856, just after the *Thornton* sailed from Liverpool. They added the middle name Alma, which would be used by later generations. Those two babies, along with Margaret Ann Steward, daughter of John and Ann Steward from Edinburgh, Scotland, and Elizabeth Ann Farmer, whose parents Edward and Morgan Farmer hailed from Spittlegate, Lincolnshire, were blessed by James Willie during a meeting held in early afternoon on June 1, 1856.[83]

Two children born on the voyage of the *Enoch Train* were named for the vessel: Christina Enoch Lyon, born to Mary Ann and Thomas Lyon, and Enoch Train Hargraves, the son of Agnes and Samuel Hargraves. Elizabeth and William Johnston named their son Hamilton, and Mary and James Sheen named their son Sydney, but this baby would die before they reached Utah.

The *Horizon*, nearly a full clipper, sailed very fast, taking five weeks to travel from Liverpool to Morcambe Bay, Boston. They "had no bad weather or storms worth mentioning," Josiah Rogerson claimed, despite other passengers' numerous reports to the contrary.[84] Aaron Jackson quoted his mother's account of that same ship's crossing. She remembered that "there was a near panic on board one day when sailors were working on the sails and an officer gave the order, 'hoist higher.' An excitable passenger thought the man had yelled, 'fire' and the passengers got panicky."[85]

Writing of the same incident, John Jaques said that early one morning "the job [jib] was split in ribbons. The main top gallant sail and the fore topsail were also injured. The noise made by the sailors on deck caused one of the guards to fancy he heard the cry of fire so he cried fire and the cry was reitered [repeated] through a great portion of the ship causing much alarm and many to jump out of their berths."[86]

It was no false alarm on the *Thornton* on May 20, 1856, when a fire did break out in the passenger's galley at 11 P.M. Although it was late at night and the event may have caused some moments of panic, the captain, crew, and many of the Mormons quickly subdued the blaze, James Grey Willie reported. Earlier that day the decks had been "well cleansed and fumigated with tar and chloride of lime."[87]

Travelers on the *Horizon,* the *Thornton,* and the *William Tapscott* reported few problems between the crew and passengers. But William Butler, a saint traveling on the *Samuel Curling,* noted "considerable trouble with the captain and crew trying to keep them from the women."[88] Patrick Twiss Bermingham gave more detail on Friday, May 9, 1856: "A gentile passenger made a great deal of noise, and was dragged from the young females part of the ship, where he had secreted himself and [then was] put into his own berth." To avoid such situations in the future, Bermingham said, "Brother Lucas and myself were placed as guards."[89]

Sixteen-year-old Fanny Fry traveled with her brother, John, and sister, Sarah Jane, on the *William Tapscott* in 1859. She had left behind in England a young man named Thomas Watson, a blacksmith apprentice. "In our last interview," she later wrote, "he tried to persuade me to stay single for two years then he would come to Zion to join me, to part no more." She made no such promise in person but intended to do so in a letter from the ship. However, her brother would not provide her any paper to write such a missive. Fanny avoided any serious bout of seasickness, but she was unable to elude thirty-one-year-old George Rowley. This married Mormon elder was "determined to have my company," although his wife, Anne, and two sons, William (thirteen) and Joseph (eleven), also were on board.[90]

"His poor wife I shall never forget," Fanny recalled. "She was sick the entire time we were on the water. I do not think she sat up three hours the entire voyage until the last few days. She wasted away until she looked [more] like a mere skeleton than anyone I had then seen." She added: "It must have been a severe trial to her to be sick so long and to know that her husband was continually running after the girls as he was."

Fanny did all she could to keep clear of Rowley's advances. "I used to go and hide in the back part of our bunk and other places to get away from him. I formed quite a dislike to him while we were on the sea. It seemed that wherever I went he was always present. There was a young man, a Swede, that I preferred before I did him. It was the Swede I liked to dance with."

Upon arrival in New York, Fanny wished to remain in the city with John, but George Rowley invited her to accompany him to Utah. First he wanted her to travel west and "become his wife when we reached Zion." But Fanny refused the offer. After further discussion with George Q. Cannon, a high-ranking member of the church, the offer was amended. "Brother Rowley said if I would consent to go with him he would pay all my expenses of the journey and he would tri and be as a brother to me, and when I got to Utah I should be as free as now," Fanny wrote. After some persuasion, "leaving my dear brother behind," Fanny elected to migrate to Utah with Rowley. In this foreign land she felt "entire[ly] alone as far as help was concerned."

CHAPTER 3

"OUR HEARTS WERE CHEERED"

The ocean travel took a toll on the immigrants as they dealt with crowded quarters, poor food, and the vagaries of weather that slowed their progress to a near standstill when the wind failed to blow or swept them through rough waters when storms caused the ocean to roil. Finally, however, they neared the end of this first leg of a journey to Zion. By June 24, 1856, "the fresh water began to stink . . . old Mr. Allen from Radcliff [died and] found a watery grave," Samuel Openshaw wrote in his diary. Just a day later the *Horizon* came "in sight of 'Yankee Land' . . . the first land that we have seen since we left sight of Ireland and truly it was beautiful." They entered into the Bay of Boston, Openshaw wrote, "to behold the rise and decline of hills beyond hills covered with green grass, cattle grazing, bedecked beautiful houses, rocks rising out of the water as if to resist the force of the waves. It was truly sublime to us to gaze upon it."[1]

Large fields of waving corn yellowing for the harvest greeted the *Horizon* when it settled opposite the Cape Cod Lighthouse, said Joseph Beecroft.[2] At 9 o'clock in the morning on June 29, a Boston doctor boarded the ship. The passengers had been ordered to clean up and be on deck. The first doctor did an inspection, left, and returned with other inspectors, who had all the passengers report to the poop deck for another review. In all John Jaques said that the travelers "were up on deck two or three hours, which was very wearing to the women and children."[3]

After weeks on the ocean, where steady breezes usually moved them along and provided some cooling relief, the travelers withered under the oppressive humidity and heat of Boston, from 96 to 100 degrees in the shade at four o'clock in the afternoon on July 1.[4]

While the captain praised the saints for their conduct during the ocean crossing, there was one point of contention. He "spoke in disapproval of the harsh conduct of the first mate and the folly of sister Williamson and him courting together." The first mate, it seems, had kept the crew in order but "had not always proper respect for the passengers." The captain had turned Mrs. Williamson out of her quarters "because of her folly with the first mate."[5]

In a later letter to Parley Pratt, Jaques said the woman remained in Boston to marry the first mate:

> How any girl, professing to be a Saint, could suffer herself to be led away by such a swearing, wicked man, ungovernable fellow as he was, I am at a loss to say. She seemed to be the only one among passenger or crew that desired his acquaintance after leaving the ship. To be sure, it might have appeared, to the Saints on the *Horizon*, a fine thing to be waited upon with a carriage and a pair of greys, but that is not the end of the matter. Such a thing is not very wonderful in this country, as it only costs a dollar or two, and dollars are more plentiful and more easily obtained here than in England.[6]

Once in Boston Joseph Beecroft purchased "a large cheese and some butter," but as a result of the high temperatures and humidity "the sweat flowed freely from us." Even so, the passengers who had gone ashore "visited the common of about 12 acres laid out in walks, grass plots, trees, flowers, all kinds, water, and every variety of garden flower and walk was there." Wandering the streets, Beecroft found the city "tastefully laid out with shops, public buildings, and so on."[7]

Jaques bought a quart of milk for five cents, several ten-cent loaves of bread, four or five pounds of ham, and other items. During the ocean voyage there had been four marriages, two deaths, and two births. A son, William Horizon, was born to Ann and William Paxman, on June 12, and twenty-four-year-old Elizabeth Hall (whom Jaques identified as Sarah) from Stratfordshire gave birth to a son on June 29, just before the ship docked in Boston. The baby's father was twenty-one-year-old Charles Hall.[8]

When the *Enoch Train* docked at Constitution wharf in Boston harbor on May 1, 1856, the Hodgetts sisters were met by their brother William Ben Hodgetts. He had taken a fast steamer to America, making it possible for him to reach Boston before the girls did. He had a letter from their mother in which she implored her daughter Maria to "come home and take care of your mother in the hour of my trial, my hours are short. Emmie, my loved one, go to Utah with your brother." Following their mother's wishes, Maria stayed in Boston only two weeks before finding transportation back to England, while Emily and William Ben continued on to Utah. They took with them the four blue chests of goods that their mother had brought on ship when she made her own attempt at immigration.[9] The siblings did not remain with the First Handcart Company. Instead William Ben took charge of a wagon train that traveled with the Edward Martin Handcart Company, the last to cross the plains in 1856. William Ben had experience crossing the plains. In 1852, when he was twenty, he had immigrated from England and lived in Utah for four years before returning to England as a missionary. Now he was again traveling to Great Salt Lake City with one sister.

A day after reaching Boston, the passengers from the *Enoch Train* debarked and climbed on nine omnibuses for a ride to the railroad station. They boarded a train that departed for New York City at 5 o'clock that afternoon. The immigration agents in America had found cheaper rail passage leaving from New York City than if they traveled to the west directly from Boston. A band played "Yankee Doodle," "Home Sweet Home," and "Auld Lang Syne" as the passengers reached New York City.[10]

There the travelers met the church's New York immigration agent, John Taylor. He asked how long it had been since they had any refreshments. "Two days" was the answer, according to Mary Powell. "I should like to see you eat before I speak to you," Taylor replied. Soon the travelers had before them bread, steak, and coffee. "I had not thought about being so hungry until then," Powell said.[11]

Not everyone who set out from England to make a handcart journey to Utah in 1856 completed the trip that year. The Crouch family arrived in Boston with no funds in hand and could go no farther. The seven-member family moved into a large tenement house. "It was in the heat of summer, we were in the depths of poverty and father out of employment. We were strangers in a strange land without the bare necessities of life," Ebenezer Crouch recalled. Within two months the children were ill. Three of them eventually died. The family had no resources, so the municipality of Boston buried these youngsters in paupers' graves. "Mother had the heart-rending experience of seeing strange men enter the house, take the bodies of her dear ones away to where she never knew. That was the last she saw of them in this life," Crouch would recall. Because of these setbacks the Crouches did not endure the overland crossing of the American continent the way their fellow shipboard travelers did. They moved to Ashland, Massachusetts, and lived there until spring 1859. The family then made another start for Utah, ultimately joining a wagon train managed by Ebenezer R. Young, who took an ox train of ten wagons loaded with merchandise to Salt Lake City.[12]

The *Thornton* docked in New York on June 14, 1856, after the tugboat *Achilles* provided a final tow to Staten Island. Marilyn Austin Smith recalled that a doctor boarded the English ship to inspect the passengers and give them a "certificate of the good health." Customs officers also boarded the vessel and "passed our luggage without any inspection. At sun down we landed at the Castle Garden, a large building appropriated for emigrants, where we were visited by Elder Felt who kindly welcomed us."[13] Castle Garden was the first immigration center in the United States. The round building formerly had been a fort and a theater but was used for immigrant processing from 1855 to 1890. Located at the tip of Manhattan in the area known as the Battery, Castle Garden at first was called Castle Clinton, named for Mayor DeWitt Clinton, and served as the headquarters of the Third Military District. This was a heavily armed fort built to dissuade the British from attacking New York City during the War of 1812. No longer needed for defense of the city, the structure was renamed Castle Garden in 1824 and became a place for public entertainment, including theatrical performances and concerts. In 1855 the State of New York leased the building for use as an immigrant processing center, as a precursor to the more well-known immigration center later established at Ellis Island, across the harbor.

When ships arrived in New York City, the area was noisy and boisterous with people stepping onto American soil for the first time (the "land" where Castle Garden stood was actually built from mounds of garbage; the castle once stood in the harbor, connected to the mainland by a bridge, but in the early 1850s landfill extended to the south and Castle Garden became part of the mainland). The day after the *Thornton* docked in June 1856 Anna Tait was "sitting in the largest house I was ever in. We all landed safe, and got in here at 7:40 P.M. yesterday. Our names were called over, and we had to state where we were going, what money we had, and other particulars, which were entered into a book, and we then passed into the house."[14]

The newly arrived immigrants spent little time at Castle Garden and other debarkation points. Facing a nearly 3,000-mile overland journey to Utah, the Mormon travelers did not tarry in the Atlantic coastal ports. They left the roll of a ship for the rocking motion and steady noise of a train. The overland journey from Boston and New York (and later from Philadelphia) to the Midwest equalized people of different classes. Squires shared carriages with tenants. One train car was a cattle pen while another had padded seats covered with crimson silk velvet, but those who rode in them were not separated by stature or financial background.[15] Certainly not all of the Mormons who traveled under the PEF (and therefore went at the lowest cost possible) had access to any cars with velvet seats, but some did.

In 1856 those traveling through New York by train paid a fare of $11.50 for each person over the age of fourteen, while children between the ages of five and fourteen were charged $5.75 for passage. Toddlers age four and under were free. They presumably did not take up much space and may have sat on the lap of an older family member. In the early companies the adults could take one hundred pounds of luggage on the train, while each child over age three was allowed fifty pounds of baggage.

Railroad travel in the 1850s was no picnic. "It was very rough traveling upon the railways in this country," wrote Andrew Smith. "It is nothing strange to be knocked out of your seat and frequently to pass heaps of cars and engines all smashed up by collision or otherwise." Smith had crossed the Atlantic on the *Enoch Train* before switching to the railroad. "The road from Devon Point to Iowa is awful. The rails are laid quite crooked," Smith said. "Luckily when we [were] traveling about 2000 miles to escape without any serious accident. We ascribe our deliverance to God our Father & thank him for his goodness to us while traveling in sea and land."[16]

Taking the train west from New York in 1856, Samuel Openshaw commented on the landscape and cities through which they passed. "We changed the Luggage into another train of cars and then got something to eat and then took a view of the city of Buffalo," he wrote on July 4. "It is a very healthy place. Streets very wide, and telegraphic wires running to ever[y] part of the city. Some of the streets had trees on each side which are refreshing in the hot of the day. It stands upon the banks of Lake Erie. Being the Fourth of July, [there were] flags on the houses and across the streets also shooting and fireworks."[17]

Most PEF immigrants took trains to Iowa, though others used a combination of trains and steamboats or packets on rivers or across Lake Erie. On June 17, 1856, Willie Company travelers took a barge from Castle Garden to arrive at the Erie Railroad Depot in New York some nine hours later. Then they took the train to Dunkirk, a distance of 460 miles.[18] They were packed tightly in the train, but Openshaw remembered that they "felt well in spirit as well as in body. The country through which we passed dotted with towns and new settlements, and which was pleasing from the contrast with the monotony of the sea." They had to procure provisions, he said, as best they could along the way.[19]

At noon on June 19, Willie's Company reached Dunkirk, New York, "feeling generally well though tired with the irksome journey by Rail." They procured provisions and that evening boarded the *Jersey City*, a "screw steam boat, bound for Toledo, distance 280 miles.... The sea was quite calm as we were on lake Erie," a contrast with the ocean voyage, they noted.[20]

Once across Lake Erie, the company divided on June 23 because there were not enough rail cars to carry all of them west at one time. The majority of the English members departed in mid-afternoon on an express train headed to Rock Island, Illinois. Those traveling on a later train came upon a railroad bridge near Chicago that had been damaged, finding "many carriages smashed, no lives lost but many injured." With the bridge damaged, the saints spent the night "sleeping in the [rail] cars."[21]

A child died the following day of "general debility" and was buried immediately. Once they reached the Mississippi River, these immigrants had another delay to transport luggage and people across the river on a steam-powered ferry. The weary travelers found accommodations in a large warehouse that the railroad superintendent allowed them to use, but it was not a restful night. "Quite a rowdy spirit was manifested by many, desiring access to the building," Willie said, "and in the evening, we had to keep a strong guard, as we received a report through some friends that a mob intended to attack us in the night and gain access to our young women."[22]

Some immigrants had unique challenges. While traveling overland to Iowa City in 1856, John Jaques wrote to Mormon elder Parley Pratt:

I've got a five gallon keg of liquor with me and I seem to be running all kinds of hazards with it. At one place the conductor called it freight, and claimed a quarter on it. At Rock Island this very morning I was told that the probability was that I should have the keg taken from me on this side of the river. In consequence of the respect the people have in Iowa for the "Maine Liquor Law." Now it will be too bad, after bringing this all the way from St. Louis, to lose it here. I say nothing to nobody, but keep it in the car with me, under careful supervision. I do not recollect that I ever before was under the necessity of being such a firm and undeviating friend to intoxicating drink. If I am questioned about this firewater, I must say that it is for medicinal purposes in a camp of emigrants across the plains, and get off the best way I can.[23]

Langley Bailey, who traveled with his family on the *Horizon* in 1856, reached Iowa City by train. He and his brother became separated from their parents as they detrained in the dark and then walked through a rainstorm to the campsite. "We were all drenched with rain," he wrote. "We were conducted to a tent, stood up with many more all night in our wet clothes. When it began to get light father and mother were out hunting us[;] this was our first experience in traveling to Zion on foot."[24]

It took seventeen days for fourteen-year-old George Harrison, a member of the Martin Company, to travel by train from Boston to New York City and then to Iowa City. "The cars were so crude and the railroad so rough we were all tired out when we arrived in Iowa City, Iowa," he said. "But our difficulties were not over when we reached the end of the railroad. They were only just begun. Thirteen hundred or more miles of journey over the plains and mountains lay before us. We must walk all of this weary way and push or pull our handcarts. Our thoughts were all centered on getting to Zion."[25]

The handcart travelers in the early years went overland from New York, Boston, and later Philadelphia to Iowa City, where they began their final and most difficult part of the journey as they picked up handcarts and began walking. By 1859 the companies did not start using handcarts until they reached Florence or other places in Nebraska, bypassing Iowa and that 300 miles of trail. Their rail journey was by a different route (ending in St. Joseph, Missouri, by 1859) before they continued up the Missouri River by steamboat to points in Nebraska where their handcarts awaited.

On May 19, 1859, Henry Hobbs, who had traveled on the *William Tapscott* with the Eighth Company, was near Quincy, Illinois: "Cooked our food out-of-doors for the first time. In the evening went with a few of the boys for a swim in the Mississippi. There was a very rough crowd down at the station. Some were returned from Pikes Peak. They were disappointed in getting gold. I hear that thousands more are returning."[26]

The later families who traveled by handcart did not go overland from Iowa to Nebraska but instead stuck to the waterways. Hobbs's group continued on to Hannibal, Missouri, and then set off by boat following the Missouri River upstream to St. Joseph. Arriving on Saturday, May 21, Hobbs rested part of the day but saw "lots of covered wagons with oxen going in different directions. Milk, meat & bread is cheap at this place." He described St. Joseph as a flourishing town, although he noted: "Slaves are sold here." Warm weather left many feeling "poorly; some with diarrhea, some from close confinement," but the boat captain "had some berths fixed up for the women which proved a blessing to some."[27]

Still on the Missouri at six in the morning on May 24, Hobbs reached Florence, Nebraska—the old Mormon Winter Quarters. Chilled because he had slept on the deck, Hobbs started a fire and "got a good breakfast out of doors & felt to thank God for the peaceful asylum we had been brought to & for being surrounded with our friends."[28]

When the newly married Danish traveler Hans Olsen Magleby reached New York City in 1859, he "went on land by means of a little steamer and found rooms in the Hotel Castle Garden, where in fact all of us had lodgings. I stood guard during the night." The New York stay was brief. The following morning the Eighth Handcart Company "entered a steamer and sailed the whole night up a river to the city Albany, where I went on land in the morning." This Danish and English group climbed aboard railroad cars for the journey on to Chicago and Quincy, Illinois. Then they took a steamboat and the train to St. Joseph, where they boarded another steamboat to sail upriver to Florence, Nebraska.[29]

One by one the first companies of 1856 and 1857 completed their travel from the Atlantic seaboard to the Midwest, where they would reorganize at Iowa City and begin taking up those two-wheeled carts that defined their overland migration. There was no overland travel by handcart in 1858. In 1859 and 1860, as reflected in the journals of Magleby and Hobbs, the first leg of the journey in America involved travel by rail and river, before loading handcarts at the Missouri River in eastern Nebraska.

For the 1856 travelers, the arrival in Iowa marked the conclusion of the initial two parts of their long journey. While the first three companies quickly outfitted and took off with their handcarts, the last two groups that went west in 1856 found no handcarts when they reached the Iowa campsite, which forced a three-week delay. "We were camped on the banks of the Iowa River," fourteen-year-old George Harrison wrote:

> While there we had a terrible rain storm which nearly washed us away, the water poured into our tent until we were all drenched. Father and mother had to work hard to keep it from drowning my little baby sister. Finally the day came when we were ordered to pack our bedding and food onto the handcart and take up our march. Some of the leaders advised against our going, but their advice was not followed. Everybody wanted to get to the Valley and go they would at all costs; so off we started with our handcart train stringing along over the old rolling hills of the Iowa trail towards the Rocky Mountain valleys.[30]

Wherever they started their journey with their handcarts, these Mormons now faced several weeks of grueling travel, pushing and pulling what Danish handcart captain John A. Ahmanson called *tohjulede Menneskepiner.* Although this has been translated as "two-wheeled man-tormentors," one historian says the translation "might be better rendered as 'two-wheeled torture devices.'"[31]

CHAPTER 4

THE OVERLAND JOURNEY BEGINS

1856

In early 1856 in England Captain Edmund Ellsworth organized the people who would form the First Company of handcart pioneers. After crossing the Atlantic on the *Enoch Train* and *Samuel Curling*, and then traversing a third of the American continent by train, Ellsworth's company regrouped at Iowa City, Iowa. There Daniel D. McArthur's Second Company and the 320 members of the Third Company, Welsh emigrants led by Captain Edward Bunker, joined them. Mormon men had been in Iowa City since early May, purchasing and preparing the vehicles for the English families to drag to Zion.[1] Now these first three companies reorganized their supplies, filled the carts that John Taylor and Daniel Spencer had bought and paid for, made ox yokes, and formed bows over which they could stretch canvas covers on both the handcarts and the wagons that would accompany them. Ellsworth led the 274 souls in his company from the camp two miles west of Iowa City on June 9, 1856. They had fifty-five handcarts, one for every five people, three wagons, three mule teams, and six yoke of oxen—plus a brass band!

Mary Ann Jones, who was nineteen when she left England on the *Enoch Train*, kept a diary of her overland journey that closely corresponded with the official account of the company led by Captain Ellsworth (whom she would ultimately marry). Her details give a more personal impression of the trip.[2] "When the brethren came to weigh our things some wanted to take more than alowed," she wrote, "so [they] put on extra clothes so that some that wore [were] real thin soon became stout and as soon as the weight was over put the extra clothes in the hand cart again but that did not last long for in a few days we were called upon to have all weighed again & quite a few were found with more than alowed."[3]

Captain Ellsworth knew that he faced challenges even in the early going. Some of the travelers, who were perhaps already exhausted from their weeks of traveling, had to be persuaded to depart from Iowa City with the handcarts. As they set out, the hills and rough roads led several of the families to desert the handcart train.[4]

Each day started with a bugle blast. "Up we rose and assembled for prayer," wrote Mary Powell Sabin. "Then we ate a scanty breakfast of dough cakes fried in the frying pan." On occasion they also ate stewed apples. When traveling through a thicket in Iowa, Mary and some little girls disappeared, ultimately coming back with a bucket of blackberries. At a trading post just five days west of Iowa City, men in the Mormon party sold tobacco and trinkets to the Indians.[5]

Forty-seven-year-old carpenter Archer Walters had helped build handcarts before the Ellsworth party set off from Iowa City. Now he had the job of constructing coffins. His wife, Harriet Cross, was quite ill when the journey began, suffering from what he called American Fever (ague). The other members of the family were Henry (fifteen), Harriet (fourteen), Martha (twelve), Lydia (six), and Sarah Walters (seventeen), identified as a servant. The first death did not occur in his family. William Lee, the twelve-year-old son of John Lee, succumbed to consumption on the seventh day of travel. Another child, Lora Preator, only a few years old, died the following morning, a victim of whooping cough, according to the company secretary. The two youngsters were buried at Little Bear Creek. The emigrants were only about thirty-five miles west of Iowa City, indicating that they were traveling an average of just five miles a day, far slower than wagon companies and nowhere near Brigham Young's estimation of twenty to thirty miles per day. The third victim of the trail also was a child. The nineteen-month-old son of Job Welling died of an inflammation in the bowels. His body was carried along the next day when the handcarts rolled west at five in the morning. The pace picked up. After traveling ten miles in just over three hours, Ellsworth halted the company, allowing the women an opportunity to wash clothes and the Welling family the chance to bury their baby.[6]

The first adult death among the handcarters recorded by the company clerk was forty-four-year-old James Bowers, who died in late June of "quick consumption." "Went to buy the wood to make the coffin," the craftsman Archer Walters said, "but the kind farmer gave me the wood and nailes." The following day, Sunday, June 22, Walters arose at daybreak to build the box. "His relatives cried very much after I lifted him in the coffin and [while] waiting to screw him down." Once the task was complete, Walters "washed in the creek and felt very much refreshed."[7] Deaths continued in the First Company of travelers, however. Emma Sheen, not yet three years old, died on June 26.

On June 11, 1856, Captain Daniel D. McArthur, with assistance from Spicer W. Crandall and Truman Leonard, rolled more than forty handcarts away from Iowa City. The Second Company included 222 handcart pioneers with 4 wagons, each pulled by 3 span of oxen. Their carts, James Gardner recollected, were of "very frail construction": they "bound the wheels with rawhide."[8] Such cart construction in one of the earliest companies to head west belies John Taylor's instructions that all carts would be sturdy and well planned for the 1,300-mile overland migration.

Although the first carts that Taylor ordered were solidly constructed, those that the saints built themselves in Iowa City and those purchased by Daniel Spencer were not. As McArthur reported, the carts were "in an awful fix." "The[y] mowed [moaned] and growled, screeched and squealed," giving notice to people for miles around that the Mormons were on the move. "You may think this is stretching things a little too much," he wrote Wilford Woodruff, "but it is a fact, and we had them to eternally patch, mornings, noons, and nights." McArthur's company set off with wagons and oxen as well as their carts. The company journal reported that they "also had 5 beef and 12 cows; flour, 55 lbs. per head, 100 lbs. rice, 550 lbs. sugar, 400 lbs. dried apples, 125 lbs. tea, and 200 lbs. salt for the company."[9]

As they moved along, the elements and local populations could make travel difficult. The wind blew the dust stirred up by the travelers with the Second Company, making it difficult for twenty-one-year-old Mary Brannigan and others traveling with McArthur even to see each other. "It looked like the imps of darkness had come to stop us from going," she wrote in an autobiography years later.[10] Almost immediately some of the saints turned around and returned to Iowa City. These included a man and his family with whom Brannigan was traveling, who took her bedclothes with them. As she pressed her back to a tree and cried at the predicament in which she found herself, an unknown man approached. After she told him she would continue on to Utah despite the abrupt departure of her traveling companions, the man brought her some replacement bedclothes. Mary learned her helper was Daniel McArthur, the company captain. Her former traveling companions later returned to the handcart group, but by then she had her own handcart loaded with "my bedclothes and my day's provisions, cooking utensils and clothes strapped on." Two other girls soon joined her in pushing and pulling the cart.[11]

The Third Handcart Company, with 320 people and 64 handcarts, managed by Edward Bunker, left Iowa City on June 23, 1856. They were two weeks behind the First Company and just twelve days behind the Second Company. Bunker, who would turn thirty-four on August 1, 1856, had become a member of the church in 1845 and joined the Mormon Battalion the following year. He took part in the Mexican-American War before traveling north to Sutter's Mill on the American Fork River in California. But he soon left California and went to Utah, where the Mormon Pioneer company had begun to establish Great Salt Lake City. Bunker continued on to Winter Quarters, where he was reunited with his wife, Emily, and their son. They eventually settled in Utah, although he continued to do work for the church. In 1856 he was returning from a mission to England, when he was called upon to lead the Third Handcart Company.

Robert David Roberts and his father and other family members set out with Bunker's Company. They made it just three miles down the road from Iowa City before the captain called a halt due to a severe storm. "We made camp on the bank of a small creek, the wind was blowing terribly, and we had to cling to our tents and poles to keep them from blowing away," Roberts said. The wind knocked down the tents as rain fell in torrents, accompanied by thunder and lightning. Soon the creek rose, flooding the camp as the rainwater puddled a foot deep around and sometimes in the tents. "We had few clothes except those we had on," Roberts wrote, "the rest having [been] left behind to be sent on later, so that we had to lay over the next day to dry our clothes. This was very trying for our first experience."[12]

Each of the handcart companies was organized in military style with a "captain" for every 100 travelers. John Parry, David Grant, and George Davies were appointed as captains of "hundreds" for Bunker's Third Company. From the start traveling was difficult and food scarce. Some Welsh immigrants deserted the Bunker Company at Newton, Iowa, and precipitated confrontations between Mormons and non-Mormons when Parry followed them to entice them back to the handcarts. The deserters had sought work in Newton, but "at last I prevailed on them," Parry wrote, and "then we started after the Camp, which was far a head." When he was partway through Newton, he said, "I was imediately Surrounded by a large croude of mobs, who was very mad, because I perswaded those that had promised to work for them, to come along." Parry added, "after a little talk the[y] did send several from the crowde to get Tar & Feathers, to put on me."[13]

About that time Mormon John McDonald, who had been shopping in one of the Newton stores, inquired as to why Parry had been detained. When the mob turned its attention to McDonald, Parry fled. Before he could reach the Mormon camp, however, "I was overcome by two rufians, who began to take hold of my colar, but I spoke very harch [harsh] and independant to them, and got from them, [and] after a while I reached the camp." This was not the only altercation between the members of Bunker's party and non-Mormons, according to Parry. "Traveling along, Great many mobs came after us some on horses and others on foot, with Revolvers, Clubs &c."[14] It is not clear how McDonald escaped the mob, but he did so and continued traveling west with the handcart company.

These attacks, combined with the variable weather and physical toil, made travel extremely difficult. Ellsworth wrote, "Nobody had any faith to give away to their neighbor, there was no energy to spare, but there was just sufficient to keep along in the journey." Even so, he believed the handcart companies would have been better served if they had no wagons supporting them. In his view the ox-drawn vehicles created a sense of weakness in the people that would "destroy their faith." Anyone who felt ill or weak would climb into one of the wagons. "I am persuaded that if there had been no wagons for such people, there would have been none sick, or weak, but that faith would have been strong in the name of the Lord."[15]

In reality, there were too many people and too few wagons, which challenged Captain Ellsworth to maintain order among his ranks. Nevertheless, the devoutly pious leader may have honestly believed that the wagons were a threat to the migration. "I have had to labor with the people incessantly to keep faith in them, to keep them away from the wagons, by showing them that there was honor attached to pulling hand-carts into the valley; by saying, I have walked 1300 miles, old and decrepid as I am, with these crooked legs of mine, and that there is honor in that."[16]

Crooked legs and faith notwithstanding, the journey took its toll, particularly on the children. Captain Ellsworth wanted the youngsters to discard their shoes and stockings and go barefoot, thus eventually toughening their feet so the pebbles and prickly pears caused no pain. But some cautious mothers insisted that their children wear foot coverings as long as they could—until the shoes fell apart from wear. Even so the daily walking soon caused blisters on the children's feet.

On one very hot day the saints asked for water from a woman who sat in a chair beside her well. The "borders" of the woman's cap, Mary Brannigan recalled, "flapped back and forth in time to her knitting" as the travelers passed by her home. Captain McArthur approached her to ask if she would allow the Mormons to use the well, but she told him he "could not have any [water] out of her well for that crow[d] of fools of Mormons, that did not know any better [than] to pull handcarts through the streets." Mary wondered how the woman felt, "refusing a cup of cold water to a crowd of famishing people."[17]

As had been predicted months earlier, the travelers began walking each morning ahead of or along with the ox-drawn wagons, but they pulled the handcarts more quickly than the wagons moved. People generally walk about three miles per hour, while oxen only cover a couple of miles every hour. Usually the families pulling handcarts stopped and rested for an hour or more in the middle of the day, allowing the wagons to catch up with them. But the walkers again outpaced oxen in the afternoon and reached camp in the evening from one to three hours before the wagons.

A month later a violent lightning storm caught the camp on the open prairie with no protection. One strike claimed the life of fifty-eight-year-old Henry Walker, of Carlisle, England. The lightning also burned James Stoddart. The force of the electrical strike knocked his father, William, and Betsy Taylor to the ground along with one other man and two women.

"VERY LITTLE FOOD TO COOK, AND WE WERE TOO TIRED TO COOK IT"

The carpenter Archer Walters worked hard for the company, spending long hours repairing carts and building coffins. He also kept a journal that was more critical of the operation than most other diarists. "Travelled 10 miles," he wrote June 24. "Very hot. Bro. Ellsworth being always with a family from birmingham named Brown and always that tent going first and walking so fast and some fainted by the way."[18] Though he referred to the "Brown" family, Walters may have meant the family of Thomas Bourne. He and his wife, Margaret Evans, had six children, including daughters Maryann (twenty-two) and Margaret (twenty).

Two days later, on June 26, Walters wrote of the travelers being "faint for the [lack] of food. We are only allowed about ¾ of lb. of flour a head each day and about 3 oz. of sugar each week. Tea good and plenty; about a ¼ of a lb. of bacon each a week." Compounding the lack of food and tiring travel, the weather turned sour. A thunderstorm that swept the region, blowing down the Walters family tent on June 28, "split the canvas and wet our clothes and we had to lay on the wet clothes and ground," he wrote. "I thought of going through needful tribulation but it made me cross."

The Walters children were "crying for their dinner" by Sunday, June 29, and had little for breakfast the following morning. That day, however, the family "got 5 lbs of flour and bakon about 1¼ lb, ¾ rice, sugar ¾ lb, and was refreshed." Still, Walters doubted that the provisions were being equally distributed. His family had "½ pound of flour each, 2 oz., of rice; which is very little and my children cry with hunger and it grieves me and makes me cross." More concerned about his children than himself, Walters wrote: "I can live upon green herbs or any thing and do go nearly all day without any [food] and am strengthened with a morsel." On July 1 he lamented another inequity: "It looked very cloudy and began to rain. Travelled about 15 miles. Walked very fast,—nearly 4 miles an hour. Brother Brown's family and some young sisters with Bro. Ellsworth always going first which causes many of the brothers to have hard feeling." To make matters worse, Walters again had to repair handcarts. Then another storm pummeled the camp. "Split the tent and not a dry thread on us."

Finally, having been ferried over the Missouri River, the party reached Florence, Nebraska, on July 8. The people could now recuperate for a few days. As additional repairs were made to the handcarts, they wrote letters to family and friends left behind in England. Having made the repairs, the people were somewhat rested when they set out across the Nebraska prairie. Walters found shellfish in a creek near Wood River, a natural bounty that supplemented the daily ration of three-quarters of a pound of flour and an ounce and a half of sugar. Walters noted that they also had a few apples and plenty of tea.

During the first 300 miles, Roberts said that the Third Company's rations of half a pound of flour to create three meals a day was "very scant."[19] They assumed they could purchase or trade for food at farms and towns along the route, which often happened. Once beyond Florence, Nebraska, they initially had a pound of flour a day per person. But the supply dwindled as they continued west and they found fewer places where they could buy or trade for food.

When these travelers crossed the Loup Fork River in east-central Nebraska, the sun bore down on them. They faced a stretch of trail with no water supply. Their faces and hands burned, and their lips became split and cracked with constant exposure in the drier air. "The sun was burning hot and it seemed to concentrate on the trail between the tall grass growing on either side. This grass grew from five to eight feet tall," Roberts wrote. "The suffering from heat and thirst was something terrible, and some of the people became so exhausted, they gave up and stopped by the way." Stronger walkers made it to the Wood River, filling their containers and returning with them to those who had collapsed from heat and exhaustion. The water thus supplied "revived them so that they could go on."

After leaving the Loup Fork River in Nebraska on July 31, the Second Handcart Company traveled twenty miles without water. "I was so exhausted with my sores and the labour of pulling that I was obliged to lie down for a few hours after arriving in camp before I could do anything," Twiss Bermingham wrote. His wife, Kate (Catherine Elizabeth), could not do any work upon arriving in camp that day. She was so fatigued that she just wanted to sleep, even without any supper. Eventually they ate a "bit of bread and a pint of milk. This is the quantity of milk we have been allowed morning and evening since we left Florence," he wrote. "Sometimes it is less. Rather little for 5 persons." A few days later, they camped on the open prairie "without wood or water and consequently had to go to bed supperless." The next morning, Sunday, August 3, they again had no breakfast and then "had to pull the carts through 6 miles of heavy sand," Bermingham said. "Some places the wheels were up to the boxes [in the sand] and I was so weak from thirst and hunger and being exhausted with the pain of the boils that I was obliged to lie down several times."[20]

The challenges continued for the family. "I was very much grieved today," Bermingham wrote, "so much so that I thought my heart would burst—sick—and poor Kate—at the same time—crawling on her hands and knees, and the children crying with hunger and fatigue." Adding to their woe, a thunderstorm deluged the region around midnight. "In our tent we were standing up to our knees in water and every stitch we had was the same as if we were dragged through the river."[21] Such was their state: cold, hungry, and sopping wet.

Beyond Wood River, Bunker's party, like Ellsworth's and McArthur's companies before it, encountered thousands of buffalo in great herds. Success at hunting meant better provisions. Finding no trees on the Great Plains, the travelers had to rely on the bison for fuel as well. As they walked, they gathered chips (manure) for use in building hot fires to cook their meager supplies of food. "At first we had a little coffee and bacon, [but] that was soon gone, and we had no use for any cooking utensils but a frying pan," Priscilla Merriman Evans said. Each handcart carried a hundred pounds of flour. "The flour was self raising," she explained, "and we took water and baked a little cake; that was all we had to eat."[22]

Elizabeth Lane Hyde traveled to Utah pulling a cart with Priscilla Evans, whose husband, Thomas Evans, struggled through the deep sands of western Nebraska on his wooden leg until he collapsed. The women put Thomas in the handcart and pulled him to Fort Laramie. Thomas's knee rested on a pad, which was insufficient to cushion it. It was "very painful," Priscilla said, "but he had to press on, or stay behind." She made no reference to his riding in the handcart, though occasionally she noted that he rode in the wagon. When Elizabeth herself "became lame" because of rheumatism in her ankles, she quit pulling the cart and was "free to walk alone."

Their company was composed mainly of Welsh people, but Priscilla could not speak the language. "Dont you think I had a pleasant journey, traveling for months with about 300 people, of whose language I could not understand a word?" Her Welsh husband, however, could "join in their festivities when he felt like it," which only increased her sense of isolation.

The travelers with the Second Company, like others after them, sang when they marched. "Some must push and some must pull, as we go marching up the hill" went one refrain. In one camp two Indian women hid behind Mary Brannigan's tent, begging for protection from white men who had come into the adjacent Indian camp, bringing whiskey with them. "The Indians were fine-looking men, most of them six feet in height, and well dressed," Mary wrote. "We met Indians often, but they were always friendly."[23]

McArthur's company had roughly thirty children, who were sent ahead of the grownups every morning. Although the youngsters had little in the way of clothing, they all wore hats, according to Thordur Didriksson, an Icelandic immigrant. "They were driven along with willows and had to keep walking as long as they could. No use to cry or complain. But along during the day when it was hot they were allowed to rest and were given food," he said. "They were often 2 or 3 miles ahead of us. It was hard for parents to see their little 5 and 6 year olds driven along like sheep." Hunger became a constant companion, though Didriksson said a beef was butchered each Saturday, providing about two pounds of meat per person for the week. The immigrants had quickly learned not to be wasteful: "Every scrap, insides and all were used."[24] They saw great herds of buffalo in Nebraska, enjoying the meat of a fine young cow but also eating tough older animals.

Mary Bathgate, who had worked in the coal pits in Scotland for forty years, became "Mother" to the younger women, recalled Mary Brannigan. As she walked across Nebraska she swung her cane shouting, "Hurree for the handkerts." The elderly woman "was the ring leader of the footmen." She walked ahead of the handcart caravan each day, usually in company with Isabella Park. According to Mary Brannigan (who in the spring of 1857 married Spicer Crandall, thirty-three, one of the leaders of the handcart company), Mother Bathgate was "instantly healed" when the church elders administered to her with consecrated oil after a rattlesnake bit her. When the snake struck Bathgate, Park sent a young girl back to get the company leader and tied her own garter around Bathgate's leg above the wound, stopping the blood from circulating. When McArthur and Leonard arrived, they "took a pocket knife and cut the wound larger, [and] squeezed out all the bad blood we could." Leaving nothing to chance, they "anointed her leg and head, and laid our hands on her in the name of Jesus." That day, for the first time on the journey, Bathgate rode in one of the wagons. Mary recalled that she "was able to cheer the company next day," indicating that she was again walking with the handcarts.[25]

Other accidents took their toll as well. On August 16 Isabella Park got too close to the wagon and fell beneath the wheels. The front wheels of the heavy wagon ran over her hips. Leonard was unsuccessful in trying to pull her from beneath the vehicle before the rear wheels reached her and ran over her ankles. Luckily, Park had no broken bones. As Twiss Bermingham recorded, "we had the most severe day's journey we had since we started and traveled over 20 miles of heavy sand hills or bluffs."[26] These two women would soon be back "on the tramp" to reach Utah. Both women "were as smart as could be long before they got here," McArthur said. "This is what I call good luck, for I know that nothing but the power of God saved the two sisters and they traveled together, they rode together, and suffered together."[27]

Mary Brannigan admitted, "I would have liked something more to eat," but she nevertheless recalled the trip as being a time when "I enjoyed myself as well as I ever did in my life."[28] Few natural landmarks graced the Nebraska prairie. More than a few travelers wandered from camp and became lost, delaying travel as the other members halted to search for those who had strayed. On July 8, for example, "old brother Sanderson" (likely sixty-five-year old Walter Sanders) of the First Company became lost. People searched for him in all directions but did not find him until the following day, when someone spied him on a hill. The saints took a mule to bring him back to camp.[29]

French-Italian immigrant Jean Pierre Stalle (one of the Waldensians, who had fled Italy generations before and become refugees in France) died on August 17, 1856, in western Nebraska just days before the company reached Chimney Rock, one of the iconic natural formations along the route. Decades later Margaret (Marguerite) Stalle Barker would make claims that Captain Ellsworth mistreated the French saints and that her father died of starvation because the captain deprived him of food. As he lay dying, according to Margaret's account, her mother, Jeanne Marie Gaudin-Moise Stalle, climbed into the wagon for a few final words but was forced out when "Ellsworth came with a rope and cruelly whipped her until she was forced to get down."[30]

Hunger has a way of making even repulsive food appealing. Mary Ann Jones wrote of killing and eating buffalo under challenging circumstances. "Some stomacks may recoil at a supper cooked with the water dug in a buffalo wallow & cooked with buffalo chips but it tasted good to us."[31] When the party reached Fort Laramie, Archer Walters traded a dagger for a piece of bacon and some salt and meal, noting that he and Henry ate the bacon raw.[32]

Snow fell in early September when Bunker's company was thirty miles west of Fort Laramie. It was not yet cold during the day, so the six inches of snow melted rapidly but left the road muddy, making it much harder to pull the carts.

Among the people in this group, besides one-legged Thomas Evans, were two blind men, a man with one arm, and a widow with five children. Louisa Rosser Evans, the adopted daughter of David and Ann Phillips Evans, did not want to head west but did so at the family's insistence. One day she and another woman lagged behind the rest of the company and fell farther and farther behind until they lost sight of the handcarts. Wolves howled around the two women, but they became truly fearful only when they saw two Indians approaching them on horses. "I became very frightened for I thought that they would kill us," Louisa said, "but Sister Roberts assured me that they would not harm us for she said, 'I put my trust in the Lord,' and to my relief the Indians rode away without harming us."[33]

Others persevered as well, some gladly. Mary Ann Jones, young and strong, crossed two rivers in a wagon with the Ellsworth Company but otherwise pushed and pulled a handcart the entire distance from Iowa City. "We waded streams, crossed high mountains & pulled through heavy sands, leaving comfortable homes, fathers, mother, brothers & sisters & what for? To be where we could hear a prophets voice and live with the Saints of God."[34] Mary Powell Sabin wrote of the daily routine: rising each morning at the sound of a bugle, assembling for prayer, eating a scanty breakfast. "Then we were ready for our march. At ten o'clock we rested one half hour. Then we traveled until we came to water. At the next meal we would eat what was left over from breakfast. At night we often went to bed without supper. There was very little food to cook and we were too tired to cook it."[35]

When the First Company reached Deer Creek about sixty miles west of Fort Laramie on August 31, 1856, they found wagons loaded with supplies sent from Great Salt Lake City. The flour was not provided without price, however. The travelers were expected to pay eighteen cents a pound. That day they buried Robert Stoddart, who died of consumption at age fifty-seven.[36] Although they now had more provisions, deaths along the trail continued. Walter Sanders, who had wandered away from the train in Nebraska, died on September 2; George Neppress (twenty-four), who had immigrated from Cardiff, Wales, died on September 7; and James Birch (twenty-eight) succumbed to diarrhea.

According to its leader, Edmund Ellsworth, the deaths among the First Company occurred because many of the immigrants were infirm and were not accustomed to the climate and the hard labor of hauling their possessions across the plains. "Some were nearly dead when they left the old country," Ellsworth wrote, "and in crossing the sea, where they had hardly exercise enough for their good, some sickened almost enough to bring them down to the graves." They walked ten or twenty miles a day overland—a physical challenge even for those who were fit. The air they breathed was pure, though sometimes dusty, but several, including five children and two young men, died along the way. Ellsworth wrote that most of the people in his company were filled with faith and therefore determined to reach Utah. But he also chronicled the actions of apostates, people who abandoned the faith. When John Lloyd and his wife and family "backed out," Ellsworth wrote that the Englishman "was very much given to drinking whisky along the road."[37] On September 8, 1856, Ellsworth halted his company near Devil's Gate, not far from the remains of Seminoe's Fort, a former trading post that had been abandoned the year before.

McArthur's Second Company had been resupplied with flour and other provisions at Deer Creek on September 2. Half a ton of flour was delivered two weeks later when the company reached Pacific Springs, just west of South Pass, still 250 miles from Salt Lake City. Mary Brannigan recalled the horseback rider, wearing a suit of buckskin, who brought the relief supplies. "The fringe was blowing in the wind. I thought of one of the Scottish chiefs. I did not tell anyone what I thought about him for fear they would think I had fallen in love with him."[38] The food provided by that relief party was welcome. At Fort Bridger the people who had walked the trail barefoot when their shoes had worn out found further aid when they were able to buy moccasins. This resupply of food and other aid fulfilled one of Brigham Young's directives when he organized the handcart migration and noted that such relief would be needed by travelers drawing their own conveyances across the trail.

The crossing was a continued challenge for Louisa Rosser Evans, but her faith remained strong. One day "as we were pursueing our wearisome march my Brother Moses became very hungry and there was very little to eat, being only one cake and a pint of mil[k] allotted." Louisa gave all the milk to Moses, believing that she could do without. Later that afternoon, she said, "I became very hungry. So trusting faithfully in the Lord I asked Him to take the hunger away and he heard and answered my prayer; and a beautiful feeling filled my heart and I didn't feel hungry any more."[39]

Crossing rivers was always a challenge. Sometimes the women and children waded through the cold waters, but men often helped them cross. John Cousins carried Elizabeth Hyde "on his back through many rivers," she recalled. "When Captain Bunker put me out of the wagon at Laramie River, [Cousins] picked me up and carried me through the water." Others seemingly found their way across through faith. At Green River, in western Wyoming, Elizabeth lagged behind the handcart company as the sun dipped low. "I sat down and thought this is the last. After a while I began to ask myself what brought you here? I called myself a coward. So I got up and asked the Lord to help me, and prepared to wade the river; and the Lord did help me, and I got safe to the camp just as they were preparing to come after me."[40]

Some were less blessed. As the First Company neared Great Salt Lake City, Mary Powell said a "lazy man in camp who had a wife and baby" climbed into a wagon of soap to ride a while. "We had been better provided with soap than food it seems." The man's ride was not smooth, though. When the wagon crossed a rough place, the wagon canted sideways. "Our friend was almost buried in soap to the amusement of the rest of us."[41] In another instance, Mary Ann Jones recalled that "one old Sister carried a teapot & calendar [colander] on her apron strings all the way to Salt Lake. Another carried a hat box full of things, but she died on the way."[42] This almost certainly was sixty-five-year-old Mary Mayo, who succumbed to diarrhea on September 13, just thirteen days before these first handcarts reached Great Salt Lake City.

Scottish traveler William Knox Aitken wrote of being "half starved" on the journey. In a letter sent to his brother from western Missouri on July 11, 1857, he said the travelers received only twelve ounces of flour per person each day, which was insufficient to sustain them while walking the 1,300 miles from Iowa City to Great Salt Lake City. Nevertheless, they made it to Utah, although "wearied and worn down, the bones almost through the skin." William told his brother that he "arrived at Salt Lake city almost used up, but my pluck as good as ever," with "my eyes wide open, my pockets empty, and without clothes or tools." He added: "All I had was my case of instruments and a rag of a shirt, having to leave all our chest behind to come on with the wagons, having paid their carriage previously. The amount paid by me for my cases, with clothes and tools, was twenty-three dollars. But the wagons were overtaken by the snow, so my goods had to be put into a hut at a place called Devil's Gate, three hundred miles from Salt Lake, so that I never saw them."[43]

Not everyone on the trail that summer traveled west, and not all church members were satisfied with their lives in Utah. Mary Brannigan wrote of apostates who were "going away from the Valley." She recalled decades later that "one of them said to me: 'You think you're going to a land flowing with milk and honey, but you will get fooled, for if you get enough to eat you will be lucky. You better go back with us.'"[44]

The handcarts were a frequent topic of discussion in Salt Lake City from the moment the first companies set off from Iowa City. Charles M. Treseder wrote to his parents from the city on September 29, 1856. While people may have been wondering where the handcarts were, and how the travelers were faring, no concrete details were available until just before they reached their destination. "The excitement in the city on the 4th and the 24th of July, to my mind was nothing in comparison to it," Treseder wrote of the First Handcart Company's approach to Great Salt Lake City.[45] The advance members of the Pioneer Company reached the Salt Lake valley on July 24 in 1847, a day then and now celebrated in Utah.[46]

The First and Second Handcart Companies set off from Iowa City just days apart and traveled closely together all across the plains, arriving in Great Salt Lake City together on September 26, 1856. President Brigham Young and Heber C. Kimball, "escorted by the minute men and a company of Lancers" and followed by general citizens who walked or rode in horse-drawn vehicles, met them as they neared the city. The Nauvoo Brass Band and Captain Dominico Ballo's band heralded the appearance of the handcarts. Residents from the city "did not forget to take them something to eat."[47]

After Young's greeting, the immigrants again picked up their carts and in a swirl of dust descended the final hill to the valley floor and Great Salt Lake City. "Folks came running from every quarter to get a glimpse of the long-looked-for hand-carts." Near Brigham Young's house, Treseder saw a row of wagons and carriages, no doubt carrying people from the city who came to greet the handcart travelers. Then he saw the handcarts themselves. "I shall never forget the feeling that ran through my whole system as I caught the first sight of them. The first hand-cart was drawn by a man and his wife, they had a little flag on it, on which were the words: 'Our President—may the unity of the Saints ever show the wisdom of his counsels.'" Treseder added: "The next hand-cart was drawn by three young women."[48]

Mary Brannigan remembered that she was the first girl to pull a handcart across the Big Mountain. The following day, as they entered Great Salt Lake City, they heard "cheering and shouting as we came down on the other side. The streets were thronged with men, women and children. When we got to the Public Square there were plenty of victuals cooked up for the two companies."[49] Tears rolled down men's cheeks as they watched the scene, which was "exciting in the extreme." Treseder added that "most everybody felt sympathetic and joyous.... amongst the women the crying was pretty near universal."[50]

The following day Brigham Young visited the handcart company twice where the people were camped at Union Square, and "an abundance of food was supplied to them."[51]

THE THIRD COMPANY ARRIVES IN GREAT SALT LAKE CITY

Throughout the journey Robert David Roberts guided his nearly blind uncle John, who had paid for his nephew's fare from England. Roberts's boots wore out by the time he reached Independence Rock, forcing him to cover the last 332 miles of the journey barefooted. The trip was too much for John, however, who died shortly after arriving in Utah.[52]

Bunker's company reached Great Salt Lake City at 6 P.M. on October 2 to almost no fanfare.[53] "We were more favored than those who came later, as we had no snow and the weather was quite pleasant," Priscilla Merriman Evans recalled.[54] Just two days later a party of missionaries returning from various assignments reached the city: Daniel Spencer, John Van Cott, Franklin D. Richards, George D. Grant, William H. Kimball, Joseph A. Young, James Ferguson, William C. Dunbar, John Daniel Thompson McAllister, Cyrus H. Wheelock, Nathaniel H. Felt, James McGaw, and Chauncey G. Webb. These men had planned the handcart migration, promoted it, and put it into action. Now they brought news to the city: "Some of the companies of Saints will be late in arriving; but we omit particulars."[55]

Although Mormon president Brigham Young knew more handcart pioneers had headed to America that year from England, he incorrectly believed that only three companies would cross the plains during the summer and that the remaining immigrants would stay in the Midwest to continue their journey the following year. A brief mention in the *Deseret News* made it clear, however, that more people were en route. The large group of missionaries had overtaken the late travelers, whom they had earlier sent out on the trail. They now brought news of their plight to the church headquarters.

The First, Second, and Third Companies had made good time in their overland trek. One thing was evident from the accounts of these early handcart travelers, however: they could not carry food sufficient to sustain themselves. Even with some relief supplies sent from Utah to points along the trail, all had gone hungry. The lack of food, combined with the demanding labor of pushing and pulling the carts and physically setting up camp each day, took a toll. Those who had died along the way foreshadowed what was in store for some of the people now still out on the plains.

CHAPTER 5

THE FOURTH COMPANY
The Willie Company, 1856

The Fourth Company, composed mostly of English, Scottish, and Scandinavian immigrants who had crossed the Atlantic on the *Thornton*, reached Iowa City in late June 1856. The company was already behind what might be considered a routine schedule for cross-country wagon trips. Most pioneers started out from locations near the Missouri River in late April or May. These Mormons, however, faced at least three weeks of travel to reach the Missouri. Even more daunting, upon their arrival in Iowa City they found no handcarts. The first three companies had taken every available cart. John Taylor had ordered more covered carts constructed in St. Louis, but those conveyances had not yet arrived in Iowa City.

With no other alternative, the men of the Fourth Company began constructing carts using the available supply of wood. Some of it was cured, but most of it was freshly cut green wood. The women started making new tents, which were finished on July 8, the day the Martin Company reached Iowa City by train. A heavy storm doused all these pioneers as members of both companies crowded into the Willie party's tents.

On July 16, 1856, Captain Willie led his party of around 500 people with 120 handcarts, 5 wagons, 24 oxen, and 45 head of beef cattle and cows from Iowa City. Getting a late start and moving very slowly, they traveled only three miles that first day. A company under the direction of Jesse Haven would follow about five days later, with 146 carts also made from unseasoned wood. A sixth company led by Captain Edward Martin pulled away from Iowa City several days after Haven's group, with 575 travelers, 145 handcarts, and 8 wagons. The Haven and Martin Companies would merge in late August in Florence, Nebraska, and become known as the Fifth Company under Martin's leadership.

Two Mormon wagon trains, one with thirty-three wagons guided by Captain William Ben Hodgetts and another with fifty wagons led by Captain John A. Hunt, also began an overland journey in late July, trailing the handcart companies. Hodgetts had overtaken his sisters Emily and Maria when they reached Boston on the *Enoch Train*. While Maria responded to her mother's request and returned to England, Emily was with her brother as the wagon train rolled west. They carried with them four blue chests filled with goods that her mother had purchased. Mother Hodgetts obviously had some means. In addition to the chests of goods, she provided funds for livestock. A Miss Benchley and Squire Thomas Tennett, acquaintances of the Hodgetts family, also had money, which William used to purchase 200 head of heifers that they would herd west as an investment. Emily said she "rode a horse and a good animal it was." William Ben, who had been over the trail before, likely told his sister that using a horse would be a more comfortable way to travel to Utah than walking or bouncing in a rough wagon. But those first days on horseback were undoubtedly tiring for young Emily, whether she rode astride or sidesaddle.

After the *Thornton* docked at the immigration center of Castle Garden in New York, Sarah Denton Moulton had jettisoned some of the family's belongings, culling them down to fifty pounds per adult, the amount allowed on the trains. On the plains, however, she needed to restrict baggage further.[1] Levi Savage, captain of one group of Willie's party, said they sold or disposed of everything exceeding seventeen pounds per person, which "makes us rather destitute for wearing apperil and Beding."[2]

The Willie Company was carefully organized into five groups of 100 people each led by a subcaptain. Scots and Scandinavians numbered about 100 people each; the others were all English. Every 100 people shared 5 round tents and 20 handcarts. The few wagons were loaded with tents and provisions, and each man was given certain responsibilities. Thomas Moulton, for example, who had been listed on the *Thornton* manifest as a farmer or shepherd, became a camp butcher.[3]

For Mother Sarah Moulton and the rest of her family, the journey started easily enough. She and Thomas pulled a covered cart. In it rode Sophia (two) and Charles (two and a half months), cradled on a pillow. Five-year-old Lottie rode too whenever the cart was going downhill. She had to walk the rest of the time, however, as did Heber, who had turned eight in early July. At times Sarah tied a rope around Heber's waist so he would not stray far from her side, but Lottie apparently stuck close to her mother without need of a tether. The older Moulton children pulled and pushed an open cart.[4] The Moultons would later report that waving grasses, flowers, and wild fruit covered the land and that the streams offered plenty of fish to supplement their food supply. Like the earlier companies, those in the Willie party who had money could trade for honey and other goods from settlers as they passed. They milked the cows they trailed.

Levi Savage did not depict such a bucolic crossing from Iowa to Florence. "The wether was very warm and the roads very dusty," he wrote on July 19, 1856. "Some of the Saints both olde and young, were nearly overcome yet they endured" better than could be expected. He noted conflicts with people living along the route, including a group of residents who threatened to "come and tear our tents down" on July 20. He recorded that six of the Saints abandoned their trek to Zion and turned back the next day. On July 24 the saints buried Mary Williams, who had died the previous day. According to Savage, several in the camp were "severely ill. Our rations are very Short *viz* 10 *oz* flour per one day. 10 oz pork per 28 days. Short rations of tea coffee Sugar. rice and aples. It is not enough. Some complaining." On another day a county sheriff searched the camp looking for women that town gossips said had been bound and forced on the journey against their will, but he found no such women. Another day, Savage said, "a goodly number of Citizens came to view our camp and hear preaching. a few ruffens als[o] came, one of whome picked up a hatchet, and put it into his pocket." This caused angry words and led to threats by local men, but "they did not put their threats into execution" perhaps because the saints were prepared "to defend ourSelves."[5]

It took the group twenty-eight days to pull the handcarts the 277 miles from Iowa City to the Missouri River. The Fourth Company reached Florence, Nebraska, on August 11. But the arrival was not without conflict. "People thronged the Street Sides, and gaze upon us with apperant Surprize. They were Sivil except a few low bread fellows, who endeavere to make sport of us the cripled and lame not excepted," Levi Savage recorded in his journal. "Some of the Gentiles, and apostates, commensed to abuse the Saints, and cure [curse] the hancart Sistem, and thost that instatuted it." One company member who defended the use of handcarts "consequently got into a fist fight," winning the altercation and receiving "no material injury to himself except geting his hair well pulled."[6]

Other difficulties arose as well. The unseasoned wood used to build the carts was already failing.[7] "The companies stay [in Florence] longer than they otherwise would in consequence of their carts being unfit for their journey across the Plains," J. H. Latey wrote in a letter published in the *Millennial Star*, "some requiring new axles, and the whole of them having to have a piece of iron screwed on to prevent the wheel from wearing away the wood."[8]

"THEIR BONES WOULD STREW THE WAY"

The delay cost precious time, and the immigrants knew it. "The elders seemed to be divided in their judgment," said John Chislett, "as to the practicability of our reaching Utah in safety at so late a season of the year." Chislett, a subcaptain with the Fourth Company, would later write a detailed account of the journey. "The idea was entertained for a day or two of making our winter quarters on the Elkhorn, Wood River, or some eligible location in Nebraska; but it did not meet with general approval. A monster meeting was called to consult the people about it."[9]

Levi Savage, an experienced trail traveler and member of the Mormon Battalion in 1846, stridently warned the 500 men, women, and children with James Grey Willie's company not to leave Florence so late in the season. It was now mid-August. More than a thousand miles lay ahead of them as they dragged their handcarts to Utah.

Four men with the party—Captain Willie, Levi Savage, Millen Atwood, and William Woodward— had been to Great Salt Lake City. Savage first headed west with the Mormon Battalion in 1846, traveling from Nebraska to New Mexico and then on to California before living in Utah. He knew well the potential weather conditions that they faced and pleaded with Willie's company to remain where it was for the winter. He told "the old, weak, and sickly to stop until another spring," George Cunningham later recalled. "The tears commenced to flow down his cheeks and he prophesied that if such undertook the journey at that late season of the year that their bones would strew the way."[10]

But they would not listen. "The emigrants were entirely ignorant of the country and climate—simple, honest, eager to go to 'Zion' at once," Chislett wrote. "Under these circumstances it was natural that they should leave their destination in the hands of the elders."[11]

Savage warned them that they "could not cross the mountains with a mixed company of aged people, women, and little children, so late in the season without much suffering, sickness, and death." Just a day after arriving at Florence, Savage wrote in his journal:

> To day we commenced preparing for our jour[ney] and ascertaining who wishes to go on this fall. and who wishes to remain here. Many are a going to Stop, others are faltering, and I myself am not in favor of, but much opposed to taking women & Children through destitute of clothing, when we all know. that we are bound to be caught in the Snow, and Severe colde w[e]ather, long before we reach the valey. I have expressed my felings, in part, to Brothers McGaw, Willey [Willie]; & Atwood. Brother Atwood Said to me last night that Since he had been a member of this Church, with all of his experience. he had never been placed in a position where things appear so dark to him, as it does to undertake to take this Company through at this late Season of the year.[12]

Despite his doubts Atwood backed the other church leaders in urging the company forward.

Determined to continue traveling west, Captain Willie exhorted the saints during a camp meeting August 13 "to go forward regardless of Suffering even to death." In contrast, Savage told of the hardships to come. "I Said that we were liable to have to wade in Snow up to our knees, and Should at night rap ourselvs in a thin blanket. and lye on the frozen ground without abed; that was not like having a wagon, that we could go into, and rap ourselves in as much as we liked and ly down." Willie and Savage traded barbs during the meeting, obviously disagreeing on whether the handcart pioneers should continue across the plains. The meeting concluded when elder Millen Atwood "spoke mildely" and "exhorted the Saints to prey to God and get a revilation, and know for themselves whether [they] Should go or Stay." Two days later, however, the handcart leaders were not sure if the immigrants were receiving the desired revelation. They held another meeting, exhorting the saints "to go forward regardeless of consequences."[13]

In Florence on August 13 nineteen-year-old Sarah Elizabeth Moulton wrote to Mark Forscutt, back home in England: "I feel it a great blessing that I am so far on my way to Zion.... I never had my health so well in my life before I walked about three hundred miles and pulled the hand cart all the way [from Iowa City] and we walked sometimes 20 & 17 miles a day and I never had a blister on my foot & cannot think to tell you my feelings when I was coursing along the road but I often think of the prophet Brighams words about the weak becoming strong." Acknowledging the discontent among the company and its leaders about continuing the trek that year, Moulton added, "some of the saints as they call themselves are going to stay here for they do not feel as though they could go through this year because it is so late.... we are going to start for the plains to morrow—and there is not any more going this year so the brethren say."[14]

Moulton's attitude reflected the viewpoint of a healthy, strong young woman. For Sarah Elizabeth and other young people the trip did not seem so bad. For the old, the infirm, and mothers with small babies (including her own stepmother), it was truly hard. It tested the physical stamina of the men, who pushed and pulled carts by day and stood guard duty by night.

"I often think of you and wish you was here with us but the time will come that you will have to come," Sarah Elizabeth Moulton told Forscutt. "Some of the saints as they call themselves are going to stay here for they do not feel as though they could go through this year because it is so late[;] well if the Lord blesses me with health and strength I will go up to Zion this year and receive the blessings and the difficulties if there is any for the children of God and I believe there is. the brethren tell us we shall be blest and I believe we shall if we do right."[15]

Despite discarding more personal possessions, the carts pulled from Florence on August 16 were more heavily laden than they had been on the month-long trek from Iowa City. Each cart carried an additional 98-pound sack of flour. "Our flour ration was increased to a pound per day," Chislett wrote. "Fresh beef was issued occasionally, and each 'hundred' had three or four milch cows."[16] The cows provided fresh milk for the children, but with only a few such animals for every hundred people only the smallest youngsters had milk to drink.

The carts were already weak, and now the weight from the extra flour broke axles and slowed the pace of travel as people stopped regularly to make repairs. Instead of eating the bacon, the pioneers used it to grease cart axles, which may have eased the screeching of dry wood rubbing against dry wood but did little to strengthen the wooden carts. Although they saw many bison, the men had difficulty killing the large beasts with any regularity. On September 3 they killed two buffalo and took the meat onto the handcarts. But when Savage and Joseph Elder went on horseback to get another buffalo cow or calf, "the olde bulls would not let us have any. They formed themselves in battle aray, ready to receive their enemy."[17]

The immigrants saw large buffalo herds in all directions on the day of Savage's unsuccessful hunt, but to no avail. That night thirty head of the company's "working cattle" or oxen stampeded in an awful storm, which forced the men to search for them the following day without success. The loss was devastating. As Levi Savage looked with other men for the missing oxen, he saw a train of Mormon freight wagons managed by Abraham O. Smoot on the south side of the Platte River. This group of 88 people had 42 wagons, pulled by 265 oxen and 15 mules. Although the oxen were in good condition, Smoot's loads were extremely heavy, including a massive steam engine that Brigham Young had had purchased for an unspecified use in Utah.[18] That evening Smoot and Porter Rockwell, who was traveling with another Mormon freight caravan that included just five wagons with eleven yoke of oxen, visited the handcart camp. "I was glad to see them," Savage, a long-time church member, noted in his journal.[19] Smoot had often crossed the plains, leading wagon trains of emigrants or hauling freight for the church. Rockwell was a henchman for Brigham Young but also an able frontiersman.[20]

The loss of the Willie Company's oxen meant the milk cows and beef cattle had to be used as draft animals. That forced yet another delay and no doubt affected milk production, as the animals diverted their energies to drawing wagons. Cattle don't naturally pull wagons, so the men had to work with them, yoking them together and then training them to respond to the gee and haw commands used by the ox drovers.[21] Routines changed whenever the company halted for more than an overnight or noon stop. Women did laundry if they had extra clothing to change into; children slept or played. Men and older boys repaired the handcarts, especially the poorly built wheels, and moved flour and other supplies from the Willie wagons onto their carts, knowing that the few remaining cattle could not haul the heavily loaded wagons.

On September 12, 1856, Willie's company reached central Nebraska (near present-day North Platte) when "a grand outfit of carriages and light wagons" overtook them from the east. These vehicles, drawn by horses and mules, carried Franklin Richards, on his return from England to Utah. He was traveling with a party of homeward-bound missionaries, including Cyrus H. Wheelock, John Van Cott, George D. Grant, William H. Kimball, Joseph A. Young, and half a dozen others.[22] Camping overnight with the handcart company, they held a general meeting. Richards rebuked Savage "very severely" for his "lack of faith in God" in response to Savage's earlier statements that it was too late for the party to set out on an overland journey and expect to arrive in Zion before winter weather closed the trail. As Chislett recalled, "Richards gave us plenty of counsel to be faithful, prayerful, obedient to our leaders, etc., and wound up by prophecying in the name of Israel's God that 'though it might storm on our right and on our left, the Lord would keep open our way before us and we should get to Zion in safety.'" He added: "This assurance had a telling effect on the people—to them it was 'the voice of God.' They gave a loud and hearty 'Amen,' while tears of joy ran down their sunburnt cheeks."[23]

Richards had managed the Mormon mission in England, so many of those traveling with the Willie Company knew and revered him as an apostle, mission president, and Brigham Young's emissary. His words gave them encouragement to continue their march west. That night Richards and the men traveling with him told Captain Willie that they wanted some fresh meat. Willie "had our fattest calf killed for them," Chislett noted, but Chislett felt "ashamed for humanity's sake that they took it." At the time the handcart pioneers "had no provisions to spare, had not enough for ourselves," he recalled. "These 'elders in Israel,' these 'servants of God,' took from us what we ourselves so greatly needed and went on in style with their splendid outfit, after preaching to us faith, patience, prayerfulness, and obedience to the priesthood."[24]

Earlier the Willie Company had come across the bodies of Almon W. Babbitt, secretary of Utah Territory and a congressional delegate, and other members of his party who had been attacked and killed by Cheyenne Indians. They solemnly buried those who had perished and then moved on. The Mormon company might encounter the Indians who had taken part in that attack, so Richards encouraged the handcart company to cross to the south side of the Platte River, which they prepared to do. After fording the stream in their carriages, Richards and the men with him waited on the opposite bank. They "watched us wade the river—here almost a mile in width," Chislett said, adding that the returning missionaries provided no assistance as "our women and girls waded, pulling their carts after them" and struggled through water two or three feet deep.[25]

Stinging from Richards's rebukes, Savage seethed in his journal as the missionaries departed: "The impression left, was, that I condemned the hand cart Skeem, which is aradiculy [ridiculously] wrong."[26] Before taking his final leave of them, Richards "promised to leave us provisions, bedding, etc., at [Fort] Laramie if he could, and to secure us help from the valley as soon as possible," Chislett wrote.[27]

The Nebraska landscape and climate changed as the immigrants transitioned from the rolling hills near the Missouri River to flat country along the Platte River and from a moist, humid climate to a much drier one. Stephen Long called this the Great Desert in 1820 when he first explored the region, in part due to the dry climate and because of the soil itself. Nebraska's Sandhills, encompassing a large diamond-shaped area covering all of the central and western areas in the state, had deep, sandy soil that made pulling handcarts particularly difficult. Brigham Young and John Taylor, who organized the handcart brigades, knew about the soil conditions: they had seen wagon wheels sink deeply into it and watched as draft animals sunk to their hocks. They had hoped to design the carts so the wheels were wide enough to roll smoothly in such soil conditions but not so wide as to drag along unnecessarily.

After Willie's Company crossed to the south side of the Platte River, the weather turned rainy and colder, with foggy mornings. Fear of Indians caused the saints to place guards around the camp each evening. When Willie stressed that the travelers must rise when they first heard the horn blow at daylight, Savage said that the immigrants, "appearently not realizeing the nessissity of our making as much distance as posible, in order to reache the valey before too Severe colde weather," complained "of hard treatment, because we urge them along."[28]

Willie led his company to the forks of the Platte River, turning to follow the North Platte through Ash Hollow, where they again stopped to repair carts and search for a woman who had become separated from the company. They walked past Chimney Rock on September 24 and camped near the old trading post run by Joseph Robidoux, just south of Scotts Bluff, on September 26—the day the First and Second Handcart Companies rolled into Great Salt Lake City. The next day Chislett wrote that older members of the company were "failing conciderably," yet they were still more than 500 miles from Utah.[29]

"EVERY DEATH WEAKENED OUR FORCES"

Sarah Denton Moulton spied the military barracks and other buildings at Fort Laramie on September 30. When two of the company leaders reached the fort, they learned that "Richards has no cattle provided for us here, & no other provisions made."[30] The party found few supplies at the fort and those that could be purchased were "exstreamly costly."[31]

Assessing the situation, Willie and his captains concluded that the people would run out of flour some 300 miles short of their destination if they traveled at the same speed at which they had been moving and ate the same rations. "The Paciffick Springs is the only place that we are Sure of meeting Suplies," Savage wrote on October 4, indicating that they expected food to be on hand when they reached the Mormon campground located west of South Pass—and almost 200 miles west of their location at Fort Laramie.[32]

Farther west in their faster carriages, the Richards missionary party did encounter wagons filled with flour intended for the travelers still out on the trail.[33] Near Independence Rock on September 23 the missionaries stopped at noon with John Smith and two other men who had a wagon filled with flour for the companies. Four days later at Pacific Springs, just west of South Pass, they met another two wagons filled with flour intended for the handcart and wagon companies. Daniel Spencer wrote to Brigham Young, "We counseled them to cache their flour and go on to meet br. Willie and his company, which they agreed to." On September 28 the missionaries met a final Mormon traveler hauling flour toward the parties still out on the plains and encouraged him to continue on toward Willie's company with the food supply.[34]

Despite this evidence that flour was sent out to the Willie Company early in the fall, nothing in the documents written by members of that party indicates that they ever saw these wagons or benefited from this flour supply. Instead some of the flour was provided to the Smoot wagon train. The remainder may have been cached (stored) and never used that year or hauled back toward Salt Lake City when the teamsters worried about the lateness of the season. Whatever the case, with no additional supply the Willie Company's food resources quickly dwindled. Captain Willie cut the flour ration from one pound to three-quarters of a pound per day per adult and implored the people to travel faster. They had already sustained several deaths on the trail, including William Reed on October 2. Two days later Benjamin Culley (sixty-one) and year-old toddler Daniel Gadd died. They were buried along with a Dane who had died the night before. To keep people from pilfering supplies, as some had begun to do, Willie ordered a guard placed on the wagons to protect the foodstuffs that they carried.[35] In addition, the saints lightened their loads yet again, throwing aside clothing, bedding, and personal items. When Thomas Moulton pitched out the family teapot lid to make the load lighter, Sarah retrieved it. She had already given up too much on this crossing.[36]

As the saints struggled onward, company leaders cut rations again—with consequences. "Many of our men showed signs of failing," Chislett wrote. "To reduce their rations below twelve ounces would have been suicidal to the company, seeing they had to stand guard at night, wade the streams repeatedly by day to get the women and children across, erect tents, and do many duties which women could not do."[37]

On October 10 the Willie Company traveled about a dozen miles to what is Evansville, Wyoming, today. By noon they were at the rough log huts where John Baptiste Richard (Reshaw) traded some with overland trail travelers. Here Willie found that Franklin Richards had purchased and left for them thirty-seven buffalo robes. They traveled another five miles that afternoon (past the site of today's Casper, Wyoming) and crossed the North Platte River near a location that would soon become the military post at Platte Bridge (later renamed Fort Caspar). The teams used to pull the support wagons were as weak as the exhausted immigrants themselves when the company set up a camp after this last crossing of the North Platte.[38] Their route the next day took them away from the river, across hills, as they continued a dozen miles to a camp that they called Mineral Springs, located near a small natural lake and spring. The place became known as Poison Spring, which feeds Poison Creek.

Now they traveled a well-beaten path. The trail, in use since 1841, when the Bidwell-Bartleson wagon train first migrated overland, was subsequently followed by hundreds of thousands of people headed to Oregon, California, and the Mormon enclave at Great Salt Lake City. From Mineral Spring the trail winds across a high plains landscape of sagebrush, greasewood, alkali pools, and rugged rock features such as the Avenue of Rocks or Devil's Backbone. The soil here (no longer sandy) is hard and compacted—unless it is wet. Then it becomes slippery, almost slimy, and cakes on boots, shoes, and the wheels of wagons or handcarts when the bentonite in it dries to a concrete-like texture.

On October 12, while traveling through this rough country, the camp butchers, including Thomas Moulton, killed one weakened cow to provide meat for the people, who had "Sharp apatites." The days were warm and pleasant, but the deficiency of food was taking a toll. Willie's company camped at the base of Prospect Hill and ate fresh beef, no doubt preparing for the following day when they would have to drag their carts past Willow Spring and then up the steep hill and on to their next campsite at Greasewood Creek (later called Horse Creek). Alkali dust swirled beneath their feet and the wheels of the handcarts as the party tramped from Greasewood to Independence Rock. They crossed the Sweetwater River for the first time using a bridge and set up camp just to the south of the granite landmark. They had neither the energy nor the desire to carve their names in that trail marker as so many other travelers before them had done. Instead they pushed on, following the Sweetwater River for a time, diverging from the watercourse to remain on the trail through a break in the Rattlesnake range of mountains just south of Devil's Gate and then following the river again toward Split Rock. "The people are geting weak, and failing very fast," Savage wrote. "A greate many Sick. Our teams are als[o] failing fast and it requires great exertion to make any

Handcart sites in Wyoming.

progress. Our rations were reduced last night, one quarter bringing the mens to 10 oz, womans to 9 oz. and the children, some to 6 and other to 3 oz each [of flour]."[39]

The children began chewing on strips of rawhide pulled from the handcart wheels or the boots of people who died. Following the Sweetwater River they stripped bark from willow trees and gnawed on it, trying to ease the hunger in their bellies. "We resorted to eating anything that could be chewed; even bark and leaves of trees," wrote John Oborn, who was twelve that year. "We youngsters ate the rawhide from our boots." Even years later Oborn said that it was "beyond my power of description to write" about the conditions they faced. "God only can understand and realize the torture and privation, exposure and starvation we went through," he wrote in his autobiography, calling those days of travel "the most terrible experien[c]e of my life."[40]

Chislett echoed Oborn's assessment. "Our old and [infirm] began to droop, and they no sooner lost spirit and courage than death's stamp could be traced upon their features," he wrote. "Life went out as smoothly as a lamp ceaes [sic] to burn when the oil is gone. At first the deaths occurred slowly and irregularly, but in a few days at more frequent intervals, until we soon thought it unusual to leave a camp-ground without burying one or more persons." Each death, he said, "weakened our forces. In my hundred I could not raise enough men to pitch a tent when we camped."[41] Thomas Moulton had his duties as camp butcher. Years later his daughter Lottie recounted a story she had heard through her childhood. "One night the wind was blowing very hard and my mother and brothers were trying to pitch a tent. As fast as she would get it up, the wind would blow it over again. My father threw his knife and stuck it in the ground and said, 'If there is not men enough in this camp to put up my wife's tent, I won't kill another beef.' Right now there were plenty of men to pitch her tent."[42]

The members of Willie's party ate the dwindling remains of their flour while zig-zagging their way through the Sweetwater Valley. Crossing and recrossing the river required them to wade through icy cold water to reach the other side each time the stream curved. "When any in my hundred died I had to inter them," Chislett wrote. "I always offered up a heartfelt prayer to that God who beheld our sufferings, and begged him to avert destruction from us and send us help."[43]

CHAPTER 6

THE FIFTH COMPANY
The Martin Company, 1856

For people who had already traveled for months and knew that they were still more than a thousand miles from their ultimate destination at Great Salt Lake, the thought of stopping at the Missouri River and waiting for at least nine months before finishing the journey may have been tempting. When camped in Florence, Nebraska, the Fifth Company heard the warnings from men who had been over the trail and now suggested that it would be better to delay. Their desire to gather in Zion, however, was stronger. That dream outweighed any misgivings about continuing to travel in the late summer of 1856. Their trust in the Lord gave them the confidence to pick up their carts and head west. This faith had been expressed by company member John Jaques earlier in the summer: "As for me and my house, we will serve the Lord, and when we start we will go right up to Zion, if we go ragged and barefoot."[1]

Little did he know.

"The Lord has promised, through His servant Brigham, that the hand-cart companies shall be blessed with health and strength, and met part way with teams and provisions from the Valley," Jaques wrote in the *Millennial Star*. Showing his great faith, he added, "I am not afraid to prophesy, that those who go by hand-carts, and continue faithful and obedient, will be blessed more than they ever dreamed of."[2] He would soon find that many blessings were needed to overcome the challenges of the overland route—physical, psychological, and environmental—that he and others would face.

John Bailey (forty-nine), his wife, Jane (forty-six), and their children Langley (eighteen), John (fifteen), and Thomas (twelve) spent two weeks in camp at Iowa City before taking up their handcarts and striking off for the West with Martin's brigade. Across Iowa they endured thunderstorms and the jeering of people living along their route. "We were wet through many times," Langley later recalled. "John and I took off our shoes and stocking[s]. This mode of travel proved too much for me." When they reached Florence, Nebraska, a doctor treating Langley Bailey's sore feet told them it was too late to make the trip. "When we reached the mountains," the doctor told them, "we would be snowed in."[3]

In another meeting similar to the one held earlier with Willie's company, Bailey said the emigrants were called together to "know their mind in regards to [whether to] stop until the next year or go on."[4] Addressing the gathered saints, Franklin Richards said: "I hear that there are saints here who fear on account of the lateness of the season and may suffer in the crossing of the Rocky Mts. in snow storms." He promised: "God will keep the way open to the faithful at heart, and we'll arrive in the valleys in safety." John Bond, a twelve-year-old traveling with the Hodgetts wagon train, said Joseph A. Young, the son of church president Brigham Young, who had experience traveling through the region, disputed Richard's premise. He feared that snowstorms would begin before they "could cross in safety." Because they were weak from constant traveling by ship on the ocean, by train, and then on foot pulling handcarts from Iowa to Florence, they "would not be able to stand the freezing cold weather in sleet snow in the higher altitudes." These conditions "would cause untold agonies, sickness and much loss of life," Young warned. "Stay here for the winter," he urged, "then go on in the spring as my father's agents have lost too much time starting the saints to arrive in the valley safely."[5] Some who knew Young from his missionary work in England cried at his words, but they did not heed his warning and instead "consented with uplifted hands to go on and take the risks."[6]

The next morning, with an extra hundred pounds of flour on the carts, bedding, cooking utensils, and other items, the immigrants bade farewell to the missionaries and struck out from Florence.

Choices shape life experiences, and almost certainly Elizabeth Whittear Sermon's decisions would have harsh consequences for her family. An English convert to the church in 1852, Elizabeth prayed for the opportunity to follow her faith to America, but her husband, Joseph, resisted. They were comfortably situated in England and owned two houses outside London, one for their own home and another that they rented. Joseph also had a steady job. Elizabeth was not the typical Victorian-era woman. She had a strong personality and eventually wore down her husband's objections to immigrating. While he did not strongly believe in the religion of the Latter-day Saints, fifty-four-year-old Joseph would not allow Elizabeth (thirty-seven) to leave England without him. In February 1856 they sold their property and with children John (eight), Robert (six), Henry (five), and Marian Elizabeth (three) sailed from England on the *Caravan*.

With money from the sale of their property in England, Joseph and Elizabeth bought railroad tickets in New York to take them west. By May the family had reached

Florence, Nebraska, where they first rented a house. As their money began to diminish they bought a tent and moved into it. During that summer the Sermons saw the early handcart companies and other traveling parties get organized and depart for Utah. Ever cautious, Joseph hesitated to leave Florence. With their money dwindling, Elizabeth finally persuaded him to move on toward Zion. Joseph's head was "full of misgivings," but he bought a team of mules and a wagon, intending to join a wagon company. Again, however, Elizabeth's strong personality and faith prevailed. "After much discussion and counsel from the Elders, we were convinced (at least I was) that it was God's will that they be sold and we buy hand carts so that more Saints could make the journey to Zion," she said.[7]

Having made the decision to sell the wagon and mules and instead use a much smaller handcart, the family began disposing of treasured possessions by selling them at auction on the camping grounds. Elders from Great Salt Lake, Elizabeth said, purchased most of the family's discarded goods. Having arrived at Florence early in the season, the Sermon family made choices now that would have serious repercussions. They not only delayed their start toward Utah but also abandoned their plan to travel with a wagon train and instead joined that year's final and tragically late handcart company. The Martin Handcart Company did have wagons, but they were "loaded with merchandise . . . for President Young's store in Salt Lake," Elizabeth said.[8] Although the Sermons had sold their possessions to lighten the load, some of their former goods may have wound up in the very wagons accompanying them, having been purchased by the Mormon elders who expected to sell them later in Utah for a profit. It is unclear why the Sermon family sold the excess baggage rather than pay a fee to have it hauled to Utah in the wagons, but their decision may have been tied to the Mormon faith-based concept that their sacrifice now would enable more people to migrate across the plains to Utah later and ultimately bring them blessings.

Martin's handcart contingent pulled away from Cutler's Park in Florence on August 25, carrying provisions expected to last sixty days. Traveling near them "to be all the assistance they could be" were the wagon companies led by William Ben Hodgetts and John A. Hunt.[9] These three parties would travel closely together across Nebraska and into Wyoming. In all, more than 600 people pulled 146 poorly built handcarts. With them were 7 wagons, a carriage for Martin, a freight wagon loaded with merchandise and supplies, and some 50 head of milk cows and beef cattle. Hodgetts had 33 wagons pulled by 84 yoke of oxen and a contingent of about 150 people. His wagon company also had some 250 head of cows, heifers, and other cattle, most of them purchased with money provided by his mother, who had attempted her own immigration to America but had been forcibly returned to live with her husband in England. John Hunt had about 240 people traveling with 50 wagons, and another 4 church wagons filled with freight, all pulled by 297 oxen and cows and 7 horses and mules.

Twenty-six-year-old James Godson Bleak kept one of the only known contemporary journals of the Martin Company crossing. On Sunday, August 24, he wrote that the Mormons held two meetings in which they "partook of the sacrament." Bleak made no mention of any discussion about whether the company should leave the Missouri River so late in the summer. Keeping brief notes day by day, Bleak's record was generally mundane: "We remained in Camp." "We traveled 4 miles." "We traveled 19 miles and slept without raising our Tents as it was very late when we camped. We had a fine view of the prairies on Fire in two places."[10]

On September 5 they met a party of Pawnee Indians traveling east. The following day Franklin Richards and other missionaries returning to Utah overtook Martin's Company, just as they did with the Willie Company (see chapter 5). When the handcarts crossed a "very heavy road" on September 8 the traveling proved difficult, with "no watering place," resulting in "considerable murmuring in Camp" that night. The company leaders put a quick stop to the complaints at a morning meeting of the company when "Martin and elder Tyler gave the murmurers a good chastising."[11]

As with the Willie party just days ahead of them, their encounter with the fresh graves of members of an overland group that included Almon W. Babbitt was unsettling. Willie's Company had found these unfortunate victims of Indian attack and buried them. Having departed ahead of the Martin Handcart Company, Babbitt had been on the trail in central Nebraska several days before he learned that Thomas Margetts and his wife, Susannah, plus James Cowdy and his wife were attacked by Cheyenne Indians near Ash Hollow in western Nebraska. Mrs. Cowdy was taken captive, while the others were killed. Near Fort Kearny Babbitt was warned not to continue west, but he did so anyway and was attacked by an Indian raiding party. The Indians killed Babbitt and two of his four teamsters, wounded another member of the party, and carried away a Mrs. Wilson after killing her child. She was later killed when she apparently could not keep up with the fast-riding Cheyennes.[12] Although the Willie party had buried the bodies of the Babbitt and Margetts victims, when Martin's group came upon the graves they found bones strewn across the prairie, dug up by marauding wolves.

Just weeks earlier, while camped at Cutler's Park near Florence, John Jaques had seen Almon W. Babbitt "dressed in corduroy pants, woolen overshirt, and felt hat." Writing twenty-two years later, Jaques recalled that at the time Babbitt "seemed in high glee, his spirits very elastic, almost me[r]curial." Babbitt started with one carriage for Salt Lake, with the mail and a considerable amount of money, bragging to those in camp that he was "confident that he should be in Salt Lake within fifteen days."[13] Such travel time from Florence to Great Salt Lake City was of course impossible, and Babbitt knew it. He had been over the trail before and certainly realized that it would take far longer to make such a journey, even with fast horses, a light carriage, and plenty of supplies to avoid delays such as hunting and restocking.

The deaths of Margretts, Babbitt, and their companions made the Willie and Martin handcart companies more vigilant. After coming upon the two disaster scenes, men in the companies took turns through the nights patrolling their camps and watching for threats. On some days travel was delayed or cut short when a company member went missing. On October 6, for example, Bleak wrote: "We traveled but 8 miles in consequence of a sister having been missed. She went for water last night but did not return. After a fruitless search this morning we found that she had been with Capt. [Hodgetts's company] all night."[14]

Out on the plains, with the carts heavily laden with flour, the children had to walk, "which greatly annoyed" Joseph Sermon and caused Elizabeth to "think, but still I drawed [the handcart forward] and said nothing, knowing I was the innocent cause of your father's troubles." He likely had a better idea than she did what they might face. "The way was rough," Elizabeth remembered years later. Soon her husband's health began to fail. "His heart almost broken, he would say [to Elizabeth], 'What have you brought us to, you, yourself in shafts drawing like beasts of burden, your children hungery and almost naked.'"[15]

Realizing that Joseph was seriously ill, Elizabeth stopped her cart one day and threw out the flour. "I told the Captain Martin that if I and my children could not eat some of it, I would not draw it any further." The captain's response was that she "must be obedient or we will leave you on the plains as food for the wolves." Angered, Elizabeth retorted: "Brother Martin, leave those two girls you have in your carriage for food for the wolves, not me." In recalling the incident nearly four decades later, she said, "I was wounded and a severe wound it was." "I was beginning to think the handcart system was not very pleasant, and I felt it was the fault of the Captains," she remembered. "On some days we made good time—other days a cart or two would break down, a child would be missing. . . . Our food was giving out, our bodies growing weak. Cold weather chilled the body, the travel was slow and hard."[16]

John Bond, with the Hodgetts wagon train, which stayed close to the Martin Handcart Company, wrote that "the saints began to show weariness of the journey by the sunken eyes and emaciated forms from constant travel." At times they did not reach camp until nearly midnight, pulling and tugging the carts, wearing shoes so worn out that their toes protruded "in a bleeding condition." Wagon train leaders

Hunt and Hodgetts deplored "the emaciated, the sunken forms and eyes too painful to behold from short rations."[17]

Heber McBride, the thirteen-year-old traveling with his family who had enjoyed the ocean crossing, was not so enamored with the overland journey. As his family moved west, they were "piled into cattle cars or box cars anything was good enough for the d—— Mormons." Upon arrival in Iowa they "had to stay 3 or 4 weeks before we could start on our journey as we were coming with handcarts their seemed to be bad Management some where." This grouching came long before his family was crossing Nebraska with the handcart brigade, where "Mother took chills and fever then our trouble began she would walk as far as she could by holding on to the cart then we would get her in to one of the wagons." As food grew scarce, Heber recalled, "the men began to give out, teams gave out, and so many [people] sick and dieing that they couldent all ride."[18]

The boy's mother was already ill. Soon his father, Robert McBride, began struggling from the travel. In western Nebraska the soil turned sandy, miring down the wheels of the handcarts and dragging at people's feet when they also sank in the sand almost to their ankles. More of the responsibility for the family now fell to Heber and his sixteen-year-old sister, Janetta. The children pushed and pulled the handcart through the soft ground, struggling more each day as the landscape changed with the climate. It was drier there but not as flat. Even small rises became difficult to traverse. The tall grasses farther east gave way to the short grasses that the buffalo preferred. Some grasses, like the one known as needle-and-thread, had sharp seed points that drilled into shoes, stockings, pants, and dress hems, dragging back and forth and causing scratches, some of them bloody, on women's legs. They needed to pay attention to the prickly pear, becoming more predominant and just waiting to stab anyone who misplaced a foot. Western Nebraska offered curious natural features and sandstone outcrops such as Chimney Rock, Ancient Bluff, Courthouse, and Jail Rocks, but all the walking took a toll on the immigrants. It was hard to appreciate the scenery as beasts of burden.

"Sometimes we would find Mother laying by the side of the road," Heber McBride recalled, "we would get her on the cart and haul her along till we would find Father lying as if he was dead then Mother would be rested a little and she would try and walk and Father would get on and ride and then we used to cry and feel so bad." Many days the McBride family did not reach camp until after dark, when they would need to "hunt something to make a fire." No one helped the children and their weary, ailing parents. "The captins of the companyes," Heber said, "was worse than brutes." As evidence of the captains' rude behavior, Heber said that he feared for his mother's life one rainy night when they reached camp late. "We thought she was going to die and we had gathered a few sunflower stalks and wet Buffloo chips and had just got a little fire started when all hands were ordered to attend prayers and because we did not go to prayers Daniel Taylor [Tyler] came and kicked our fire all out and spilled the water that we was trying to get warm to make a little tea for Mother." Furious, the boy lashed out. "I then told him if I ever got to be a man I would whip him if it was the last thing I ever did on this earth."[19]

John Jaques may not have said anything during the journey, but years later he supported McBride's assessment:

The weary emigrants needed rest and refreshment, night and morning, to recruit their exhausted energies after tugging at those handcarts all day long, and some of the men having to stand guard half the night in addition to their regular day's work. It would have been much better for the occupants of each tent to have had their daily prayers at such time as best suited them and the whole camp to have had public meetings only when absolutely necessary or really advisable. There is no more necessity for a large company of traveling emigrants to be required to attend public meetings and preachings twice a day than there is for a community or a ward to be required to do the same.[20]

Most of the companies held at least one or sometimes two meetings daily. The gatherings lasted up to an hour, during which company leaders shared information, prayed, and preached. The days routinely began with prayer, then breakfast, followed by packing the camp, and lining the carts in single file as they headed out on the trail west. The march halted at noon for a meal composed of extra biscuits, gruel, or other food left from the morning's meal (or sometimes the prior night's supper). After a brief rest, travel resumed as the companies tugged their carts to a new campsite, where they set up tents, built fires (often using buffalo chips they had gathered during the afternoon walk across the prairie), and cooked their meager rations. Camp meetings and prayer sessions also were held most evenings.

"We had to go out to the meetings to hear them harrangue when we should have been in our beds getting our rest," Elizabeth Sermon said, "but the beast would threaten and carry out his threats and pull the tents down to make us go to prayers." Working a rotating schedule as camp guards meant that some of the men only got a few hours' sleep each day. "I have seen [leaders] take poor, half starved, weak men by the arm and . . . drag them out of their tent to stand guard over poor cattle who could hardly stand themselves," she added.[21]

"It might be their lot to be worked and wearied and worn down to death," John Jaques lamented, "or starved to death, or frozen to death, or wasted to death by diarrhoea and want and weakness, but surely that was enough. It hardly seemed fair that they should be harassed to death with needlessly frequent public meetings, and preached to death while they were at the meetings. For, of all deaths, to be prayed to death, or preached to death, or talked to death in any way, is not the easiest kind of death to die."[22]

Elizabeth Sermon resented that some of the captains had advantages over her family and friends: "By our going around camp at night where cooking pots of some of the Captains could be seen, they looked pretty full and smelled quite savory. In fact the Captains fed well while we drank *ours* in porridge for I could not make bread with the small allowance of flour." At times the captains "had the power to 'Lord it over us,'" she wrote, specifically calling out a butcher who became captain over her group of saints.[23]

Reaching Fort Laramie on October 8, Martin's Company did some brief trading but did not lay over to rest, unlike some westbound parties. After selling (or exchanging) watches and other valuables for provisions they pushed on, no doubt driven by the company leaders, who must have been wary of how the weather could change.[24] When crossing Nebraska these immigrants sometimes traveled only six or eight miles in a day, but with supplies running low and days growing shorter they made twenty or even twenty-two miles in a day in Wyoming, traveling at least six to eight hours daily to cover that distance.[25] Even so they moved fewer miles each day than the Willie Company, allowing the Fourth Company to put ever greater distance between the two handcart groups.

The Hodgetts wagon train rested two days at Fort Laramie, washing clothes, shoeing the draft animals, making repairs, and lightening their loads. Bond remembered Hodgetts's advice to "leave all heavy things at the fort to help you and our loved children so they may have a chance to ride once in a while," since the teams were becoming "more foot sore, thin, and tired." As with the handcart immigrants, the food supply was inadequate to provide for the wagon travelers until they reached Salt Lake. Bond's father, for example, abandoned a No. 8 Charter Oak stove, along with other heavy possessions. The days rapidly grew shorter, the nights colder, the food supply smaller. When Martin and his company reached Deer Creek on October 17, they deliberately discarded baggage, bedding, and cooking utensils to lighten their loads, no doubt because they'd been implored to travel more quickly. They burned some of the discards and buried other items, perhaps believing that they would return the following year to retrieve them. Now they had only ten pounds of goods per person over the age of eight and just five pounds of gear for the youngsters, no greater than a 10-pound sack of potatoes for an adult and only half that much for children.[26]

The sight of snow on Laramie Peak was alarming, as was the monotonous howling of the wolves that began following the trains, perhaps to raid the shallow graves of victims as they had done with the Margetts party farther east in Nebraska. "The snow caped Peaks bring much alarm," wrote Bond, who was traveling with the Hodgetts Company. He feared for the handcart travelers who lived in tents and had only worn bed coverings and clothes. "God pity them. He knows of their wounded and aching hearts." The Hodgetts wagons and cattle herd had made only short daily drives since leaving Fort Laramie "so as to be near to the Hand cart Saints, to be helpful to them should they need it."[27] Hunt's wagon company also traveled near the handcart brigade. As these parties approached the Reshaw (John Baptiste Richard) Bridge and then the last crossing of the North Platte River six miles to the west (at present Casper), many of the handcart people pulled close to Hunt's wagons. "It was enough to draw forth one's sympathy for them," the Hunt company clerk wrote, "seeing the aged women and children pulling their handcarts, many of them showing haggard countenances."[28] They were still 384 miles from Great Salt Lake City.

"WINTER CAME ON ALL AT ONCE"

On October 19 everything suddenly turned worse. A winter storm blew across South Pass and swept down the Sweetwater Valley, slamming the Willie Company encamped at the Sixth Crossing. It then roared east with bitter cold winds blowing into the Martin, Hunt, and Hodgetts Companies as they passed Reshaw's trading post.

Fall storms can hit this area of Wyoming with little warning. The nights are cold and mornings are crisp and cool, but the sun creates enough warmth during the day that coats are not needed. Autumn, however, can bring unexpected change. Wandering along the Sweetwater River through a valley protected by rocky mountain outcrops to the east and higher, pine-covered mountains to the west, Willie's company may not have realized that clouds building to the west represented a wintry blast that would pour over the continental divide and whip down the river valley, striking them with such force that it literally took their breath away.

"We were overtaken by a snowstorm which the shrill wind blew furiously about us," Chislett wrote. "The snow fell several inches deep as we travelled along, but we dared not stop, for we had a sixteen-mile journey to make that day, and short of it we could not get wood and water."[29] In struggling to the Sixth Crossing of the Sweetwater River, they ate the last of their flour. Willows were the largest trees in the area and bitter to the taste, but the children had been stripping off bark and leaves to chew on for sustenance. Lack of timber meant no good wood for fires, either for cooking or for staying warm. A foot and a half of snow covered their camp overnight.

While Willie's party shivered and suffered at Sixth Crossing, the Martin Company, eighty miles farther back on the trail, reached the last crossing of the North Platte River on October 19, where they waded through waist-deep water with mushy blocks of ice floating in it. James Bleak said the final crossing was "very trying in consequence of its width and the cold weather." Some women, Bleak noted in an otherwise sparsely worded journal, "tied up their skirts and wade[d] through" but others, too frail or fearful, begged for mercy.[30]

Bond, with the Hodgetts wagons, said the handcart pioneers pleaded with Captain Martin to unload a wagon so that they could ride across the stream, rather than ford the icy channel. "The saints pleaded so earnestly," he said, "We could hear their appeals on the opposite side of the river." But they cried out in vain. "The captain still gave them a deaf ear to their pleadings." Instead Martin "sat on his mule and saw those innocent ones, who had pleaded so, fall in the river as the current was carrying the weak ones off their feet." Some of the stronger men assisted the "helpless and weakened ones" by carrying them across on their backs, many making more than one trip through the river.[31]

When Aaron Jackson reached the North Platte, he valiantly waded into the cold water. He "had only gone a short distance," his wife, Elizabeth, remembered, "when he reached a sand bar in the river on which he sank down through weakness and exhaustion." Elizabeth's sister, Mary Horrocks, walked into the icy stream to help him before a man on horseback came along and carried him across. Mary then returned to help Elizabeth pull the handcart, burdened with three of the Jackson children and other goods, through the icy river. Once they were across, Aaron, completely exhausted, was placed on another handcart and hauled to the night camp, a short distance from the river. His legs had completely given out, and he would not walk another step toward Zion.[32] Just as they made it across the North Platte, the cold wind became a strong winter storm swirling from the northwest. As Jaques later remembered, it was a "bitter cold day. Winter came on all at once, and that was the first day of it."[33]

Snow continued to fall the next morning, October 20. With people and animals suffering and exhausted, the Willie party faced calamity: farther to the west but mired in the deep snow, with no food and little opportunity to build and feed campfires. "Starvation was taking its toll," John Oborn wrote. "It seemed only a matter of days before all would parish."[34] Savage agreed: "Except we get assistance, we Surely, can not move far in this snow."[35] The Hunt and Hodgetts wagon trains were similarly stranded near the North Platte River. The deadly winter weather that experienced trail travelers had warned about had now settled in. Without aid, sheer survival was in doubt.

Robert McBride was so weak that he could barely sit up, so his son Heber found a place for his father to ride in one of the wagons as soon as they crossed the river. It was snowing so hard when they reached their camp west of the North Platte River that Heber struggled with sister Janetta to pitch their tent and find a few willow branches to burn for heat. After making their mother as comfortable as possible, Heber and Janetta "went to try and find father but the wind was blowing the snow so bad that we could not see anything and the wagons had not got into camp and it was then after dark so we did not find him that night."[36]

"The evening we crossed the Platte river for the last time it was very cold," Heber would later write, "and the next morning there was about 6 inches of snow on the ground and then what we had to suffer can never be told."[37] That morning Janetta prepared "our little bite of breakfast" while Heber went to search for his father. He found him "under a wagon with snow all over him and he was stiff and dead. I felt as though my heart would burst. I sat down beside him on the snow and took hold of one of his hands and cried 'oh Father Father.' There we was away out on the Plains with hardly anything to eat and Father dead and mother sick."

Young Heber said he had a "cry out" before returning to the tent to tell his mother and siblings that their father was dead. The McBride family never knew if Robert had died in the wagon and was then lifted out and placed beneath it or if he climbed from the vehicle to go in search of his wife and children then fell and froze to death under it.

The toil of crossing the river, combined with freezing weather and lack of food, contributed to every passing. As Heber would later say, "tounge nor pen can never tell the sorrow and suffering."[38] At least a dozen other men died in the camp that night. With aid from her sister, Elizabeth Jackson had cared for her children and ill husband, Aaron, as best she could. At the first camp after crossing the river, Jackson's husband "tried to eat but failed. He had not the strength to swallow." She put Aaron to bed and joined him there. Lacking bedding, they did not disrobe, but kept their clothes on for warmth. Even so she woke in the night because she was "extremely cold." The weather, she said, "was bitter. I listened to hear if my husband breathed—he lay so still. I could not hear him. I became alarmed. I put my hand on his body, when to my horror I discovered that my worst fears were confirmed. My husband was dead. He was cold and stiff—rigid in the arms of death. It was a bitter freezing night.... I called for help to the other inmates of the tent. They could render me no aid; and there was no alternative but to remain alone by the side of the corpse until morning."[39]

In the morning men who still had strength built a fire. Its heat thawed the ground enough that they could dig graves for those who had perished, including Robert McBride and Aaron Jackson. Some of the dead were placed in a common grave, Heber

McBride recalled, "side by side and on top of one another any way to get them covered for I can assure you that the men had no heart to do any more than they had to."[40]

Many years later Josiah Rogerson Sr. wrote of Elizabeth Jackson's loss: "[She] was sitting by the side of her dead husband. Her face was suffused in tears, and between her bursts of grief and wails of sorrow, she would wring her hands and tear her hair. Her children blended their cries of 'Father' with that of the mother. This was love; this was affection—grief of the heart and bereavement of the soul—the like of which I have never seen since."[41] Jackson herself wrote: "I will not attempt to describe my feelings at finding myself thus left a widow with three children, under such excruciating circumstances. I cannot do it. But I believe the Recording Angel has inscribed in the archives above, and that my sufferings for the Gospel's sake will be sanctified unto me for my good." Her sentiment echoed a common Mormon teaching at the time: through faith and suffering people would ultimately earn salvation. "Six or seven thousand miles from my native land, in a wild, rocky, mountain country, in a destitute condition, the ground covered with snow, the waters covered with ice, and I with three fatherless children with scarcely nothing to protect them from the merciless storms," it is little wonder that Elizabeth "became despondent." Her despair led her to "appeal to the Lord alone . . . and he came to my aid."[42] The aid was not physical but spiritual: Jackson drew strength from her faith even while her challenges mounted.

A piercing north wind drove snow, sleet, and hail down on the people in their new camp.[43] They picked up their carts the following day but were only able to struggle a few miles to near Red Buttes, where the storm swirling around them forced another halt. This time they saw little relief and huddled in frozen misery, praying and waiting for the storm to abate. It would be days before the weather improved.

Elizabeth Jackson's only familial support was her sister, Mary, who was also ill. "So severe was her affliction that she became deranged in her mind, and for several days she ate nothing but hard frozen snow," Elizabeth wrote.[44] This state of incomprehension may have been a harbinger of hypothermia, a state in which the body undergoes profound physiological change due to cold. People no longer shiver, as a feeling of warmth, even euphoria, overcomes them. Individuals suffering from hypothermia have been known to discard warm clothing and wander aimlessly, before eventually succumbing to the cold.

"I remember distinctly when that terrible snow storm came how dismayed the people were," Jane Griffiths recalled. "We were in a pitiable condition before, but the snow made it look hopeless. My stepmother took my little brother six years old by the hand and myself and helped us along the best she could while sister and Father floundered through with the hand cart. How we did flounder through that snow, tumbling over sage brush and crying with the cold and hunger."[45]

They moved only five or six miles west of the North Platte before setting up their new camp, huddling there in misery. As James Bleak recorded on October 23, "For several days we have been weather bound in consequence of a heavy fall of snow."[46] Most of their sixty-day supply of food had been consumed. For the next nine days they stayed in their forlorn camp near Red Buttes, too weak, cold, exhausted, and hungry to break camp and move out into the frigid, snowy landscape.

Conditions were frightful. The older brother of Jane Griffiths died during one of those bitterly cold nights, along with others. "In the morning we would find their starved and frozen bodies right by the side of us; not knowing when they died until day light revealed the ghastly site to us."[47] The company could barely sustain itself to keep fires burning and make meager meals. "It seemed as though death would be a blessing," Heber McBride wrote. "Our clothing almost worn out and not enough of bedclothes to keep us warm[;] we would lay and suffer from night till morning with the cold." The oxen used to pull the wagons "began dieing," he said, "but [every animal] that died was devoured very quickly and us little boys would get strips of rawhide and try and eat it." The boys would take a strip and "crisp it in the fire and then draw a string of it through our teeth and get some of the burnt scales of[f] that way and then crisp it again and repeat the operation till we would get tired."[48] Death was foreshadowed. "The gaunt form, hollow eyes, and sunken countenance, discolored to the weatherbeaten sallow, with the gradual weakening of the mental faculties," Jaques remembered, "plainly foreboded the coming [death]."[49]

The travelers huddled in their canvas tents at the Red Buttes camp, prostrated by the toil, unable to drag the carts any farther. "Captain Martin looked sorrowful and care worn," wrote Bond, "but was as firm as the hills that assistance would soon arrive to help all the famishing ones."[50] In spite of their desperate plight, most of these people did not lose faith. Some, however, knowing they were still hundreds of miles from Utah, began to give up hope. As Heber McBride noted, "We used to pray that we might die to get out of our misery."[51]

Edmund Ellsworth, captain of the First Handcart Company.
(Church History Library, MS 25545)

Daniel McArthur, captain of the Second Handcart Company.
(Church History Library, PH 1700)

Edward Bunker, captain of the Third Handcart Company.
(Church History Library, PH 170)

James Grey Willie, captain of the Fourth Handcart Company.
(Church History Library M205)

Edward Martin, captain of the Fifth Handcart Company.
(Church History Library, PH 4888)

Christian Christiansen traveled with the Seventh Handcart Company
and was captain of the company from Florence, Nebraska, to Salt Lake City.
(Church History Library, PH 2490)

Brigham Young, president of the Church of Jesus Christ of Latter-day Saints,
conceived the idea of having people travel overland using handcarts
for their possessions in 1855. The migration started the following year.
He is shown here with one of his wives, Margaret Peirce Young.
(Church History Library, PH 914)

Sarah Elizabeth Moulton and John Bennett Hawkins. Sarah, eldest daughter
of Thomas Moulton, came from England with her father, stepmother,
and seven sisters and brothers. They traveled with the Willie Handcart
Company in 1856. They endured freezing cold temperatures,
inadequate food, and a seven-month journey to Salt Lake City.
(Moulton Family Photo)

Sarah Denton Moulton, wife of Thomas Moulton, saved money for years before she and her family had the opportunity to leave England and travel to Utah in 1856 with the James Grey Willie Handcart Company. She followed her sisters to Utah and brought her seven children, including her infant son Charles, who was born on the ship shortly after the family sailed from Liverpool, and stepdaughter Sarah Elizabeth.
(Moulton Family Photo)

Born on the ship *Thornton* shortly after sailing from England,
Charles Alma Moulton was carried by his mother or rode in the handcart
as his family traveled with the Willie Handcart Company in 1856.
All ten members of the Moulton family survived the trip to settle
in Heber Valley, Utah. As an adult Charles moved to Idaho.
His son Thomas Alma later homesteaded in Jackson Hole, Wyoming.
(Moulton Family Photo)

John Taylor directed the handcart migration from New York City,
arranging for train transportation, campsite logistics in Iowa City, and
the purchase of the earliest carts used by the first three companies.
(Church History Library, PH 4468)

Many of these Mormon missionaries played a significant role in the handcart migration. The image was taken in England in 1855 when the men, all filling missions in Great Britain, met to plan for the immigration. Back row, from left: Edmund Ellsworth, Joseph A. Young, William H. Kimball, George D. Grant, James Ferguson, James A. Little, Philemon Merrill. Middle row, from left: Edmund Bunker, Chauncey G. Webb, Franklin D. Richards, Daniel Spencer, Dan Jones, Edward Martin. Front row, from left: James Bond, Spicer Crandall, William C. Dunbar, James D. Ross, and Daniel D. McArthur. (*Church History Library, PH 1900*)

Frederick Piercy drew this sketch, "Leaving Liverpool," for
Route from Liverpool to the Great Salt Lake Valley Illustrated, published in 1855
and used as a guidebook for English immigrants.
(Author's Collection)

A seemingly endless serpentine of handcarts rolls across
the Iowa hills in this artist's rendition of the migration.
(Utah State Historical Society)

Carl Christian Anton Christensen traveled with the Seventh Handcart Company.
He later became an accomplished artist. This scene titled "Handcart Pioneers" (1900)
depicts the handcarts crossing a stream in Iowa. It is a representation
of the early days of travel, almost bucolic in nature.

(Church History Library)

Danquart Anton Weggeland painted this image: "Handcart Pioneers."
(Church History Library)

Chimney Rock in western Nebraska became the first signature landmark
along the Mormon Trail. Most travelers remarked on its conical shape
in letters home, in journals, or in later reminiscences.
(Library of Congress, 3b39113u)

Independence Rock is a signature landmark along the Mormon Trail,
located in central Wyoming. The two horseback riders give perspective to the site
of the granite outcrop where pioneer-era travelers carved or painted their names.
William Henry Jackson captured this image in 1870.
(L. Tom Perry Special Collections, Harold B. Lee Library, Brigham Young University)

The view east from Independence Rock shows a small camp of wagons and tents and the Sweetwater River as it flows toward the North Platte River. The camp is the one used by photographer William Henry Jackson. (*L. Tom Perry Special Collections, Harold B. Lee Library, Brigham Young University*)

The Sweetwater River stretches to the west as seen from a vantage point atop Independence Rock. Note the men on the rock in the foreground, and the wagon beside the river, no doubt part of photographer William Henry Jackson's party. (*L. Tom Perry Special Collections, Harold B. Lee Library, Brigham Young University*)

The rugged defile of Devil's Gate is a signature landmark along the Sweetwater River in central Wyoming. William Henry Jackson took this image in 1870.

(L. Tom Perry Special Collections, Harold B. Lee Library, Brigham Young University)

This illustration, titled "The Hand Cart Train—Brigham Young's 'Divine Plan,'"
depicts the Mormon emigration, showing how the people struggled in the snowstorms
that hindered their crossing in the fall of 1856. The etching appeared in *Wife No. 19
or the Story of a Life in Bondage* by Ann Eliza Webb Young, published by Dustin,
Gilman and Co., Hartford, Connecticut, in 1875.
(Utah State Historical Society)

A Mormon wagon camp in Wyoming near the end of the trail era, in 1866.
(Church History Library, 018)

William Henry Jackson painted this image of a Mormon handcart company
crossing the Blacks Fork River near Fort Bridger in western Wyoming.
He accurately depicts the people pushing and pulling the handcarts, with
children both walking and riding in the carts, and support wagons.
(National Park Service)

Jim Bridger's original trading post served travelers on overland trails after 1843. Bridger operated the post until 1853, when the Church of Jesus Christ of Latter-day Saints took it over. The church members maintained a presence there until 1857, when they withdrew to Salt Lake City as the U.S. Army approached during the Utah War.
(Wyoming State Archives, Department of State Parks and Cultural Resources)

Great Salt Lake City, established by the Church of Jesus Christ of Latter-day Saints in 1847, was already a developed community by 1853 when this image was made showing the view looking south. It was originally published in 1855 in *Route from Liverpool to Great Salt Lake Valley Illustrated* by James Linforth, with illustrations by Frederick Piercy.
(Author's collection)

The Mormon Handcart Historical Site, Natrona County, Wyoming, is the location
where the Martin Handcart Company took refuge during harsh weather in 1856.
The Church of Jesus Christ of Latter-day Saints now owns the land, once a private ranch.
(Candy Moulton)

Wagons still stir dust along the trail in central Wyoming. This stretch of the
Mormon Trail is on public land just a mile east of Independence Rock. These
three wagons were part of a small wagon train reenacting trail travel for the
filming of *In Pursuit of a Dream*, a documentary for the Oregon-California
Trail Association, written and produced by Candy Moulton.
(Candy Moulton)

A setting sun highlights the Rattlesnake Range and Split Rock,
one of the prominent natural markers for trail travelers. The Sweetwater River
meanders through the valley, which required overland travelers to ford
it several times as they worked their way west.
(Candy Moulton)

This original handcart was on display at the Church History Library in 2014.
(Candy Moulton)

This elderly man with his replica handcart shows how the carts used
during the migration from 1856 to 1860 would have been built and loaded.
The man is unknown, but the photo was taken by L. C. Thorne.
(Uinta County Library Regional History Center)

CHAPTER 7

"GO AND BRING IN THOSE PEOPLE"

Franklin Richards's missionary party, which had overtaken the two handcart companies earlier that fall in Nebraska, traveled quickly and arrived in Great Salt Lake City on October 4. That day Willie's party was camped on Horseshoe Creek about forty miles west of Fort Laramie, while the Martin Company was at Scotts Bluff. The Hunt and Hodgetts wagon trains were still in western Nebraska as well. Fifteen days later the massive snowstorm would sweep over South Pass and hammer into the Willie Company at Sixth Crossing before subsequently hitting the Martin Company as they crossed the North Platte River.

After his arrival Richards immediately met with Brigham Young and explained that more than a thousand people remained out on the plains without adequate food, shelter, or clothing. He had purchased buffalo robes that the Willie Company would find when they reached the Reshaw (Richard) Bridge crossing of the North Platte, but he knew that was not enough and there had been little food to buy. Richards's appearance in Great Salt Lake City coincided with the semiannual Church of Jesus Christ of Latter-day Saints Conference, a gathering that always drew people to the Mormon headquarters. Speaking in the Bowery on Sunday morning, October 5, he gave another warning: "Many of our brethren and sisters are on the plains with handcarts, and probably many are now seven hundred miles from this place, and they must be brought here, we must send assistance to them."[1]

Richards's message was full of ambivalence and cross-purposes. He appealed to those gathered in the Bowery to help and even admitted that crossing so late might have been a mistake (not mentioning that he had urged all those now in peril to continue their journey that year), but he also stressed his belief that faith would bring them through. "The Saints that are now out upon the plains . . . expect to get cold fingers and toes," Richards told those gathered in the Bowery. "They have this faith and confidence towards God that he will over-rule the storms that may come . . . that their path may be free from suffering more than they can bear. They have confidence to believe that this will be an open fall." We may wonder whether Richards truly believed his rhetoric or said these things to assuage his own conscience after having urged the saints forward weeks earlier in Nebraska.

Speaking directly to the women in Utah, Richards reminded them of their own journeys across the plains: "Sisters think of those fatiguing times, and stir up your good men in behalf of those who are footing it, and pulling hand-carts [1,300] miles, instead of riding 1000 as you did. . . . Many of those now back are poor . . . they have scarcely a change of clothing. If they can have some shoes sent out to them, and a few blankets to make them comfortable at night, and flour enough, with what beef they have along, to make them a good meal in the morning they will make those hand-carts work powerfully."

Richards told them that "ten to one they will have storms to encounter; though the Lord will not let them suffer any more than they have grace to bear." He added that no measure "filled up my soul with joy, faith and energy so much as this plan for the gathering of the honest poor." Richards was totally faithful to Brigham Young and the church. It was his job to see that any undertaking presented by the church leader be implemented, so he announced to those gathered at the Bowery that day: "We did not stop to enquire whether the plan was a feasible one or not, that was none of our business." Richards, it would seem, was already laying the groundwork to avoid blame for his overzealousness and for contributing to what he must have realized was a disaster in the making. The handcart endeavor was "an experiment," Richards said. "We cannot yet tell you exactly what it costs to come through in that way; but we know that it is going to cost those on the other side of the mountains cold feet and a great deal of affliction and sorrow, unless we help them."

Daniel Spencer, who had not provided an adequate number of handcarts for all of the travelers who needed them that year, also told those gathered in the Bowery on October 5 that they had "the power to help them." Spencer acknowledged that the "emigration is late, quite late, but it is useless for me to undertake to explain why it is so." He spoke about the experiences of the handcart pioneers when they reached Iowa and in starting their journey to Utah but cut his talk short: "I will not dwell longer upon this subject, but simply admonish you to do all you can to help those poor brethren and sisters who are out upon the plains."[2] He may not have wanted to acknowledge that the dearth of handcarts—which had been his responsibility—had delayed the Willie and Martin parties in Iowa longer than was prudent but that they still sent the late companies west.

When church president Brigham Young took the podium, he called upon the bishops for aid:

I shall not wait until tomorrow, nor until the next day for 60 good mule teams and 12 or 15 wagons, I do not want to send oxen I want good horses and mules. They are in this Territory, and we must have them. Also 12 tons of flour and 40 good teamsters, besides those that drive the teams. . . . To take charge of the teams that are now managed by men, women and children who know nothing about driving them. Second, 60 or 65 good spans of mules, or horses, with harness, whipple trees, neckyokes, stretchers, lead, chains, &c. And thirdly, 24 thousand pounds of flour, which we have on hand.

Noting that faith, religion, and the "profession of religion" would not save the people, Young implored the faithful, "Go and bring in those people now on the plains." Young wanted the relief mission to begin immediately. "I want the sisters to have the privilege of fetching in blankets, skirts, stockings, shoes, etc., for the men, women, and children that are in those handcart companies [plus] . . . hoods, winter bonnets, stockings, skirts, garments, and almost any description of clothing." This came from the man whose handcart plan just a year earlier had suggested that people should "only bring a change of clothing."[3]

Young's words brought action. The quickly organized relief train led by George D. Grant, with William H. Kimball and Robert T. Burton assisting, camped at Big Mountain, just east of Great Salt Lake City on October 7, the first night of their mission. These men had been in the missionary party that had traveled so quickly from Nebraska to Utah earlier in the fall. They were intimately familiar with the route and knew just how many people—old, young, healthy and infirm—were out there somewhere on the trail.

Richards's report to Brigham Young in the President's Office goes unrecorded in the journal kept for Young's office. But on October 8, 1856, the journal includes the notation: "Bro Franklin Richards gave a report on his mission . . . to England from which he just returned." That same day Young granted four divorces. The next day he reprimanded a Welshman who had failed to repay a woman who had provided funds for the man to immigrate to Utah. Young dealt with other routine business until October 11, when he "signed some special orders as he was preparing to meet the Emigrants on the road. The president will be accompanied by his counsellors and others when he goes."[4]

The first rescue unit made it the 113 miles from Salt Lake City to Fort Bridger by October 12, just a week after Young's plea. That same day the Willie Company, just past Devil's Backbone, killed a cow for food, one of their last animals. The Martin handcarts were midway between Fort Laramie and the last crossing of the North

Platte River. On October 13 President Young and several others, including one of his wives and the wife of Heber Kimball, "left G. S. L. to meet the coming Emigrant and make a short visit at Fort Supply and Fort Bridger." On October 15 the rescue team vanguard reached the Green River, another fifty-three miles back along the trail. Young indicated that he was ill, however, so he and Kimball returned to the city with their party. By the following day the official journal reported that Young's health was "very much better."[5] The cause of his illness was not recorded, but he suffered periodically through the winter. At Green River the rescue team found no sign of the Willie Company or those behind him and sent out scouts on horseback who could travel more quickly than the relief wagons. Young continued to call for relief resources in Great Salt Lake City and men and wagons to haul them toward the beleaguered handcart companies.

East of the Green River George D. Grant and the rescue wagons met Smoot's westbound teams. That wagon train had camped near the Willie Company back in Nebraska but with experienced teamsters made good time along the North Platte River route and through the Sweetwater Valley and thus avoided being bogged down by the storm east of the Continental Divide. Now the Grant and Smoot groups camped together at Big Sandy in western Wyoming, west of South Pass. Although Grant was hauling goods intended for the Martin and Willie parties, he shared flour and beef with Smoot and even provided the Mormon freight company with "teams and 18 men" to aid them in their journey toward Great Salt Lake, thus depleting his own resources meant for the handcart companies.[6]

WELCOME MESSENGERS FROM THE COURTS OF GLORY

Willie's party took no time to mourn the death of thirty-two-year-old Eliza Rowley on October 19. By noon they were near Ice Slough when the clouds heralding a cold wind and the first snow of the season descended on them. This location, nearly eighty miles west of the Martin party, was a recognized trail point, known for the peaty bog that protected an ice field where travelers could dig down and get ice even during the middle of summer. They pushed on several more miles to the Sixth Crossing of the Sweetwater River, where freezing cold and heavier snow blanketed them, forcing a halt. Twelve-year-old John Oborn had sustained himself in part by eating willow leaves and rawhide from his boots. He remembered that the members of the party had reached the end of their resources and all feared that they might perish. They were in desperate straits when "like a thunderbolt out of the clear sky, God answered our prayers."[7] Advance scouts from the Grant rescue company—Cyrus H. Wheelock, Joseph A. Young, Abel Garr, and Stephen Taylor—had found them. "More welcome messengers never came from the courts of glory than these two [sic] young men were to us," Chislett wrote.[8] The immigrants knew the men from missionary work in England and from having seen them on the trail in Nebraska weeks earlier. They "reported forty wagon loads of flour one day in advance of us," Savage wrote. "This was joyful news to us for we had eaten the last of the flour, having only six small beefs and 400 pounds of biscuits to provision over 400 people."[9]

The news that they would soon have food and warm clothing was a godsend. "Those of you who have never had this experience cannot realize its intensity," recalled Oborn, who remembered shoveling the snow out of their tent, using a "tin plate belonging to my mother's mother."[10] They remained at the Sixth Crossing that night and issued the last of their provisions: the hard biscuits purchased at Fort Laramie. These biscuits, also called hardtack, ship's biscuits, and pilot bread, were a staple of nineteenth-century travel diets. Made of flour, water, and a little salt, they were rolled to about a quarter-inch in thickness and three inches square, had holes punched in them with a small cutter, and then were cooked in hot ovens until they were as hard as a hockey puck. This hard, dry state meant they not only kept indefinitely but also traveled well. They could be softened with bacon grease or dunked in hot beverages to make them more palatable. Lacking bacon and hot drinks, however, the Mormons simply gnawed on them until they softened enough to be chewed and swallowed. The news that relief was near was welcome but came too late for many. In addition to Eliza Rowley and Daniel Osborn, several others died on October 19, including Eliza Smith (forty), from Eldersfield, Worchestershire, England; John Kockles from Norwich, Norfolk, England; and Rasmus Hansen from Falster, Denmark.[11]

The next day, October 20, members of the Willie Company awoke to find several inches of snow on the ground, their oxen scattered, and the lifeless body of Anna F. Tait (thirty-one) from Glasgow, Scotland. That morning Captain Willie and Joe Elder left camp, riding west in search of the relief wagons. "We rode 12 mile where we expected to find them," Elder wrote, "but they was not there [so] we ascended the rocky ridge the snow and an awful cold wind blue in our faces all day."[12] Snow continued to fall, so Willie's party remained in camp at Sixth Crossing. Meanwhile Martin and his party were eighty miles farther east that same day, struggling through the snow to Red Butte camp.

At Rock Creek, a few miles east of South Pass, Willie and Elder found the rescue company's camp, twenty-seven miles west of the Willie Company travelers. If it had been a long day for Willie and Elder, the situation back at Sixth Crossing was almost unendurable. Having devoured the last of the hard biscuits, the Willie Company did not move that day. One immigrant recorded: "It continued snowing severely."[13]

As temperatures plummeted and the wind howled, they watched for the relief party and their company captain. Amid conflicting emotions of hope and despair, they saw nothing. Not until the following day would Willie and Elder, with the rescue party in tow, begin retracing their route to the stalled camp, but they did not arrive until evening.

━━━━━━━

Rescue party member Harvey Cluff wrote of the first sight of the stranded travelers in Willie's party. "It was about sunset when we came in sight of the camp: which greatly resembled an Esqumeax [Eskimo] Village fully one mile away. The snow being a foot deep and paths having been made from [each] tent gave the camp that appearance."[14] When the rescue wagons reached Willie's party on October 21, "shouts of joy rent the air; strong men wept till tears ran freely down their furrowed and sun-burnt cheeks," Chislett wrote. "Restraint was set aside in the general rejoicing, and as the brethren entered our camp, the sisters fell upon them and deluged them with kisses."[15]

"We found them in a condition that would stir the feelings of the hardest heart," wrote rescuer Daniel Webster Jones. The valley they were in has a rugged rocky range to the east and a higher rise of mountains—the Continental Divide—to the west. The landscape along the river itself is relatively flat, covered with sparse grass and sagebrush and a few willow trees at places near the river. No trees much larger than a willow stood anywhere closer than a day's ride away. At some points along the Sweetwater River the view stretches for miles, but the Sixth Crossing is in a small hollow with slight hills rising to both the southeast and the northwest. The experienced travelers with Willie's party no doubt told the immigrants that the terrain would become steeper and more difficult as they ascended the final miles to South Pass. The open valley with mountains rising in both the east and west acted as a wind corridor. Wind, nearly constant and often gusting, blew snow over the immigrants and drew any heat generated by the small campfires away from them. Although late-season grass could have sustained livestock, few animals survived in the Willie Company. Those that did had to paw their way through the snow to get at meager nourishment. "They were in a poor place, the storm having caught them where fuel was scarce," Jones wrote. "They were out of provisions and really freezing and starving to death."[16]

Their camp, a huddle of tattered canvas tents, with small fires strategically located, was not only buried in snow and destitute of food but also filthy. While stranded by the weather the men, including Thomas Moulton, had "killed more cattle and issued the meat," Chislett wrote, but that did not satisfy their hunger. "To those who were suffering from dysentery it did more harm than good.... The camp became so offensive and filthy that words would fail to describe its condition, and even common decency forbids the attempt."[17] The people had no energy to leave camp to take care of natural needs. As a result snow was yellow and covered with excrement. Only the cold kept it from reeking like an outhouse. The rescuers used their horses to find and drag wood to the cluster of tents. They prepared food for the Willie Company, using the flour, potatoes, and onions that they brought in their wagons. They also had a limited supply of warm clothing plus quilts, blankets, and buffalo robes that they distributed to the destitute and freezing immigrants.

The rescue had lifted the travelers' spirits. There was a bit of music in camp that evening, but the celebration was short-lived. The assistance was too late for some, who were "already prostrated and beyond all human help," wrote Chislett. "Some seemed to have lost mental as well physical energy."[18] Four people died that night. The food and fires and warm bedding were a blessing, but the rescuers told the weary travelers that they had to keep moving west. They did not know precisely where the Martin Company was but knew that it was farther back on the trail.

The Willie Company moved about ten miles on October 22, camping beside the Sweetwater in a sheltered area at the foot of Rocky Ridge, a steep, northeast-facing hill that must have seemed all but insurmountable. The trail was barely defined as it ascended slick rocks jumbled and stacked almost like a natural staircase with extremely uneven steps. Snow had filled in cracks and crevices and buried smaller stones, so the people could not even see all the obstacles in their way.

On October 23 the Willie Company "beried our dead, got up our teams, and . . . commenced ascending the Rocky Ridg[e]," Savage recorded.[19] It was a brutal day. They struggled with the carts in the snow, which caked in the wheels and became a drag on the people pulling and pushing. Under William Kimball's direction, they faced the rugged Rocky Ridge. In the bitter cold they found it steep, slick, and miserable, falling down or collapsing on the icy ground and uneven rocks. Many suffered frostbite on their hands, feet, and faces. Eight-year-old Heber Moulton trailed along, pulled by the rope around his waist that kept him near his mother, until a woman in the company took his right hand and helped him up the hill. The warmth and protection of her hand saved his right hand. The left one, exposed to the freezing temperatures, was severely frostbitten. He later lost some fingers.[20] The three youngest Moulton children were probably in the cart that day, huddled under blankets to keep them from freezing. Their parents and older siblings struggled up Rocky Ridge one footstep at a time, pulling their two carts over the hills and wading through more than one stream on their way to the next campsite.

Chislett, bringing up the rear that day, helped one cart after another to ascend Rocky Ridge. "I overtook a cart that the folks could not pull through the snow, here about knee-deep. I helped them along and we soon overtook another [cart]. By all hands getting to one cart we could travel; so we moved one of the carts a few rods, and then went back and brought up the other." Before reaching the apex, Chislett and the few people who could help him "had six carts, not one of which could be moved by the parties owning it."[21] Anyone stopping to rest, Savage said, "became chilled, and commenced to frieze" while those riding in the wagons were so crowded there was a fear that "some would Smuther."[22] During the day they crossed several streams, winding ever higher in elevation as the trail led toward South Pass.

After hours of toil, the rear guard, by then consisting of eight handcarts, three wagons, and forty or so people, came to yet another stream, this one frozen with a coat of ice. When oxen pulling one of the wagons started to cross, the animals broke through the ice and stalled there in the stream. "No amount of shouting and whipping could induce them to stir an inch," Chislett said. Afraid to try crossing the creek with the other ox teams and without wood for fires, the people faced potential calamity. Chislett, who had wet feet from crossing the icy stream (most likely Rock Creek, although it also could have been Strawberry Creek), set off on foot to find the camp farther ahead on the trail. He overtook other straggling members of the company and finally reached the new camp beside Willow Creek near midnight. Hearing of the situation back on the trail, "The boys from the Valley started back about midnight to help the ox-teams in. The last of the travelers finally made it to the new camp before dawn." The night was "very severe," he wrote, "and many of the emigrants were frozen."[23]

Those last teams reached Willow Creek camp just before sunrise, the coldest hour of the night. The stronger men had moved the tents from their initial locations to a better shelter in some willows, which gave some protection from what Savage described as "the scre[am]ing wind, which blew enough to bearce [pierce] us through."[24] Some early accounts of this crossing from the October 22 camp at the base of Rocky Ridge to the new camp on October 23 placed the second campsite on Rock Creek, but more recent historians have placed it on Willow Creek.[25] Thirteen casualties in the Willie Party, some of whom froze to death, were buried there on October 24 in a single grave. Chislett, who was part of the burial detail, said that the bodies were placed "three or four abreast and three deep." "When they did not fit in, we put one or two crosswise at the head or feet of the others." He added: "We covered them with willows and then with the earth." Relatives of some of those who had died seemed to care little about their loss. "The numbness and cold in their physical natures seemed to have reached the soul."[26]

Meanwhile the Hunt wagon train had spent the days immediately after the October 19 storm in camp near the North Platte River. Fording the river on October 22, it moved on to Red Buttes, camping with the Martin party, which remained stranded there. The Smoot wagon train—which the Willie Company had encountered in Nebraska—was now several days ahead of the handcarts. After receiving food and the assistance of teamsters and teams, Smoot was at the Green River on October 19 when winter weather hit the entire region. Three days later the wagon train was descending toward the Bridger Valley.

Near the confluence of Willow Creek and the Sweetwater River Willie's company was on the brink of crossing South Pass. They had food, warmer clothes, and assistance from rescuers, but they were still weeks away from Salt Lake. Two more men died at that camp and were buried beside the larger mass grave. Even with the rescuers' help, the immigrants found the twenty-seven-mile journey from Sixth Crossing to Willow Creek a constant struggle. Walking in snow in worn-out shoes resulted in "feet so badly frozen that they could not walk," Chislett wrote, and forced many to be carried or hauled in wagons. "Some got their fingers frozen; others their ears; and one woman lost her sight by the frost. These severities of the weather also increased our number of deaths, so that we buried several each day."[27] Digging graves was almost futile. To thaw the frozen ground, men built campfires. Once the fires burned down, they moved the coals to the side and hacked shallow holes for the bodies. Sometimes they simply buried the people in snowbanks, knowing that wolves trailing them would find the corpses. As deaths occurred, clothing was removed from the deceased and given to those who still survived. In one case Chislett himself took a pair of medium-heavy laced shoes from a victim to replace his own dilapidated boots.[28]

On October 25 Willie's Company shrugged off the snow at Willow Creek and "commenced our march again," Savage wrote in his last journal entry of the trip. That day they crossed South Pass. On that same day Brigham Young in Great Salt Lake City had a message from Charles Decker, who was with the men sent out to rescue the handcart companies. He told Young had there was no feed for the horses due to the deep snow and implored him to send some grain. By the end of October more than 250 teams were on the road with aid, many of them handled by the missionaries who had overtaken the Willie and Martin Companies earlier in the fall.[29] Savage stopped writing a daily log after October 25, which leaves the record void of contemporary details regarding what happened to the Fourth Company in the long miles from South Pass to Fort Bridger.

CHAPTER 8

"THEY ARE ANGELS FROM HEAVEN"

The snowstorm that blew in from the northwest just after the Martin Company waded through the icy waters of the North Platte River, combined with inadequate food and general exhaustion, devastated the members of the last handcart company on the trail that year. Camping near Red Buttes, they suffered in the cold, lost people every day, and buried them as best they could in frozen ground. Campfire locations became burial grounds. Once the fire burned down, the men, like those in Willie's Company ahead of them, took advantage of the area where the ground had been warmed and thawed to dig shallow graves.

Some in Grant's rescue party, after aiding Captain Willie at the Sixth Crossing of the Sweetwater, had continued traveling east, fully expecting to find Martin's Handcart Company close behind. But at Split Rock and then at Devil's Gate they found no sign of the Fifth Company or the Hodgetts and Hunt wagon trains. The rescuers questioned whether those travelers had perhaps halted much farther back on the trail, perhaps even at Fort Laramie. Grant stopped his wagons but sent Joseph A. Young, Abel Garr, and Daniel Webster Jones farther east in search of the missing immigrants, ordering these scouts to continue to Reshaw (Richard) Bridge at the North Platte River. Once the handcarts were found, the vanguard would return to tell the remaining members of the rescue companies, who were themselves becoming weary and whose teams were suffering from lack of feed and difficult grazing on the snow-covered ground.

At the Martin camp near Red Buttes, still 274 miles from Great Salt Lake City, the newly widowed Elizabeth Jackson, with little support from her distraught sister and caring for her three now fatherless children, prayed for relief from their situation. On the evening of October 27—just two days after the Willie Party crossed South Pass with the assistance of the rescuers from Salt Lake—Elizabeth "had a stunning revelation" while lying in her cold bed. "In my dream my husband stood by me and said—'Cheer up, Elizabeth, deliverance is at hand.'"[1]

Mentally and physically worn down, Martin's group could do little more than huddle together for warmth and pray for aid. That help arrived as apparitions through the snow more than a week after Martin and company had first pitched their camp near Red Buttes. Mary Scott saw them first and "sprang to her feet in the wagon and screamed out at the top of her voice. 'I see them coming! I see them coming! Surely they are angels from heaven.'" As the people in camp strained to look westward, they saw "men on horses driving another slowly in the deep crusted snow, and the wolves were howling in all directions." When rescuers Young, Jones, and Garr reached the camp, the people surrounded them, tugging at their coats.[2]

One of the young boys in the Martin Company described Young—who had earlier warned them about starting out so late in the year—as a "big blue winged angel flying to our rescue."[3] The three men had a pack mule and a few supplies with them but nothing that helped the stranded travelers significantly other than the knowledge that some sixty miles to the west were wagons filled with food, warm bedding, and clothing. These were part of the rescue wagons that had bypassed Willie's Company in order to continue toward Martin's group. They appeared not to acknowledge that the Hodgetts and Hunt wagon trains, traveling with or near them, had possessions being hauled to Utah. These items were goods for Brigham Young, Salt Lake City merchants, and the missionaries, including Franklin Richards, John Van Cott, and others. Much of it was freight for men who intended to sell it at the end of the trail, though some was excess baggage that belonged to people in the earlier handcart companies traveling west that year.

Although many people had died at or near the Martin camp at Red Buttes, the arrival of these advance rescue scouts cheered the immigrants enough that the following day the Martin Company survivors broke camp and pushed west toward Avenue of Rocks or Devil's Backbone, a natural uplift where a spine of rocks resembling the broad curved back of a Triceratops juts into the sky. The rescue scouts precipitated the move by stressing the urgency of resuming their walk west. They knew that winter weather could be expected to continue and that the relief supplies would last only a short time. The immigrants could not survive the coming winter where they were, so they dutifully picked up their carts and trudged through the snow, following the trail that would take them to the Sweetwater River Valley. Jones and his rescue companions continued east to William Ben Hodgetts's wagon train, which had halted near the Reshaw Station. They told the members of the wagon company that no supplies would be coming this far east from Great Salt Lake, so they also needed to resume the march west or face starvation.

Young and Jones, quickly reversing course to help the handcarts and Hunt's wagon train, overtook the immigrants as they ascended a long, muddy hill. "A condition of distress here met my eyes that I never saw before or since," Jones said. With the train strung out over two or three miles, old men were "pulling and tugging their carts, sometimes loaded with a sick wife or children—women pulling along sick husbands—little children six to eight years old struggling through the mud and snow." Jones felt helpless in seeing the hundreds struggling up the hill, as mud and snow froze to their feet and clothes. Unrolling his lariat, he tied it to one cart after another and with the power of his horse "helped as many as we could into camp on Avenue hill."[4]

Here Jones and Garr split away from Martin, returning on their faster horses to the relief party commanded by George D. Grant. The slow-crawling handcart company continued unaided to Greasewood Creek (now known as Horse Creek), where they set up another camp and gathered sagebrush—which at least burned hot—for their fires. They were now about thirty-five miles west of Red Buttes, where the advance rescue team had found them, and less than twenty miles from Grant's rescue wagons at Devil's Gate. Informed by Jones and Garr that the struggling converts had been found and were even then moving west, some of the men at Devil's Gate hitched teams to their wagons and set out to intercept the handcart brigade, including Grant, Robert T. Burton, Charles Decker (the man who had sent the message to Brigham Young, pleading for grain to be sent for the horses and mules), and Chauncey G. Webb, all experienced frontiersmen.

Eastbound rescue wagons met westbound handcart immigrants at Greasewood Creek. In their six wagons the valley men had clothing, boots, flour, and onions. They had more stamina than the worn-out travelers. As Heber McBride recalled, the men from Utah "put the tents up and got wood and took care of Mother and the 3 little ones." Knowing there was more help still ahead, "we received an extra half pound of flour and orders to start out in the morning," McBride said.[5] The combined party camped together that night at Greasewood Creek, the site that would become a Pony Express station in another four years. Helped by the relief party the following morning, the Martin Company "started homeward." The weather had warmed slightly, melting some of the snow, "and the news of wagons waiting for us seemed to put new life into every one of us." McBride said. "The 10 wagons releived us of some of our load by taking the sick into their wagons and a fiew other things such as tents and cooking things."[6]

Although "the sick, the children, and the infirm" now rode in wagons, their troubles were not over. Most of their baggage remained in the carts that were still pulled by the strongest of the immigrants. Snow began to fall again and piled eight inches deep as they struggled past Independence Rock and on toward Devil's Gate. As temperatures plunged, the people fainted "by the wayside; falling, chilled by the cold; children crying, their limbs stiffened by cold, their feet bleeding," George D. Grant wrote. "The sight is almost too much for the stoutest of us; but we go on doing all we can, not doubting nor despairing. Our company is too small to help much. It is only a drop to a bucket . . . in comparison with what is needed." The rescue party was composed of men intimately familiar with the route and the conditions found along it. "Brother Charles Decker has now traveled this road the 49th time," Grant said. "He says he has never before seen so much snow on the Sweet Water, at any season of the year."[7]

The harsh start to winter continued to work against Martin's Company and against the two Mormon wagon trains still out on the trail as well. A foot to eighteen inches of snow had fallen at the Sweetwater Bridge near Independence Rock when Martin's Company arrived there. Lacking shovels, the people used "their frying pans, or tin plates" to move the snow enough to pitch their tents, but driving tent stakes into the frozen ground proved almost impossible.[8]

On November 2 the Martin Company and rescue wagons moved six miles from Independence Rock to Devil's Gate, where many of them took refuge in the log cabins known as Seminoe's Fort. Ahead of them, Willie's Company and those helping it approached Fort Bridger. They would reach Bear River on November 4 but remained a week's journey from Salt Lake City. On that very day Brigham Young told people gathered at the Tabernacle that the handcart companies should "start in season." He also began "assigning blame" to Franklin Richards for the plight of the Willie and Martin Companies.[9]

Four years earlier, in 1852, Charles and Basil Lajeunesse had built the crude Seminoe's Fort structures now sheltering Martin's Company. Basil, a French voyageur, first saw the country when traveling with John Charles Frémont in 1843. That year he had led the way to the top of Fremont Peak, the highest point in the Wind River Mountain range to the west, before following the Sweetwater River east and meeting with near disaster in a rubber boat as they swirled into the rough chasm just below the confluence of the Sweetwater and North Platte Rivers. The place was later named Fremont Canyon.[10]

Charles Lajeunesse made a name for himself as a booshway (bourgeois)—a leader of mountain men—in the American Fur Company. His surname may have been Simond, though he was called Simono, and Francis Parkman, the early explorer-writer, gave a nod to his French voyageur roots in referring to him as Cimoneau. While operating a trading post near Fort Bridger, Charles Lajeunesse married a Shoshone woman and had two sons. He sold his Fort Bridger area post to Jim Bridger for $400 and then moved into the Sweetwater country. There he constructed the bridge at Independence Rock and with his brother built a trading post at Devil's Gate, which became Seminoe's Fort.[11]

The significant number of travelers on the overland trails through the Sweetwater valley—people headed to Oregon, California, or the Mormon settlement at Great Salt Lake—created opportunities for Lajeunesse and the trading fort at Devil's Gate. The post consisted of some fourteen buildings constructed of hewn logs, featuring sod roofs, all arranged in a square just a few hundred yards from the Sweetwater River. With fewer people traveling the trails, the fort was abandoned a year before the handcart brigades arrived. The rough structures remained, however, and the saints would put them to use. They provided the first substantial protection since they had left Florence, Nebraska, in early September.

As the Fifth Company traveled toward Devil's Gate, it "was so cold all day we could hardley make it but when we got there the tents were up and big fires burning," Heber McBride said. "Sister and I cried for joy it seemed so nice to have nothing to do." Their joy was short lived, however, for the next morning there was more snow "and the north wind blowing hard and cold."[12]

Relief Captain Grant on November 3 directed Abel Garr and Joseph Young to ride quickly to Salt Lake to report on "the situation of the emigrants." In preparing to leave the larger group, Young "put on three or four pairs of woolen socks, a pair of moccasins, and a pair of buffalo hide overshoes with the wool on." He wanted to at least keep his feet from freezing.[13] Grant instructed Young and Garr to give Brigham Young a message: "I never felt so much interest in any mission that I have been sent on." Grant, determined to get the Martin Company to Salt Lake, added: "We will move every day toward the valley, if we shovel snow to do it, the Lord helping us."[14]

Back in Salt Lake City that same day Brigham Young and Heber Kimball, one of his closest advisors, met with J. W. Young, instructing him to take two yoke of oxen and head out on the trail to meet Abraham Smoot's wagon train. They had word that Smoot's wagons had also become mired in the winter snow and had left behind their weakest teams—along with some of their wagons, including the heavy steam engine.

After receiving aid from the Grant rescue party in the form of livestock and men as well as food and other supplies, Smoot had continued moving his wagon train through the Green River Valley. Struggling in the deep snow that hit on November 19, he finally reached Fort Bridger, where some of the teams gave out completely, the "long & tedious snow storm" having taken its toll on them. Smoot wrote Brigham Young that he was at "quite a loss" to determine how to proceed. He told Young he could store some of his cargo at Fort Bridger, such as "the Books, Thrashing machine, your Engine & fixtures & a part of the nails, glass & groceries & perhaps a portion of the Dry Goods."[15] Young rejected that plan. Instead he instructed Smoot "to bring all the goods in and if he had not enough teams to call upon the brethren who were out in the mountains with ox teams to assist the hand cart emmigrations, to assist in bring[ing in] the wagons."[16]

By late October 1856 the stream of Mormons traveling toward the handcart companies and those returning to Great Salt Lake City provided Brigham Young with regular communication—though no intimate details and specifics—regarding the situation out on the trail. News of the disaster was slow to reach the wider populace, however. The early reports did not appear in publications in the Midwest and on the East Coast until January or later.

The Shoshone Mission journal kept at Fort Bridger that fall provided some early commentary on the migration. On October 22, just as Willie's party prepared to cross Rocky Ridge, that journal reported that Smoot had come to Fort Bridger seeking "help to move the train of goods belonging to the Church that he had gone to the states to bring up."[17] These goods included books, nails, glass, groceries, dry goods, a thrashing machine, and a massive steam engine.[18]

On October 24, not knowing where the handcart companies were, Young wrote to the Mormons in the Bridger Valley urging them to prepare to assist the late travelers. "If it should continue cold and stormey and those emigrating with the Handcarts come along needing help at Fort Supply and bridger do their utmost for their releif, let them pick up women and children and the infirme and bring them in." Five days later Abel Garr and Joseph Young, carrying the message from George D. Grant addressed to Brigham Young, arrived at Fort Bridger with the first news of the plight of Martin's Company. Having overtaken Willie's group east of the Continental Divide, they said that the Martin Company, then on the Sweetwater, was in a "deplorable Situation" with snow "a foot deep & weather very cold—32 had died in 5 days."[19]

On October 31 the *Baltimore Sun* reported "dreadful accounts of the sufferings among the Mormon emigrants by the hand-cart train, which is now in the mountains." The train "contained 350 souls," said the *Sun*, which likely prepared its report on the basis of accounts from eastbound trail travelers who had encountered the handcart companies. This information was almost certainly not about the Willie and Martin Companies but instead referred to the Third Handcart Company, which had run into early cold weather and a snowstorm while traveling near the Bear River west of Fort Bridger. The newspaper report claimed heavy deaths among the travelers: "One-seventh are already dead, and they are dying at the rate of fifteen per day." While some travelers in the early companies perished, the tally was certainly not that high. Other parts of the account provided somewhat accurate information: "There are some 600 more behind, of which we have heard nothing. We hope that they stopped at Laramie. It is impossible for them to get through this fall. The Mormons estimated that there are not less than 1500 of their brethren yet to come in, and the snow is reported to be not less than 3 feet deep in the mountains."[20]

The shelter at Seminoe's Fort, although welcome to the members of Martin's Company, was wholly inadequate for so many people, especially after they pulled down some of the wood structure to fuel their fires. On November 3 they decided to cross the Sweetwater River and set up a new camp close to the rocky outcrop of the Rattlesnake Range. The company went into a sheltered area they called Martin's Ravine, which became known as Martin's Cove in later years. To get there the immigrants walked onto an ice-covered Sweetwater River, but their weight broke the thin ice and plunged them into intensely cold water.[21] As had happened at the North Platte crossing, the women tied up their skirts and waded the Sweetwater if they were able to walk. Those who could not walk were taken into the arms of stronger men and carried across. With so many of the male handcart immigrants themselves struggling, the duty of carrying women, children, and even men through the icy water that day fell to the rescuers, some of whom made multiple trips across the river.

Getting the carts across the river proved difficult as well. John Jaques recalled one handcart being pulled by a lone man who "rolled up his pants as high as he could, pulled off his stockings and boots which he had happened to receive at Greasewood Creek, and put on a pair of old shoes he carried with him." The cart, filled with pots and kettles, was heavy, however, and soon became mired in the soft streambed. The man was unable to pull it out without aid from two of the valley men. Once across, though, he pulled the cart single-handedly to Martin's Ravine.[22]

After leaving the structures at Seminoe's Fort, Heber McBride said that they traveled about two miles before turning toward the Sweetwater River. "When we saw that we felt very bad to think we had to ford that stream and I dont think we could have made it in our weekned condition but when we got there we was very much surprised for there were some men there they carried us across." By the time Heber and Janetta McBride reached the new camp, they found that "the tent was up and Mother and Mrs barton [were] sitting by a good fire" that the rescuers had built for them.[23]

Clouds and snowstorms obscured the sun as the travelers huddled in their dilapidated tents in the new campsite. Thus hunkered down, they were slightly more sheltered from the wind blowing through the Sweetwater Valley than they had been at Seminoe's Fort, but their troubles were far from over.

Meanwhile Willie's Company, with many of the people now riding in wagons that had met them at Fort Bridger, camped at Bear River on November 4. That same day

Smoot train teamster Franklin Benjamin Woolley, at Bear River with Willie's Company, learned that the remainder of the Smoot train had become stranded at Fort Bridger. William Woodward wrote in the Willie camp journal that Woolley had word from Brigham Young that "some freight still lying at 'Fort Bridger' was to be brought in this season & that some teams and men of our company were needed to go on to 'Bridger.'" With the suffering Willie party still eighty miles from Salt Lake City, "several teams & men were selected for the trip," Woodward wrote. The chosen wagons and teamsters abandoned the beleaguered Willie Handcart Company to retrieve the Smoot cargo. Now with less help, the Willie brigade continued slogging its way toward the valley. For some the end of the trail came before the end of the journey. Eight more people, four of them children, died before the company reached the valley.[24] Meanwhile someone recorded in Young's President's Office Journal that 40 bushels of corn were sent out of Great Salt Lake on November 7, apparently intended for Smoot's wagon train, not the Willie Company.[25]

Farther back on the trail the frigid, gusty weather made it impossible for Martin's Company members to move from the ravine where they had taken refuge. Instead they reduced rations while the stronger men and rescue party with George D. Grant "began killing the poor oxen that had not died and distributing the hyde and bones among the people to try and keep them from starving." Heber McBride recalled that "nearly all the children would cry themselves to sleep every night. My 2 little Brothers would get the sack that had flour in [it] and turn it wrong side out and suck and lick the flour dust of it[;] we would break the bones [of the beef] and make a little soup by boiling them and put in what little flour we had for we did not get enough flour to make bread."[26] According to Elizabeth Jackson, "The sufferings of the people were fearful. nothing but the power of a merciful God kept [us] from perishing."[27]

The weather turned bitterly cold. Robert T. Burton reported that the thermometer dipped to 11 degrees below zero on November 6.[28] With the men from Salt Lake able to take on some of the heavy chores, such as finding firewood, Heber McBride recalled, "my Sister and me had nothing to do only try to keep ourselves and Mother and our 2 Brothers [and] little sister from friezing."[29]

Deaths had occurred all along the route. Many succumbed in those first few days after crossing the North Platte River for the last time, and more died in the twelve days it took to travel from Red Buttes to Martin's Ravine. Somewhere near Devil's Gate and Martin's Cove, Joseph Sermon's health failed. He died in Elizabeth's arms. Before he and eight other men who died at that same time were placed in a common grave, she "sewed him up in a quilt with his clothes on." Elizabeth kept his boots—wearing them herself when she continued on toward Salt Lake with the children.[30] How many people died in the cove remains a mystery. According to Josiah Rogerson, while at Martin's Ravine, "our appetites (if it were possible), were getting keener, the weak getting weaker, and roasted rawhide eaten with considerable relish."[31] While the Martin Company huddled in the cove, Hunt's wagons were at Devil's Gate and the wagon train led by William Ben Hodgetts finally reached Independence Rock.

A BREAK IN THE WEATHER

The Willie party camped November 7 in the area between Little Mountain and Big Mountain—two of the last landmarks on the overland trail to Great Salt Lake City. Forty bushels of corn had been sent east that day from Salt Lake, intended not for Willie's Company but rather for the Smoot wagon train. The following day Young's official office journal noted "trying weather," but word reached the city that "Bro Willey Company were between the mountains, and that Bro Smoot and Company were on the bench."[32]

Back at Devil's Gate, George D. Grant had told the teamsters and emigrants with Hunt and Hodgetts that their wagons were needed to transport the people so they should leave their goods at Seminoe's Fort. The companies unloaded their wagons and cached the cargo in the dilapidated buildings at Seminoe's Fort then prepared to get back on the trail with the Martin Company. All they needed was a break in the weather. Included in the cache were stoves, boxes of tools, clothing, and more, including the four blue chests that belonged to Emily Hodgetts. "Only take along sufficient clothing to keep warm," Grant told them.[33] The freight was considered valuable property and could not simply be abandoned, so twenty men, including three rescuers and seventeen men (some of them teenagers) who had been traveling with Hunt and Hodgetts, remained behind when everyone else resumed the journey to Utah. Daniel Webster Jones, the express rider who first came upon both the Willie Company and later the Martin Company with Abel Garr and Joseph Young, now took charge.[34]

According to a much later account written by Josiah Rogerson, the suggestion to leave the goods and a party to guard them came from discussion involving Daniel Webster Jones, Al Huntington, and Stephen Taylor. When the men approached Grant with the idea, the captain reportedly responded: "I have thought of this, but there are no provisions to leave and it would be asking too much of anyone to stay here and starve for the sake of these goods; besides, where is the man who would stay if called upon?" Jones responded: "Any of us would." Perhaps he did not expect the captain to endorse the suggestion, but Jones was indeed one of the men selected to remain behind. He later said that he was chosen because he was "the best cook in the camp," a rather ironic statement since they had so little to cook. Later Jones wrote, "there was not enough money on earth to have hired me to stay." Obviously, keeping his word was more important to Jones than money, so "I could not back out."[35]

We can only imagine what measure of suffering might have been avoided had the goods in those wagons been removed or even distributed earlier. The clothing and supplies in the wagons belonged to other immigrants, to the church, to missionaries, or to storekeepers in Salt Lake City. As people suffered in the cold, the use of some of those cloth goods might have provided warmth enough to prevent some from freezing limbs or even freezing to death. Furthermore, the goods included stoves and other heavy items. If they been removed and cached earlier on the trail, perhaps space could have been made for the suffering pioneers to ride at least part of the time, allowing them to save energy and possibly survive the journey, rather than end their lives in shallow graves along the road.

Almost everyone was on the move on Sunday November 9. As the weather broke and they left their limited shelter at Martin's Ravine, members of the Martin Company abandoned most of their handcarts. Many piled into twenty-four wagons, although most still walked. Leaving their shelter at noon, they traveled only five or six miles, crossed the Sweetwater River once, and then set up camp in the late afternoon, making little more than a mile an hour on this first day of resumed travel. Ahead of them were another 327 trail miles, including river crossings and mountain passes. More snow, wind, and cold weather likely awaited them as well. Meanwhile the vanguard of the Smoot wagon train reached Great Salt Lake City, followed by the Willie Handcart Company.

Like many others traveling with Willie, the Moultons abandoned their handcarts and accepted the offer to ride in wagons sent by Brigham Young and driven by rescuers. At the foot of Little Mountain in Emigration Canyon they met Samuel Cussley, the husband of their mother's sister, who had immigrated to Utah a year earlier. Years later Lottie Moulton recalled, "When the relief trains came to meet us one of the men [asked], 'Is there a Thomas Moulton in this company?' and to their surprise it was my mother's brother-in-law by the name of Cussley. He had, oh, so many of the good things that children like, pie, cake, etc., but there was nothing looked so good as the good bread and butter."[36]

At about noon on November 9 the Willie handcarts finally stopped in front of the old tithing office in Salt Lake City. Sarah Denton Moulton stood there with her family. The blessing that they had received in England before beginning the trip came true. Some seventy people traveling with them had died, but all of the Moultons survived.[37] Less than a month later, on December 5, 1856, Sarah Elizabeth Moulton married John Bennett Hawkins, one of the men who had helped in their rescue.[38]

As momentous as getting to Salt Lake was for them, their arrival merited only a brief mention in the President's Office journal: "Bro Willey hand cart company arrived also Bro Smoot and train arrived." The Willie Company was in deplorable condition. "Brother John Sharp reported that one woman that came by the hand cart company had her eye froze out and many more not only were covered with lice but their skin was eaten with the vermin."[39] The wagons hauling the steam engine and other goods were still back on the trail, however, and would not reach Salt Lake for weeks.[40]

Chislett later wrote that as soon as people in Great Salt Lake City heard about the condition of the suffering handcart immigrants, "the most fervent prayers for their deliverance were offered up. . . . Prayers in the Tabernacle, in the school-house, in the family circle, and in the private prayer circles of the priesthood were constantly offered up to the Almighty, begging Him to avert the storm from us."[41]

Few records document the Martin Company's journey after leaving the Devil's Gate/ Martin's Ravine area, although the camp journal kept for the Hunt wagon train provides some detail. The sun was low on November 10 when Ephriam K. Hanks, who had left additional rescue wagons and was now traveling east from South Pass, "spied somethin[g] in the distance that looked like a black streak in the snow." Upon riding his horse closer, he could tell it was the "ill-fated train," which had just camped for the night. "The sight that met my gaze as I entered their camp can never be erased from my memory! The starved forms and haggard countenances of the poor sufferers, as they moved slowly, shivering with the cold to prepare the evening meal, was enough to touch the stoutest heart."[42] Hanks, traveling ahead of more rescue wagons, had killed a buffalo that day and shared the meat that he had been able to carry with him. As Elizabeth Jackson noted, "we eagerly devoured it."[43] Even so, by the time the additional rescue wagons arrived, the Martin Company had buried well over a hundred people.[44]

When they set out again, Heber and Janetta McBride helped their mother and younger siblings into one of the wagons, but the two young people continued to walk. "There was snow on the ground every place we camped and some bitter cold weather," Heber recalled. "There was a great many froze their toes and feet."[45] The early stages of frostbite—extreme cold skin that becomes numb—eventually turn into severe frostbite: the skin and underlying muscle actually freeze and the extremity turns pale and then hard. The dead skin may be cut away to reduce the decay and avoid infection.

One of those whose feet froze was five-year-old Robert Sermon. In the days ahead his mother "had to take a portion of Robert's feet off—portions that were decaying."

Using her scissors she cut away the dead skin "until the poor boy's feet were nearly all gone." Doing her best to care for the children she would clear the snow away from their tent using a tin plate, gather what wood she could find, and make whatever meal she could muster from limited flour and other supplies. "We went to bed without supper so that we could have more for breakfast," Elizabeth Sermon recalled. "I found it some help to toast the rawhide on the coals and chew it; it kind of kept the terrible hunger away, for I assure you, I was feeling it rather keenly now."[46]

The cold did not spare Sermon's nine-year-old son John either. His feet and Elizabeth's also began to freeze. "But thank god none had to be cut [from her or John's feet] as much as Robert's."[47] She does not refer to the suffering of her two-year-old daughter, Marian. Most of the time she rode in the cart, covered with clothing and other items, which apparently protected her from the freezing cold weather. Elizabeth may well have questioned how different her life might have been if they had left earlier in the year or at least traveled in the wagon that they purchased rather than by pushing and pulling a handcart.

Deaths continued to mount as the combined Martin Handcart Company and Hodgetts and Hunt wagon companies pushed west. On November 11, Mary Hutchison (seventy), and James Reese (sixty) died. The following day fourteen-year-old Sophia Turner "was found dead in bed having been suffering with diarhea for some time past." Her brother John (twelve) would die four days later.[48]

One day Elizabeth Sermon asked for a cob of corn from one of the rescuers. "He looked so pitiful and said, 'Oh, Sister, I hate to refuse you, but my horses have not enough to eat now and I do not know how we will get back to Salt Lake if the horses give out.'" She apologized for even asking but told him, "my children [and] myself are so hungry." When the man told her to "keep up your faith," she thought: "A loaf of bread would have given me great faith then and would have satisfied a hungry stomach as well."[49]

Almost a month to the day from the time when the Willie Company found itself out of food and stranded at Sixth Crossing, the Martin Company reached that area. As Martin's group climbed over Rocky Ridge, the weather was eerily similar to what it had been for Willie's group. Snow was falling fast, and a piercing north wind raked over the landscape. With the aid of the rescue wagons and stronger men from Salt Lake City, however, they did not suffer nearly so badly there as Willie's Company had.

The struggling Martin Company was not yet at South Pass when Young again spoke in the Tabernacle on November 16. He suggested that more people had died of

cholera while crossing the plains in earlier years than with the handcart companies
that year. "With regard to those who have died and been laid away by the roadside
on the plains, since the cold weather commenced, let me tell you that they have not
suffered one hundredth part so much as did our brethren and sisters who have died
with the cholera."[50] Young's assertions likely reassured those in Utah and potential
immigrants as well. He knew that efforts were already underway to bring even more
people to America and have them travel by handcart. He may also have wanted the
eastern press to have more of his side of the story as a way to garner favor. Young knew
that issues other than immigration were pressing on life in Utah just then. The federal
government was already making changes in appointees serving in the territory that
seemed to undermine Young's influence. As a result the church leader desperately
needed positive news.

In remarkably insensitive comments, Young added: "Some of those who have
died . . . would be singing, and before the tune was done, would drop over and breathe
their last; and others would die while eating, and with a piece of bread in their hands. I
should be pleased, when the time comes, if we could all depart from this life as easily."
Unbelievably, given the privation that the Willie party members must have reported and
their obviously poor physical condition when they arrived in Salt Lake on November
9, Young said that he wanted to "forestall indulgence in a misplaced sympathy."

The exact number of deaths in the Martin Company and where they occurred
before the group reached South Pass on November 18 are unknown, but a review
of the official accounts, diaries, and reminiscences places the number at nearly 150,
maybe more.

Five days earlier Joseph A. Young had arrived in Great Salt Lake City with his
message from George D. Grant at Devil's Gate.[51] He reported to his father, Brigham
Young. In their ride west Joseph Young and Abel Garr had met additional relief wagons
and urged the teamsters driving them to hurry east.[52] But they had also overtaken
some relief teams and wagons that had abandoned the eastbound route and were
returning to Great Salt Lake City, whose teamsters apparently placed more value on
their own lives than those of the poor people with the handcart companies. A week
earlier Brigham Young had ordered W. H. Kimball, Hosea Stout, Joseph M. Simmons,
and James Ferguson to take a letter of instruction to the men who had been sent to
aid the stranded immigrants but were known to have turned their wagons around
before reaching the beleaguered travelers. Young ordered the wagons to "turn back the
brethren who were coming on without seeing or finding out where the Emmigration
had got to."[53] It is not clear when Kimball and Stout reached the returning rescue teams
and turned them back around, but it was almost certainly days after they received the

instruction from Brigham Young (and some never did turn back to help the handcart travelers).

An article in the New York publication the *Mormon* on November 22 echoed Young's position: "The emigration to Utah of late years has been continued till the summer was far advanced, and at risk and in convenience which could be altogether prevented, if the Saints would take time by the forelock and carry out the counsels they receive from those who are placed to counsel them."[54] This statement contradicted the fact that the missionaries and planners of the handcart migration had urged the late-season travelers to set out on the trail when most of them must have known the risks. Furthermore, the early planning had clearly called for no travelers starting a cross-country trek late in the summer. There had also been plenty of advance directives indicating how much food and other supplies each company should have. Despite all this, only one experienced trail traveler—Levi Savage—had stridently urged the Willie Company to remain in Nebraska. He was castigated for his position when Franklin Richards overtook that party out on the western plains of Nebraska. Joseph A. Young, with the missionary party in Nebraska, also had urged caution to the Martin Company before that group departed from eastern Nebraska. After reaching Salt Lake City, Young had quickly joined the rescue teams and was with the vanguard who found the Willie and Martin Companies.

In issuing early directives about the handcart migration, Brigham Young had recommended that the travelers depart early in the season. John Taylor supported that plan with his work in New York. Other men traveling with both the Willie and Martin Companies, however, including the agent on the frontier and the missionaries, had urged the saints to continue westward from the Missouri River. In Florence, Nebraska, Franklin Richards not only told the people to resume traveling but also promised them blessings if they would continue their trip despite it being so late in the season. Richards stressed to them that no challenge would be too much for them to overcome or endure if they had enough faith. He was one of only a few men in his missionary party that overtook the handcarts on the plains of Nebraska who did not later join in the rescue. He remained in Great Salt Lake while others from that missionary group quickly returned to the trail to help.

The first contingent from the combined Martin, Hunt, and Hodgetts Companies crossed South Pass on November 19. The following day they divided into smaller groups, possibly finding it easier to keep moving when traveling in more compact units. Some of the wagons delayed crossing the Continental Divide to wait for more teams to arrive from Great Salt Lake City. That happened on November 21, when wagons pulled by four-horse teams encountered the struggling people. These wagons provided space for more people to ride. The additional teams could now be used to pull the wagons that had been crawling west from Martin's Ravine. There is no record of travel for the next few days, but most likely the vanguard of the Martin Company reached the Green River on November 21. Oxen brought from Fort Bridger met the Hunt and Hodgetts Companies on November 22, providing relief for the teams already pulling the wagons that were heavily loaded with weary travelers. The following day Martin's whole group reached Fort Bridger. The company finally made its way into Great Salt Lake City on November 30.[55]

In an address at the Tabernacle on November 30, 1856, Brigham Young said that many in the Willie and Martin Companies "would have been dead long before this, had it not been for the assistance of br. George D. Grant and those who went back with him. The rear companies would never have got over Rocky Ridge, or seen the upper crossing of the Sweetwater, had they not been helped from here." The church president spoke of people "with their feet frozen to their ankles; some are frozen to their knees and some have their hands frosted." Then he added: "Prayer is good, but when baked potatoes and pudding and milk are needed, prayer will not supply their place."[56]

The condition of the Martin Company "beggars all description," said the *New York Semi-Weekly Tribune* in an article datelined Great Salt Lake City, December 4, 1856. Echoing Young's comments, the paper said: "Had not the relief which was sent from here reached them, every one of them would have perished."[57] If all the rescuers who departed Salt Lake City upon hearing Brigham Young's call for aid in October had traveled as quickly and determinedly as the vanguard commanded by George D. Grant, however, more might have been saved. The first group moved expeditiously, and a second wave of rescue teams and wagons left Utah about three weeks later.[58]

The lead group with Grant and the next wave of supporting wagons provided critical aid to the handcart companies, but not everyone who set out from Salt Lake City helped. Rescuers with seventy-seven wagons turned back before they had gone far back down the trail. Others, as noted, were diverted from their mission of helping the handcart companies to provide aid instead to the Smoot wagon train—including bringing in that heavy steam engine. Among those who started out to help but then turned around without giving aid to the Martin or Willie Companies was John Van Cott, who said, without knowing where the missing companies might be, that it was no use to continue on and perhaps "lose his own team and starve to death himself & do no good after all."[59] Van Cott owned a substantial amount of the freight being hauled west in the Hunt Wagon Company.

Reports reaching New York newspapers from observers on the ground had a decidedly different cast than those published in the church newspaper, the *Deseret News*. With hundreds dead on the trail behind them, those who finally arrived in Salt Lake City were destitute and still faced serious health concerns. "When they reached here [Great Salt Lake City]," an unnamed observer told the *New York Tribune*, "there were not 50 in the train who could help themselves; the rest were stowed in the bottoms of the wagons which had been sent for them, ragged and filthy beyond conception; helpless and despairing they could or would not get out of the wagons to attend to the calls of nature, and if the weather had not been intensely cold it would have bred a pestilence. I never imagined such a scene." The *Tribune* indignantly added: "*The Deseret News* has the effrontery to tell the world that they came through well."[60]

John Jaques recalled that "the meeting of the emigrants with relatives, acquaintances, and friends was not joyous." Indeed, he said the occasion was solemn. "Some were so affected that they could scarcely speak, but would look at each other until the sympathetic tears would force their unforbidden way." The emigrants were taken into friends' houses and made "as comfortable as circumstances would permit them to be while they thawed the frost out of their limbs and recruited their health and strength." Thus ended "this unfortunate expedition." He added: "I think that none of the emigrants would be willing to endure another such a journey under any circumstances whatever. One in a lifetime is enough."[61]

Meanwhile the Hunt and Hodgetts wagon trains, which now included people from the Martin Handcart Company, struggled westward. They crossed the Green River on November 29 and 30. The last of the wagons rolled in to Fort Bridger on December 4. Even more teams of horses, mules, and oxen with skilled drivers went east on the trail from Salt Lake City, meeting with the wagon trains and bringing them to Fort Bridger and ultimately to Utah by mid-December.[62] In making the final crossing of the Wasatch Mountains, the oxen struggled through deep snow and were able to complete the journey only because teams sent from Salt Lake City had broken and packed the trail. Floundering through four-foot to five-foot snowbanks "the train goes on slowly," John Bond wrote. "Every little while the lead team [that] had pulled the wagon while wallowing in the snow [would be replaced], the next team would wallow a while going on in this way until all had a turn breaking the snow down." Reaching Emigration Canyon and catching their first glimpse of the valley "brought many tears to the eyes of the saints to know that their journey was drawing to a close."[63]

Of the final painful weeks of travel the immigrants endured that fall and winter, John Bond would write that "the men in high standing with high priesthood power are yet to meet the innocent ones before the bar of God to answer to Him for the atrocities of inhuman advice."[64] Although about 75 members of the Willie Company and about 145 to 170 members of the Martin Company had died on the trail, the ordeal of 1856 was not yet over. Daniel Webster Jones and his nineteen companions were still on the Sweetwater at Devil's Gate.

CHAPTER 9

"I WILL NOT HAVE SUCH LATE STARTS"

Even before the members of the Willie and Martin Handcart Companies reached Great Salt Lake City, Brigham Young and his counselors were putting together a narrative to explain the situation then unfolding on the plains. Young, at a Tabernacle gathering on November 2, 1856, said the First Presidency had urged the migration to "start in season," but added that it was not expressly forbidden to start late. "Hereafter," he said, "I am going to lay an injunction and place a penalty, to be suffered by any Elder or Elders who will start the immigration across the plains after a given time; and the penalty shall be that they shall be severed from the church, for I will not have such late starts."[1] By this time Young knew the situation on the trail was deadly. He had word on October 31 that thirty people traveling with James Gray Willie had perished before the rescue companies reached them east of South Pass and that another thirty had died in the first days after their "rescue."[2]

When Young addressed the Mormons on November 2, he spoke of other parties crossing the plains, saying the church would "allow them three months in which to perform the journey."[3] He would have known that this was the typical amount of time for a wagon company to travel the 1,131 miles from the Missouri River to Utah. Yet by their own accounts members of the Willie and Martin Companies had supplies expected to last for just sixty days. There may have been expectations of resupplying them at stations along their route, but the church had not set up such a supply line in time for the 1856 migration, although some resources had been delivered for use by the first three handcart companies. Places that did exist, such as Fort Laramie and the Reshaw post, were operated by non-Mormons and not sufficiently stocked to provide aid to such large numbers of travelers. Church records show that 4,326 members traveled from England that summer, including 3,318 in the ships that carried people in the handcart companies.[4] Of these some 1,948 actually traveled with the handcarts from Florence to Great Salt Lake City, with more than half of them (512 and 641, respectively) in the Willie and Martin Companies. The remaining people had stopped at various points along the route, electing not to continue their journey to Utah that year, quite often because they did not have the resources to do so.

In his November 2 address Young strove to distance himself from the tragedy. Franklin Richards, he said, had "but little knowledge of business," while Spencer was a man of "age and experience. . . . I do not know that I will attach blame to either of them. But if, while at the Missouri river, . . . even a bird had chirped it in [their] ears . . . they would have known better than to rush men, women and children on to the prairie in the autumn months, on the 3d of September, to travel over a thousand miles." Again to provide cover for himself, Young added: "I do not believe that the biggest fool in the community could entertain [the thought] . . . that all this loss of life, time and means was through the mismanagement of the First Presidency."[5]

Young said it was costing more in time, effort, and goods to go out and help the people come in from their precarious position on the plains than it would have cost to have kept them for the winter somewhere near the Missouri. Even as he laid a defense to show how the First Presidency should not shoulder blame, Young warned of how the rescue effort was diverting resources and could affect future conditions in Utah. "We need all our teams and [men] to prepare for those persons who are coming, instead of crippling us by taking our bread, men and teams and going out to meet them. And if the present system continues, this people will be found like the Kilkenny cats, which eat up each other clear to their tails, and they were left jumping at one another; such operations will financially use us up."

With ever-greater determination to deflect blame to others, Young declared: "Are these people in the frost and snow by my doings? No, my skirts are clear of their blood, God knows." Instead the church president appropriately targeted Richards: "If a bird had chirped in br. Franklin's ears in Florence, and the brethren there had held a council, he would have stopped the rear companies." Young suggested that the men who had made decisions—and exhorted the travelers to continue their journey so late in the year—had the "big head" that overshadowed common sense. Still shifting blame Young said: "The very spirit some have in them of pride, arrogance and self esteem, has led men and women to die on the plains by scores." But in their defense Richards and other church elders who had encouraged the immigrants to continue west that year had long since established reputations for supporting church missions and goals and certainly wanted to please Brigham Young. Then again, the travelers themselves had stepped onto ships in Liverpool, England, demonstrating their unwavering (some might say blind) faith that God would take care of them as they headed toward Zion.

The *Mormon* reported in late November that the Martin Company's arrival at Fort Laramie in early October meant: "If favored with a long summer and a favorable 'Indian summer,' after it, they may all arrive before the snow begins to fall on the mountains, otherwise they may have cold fingers and other inconveniences."[6] This punctuates the concern by Mormons like John Taylor in New York, who recognized that a delayed start could have hard consequences. This late reporting also was an attempt to send a message that the trail journey did not necessarily need to be overly difficult to church members who may even then have been planning to immigrate to America from England, Scandinavia, and other foreign locations with the next wave of handcart travelers.

Some church spokesmen attempted to swing the blame for the plight of the Willie and Martin travelers onto the immigrants themselves. "The emigration from Europe and from the States has been prudently conducted by the authorities of the Church to whom the business has been confided," the *Mormon* reported in late November 1856, "but by dilatoriness on the part of some Saints; the former have labored frequently under disadvantages in making the most suitable arrangements, and at the more convenient time for the journeying of the latter by sea and land, and not unfrequently those who were dilatory in sending the names and their money, were the first and the loudest in grumbling about the inconvenience which their own backwardness had entailed upon themselves and others."[7]

Late that fall Brigham Young wrote two letters targeting New York church agent John Taylor with a measure of responsibility for the disaster, accusing him of "saving one and incurring three dollars expence."[8] Taylor quickly countered the charge that he had wasted church money. "You must have been mistaken," he wrote Young. Such an accusation was "without any foundation or semblance in truth." Taylor told Young: "The Hand-Cart system was to me, and to us all, a new operation." As twin faults he pointed to the missionaries in England who sent the immigrants and the lack of money to make preparations until it was too late in the year. The lack of funds that year, he stressed, meant that he could not prepare in a way that would ensure a safe journey for all of the travelers. Because he "knew of the weakness of many women, children and aged persons that were calculated to go, I did not consider that a few dollars were to be put in competition with the lives of human beings."[9]

After arriving in Great Salt Lake City, John Chislett, who had traveled with James Willie's Company, became aware of concerns that had been raised even while he and his fellow travelers struggled in the cold along the Sweetwater River. "Immediately that the condition of the suffering emigrants was known in Salt Lake City, the most fervent prayers for their deliverance were offered up. There, and throughout the Territory, the same was done as soon as the news reached the people," wrote Chislett, keeper of the Willie Company's official journal. "Prayers in the Tabernacle, in the school-house, in the family circle, and in the private prayer circles of the priesthood were constantly offered up to the Almighty, begging Him to avert the storm from us. Such intercessions were invariably made on behalf of Martin's company, at all the meetings which I attended after my arrival." He added: "But these prayers availed nothing more than did the prophecies of Richards and the elders. It was the stout hearts and strong hands of the noble fellows who came to our relief, the good teams, the flour, beef, potatoes, the warm clothing and bedding, and not prayers nor prophecies, that saved us from death."[10]

Brigham Young likely would not want to admit it, but he had his own direct role in escalating the disaster. He had indeed organized the rescue teams and sent them east, but when Young learned that Abraham Smoot's wagon train—which was hauling the huge steam engine and other church freight toward Salt Lake City—was stranded near Fort Bridger, unable to continue due to the difficult weather, the church leader shifted resources. He ordered the rescue teams to divert from aiding the Willie handcart travelers to support Smoot and keep the steam engine moving toward the Mormon capital.[11] Why he did this is unclear. He may have considered the freight necessary for the future welfare of Utah and had long advocated obtaining resources to advance conditions in the region. Possibly he took the action simply because he wanted all Mormon travelers on the trail during the harsh weather to reach their destination.

Even the stragglers in Edward Martin's Handcart Company had reached Salt Lake City by the time church president Brigham Young issued the Fourteenth General Epistle of the church on December 10. Saying that the experiences of the year would help improve future operations, Young, speaking of the first three companies, again ignored reality when he claimed that the handcart plan "has been fairly tested and proved entirely successful." Those companies completed their crossing from Florence to Salt Lake in a little over two months, he said, and could have traveled even more quickly "had they not been hindered by the few ox teams which accompanied them."[12] Their journeys had been made quickly at little cost, which was a success in Young's opinion. He made no reference to the deaths sustained in those early companies or their own inadequate food supplies.

Young made further remarks, what could be termed early-day public relations statements, to support the continuation of handcart travel in future years. Here, too, his contentions belied the facts of the Willie and Martin Companies: "The Saints who have come this way have been healthier, more contented and happier, and have encountered less trouble and vexation [than] those with teams and have, moreover, manifested to the world their faith, perseverance and good works."[13] He made no comment regarding the hundreds of people who lay dead and buried along the trail in large part because they had frozen and starved to death. Nor did he speak of those who had suffered terribly and yet somehow made it through. One woman who traveled in 1856 later told Hannah Lapish that she was so exhausted that she felt she could not move another step but "they kept beating and whipping her so that she would move along and not freeze to death. Finally, she took hold of the back of one of the provision wagons and it seemed as if her hands frose there. She could not get away and although nearly dead, she was compelled to continue her journey."[14]

However he chose to interpret the disaster, Young knew that the lessons had been hard learned. Future handcart companies, he said in one address, "must start earlier in the season . . . no company must be permitted to leave the Missouri river later than the first of July." They would need stronger handcarts, lighter loads, and an extra supply of good shoes. Elderly or ill individuals should not be part of the handcart companies but rather be transported in wagons. Young, always the micro-manager, recommended that there be no delays in travel, with a few miles covered every day. "On the Sabbath, after meeting and resting during a portion of the day, it will generally be better to make a short march," he said. "Move on every day, if you wish to accomplish your journey in due season."[15] This directive totally discounts the reality that people need rest, particularly when they are under extreme physical exertion when walking from ten to twenty miles daily, while pushing and pulling heavily laden handcarts, carrying children, fording creeks and rivers, and setting up a new camp every day. Just the exertion of cooking even meager meals and gathering buffalo chips, sagebrush, or willows for fires added to the exhaustion that these travelers felt each day.

Responding to Brigham Young's remarks about the late start of the Willie and Martin Companies, John Taylor wrote in the *Mormon* in February 1857: "It was our own fixed, decided opinion that the hand-cart trains should start early." There must be no delay, he said. "I believed that additional sickness and expense had occurred the year before in consequence of the emigrants laying in camp so long, and that this must be avoided."[16]

Reports of the Mormon trail difficulties that year were slow to trickle out to the nation. The *Zanesville Gazette* published an early report in February 1857 that was picked up and repeated in other newspapers. "It is greatly to be feared that the next tidings from them will inform us that the whole company, several hundred in number, have perished. . . . they were suffering beyond measure for want of provisions and on account of the cold—They were badly clothed, and in consequence of the hardships many of them were dying."[17] This newspaper did not report that the majority of the handcart travelers survived the trip, which is another indication how slowly information made its way from west to east in that period.

The *Daily Gazette* in Vincennes, Indiana, used newspapers received from Utah to prepare an account of the handcart migration. Published on March 13, 1857, the *Gazette*'s compilation noted that the Abraham O. Smoot wagons and the handcart company led by James Grey Willie had arrived in Salt Lake City on November 9, 1856. Perhaps having no way to verify or question the reports, the *Gazette* did not deviate from the Mormon narrative. "The eminent feasibility of the handcart movement had been previously demonstrated; its healthfulness is now proven by the experience of this company, late though they were, and in storms, cold and snow."[18]

John Taylor, initially unaware of the late start of the Willie and Martin Companies from Iowa City, responded to criticism of his actions: "In regard to our being uninterested, the following letter will exhibit what our feelings were on that subject." He then quoted his own letter written to Daniel Spencer (whom Richards had placed in charge at Iowa City) on June 5, 1856, wherein he had outlined the need for sixty pounds of bread and extra flour for every person and suggested that wagons should be filled with supplies and then sent ahead and stockpiled along the route near Fort Laramie.[19]

In 1856 Taylor had objected when Franklin Richards requested that George Grant, who had been assigned to help with preparations in Iowa City and in Florence, go instead to St. Louis. Taylor disapproved the reassignment: "I was not willing that the emigration should be delayed on any consideration."[20] Taylor then wrote to Richards: "I wished to have your instructions attended to there; but could not, of course, see the business of emigration interrupted."[21]

It was generally recognized that the Fourth and Fifth Handcart Companies had left Florence, Nebraska, too late in the year. However, the *Mormon* was a church publication that not only reported the news sent from Utah but also was charged with building up the faith of the Mormons in the East. It always stuck to the church narrative when reporting. "The relief so promptly, freely, liberally and timely sent from here was so blest in rescuing them, that but few comparatively, have suffered severely," the paper said, "though some had their feet and hands more or less frosted; yet the mortality has been much less than often attends well fitted animal trains traveling in good season." Claiming there was a "comparatively small amount of suffering" among that year's travelers, the paper added, "[one] thing is evident; that if according to President Young's instructions the hand-carts had started earlier, there would have been comparatively no suffering."[22]

Such reporting was blatant church propaganda. It may have been too painful to report that 75 or more people had died with Willie's Company while traveling from Florence to Great Salt Lake City and from 135 to 170 members of the Martin Company perished on that same route, mainly from the combined effects of starvation, exhaustion, and exposure. Then again, during that period it would have been an extreme breach of faith had the church publication even hinted at any criticism of Brigham Young and his closest advisors. This was especially true at this particular time, because Young was facing increasing criticism and scrutiny from federal officials and the national press, which had concerns about Young's administration of federal law in Utah and the Mormon proclivity to practice plural marriage. The issues were rising to the highest levels of the federal government in Washington, D.C., and would soon spill westward.

Not accounted for in the church reporting were the deaths of dozens of members of the Willie and Martin parties on board ship, while en route to Iowa City, while camped there waiting to begin their handcart journey, and then while traveling across Iowa. There also had been deaths in the three earlier handcart companies as they came by ship across the Atlantic and then walked more than 1,300 miles from Iowa City to Great Salt Lake City. The inescapable common denominator in all cases was a lack of food combined with the need for human power to draw the carts across a rugged landscape. For the Fourth and Fifth Companies, the onset of cold winter weather compounded the suffering and deaths. People familiar with the frontier region should have anticipated that fate—and avoided it. Other newspapers less favorable to Brigham Young, such as the Cleveland Plain Dealer, reported: "Under delusion, they left their homes in foreign lands; and, to satisfy a whim of the Governor, undertook a journey of thousands of miles, not half provisioned or fitted for a trip that, even in good weather, is difficult enough, let alone this inclement season of the year."[23]

Even as the last Martin party stragglers came into Utah, the planning went ahead for the 1857 migration. British mission president Orson Pratt noted that the last company should leave England no later than March 25 in order to reach Iowa City, where they would outfit for the handcart trek across the plains by early May.[24] To prepare for the 1857 migration, church members in England were urged to send their deposits to Pratt before January 1. The British Mission Presidency of 1856, led by Richards and his counselors, had obviously failed to get the saints off from England early enough in the year. The new presidency did not intend to make the same mistake again.

For years church leaders and those who had lived through the handcart disaster of 1856 spoke little about it. As with other painful events, they may have wanted to forget. But some, like John Jaques, did speak out. "The grand mistake in the management of the fifth company of handcart emigrants in 1856," he said, "was the late start on the handcart portion of the journey, throwing the last third of the same into a semi arctic winter and thereby causing the expedition to be one of the most painful, disastrous, and costly character."[25]

Jaques considered the 1856 experiment "cruel to a degree far beyond the power of language to express, and the more so for the reason that the worst parts of the experience were entirely unnecessary, avoidable by timely measures and more sagacious management." He added, "The affair, was one of those disagreeable things, like some hateful dream, or dreadful vision, or horrible nightmare, that people seem indisposed to refer to but rather tacitly agree to forget, as much as possible, at least for a time."

Jaques continued: "The question may be asked, whom do I blame for the misadventures herein related[?] I blame nobody. I am not anxious to blame anybody. I am not writing for the purpose of blaming anybody, but to fill up a blank page of history with matters of much interest." Even so, he suggested, "it would be entirely proper for the president of the Perpetual Emigration Fund company and his assistants to be asked to freely and fully cancel the indebtedness for passage, if any remains, of every member of this unfortunate and sorely tried emigrant company, and it would be a righteous, beneficent and graceful act for those gentlemen to readily accede to such a request." These debts were not quickly forgiven, however, and the immigrants remained liable for the aid that they had received until 1880, when church president John Taylor expunged half the amount of any outstanding PEF funds owed to the church.

CHAPTER 10

FACING THE DEVIL

The Hunt and Hodgetts wagons containing "all that many poor families had on earth" were unloaded at Seminoe's Fort in early November 1856. These goods were then stored in the fort or buried (cached) in pits dug by the men. As they moved the freight, the men attempted to account for ownership before they stored everything, excepting "a change of clothing, some bedding and light cooking utensils."[1] Daniel Webster Jones claimed that two hundred wagons were unloaded, but without doubt his figure was seriously inflated. Fewer than one hundred wagons were known to be with the Hunt and Hodgetts wagon companies and Martin's handcart company. The Martin wagons had few goods in them. They had been used for hauling ill or injured travelers after the food ran out; only one of those wagons had any church freight in it.

When the Martin Company and the wagon trains continued west on November 9, Jones and nineteen other men remained at Devil's Gate to guard the goods cached there. Jones was chosen not only for his ability to cook but also because he was a frontiersman and a natural leader. George D. Grant instructed Jones to select two other rescuers to stay behind with him. "I had a great mind to tell him I wanted Captains Grant and Burton," Jones wrote later. These two men were undoubtedly among the most experienced frontiersmen in the rescue party, which may have been why Jones preferred them, but he knew that they were needed to assist the struggling Martin Handcart Company, so he instead selected Ben Hampton and Thomas Alexander (49). Another seventeen men, teamsters from the Hunt and Hodgetts wagon trains, would complete the party left at Devil's Gate.

"There was not money enough on earth to have hired me to stay," Jones wrote. But stay he did, because earlier he had said that any of the men would remain at Devil's Gate to guard the goods if called upon to do so. Jones must have known that his decision could have had deadly consequences, but he did not back down from the assignment, clearly demonstrating his sense of honor.

Once the immigrants moved on, Jones gathered the men with him at the old trading fort. If they were not prepared to eat the last bite of the poor cattle (the remnants of the 250 head of heifers in the investment herd being taken to Utah with the Hodgetts wagon train) "hides and all, suffer all manner of privations, almost starve to death," he told them, they could leave Devil's Gate and catch up to the handcarts. None of the men would go. Instead they all "voted to take their chances" (50).

The stormy weather abated enough for the handcarts and wagon companies to leave Martin's Ravine and strike out west through the Sweetwater Valley toward Great Salt Lake City, but full winter soon settled in to isolate the men at Devil's Gate. They had the worn-out yearling and two-year-old heifers, which were expected to sustain the men over the coming winter. Besides the poor beef, they also had a few crackers and other provisions, which they thought would last for twenty days. It was not much. Jones must have known that winter conditions would remain at least through March or April—fully five or six months hence.

Most of the cattle in the Hodgetts herd soon died of starvation and exposure. The carcasses attracted more wolves. Not content to eat the carrion, the wolves attacked the living cattle, easily killing the weakened animals. After a week of significant losses, the men realized that they could not save the cattle, so they "killed them to keep them from dying" under attack by the wolves (76). They butchered the carcasses, expecting to use the meat to trap wolves, but instead devoured it themselves.

The men had covered the floor of the roughly built Lajeunesse trading post with ox yokes and again rearranged the goods left behind. They found sugar, coffee, some fruit, and a roll of leather plus some candles and soap, all of which they kept out for their own use, documenting what they took. Most of the goods were the property of several Mormon elders, including Franklin D. Richards, Daniel Spencer, Cyrus Wheelock, and John Van Cott (who had abandoned his effort to reach the stranded travelers).

Having little success at hunting, the men ate the poor beef and other limited supplies, lacking salt but generally managing without undue hardship until just before Christmas, when Ephriam Hanks and Feramorz Little arrived, carrying the mail from Great Salt Lake City.[2] In the packet was a letter from Brigham Young, dated December 7, telling them to be "constantly on the alert" and to remain "firm, steady, sober-minded, and sober-bodied, united, faithful and watchful, living your religion." He further urged the men to "use all due diligence for the preservation of your stock," not knowing that the wolves had already forced the men to kill the cattle. Young told them the church would "send teams to your relief as early as possible in the spring."[3]

Others traveled the trail that winter, including a west-bound mail company that left its coaches at Devil's Gate and continued from there using packs. These men turned around east of South Pass, however, when deep snow halted their progress. Daniel Webster Jones killed a buffalo the day the mail party returned to the Mormon camp at Seminoe's Fort, shooting the beast as it moved toward him on a snowy trail a dozen miles from camp. It took three days to haul the meat to the rough buildings they called home for the winter. The mail company continued east, heading back along the trail to the Reshaw post even though the men at Devil's Gate must have told them that they would not find much to eat there. The Mormons knew this because some of them had already made the 120-mile round trip without obtaining any significant aid. As Jones wrote, "We barely got enough to last us back." The mountain men who were staying at Reshaw's Bridge had no flour for bread but "lived by hunting" (57).

Early in 1857, with winter snow and wind pummeling the region, the men faced the worst conditions imaginable. They had no supplies other than some sugar and coffee, which they did not like. Having eaten all their meat and facing starvation, they resorted to boiling the hides that they had pulled from butchered cattle. "A lot was cooked and eaten without any seasoning and it made the whole company sick," Jones wrote. They tried again, cooking the hide and then soaking it and scraping the hair off until the hide was soft, which they consumed "glue and all." But this meal was "rather inclined to stay with us longer than we desired." Ultimately, they did as the little children had done: they scorched and scraped the hair off before they boiled the hide, disposing of the gluey water. After washing the skin in cold water, they boiled it again and ate it "with a little sugar sprinkled on it"—a lot of effort for a poor meal, as Jones said, but "better than starving" (57–58).

The men killed wolves that had preyed upon the cattle, stacking the dead predators not far from the fort. At one point when they became most desperate for food, they eyed the carcasses, likening them to mutton. Despite their need for sustenance, they did not eat any of the wolf meat. There is no account of them killing and eating any of their horses either, perhaps because they viewed the horses as their way to get home in the spring. Unlike cattle that needed grass for survival, the horses could sustain themselves by eating the willows that grew along the river.

In his December 7 letter Brigham Young had warned the men to remain on guard against Indians, who could be in the region during the winter. When the first Shoshone actually showed up, however, the men welcomed him. "At the time of his arrival we were out of everything, having not only eaten the hides taken from the cattle killed, but [we also] had eaten the wrappings from the wagon-tongues, old moccasin-soles . . . and a piece of buffalo hide that had been used for a foot mat for two months," Jones wrote (58).

The same day the Shoshone arrived, the McGraw mail company again tried to travel west from Platte Bridge and reached Devil's Gate. The French-Canadians with the mail coaches shared their limited supplies. Even better, at least one French-Canadian and the Indian went hunting, returning to camp with their horses "loaded with good buffalo meat." There were more days with sparse rations as the long winter continued. "Some may ask why we did not leave," Jones wrote. "There was no time during the winter but the attempt would have been certain death to some of us" (60). Brigham Young had instructed them never to leave the fort with less than ten men, to protect against any attack by Indians or other renegades, but, as Jones wrote, "There never had been a time when we had that many able men" (63).

When returning to camp after one unsuccessful hunting trip, Jones decided that he would head out alone for Reshaw's, seeking supplies. With no food at all the men faced starvation even as they guarded the freight. But on arrival at Devil's Gate the skunked hunters found William Hickman of the Y. X. Express—the new mail service launched by Brigham Young. Hickman had not only crossed South Pass but also killed a buffalo and hauled some of the meat to the fort.

Jones would later write that when Hickman arrived the company at Devil's Gate was soaking the packsaddle, in preparation for cooking it to gain whatever nutrition might remain in the rawhide cover. One man would later say that Jones was the "man that ate the packsaddle," but Jones himself wrote, "this is slander . . . I think if they had not arrived, probably I would have taken a wing or leg, but don't think I would have eaten the whole of it" (64).

Before eating any of the buffalo, Jones drank a pint of salty broth, made from boiling the salt pork brought by the mail company. The rescue party, now rescued from their own desperate situation, paid for the supplies provided by the mail party with goods that they were guarding, "paying mostly in calico and domestics" from boxes owned by John Van Cott. Among the supplies they obtained were two mules, which, if nothing else, could be butchered and eaten. But first Jones and Ben Hampton would go to Reshaw's post to see if they could find other supplies. They had not ventured far when they encountered men traveling west with some beef for the Mormons. John Baptiste Richard, upon learning of the Mormons' plight from the Indians, "had butchered several of his oexen and sent them by pack train to Devils Gate."[4]

As winter waned, more Shoshone and Bannock Indians traveled east through the Sweetwater Valley. They, too, aided the saints by bringing more meat, which they traded for clothing and other supplies that the Mormons took from the stores they guarded.[5] When spring finally came, the Mormons killed some antelope and further enriched their diet with thistle roots. The Indians brought them buffalo meat and then the weather broke, making the trail passable once again. Additional riders with the Y. X. Express came through, along with other travelers, including a group of Mormon missionaries pulling handcarts east.

When wagons sent from Salt Lake to haul the goods stockpiled at Devil's Gate finally arrived, they were loaded and soon after the twenty men who had spent such a difficult winter at Seminoe's Fort set off for Utah. William Ben Hodgetts was one of the men who returned to the winter camp to reclaim goods. His sister Emily would later write: "We left our belongings in the old fort in our four blue chests. The next summer Ben went back for them and for some freight for the church. Of the four chests, we only got one back. The blue box is the only relic of my childhood home."[6]

Spending the winter at Devil's Gate had been a demanding task that put the men in danger of starving to death themselves. Astonishingly, Jones and the men with him later were accused of improper use of some of the goods that they had been left behind to guard, apparently because they had used them to trade for food. Following a church investigation, Jones and the others were cleared of any wrongdoing.[7]

We might wonder at the mindset that led those twenty religious men to put themselves in such imminent danger of death by starvation just to guard material possessions. We might also question how the men who owned the goods and were safe and warm in Utah could have had the audacity even to suggest that anything had been improperly used for survival. Those property owners in Utah presumably had enjoyed full dinners every day, while the men with Daniel Jones had survived on glue-infused soup made from boiling cattle hides.

CHAPTER 11

THE SIXTH AND SEVENTH COMPANIES

1857

For the Mormons, traveling to Zion was a calling tied to faith. As twenty-two-year-old Robert Fishburn said, "We felt that the Lord would preserve us and would give us strength and power of endurance sufficient to enable us to go through."[1] He walked with the Israel Evans Company, the first handcart contingent to set off on the road to Utah in 1857. Although the journeys of the Willie and Martin parties the year before had been disastrous, the 1857 travelers had little inkling of their plight, in part because the church public relations campaign had spun the news in such a positive manner, not reporting the negative aspects of the trip in church publications. Also, it took weeks if not months for news to circulate in those years before a transcontinental telegraph.

The *Lady's Newspaper* in London published one early report about the handcart migration on February 14, 1857, basing the account on a letter written by William Hartle on December 27, 1856, when he was in Leavenworth City, Kansas Territory, to his brother and sister still in England to "acquaint you with our sufferings and loss." The Hartle family had traveled with Edward Martin's Fifth Company. Once they reached Florence, Nebraska, William said that he "tried to persuade my wife and parents to stay there during the winter, as I thought it was too late in the season to cross the plains." After Franklin D. Richards and other American elders "gave us good instructions and cheered us up," the family pushed on, only to pay a costly price for the decision. Hartle's mother, Lydia (seventy-one), after "walking sixteen, eighteen, or twenty miles a day for weeks, without a ride or any assistance, until she was exhausted," soon could walk no more. Hartle put her in his handcart and continued traveling west, but "she was quite wore out, wished to give up, and died one morning before we started out. We buried her beside the roadside without a coffin."[2]

That was the family's first death. Eight or nine days later William's sister Mary died. Then his infant son Ephriam perished when they were between Scotts Bluff and Fort Laramie. William's letter continued: "My father kept pushing and pulling the hand-cart with sore feet, until he was worn out, and had to go to the waggons to ride. My wife pushed at the hand-carts until she fell sick, was worn out, and had to go to the waggons to ride. My son William fell sick of the fever and ague and his mother was ill of the same complaint." When the company reached Fort Laramie, William, hungry and completely exhausted, stayed behind with John Barlow, a young man from Manchester. As he later said, "If I had gone on another week I should have been a dead man."

Hartle's family continued on to Salt Lake City with the Martin Company, while William stayed at Fort Laramie for six days until he joined an ox-train operated by Alexander Majors and William Russell headed east to Leavenworth, Kansas. (Majors and Russell had a freighting company working along the trail and a few years later joined with William Waddell to organize the Pony Express.) Writing his letter from Leavenworth, William Hartle said that he was "staying at a boarding house, paying three dollars per week, chopping wood, and getting along the best way I can, until Spring, when I hope, by the help of God, to get to Salt Lake to my family." Hartle's family did not fare well after he halted at Fort Laramie. His son William (three), who had been ill when his father dropped out of the company, and son John (twelve) completed the journey, but William's father, John, wife, Elizabeth, and son Samuel (six) all died.

The *Christian Cabinet*, published in London as "A Weekly Newspaper for the Churches," on March 6, 1857, gave another account of the Mormon handcart migration that would have provided a warning to anyone in Great Britain considering their own migration. The long-delayed news provided details that the Third Handcart Company was "suffering dreadfully from cold and hunger." At that time (in mid-September 1856) the Third Company was traveling between the Green and Bear Rivers, in the vicinity of Fort Bridger. In further warning, the paper added: "Of the Fourth, Fifth and Sixth Hand-cart Companies we have heard nothing. They are far in the rear, and if they have not stopped at Fort Laramie will all perish. Besides these there are several waggon companies, and the number of emigrants yet on the Plains is estimated at 1,200."[3]

This account is very similar to the information reported the previous October by the *Baltimore Sun*, perhaps another indication of how long it took news to travel.

Despite these concerning reports, hundreds of converts to the church were even then packing their bags and preparing to sail to America, anticipating their own faith-based journey to Zion.

John Taylor, who had directed aspects of the 1856 handcart operation from New York City, was in Philadelphia in May 1857, arranging for the first leg of overland emigration by the saints who would be part of the Sixth and Seventh Handcart Companies.

After organizing transportation for the Danes who would become part of Christian Christiansen's company, Taylor himself traveled west, arriving in Iowa City on May 30. The Evans Company, composed of travelers from England, had already departed for Florence, Nebraska, but there were other Mormons at Iowa City.

"The camp is beautifully situated on a gentle elevation on a rolling prairie," Taylor wrote. "The white wagon sheets and tents, the order of the camps, and some pretty looking wagons, presented a beautiful and picturesque appearance." The grass was slow to grow that spring. But according to Taylor "everything here is business and bustle," in part because "this is at present the terminus of the railroad west—the jumping-off place."[4]

There were changes in the handcart operations this second year of travel. With a new federal contract, the church started its mail delivery service, the Brigham Young Express and Carrying Company (also referred to as the B. Y. X. Company or more commonly, the Y. X.), and established stations that also provided assistance to the LDS church members journeying overland. In traveling west with the Sixth Handcart Company, Evan Morgan later reported on these stations, noting that at Horseshoe Creek, a day's travel west of Fort Laramie, eighteen "brethren from the Valley" built houses to serve the saints. Farther west, at Deer Creek, another sixty Mormons under direction of Nathaniel V. Jones made a new settlement. At the old Seminoe's Fort near Devil's Gate, which had housed Daniel Webster Jones and his men guarding freight during the previous winter, eighteen church members would be on hand and provide aid as the Evans Company moved through the Sweetwater Valley.[5]

Robert Fishburn said that in their company of 149 people, who had 28 handcarts as they left Iowa City, the strength of the men, women, and children was "divided out to the best advantage, the single young men being used where they were most needed so as to help those who were not so strong."[6] The travelers this year were generally younger and stronger than those who had been part of the 1856 migration. Evan Morgan joined the Sixth Handcart Company when one woman become sickly and decided to drop out in Boston. "She had paid for her handcart fare in Liverpool . . . [and] gave me the opportunity of going in her stead." Lacking money for his train fare from Boston to Iowa City, Morgan borrowed $5 from Grace Jones. Once in Iowa City he "worked in the neighborhood, wherever I could find employment to make a little means."[7]

Three weeks after arrival at Iowa City the Sixth Company, now pushing and pulling carts, rolled away across the hills of Iowa toward Florence, Nebraska. In addition to their handcarts, the company had one wagon with two span of mules to haul tents, cooking utensils, and other supplies. The people had sixty pounds of flour each plus bacon, dried fruit, and tea.

The Seventh Company, with 330 individuals, 68 handcarts, and 3 wagons, would be the last handcart brigade to cross the plains in 1857. Kersten Erickson (twenty) became separated from this Danish party while traveling by railroad from Philadelphia to Iowa City, later saying she was "a young girl in a strange land [who had] no friends and could not speak English or make my wants known." But the company leaders realized that she had been left behind. Using a description of her clothing, they located the young woman and arranged for her to get on another train that would bring her to Iowa City.[8]

At Iowa City these foreigners found that the church had not provided supplies for them, so they took up a collection to purchase tents, baking kettles, and other goods, plus wagons that were pulled by three-mule teams and an ox team driven by Carl Christian Anthon Christensen, a man who would eventually become a well-respected folk artist. Even with the wagons the Scandinavians needed to limit the goods that they would haul on their handcarts. "At the campground we encountered our first trials, in that we had to give up books which were bound and had been kept carefully for a long time, particularly our *Skandinaviske Stjerner* [*Scandinavian Star*]," Christensen wrote.

> We were only allowed to take with us fifteen pounds in weight for each person who was to travel with the handcarts, and that included our tinware for eating, bedding, and any clothing we did not wish to carry ourselves. Thus I remember that I sold my best trousers to a passing ox driver for twenty-five cents, and others had to leave valuable articles behind at the campground without any compensation. Books were left there in large numbers, and their loss has been felt afterwards with sorrow by others as well as myself.[9]

Although there almost certainly had been a grapevine passing on information from the prior year's handcart migration, the need to discard excess baggage was "quite a puzzle." Before leaving Copenhagen the company had heard of the limit on goods, but the people "supposed it meant fifteen pounds of wearing apparel and not everything," recalled Frederick Hansen. "When father came to that," he continued,

> he did not know what to do. Mother was sick, bedfast. The railroad journey from Philadelphia was too much for her weak body. Father thought for awhile [that] we would have to stay in Iowa City. Mother called us children to her bedside one afternoon, and I being the oldest, she talked mostly to me, telling me she could not live to get to Zion and wanted me to help father with the younger children. ... When our three days of preparation had passed, father like many others had solved that awful problem of fifteen pounds by throwing away and leaving good clothing that he knew would be needed before spring.[10]

People left many valuables, including feather beds, before they left the camping ground.[11]

Scottish missionary James P. Park became the leader of the Seventh Company. According to wagon driver C. C. A. Christensen, "The less said about this unfortunate choice of a leader for such a people as us, the better for him. We suffered greatly the first two or three hundred miles, traveling through the state of Iowa until we reached the Missouri River."[12] Park did not know Danish and set a relentless pace perhaps because he did not want to get behind schedule and arrive in Salt Lake City late in the year, which would have earned him the wrath of Brigham Young.

Each day the wagons and experienced trail leaders set out ahead of the handcarts and, according to John Frantzen, often outpaced the immigrants. Unlike the trip the year before, when wagons traveled behind the walkers, if someone in this company could not continue walking there was no wagon coming along to help. "We were all strangers in a strange land, and as our leaders and guide generally traveled with more ease and rapidity than [we] could with our carts, [they] were so far in advance so as to be out of our sight, hence it sometimes happened we took a wrong road, which [was] greatly to our inconvenience."[13]

Not many days out on the trail, the company reduced its gear and supplies by another two pounds, to just thirteen pounds per person. Each day people collapsed along the road. Some climbed into the wagon that Christensen drove, but others were left behind until late in the day, when young men were sent back to help them to the new camp.[14]

While crossing Iowa these Scandinavians endured hot weather and rain that caused "almost bottomless roads" while also adjusting to an unfamiliar diet and a drastically increased level of exertion. Those difficulties were enhanced by "the unreasonable, inconsiderate course of action" pursued by Park, which Christensen said "brought about much sickness and deaths."[15] In addition to his proclivity to strike out fast and ahead of the handcarts, Park had to rely on Ola Nilsson Liljenquist, who spoke both English and Danish, to act as interpreter.[16]

Although his mother initially was bedridden and rode in the company wagon, Frederick Hansen said that she and other elderly or ill people were soon forced out of the wagons and required to walk up the hills. Eventually these weak people were hiking part of the route every day, generally setting off ahead of the handcarts and wagons and then climbing aboard as the vehicles reached them, as had been the pattern in 1856. One day his mother and a few others "had walked as far as they could, so sat down to rest and wait for the wagons." But when the wagons and carts overtook them, they did not stop "and left mother and her companions sitting by the roadside." In camp later that day Hansen realized that his mother and others remained out on the plains. "Father went at once, to see our interpreter who was also first counselor to the captain and demanded to know what this kind of treatment meant. The brother told father to be quiet—that his wife was not the first one to be left on the prairies by the roadside."

Even so, responding to Hansen's father, Park had a four-mule team hitched to a lumber wagon and sent it back along the trail to pick up the ill and elderly who had been abandoned. The ride to camp was quite uncomfortable for Mrs. Hansen, who "took her thick calico apron and folded it to put behind her knees and then caught each side of the wagon with her hands." The wagon "hit all the high places" as it rolled over the rough road, finally arriving in camp at midnight. "This act of cruelty hurt father and weakened his confidence in our company leaders," Hansen said. "I think from that time on he planned some on pulling out at Florence."

As they struggled across Iowa, Carl Dorius "was the Samaritan among the sick; the encouraging, helpful friend and brother to the despondent and the exhausted," Christensen said. But Carl did not do it all alone. "He has help from his young wife, and other newly-married wives and of J. F. F. [John/Johan Frederick Ferdinand] Dorius."[17]

John Frantzen also aided those who were having difficulty traveling with the Danish handcart company. "A great many of the emigrants took sick," he said, "quite a number of whom were left along the road side during the day until we camped for night, when a sufficient number of young men was sent back to bring them to the night quarters, and a few died. I was generally fortunate enough to be well and able to perform this duty and mostly called on for that purpose every time, and this occurred nearly every day." Providing all this aid, Frantzen, who described himself as "young, full of vigor and life," admitted that sometimes he was tired after pulling the handcart.[18]

"We were told that it would be pleasant to travel without having the oxen to care for twice a day and that there would be greater blessing for those who made the greatest sacrifice," Frederick Hansen later reminisced. "I well remember that President Young (as he was called by those people) in an article that came out in the *Scandinavian Star* said prophetically that the time would come when the saints would be willing to go to Zion with a bundle on their backs and be glad to have that privilege. However, that prophetic statement has not yet been fulfilled." Hansen said that traveling with a handcart "proved to be unwise, and never provided for by the great god above."[19]

On July 1 Soren Jacobsen (twenty-six) wrote in his journal: "In the morning a child died and was buried. I believe that was the twelfth [death] since starting. Campt at noon and a [boy] died. That afternoon close to evening we reached a spot near Council Bluffs but we were not permitted to go through the town."[20]

In crossing Iowa the travelers passed near or through towns where residents "would come out in mass to look at [these] wonderful pilgrims, consisting of men, women and children, old and young, blind and cripples, pulling their hand carts and bound for the rocky mountains, called Zion." But there was no conversation, mainly because the Scandinavians did not speak English and the residents of the settlements could not speak or understand Danish.[21]

It took three weeks for the Sixth Company to travel from Iowa City to Florence, reaching that point on June 13. The Missouri River town bustled as church workers gathered supplies and prepared for the arrival of travelers who would be headed west. At the same time, missionaries traveling from Great Salt Lake to locations in the East and then on to foreign countries arrived daily. Perhaps to show that handcart travel could be accomplished efficiently—and safely—a large party of church missionaries departed from Great Salt Lake City that spring, pushing and pulling their own handcarts. They arrived in Florence on June 9, Amos Musser recorded in his diary. They made the eastbound trip in just forty-eight days. Their early crossing of South Pass was likely made possible by the efforts undertaken from Salt Lake City to reach the men who had remained at Devil's Gate for the winter.[22] It is difficult, if not impossible, to equate their eastbound journey with the trip being made by the westbound immigrants. The men from Great Salt Lake City were young, strong, and familiar with the landscape. Many of them had already crossed the trail one or more times as they responded to missionary calls. They traveled with lightly loaded carts, had the wind at their backs, and, as skilled frontiersmen, could hunt and fish with moderate to good success, enabling them to maintain a healthy diet while traveling. Brigham Young conceived their journey to demonstrate his continued support of handcart travel and perhaps to reassure those immigrants who would pull their own carts to Utah later that summer.

Musser had been in Florence since earlier in the year, preparing for west-bound immigrants to arrive. On June 12 he worked in the church warehouse, arranging supplies for the companies, while anxiously awaiting the arrival of the first westbound handcart company of the year. "I trust they will make their appearance as the season is advancing fast," Musser wrote.[23] Everyone, it seemed, recognized the need to get the handcarts on their way across the plains quickly to avoid a repeat of the prior year's calamity and ward off the harsh consequences that Brigham Young had set forth: if companies started too late in 1857 or subsequent years, those responsible for the late start would be excommunicated.[24]

At midday on Saturday, June 13, Musser said the "H. Cart train made its appearance on the opposite bank of the river. [I] Immediately crossed and welcomed them to Florence." That evening Musser performed a wedding ceremony for twenty-seven-year-old Elias Crane and twenty-six-year-old Elizabeth Smith. Just days after the Sixth

Company, led by Israel Evans, reached Florence, the steamer *Silver Heels* docked at the city "ladened with a goodly cargo of Saints & freight for the Saints."[25]

The Seventh Handcart Company reached Florence, Nebraska, on July 3. Musser wrote in his journal that both this company, headed by James P. Park, and the earlier Evans Company "lost several of its emigrants between this & Iowa City." Musser was seeing not only the large numbers of Mormon travelers setting off for the west but also missionaries coming east. Others were on the trail and passing through Florence that spring and early summer, including some individuals who had left the Mormon faith. "Apostates are becoming as thick in this country as the lice were in Egypt in the days of Phareoh," Musser said.

On the Fourth of July, violence rocked the bustling city of Florence: a man "went to work & stabbed another adulterous animal by the name of Kingsley, who . . . had been in the habit of cuddling Ro's wife." Musser's diary entry is a bit unclear, but the man doing the stabbing apparently "afterwards committed suicide himself." Musser, whose job had been to make sure that the handcart companies got off from Florence, now left behind the hard work of outfitting the Mormon companies—and the violence of the community. On July 12 he took his "good Chicago wagon & 2 yoke of oxen, a good stove & many other things to make me comfortable" plus four female passengers and set off across the plains for Utah—home.

After six days in Florence, no doubt to rest a bit and gather more supplies, possibly including some that had been hauled upriver on the *Silver Heels*, the Evans Company members again picked up their handcarts and set off across Nebraska.

Meanwhile the Seventh Handcart Company, now in Florence, rested and reorganized. Christian Christiansen was appointed as the new leader, replacing the unpopular Park. "Which appointment met with the hearty approval of all concerned," Frantzen recalled. Christiansen had been in the United States for some time but remained a fluent Danish speaker, which was "a great comfort and satisfaction" to the Scandinavian immigrants.[26] He was not related to the similarly named C. C. A. Christensen.

Musser was appointed clerk of the William G. Young Wagon Company, which consisted of fifty-five people using nineteen wagons. There were now seven companies of Mormon travelers on the plains, he wrote:

2 of these are hand cart cos. One contains about 330 souls & the [other] 149 souls[.] The first Co. [Evans] was furnished with 60 lbs flour[,] 10 lbs Bacon, 5 lbs sugar, 1 lbs rice, 1 lbs peaches, 2 lbs salt & 1/2 lbs tea to each souls old & young. The 2d or Danish Co. [Christiansen] got 58 lbs flour, 5 lbs rice, 4 lbs Bacon, 2 lbs

D. Beef, 4 lbs Sugar, 3 lbs peas, 2 lbs salt, 2 lbs Coffee 8 good mules & 2 wagons, tents &c[.] The first had but one 4 mule wagon. These [seven] Cos. have in all 1214 souls, 157 wagons, 646 hd of oxen, 75 cows, 18 mules, 20 horses, 19 loose cattle & 97 H. Carts. Add to these isolated emigrants with Bros. Tyler [Taylor] & others we have the sum total of our this years emigration.[27]

As the Seventh Handcart Company prepared to get back on the road, it became clear that not all those who had come from Denmark and traveled together from Iowa would continue west. James Jensen, a youth at the time of the crossing, wrote that "aged people and those in poor health" were turned back, even though they were "eager to proceed and willing . . . to take their chances against the certain failures before them." The harsh lessons of the 1856 migration, which left hundreds dead in Wyoming, were not forgotten. Christiansen and his counselors remembered "the intense suffering" and did not want a similar outcome in 1857. While they were at Florence "every effort was made to thin the ranks by requiring those who were not suitably prepared for the journey to return to Florence and await later opportunities to reach the Valleys."[28]

The weakest people included the family of Frederick Hansen, whose father "sold out his share in the company to three young men that wanted to go to Zion."[29] Also among those who were told that they could not continue was Christopher Hultberg, Jensen recalled. Hultberg's wife, Karna, was believed to be too feeble to cross the plains. The couple had two small children, Anna Catrina (seven) and Anders (three). "The disappointment was more than [Hultberg] could endure," Jensen said, "and after the company had started on he determined to proceed in its rear undetected until it would be too late for him to look backward." Hultberg indeed allowed the handcarts to move ahead while he and his family followed at a distance. Once they had gone about fifty miles, Hultberg rejoined the company. He took the gamble that the distance would be too great for the handcart leaders to reconsider and force him to go back. For much of his solo journey, "he had carried his children and even his wife upon the cart," Jensen recalled, "which he was able to pull by means of his superior strength and irresistible desire to reach the land of Zion."[30]

Kersten Erickson, the young woman who had been separated from the Danish party while traveling by train from Philadelphia to Iowa City, faced her own difficult parting. The crossing from Iowa City to Florence, she remembered, "had proved that my Father and Mother and Grandmother, who was 75 years old could not stand the journey. I could not leave my aged parents in a strange country and so made up my mind to stay with them." But Christiansen advised her to leave her family behind and resume her journey, telling her, "if I would do so, God would bless me and them and preserve us.—This was a very sore trial for me."[31]

When the Scandinavian company resumed its journey from Florence, it included several men to assist Christian Christiansen, including Parks and Lorenzo Dow Rudd. C. C. A. Christensen, Johan F. F. Dorius, Ole C. Olsen, and Carl C. N. Dorius each served as a captain over sixteen or seventeen handcarts and about one hundred people. At least some of these people knew Christiansen. He had joined the church early, served as a missionary in Denmark, and immigrated to Utah in 1852. Before his own relocation to America, he encouraged some of the people now traveling with the handcart company to join the Church of Jesus Christ of Latter-day Saints, including the Dorius brothers, who both said that he "acted as a father to us."[32]

On Captain Christiansen's advice, Kersten Erickson left her family in Florence on June 15, 1857, "put my trust in God and the promises of His Priesthood," and set off on the final leg of the journey, pulling a handcart. It was "a day I shall never forget—full of sorrow in parting from my parents." Not many days later, physically exhausted and "discouraged because I did not believe that I could stand the journey," Erickson "came to the conclusion that I might as well die there as suffer longer—and I was lonely for I had no relatives in the company." The girl dropped out of the line of march and "laid down in the grass expecting to die there."[33]

Still out on the trail himself, Christiansen found Erickson, helped her reach the camp, and promised that he would continue to look out for her. He assured her that if she needed help he would be there to aid her in pulling her cart. He kept his word. To compensate for the poor condition of travelers like Erickson, Christiansen "began with very short daily travel and walked the entire way himself in order to better be near at hand and to be able to assess the strength of the people.... His gentle, fatherly treatment will never be forgotten by those whom he led across the plains and the mountains in 1857," wrote his fellow traveler C. C. A. Christensen.[34]

They faced challenges, to be sure. At a large Indian village at the Loup Fork River in eastern Nebraska several of the young girls were ferried across the stream "by sitting behind a half-naked Indian on horseback, having to hold on to him around the waist in order not to fall off."[35] The immigrants who waded the swift stream held tightly to each other to avoid being swept downstream. Some did not make it. Due to their sickness, two families in the Seventh Company had to be left at the Mormon support settlement that was being developed. Hultberg's family was not one of them. His determination to continue west was paying off.[36]

Anna Marie Anderson Sorensen gave birth to a daughter, named Iowa, when the company reached Wood River. Some accounts say that she "retired into the brush where her accouchment was accomplished by the aid of devoted friends." Others remarked that the next day she appeared "with her infant in her apron" ready to continue traveling. Although Anna Marie may have planned to walk that day, a place was found for her and the infant in one of the company wagons instead.[37]

The limits on personal possessions meant that the travelers had little excess baggage. As Kersten Erickson's shoes wore out, she took a piece of hide from a dead cow found alongside the road and made new ones. Crossing creeks and rivers "would make the Raw Hide Soft and the hot Sun and Roads would make them hard and our feet were nearly all the time sore and bleeding," she said. She had no bedclothes but slept wrapped in an old shawl.[38]

John Taylor may have directed the handcart migration but did not *participate* in that form of travel. The one time he "took hold of a hand-cart alone to pull it up a hill," he said that he "found it rather heavy." But to justify using human power to draw the carts, Taylor added: "The opinion of most persons who are experienced in the matter is that those who are inexperienced in cattle can travel the road easier in this manner than to have the charge of a team."[39]

The traveling was tedious and often challenging. Robert Fishburn, a young, single, and healthy man, recalled the Sixth Company's journey. They moved across Nebraska "through mud holes and swamps, uphill and downhill, and over the sand hills," but they "got along first rate . . . for we were both cheerful and happy and were disposed to make the best of everything." This company moved at a slower pace than the groups in 1856 led by Ellsworth, McArthur, and Bunker and did not face the difficulties of a late start as both the Willie and Martin Companies did. Accounts of the handcart journeys of 1856 show little evidence that the travelers did much more than walk, push and pull the handcarts, make repairs to them, and generally deal with the day-to-day grind of their journey, with only occasional moments when they relaxed to enjoy music or other casual pursuits. But the atmosphere was more relaxed in Evans's Company of 1857. "We enjoyed ourselves in various ways around our camp fires at night, after having had supper," Fishburn remembered. Gathered around the fires, the travelers "would entertain themselves in recounting the incidents of the day, singing and reciting, and very frequently, when not too tired, we would have a dance."[40]

Music helped the 1857 travelers cope with the drudgery of walking mile after mile each day. Fishburn had his fiddle and shared handcart-pulling duties with Eliza P. Noble, Elizabeth Walker, and Sarah Pollard. On the trail they "sang for miles, which used to make the time slide along pleasantly and would also make our burdens seem lighter," Fishburn said. The music and singing "not only made us feel more cheerful and happy, but it had the same good effect on all the company."[41]

One thing that had not changed since 1856 was the great faith maintained by most of the Mormon travelers. C. C. A. Christensen likely spoke for many when he observed:

> For me it is beyond all doubt that the angels of the Lord were with us, though they were unseen, for we were walking defenseless in a long, spread-out row, in what was then the land of wild Indians, and many times we were among great herds of buffalo that could have totally annihilated us if they had been startled or for one reason or another had been led in the same direction we were traveling. But they seemed to be held at a suitable distance the whole time, although they were often only a gunshot away.[42]

Like the travelers of the previous year, they lacked sufficient supplies. Christiansen's handcart travelers were "poorly supplied with provisions" as they drew their carts away from Florence. They had smoked pork, dried beef, sugar, coffee, salt, and other seasonings that lasted for the first three weeks of travel, but "after that there was naturally flour, flour, flour, and only flour to eat." They turned their flour into bread and had porridge, gruel, and pancakes, Christiansen said, "but still it was just flour, flour and flour; and at one point the flour was scarce, too." With no wood for fires, they used buffalo dung, *ko kasser* (droppings) in Danish, as a fuel source.

Such lack of variety created some peculiar situations. A man who could no longer smell (and perhaps had failing eyesight) brought a skunk to camp, "which he counted on cooking for soup." Those in the camp who still had their sense of smell were not inclined to cook and eat the offering and may have shunned the man for a few days too.

Sometimes the travelers got lucky. The killing of a buffalo "happened almost like a miracle, for it had lagged behind the rest of the herd," Christensen said. He added that they dared not attack the great herd, which had been around them for many days. "If they had been alarmed and charged, that would have been the end for us, just as we could have been swept away by a tornado. But the Lord held his hand over our defenseless emigrant company, and we were not molested by either wild people or wild animals."

Each morning all the little children and some of the older girls were sent ahead of the handcarts, "partly to avoid the dust and partly to walk as far as possible before the burning sun and exhaustion would make it necessary to put them in the handcart," Christensen said. As the immigrants' footsteps marked their progress, their clothing deteriorated. "Our hats, or what might have once have been called hats, assumed the most grotesque shapes, seeing that the sun, wind, and rain had the superior force. The ladies' skirts and the men's trousers hung in irregular trimmings, and the foot coverings proportional to the rest, with or without bottoms." The travelers' bodies also took a beating. "Our faces were gray from the dust, which sometimes prevented us from seeing the vanguard; our noses with the skin hanging in patches, especially on those who had as much nose as I have; and almost every lower lip covered with a piece of cloth or paper because of its chapped condition, which made it difficult to speak and particularly to smile or laugh."

The members of the Sixth Handcart Company moved into the buffalo country along the Platte River on July 8, killing one animal that they butchered and divided among themselves. "There were large herds of buffaloes to be seen now mostly daily, coming down from the foothills to the Platte River for a drink," Evan Samuel Morgan wrote. "As there was scarcely any wood along the Platte River, we had to use what was commonly called 'buffalo chips,' which was the droppings of the buffalo, for fuel to cook with, which made [a] fair fire when dry, but as it rained very hard . . . they would not burn. Then we were liable to go hungry."[43]

The supplies these saints carried held out longer than in 1856. Still, by the time they neared Fort Laramie they were destitute. Their condition required hard decisions. Captain Evans assured them that they would not go hungry for long because supplies were being sent from Great Salt Lake City to replenish the depleted stores they had carried on their carts. "He then asked us how we felt about handing over our outfits, which consisted of our handcarts, teams and wagons, tents, cooking utensils, etc., to the Church when we arrived in Salt Lake City, if we were provided with provisions through the remainder of our journey," recalled Robert Fishburn. "These things belonged to the company, having been bought with their money and not with Church funds." In reality, the saints had little choice: without food they faced certain hardship and perhaps death. "We very willingly agreed to hand them over rather than starve," he explained.[44]

By July 25 the company was just a couple of miles west of Fort Laramie, again facing food shortages. "We are finding out now that the amount of food allowed us at the start was not nearly enough for the journey," Morgan said. "We are mixing pig-weeds and berries with the flour to help it out. The meat is about gone."[45] The travelers felt "somebody was at fault for the scanty supply of provisions furnished us" but no condemnation or anger was directed toward the highest leadership of the church. Fishburn said that they believed the hand of a "kind and over-ruling Providence" had blessed church president Brigham Young with "wisdom and foresight sufficient," leading to the stockpiling of supplies along the route. "Had such relief not been afforded to us, we certainly must have perished on the way."[46]

At Horseshoe Creek, a day's journey west of Fort Laramie, Evans's party found those relief supplies. "Flour was soon served out, and as quickly as possible made into bread and baked, and then eaten with a good relish until all were satisfied," Fishburn said. "Though we had nothing else to eat, we counted this very sweet and were thankful to get it."

Upon reaching Deer Creek a few days later, the company saw a beehive of activity: many people from Salt Lake had arrived and were industriously building log houses in a fortlike fortress, to be "prepared to protect themselves from Indian depredations." This fortress was a post for the new Y. X. Company, an aid station for the handcart companies, and a defense against an anticipated federal army that the Mormons knew was traveling their way. For Fishburn and his fellow travelers, Deer Creek was a spot to rest or "recruit." They stayed in camp there for a few days, butchering a beef and distributing the meat among the company. They were singing again as they pulled their carts away from Deer Creek, bound for the last crossing of the North Platte River and then Devil's Gate, where they received another supply of flour.

They found the best treat along the trail at Fort Bridger: a wagonload of potatoes brought from nearby Fort Supply, another Mormon-owned and operated post. Fishburn baked some of the potatoes and shared them with his traveling companions. He kept one for himself. "I don't know that I ever enjoyed anything more than I did that potato, for we had not seen one since we left the ship at Boston, being a period of about five months." Freshly killed beef added to the bounty the following day. Then Evans's party set off on its last days of travel to Great Salt Lake City. Although the journey tested the saints, the ever faithful Fishburn said that they were "abundantly blessed of the Lord. He gave us strength and the power of endurance sufficient to enable us to go through."

Evans brought the Sixth Company, which was better supplied and traveled earlier in the year than some of the 1856 companies, through with only one death among the adult travelers. Twenty-nine-year-old James Reader had died in Nebraska, leaving behind a wife and two-year-old son.

CHAPTER 12

CONDITIONS AT FLASH POINT

Other travelers were on the trail in 1857. John Frantzen, a member of the Seventh Company, claimed that the "Buchannan army" was "out on the prairie after the Indians."[1] The federal military force, authorized by newly elected U.S. president James Buchanan, actually had a far different mission that year: a march toward Utah to install a new governor. Trouble had been brewing in Utah for years before Buchanan's election. Young's position as both church president and territorial governor had vested in him unprecedented authority over the region. In addition to the territorial and political issues, another concern was the volatile sectarian issue centered on the Mormon practice of polygamy.[2]

After "nearly a decade of corrosive incidents, deteriorating relations, and grossly differing philosophies of governance—one secular, conventional and republican while the other was authoritarian, millennial, and theocratic," conditions reached flash point. The Mormons threw their support behind Buchanan, the Democrat who had earlier faced his party opponent, Illinois senator Stephen A. Douglas. Meantime the newly organized, antislavery Republican Party ran John C. Frémont, whose platform called slavery and polygamy "the twin relics of barbarism."[3]

After Buchanan's inauguration, individuals close to the new president, including Robert Tyler, son of former president John Tyler, advised Buchanan that Mormonism "should be put down and utterly extirpated."[4] Facing unsettled conditions—and under pressure from Brigham Young—all but one non-Mormon official (Garland Hurt, who served as an Indian agent) fled Utah early in 1857. Among those who left were federal judge George P. Stiles, territorial surveyor general David H. Burr, and U.S. marshal Peter K. Dotson. Judge William W. Drummond—who was highly critical of the LDS regime—was on his way to California by April and then on to Washington, D.C. He charged Mormon leadership with the murders of Judge Leonidas Shaver and government survey company leader John Gunnison and claimed that the church was a "blind and treasonable" organization that demonstrated disloyalty to the United

States. By April only two Indian agents remained at their posts in the territory leading Buchanan to claim that the only government in Utah was the "despotism of Brigham Young."⁵ The Shaver death was later ruled to be the result of natural causes.

While Buchanan sought advice and ultimately gave his secretary of war, John B. Floyd, authority to take action, Brigham Young also made preparations. He had begun stockpiling lead ore in the fall of 1856 and was manufacturing pistols by the spring of 1857, just months after the January 14 action by the Utah legislature that reorganized the Nauvoo Legion, the territorial militia. Young and a large contingent left Salt Lake City in April and traveled north into Oregon Territory to visit Fort Limhi, a missionary outpost on the Salmon River along the present Idaho and Montana border. While Young claimed it was a "pleasure ride," most recognized it as something altogether different. Young nurtured friendly relations with local Indian tribes, and this trip north was a reconnaissance to find an escape route from the oncoming federal troops.⁶

On May 20, 1857, Buchanan took action. The federal troops were already being massed in Kansas and would soon march west in order to install a new governor, Alfred Cumming, who was appointed by Buchanan on July 13, 1857.⁷ Three weeks earlier the word had reached Utah that a federal army was then en route to Utah, but Brigham Young controlled the information until July 24, 1857, the day of the annual celebration in Utah known as Pioneer Day. As hundreds of people gathered to recognize the day when the advance members of the Pioneer Company had first reached Great Salt Lake City a decade earlier, four powerful leaders in the church, including Abraham O. Smoot, thundered into town in a buckboard. They quickly announced cancellation of the territory's mail contract and shared the unsettling news that 2,500 men in the federal army were expected to start for Utah, bringing with them new judges and a new governor to replace Brigham Young.⁸

Prepared for the news, Young was nevertheless surprised that the approaching army was now under command of General William S. Harney, a man with a reputation for cruelty who had been court-martialed repeatedly. In response Young sent the Nauvoo Legion into the field and urged vigilance among the Mormons at Fort Supply and Fort Bridger as well as along the route leading over the Wasatch. The Mormons began fortifying their holdings and making plans for an all-out retreat if necessary. In fact Harney had remained in Kansas, where tension over slavery issues (beginning in 1854 and continuing through 1856) had caused continued unrest and militant attacks in what was then called Bleeding Kansas. In 1857 Kansans were writing a proslavery constitution that was supported by President Buchanan. But that document was hotly contested while it was under consideration by Congress (a new vote was required after charges of voting irregularities). Free State promoters wrote a third constitution, which would be approved in 1858 but was never ratified by Congress.

All of these political dealings, while delaying Harney's arrival to join the troops, had no direct influence on the families even then tugging their handcarts across Nebraska and Wyoming, headed toward Utah. Near South Pass the Sixth Company encountered seventy-five horsemen traveling east under command of the Canadian Mormon Robert T. Burton "to watch the movements of the U.S. Troops (or mobs) sent hear by President James Buchanan to destroy the Servants of God, And scatter the saints," Griffith Roberts wrote.[9]

The Scandinavian saints may not have spoken English well, in some cases not at all, but they also were aware that a "considerable military force was also on the way to Utah," C. C. A. Christensen said, although "providentially they never came near us, in that they marched along the other side of the Platte River, where we could see them, and their weapons shone in the sun."[10] Kersten Erickson said their handcart company was "overtaken by the U.S. Army . . . going to war with our people but they treated us kindly."[11] Carl Dorius also remarked on the army marching toward Utah. His comment may reflect the degree of understanding that most of the handcart travelers had: "Little did we know who they were or what their purpose might be."[12]

John Frantzen, traveling that summer with the Seventh Handcart Company, wrote of seeing Indians who "never troubled us any." He also saw the first soldiers sent toward Utah, which he erroneously reported was "some 6000 or 7000 men." It was, he said, "fitted out the best army pertaining to provisions, implements of war and in fact everything else necessary to accomplish the object for which the[y] were sent—to bring the Mormons into subjection to the laws of the U. States." The federal army traveled ahead of the Seventh Handcart Company for a time, but ultimately the handcarts overtook and passed it "without interference," Frantzen recalled.[13] Carl Dorius also saw the army on the plains that year. "We appreciated the fact that at one time when our company was nearly without food, almost like a miracle, the Army came to our rescue."[14]

Amos Musser, traveling with the Young wagon company ahead of the handcarts, wrote about the federal force. Their wagons had overtaken a number of California emigrants in western Nebraska on August 4. A week later they neared Chimney Rock and Scotts Bluff. "We have been passing amid picturesque & grotesque natural mountain & hill scenery," Musser wrote on August 12. In their travels they gleaned news from others on the trail. Concerned about the stories that they heard, they unanimously agreed to have William G. Young, a nephew of Brigham Young, take a mule and travel straightaway to Utah to report on conditions, including the presence of the troops along the trail. They stopped for a noon meal that day at a trading post, possibly the post near Fort Laramie, where they learned that "the Utah mail has been stopped by order of the postmaster general."[15]

"We learn that the company of soldiers, set apart to straighten the Utonians out, have lost 800 head of cattle, through stampedes; 60 head had been recovered," Musser wrote in an August 19 letter. In response to the federal action of halting their recently launched delivery service, the Mormons abandoned and often burned the new stations that they had been erecting along the trail to Salt Lake to serve their mail and freight service and provide aid to the handcart travelers. On Sunday, August 23, Musser reached what he called Porter's Station about thirty-five miles west of Fort Laramie, most likely the Mormon mail station on lower Horseshoe Creek. "The brethren in a very short time have built a number of good comfortable log houses & a good Korrell [corral] at this place," Musser wrote. "Now they have to go off & leave it all & as they have been remanded by our mutually beloved & esteemed Prest. Brigham Young. The news from the valley is most cheering. Bro. Brigham & Heber &c have come down upon the United States Authorities like a 1000 of bricks for stopping the mail & sending troops to Utah." This, of course, was simply bravado. At that time the Utah saints and their Nauvoo Legion had engaged in no direct conflict with the federal army in the situation sometimes called the Mormon War and other times referred to as the Mormon Rebellion.

As Musser's wagon company prepared to depart from the station, the saints there also packed up and headed toward Salt Lake. A few days later he noted: "We are making some large days drives & purpose continuing our course with all possible expedition as our as Bro Brigham's instructions to this effect are most urgent. This day drove about 25 m. & camped on Deer Creek." The call for urgency may have been in response to the 1856 difficulties, but more likely they hurried along because of the troops marching toward Utah.

At Deer Creek the westbound travelers found that the saints who arrived in June "have made an excellent correll & have commenced a hewed log fort laid out & planned most admirably. They also have made many much ditching for irrigating farm & have very planted 7 acres of corn." All these efforts were to support the handcart travelers then headed west, but Musser said that those at Deer Creek would abandon the new station now and return to Utah.

The people retreating from the stations along with the members of the Young wagon company would have ice on their buckets in the morning by the time they reached western Wyoming and be using both sagebrush and buffalo chips for fuel in their fires. There they encountered James M. Barlow, who led a small detachment of the Mormon militia east from Salt Lake to provide a defense against the oncoming army.

"We camped near them for the day & enjoyed their society," Musser said of Barlow's group, adding on September 8 that "Antelope, Sage Hens & Hare all very numerous." A week later his wagon company was at Fort Bridger, where the Mormons had made fortifications to hold off the federal army.

The handcart company John Frantzen traveled with reached Salt Lake City four days before the last companies of the Utah Expedition left Fort Leavenworth. Colonel Albert Sidney Johnston took command from General William Harney then "ordered the dragoons to march on 17 September and waited until the following day to make sure they were under way before leaving himself."[16] Johnston, however, would not be with the army until early November, in western Wyoming.

As the conflict played out along the trail, the handcart companies continued their walk west under predictably difficult circumstances but remained ahead of the army. "None but those who have experienced such a trial of patience, faith, and endurance can form an idea of what it meant to pull a handcart," Christensen wrote. "Extreme heat and lack of humidity, which could cause the [wood of the] cart to split," threatened to collapse the carts, which in turn would "thus deprive them of the last means they possessed to bring with them their absolute necessities."[17] Added Carl Dorius: "Our shoes were entirely worn out." The women had to use burlap around their feet, a hardship "which my wife Ellen could never forget. When we crossed streams the thin ice would tear our bleeding feet which became infected and swollen."[18]

Along the trail Christensen noted "the skeletons of worn-out oxen." The men and women "with their lips half eaten up by saleratus dust, and clothed in rags, with almost bottomless shoes on their feet," nonetheless "greeted with songs of delight the rising sun which let them see Salt Lake City for the first time."[19] But high spirits were not always the rule. "There was both joy and sorrow in that trek," Dorius noted. "We danced barefoot and sang in the evenings; and tried to be happy. We witnessed a thrilling though frightening, and never to be forgotten, buffalo stampede. We ran out of food and sent to Salt Lake City for provisions which came too late to help."[20]

The Sixth Handcart Company led by Israel Evans had departed Iowa City on May 22 and arrived in Salt Lake City on September 12. Traveling much more quickly, even though it was twice as large and had left Iowa City three weeks after Evans's group, the Seventh Company, which had set out under Park and ended the trip led by Christian Christiansen, reached Salt Lake City just a day later, on September 13. C. C. A. Christensen wrote: "One can perhaps form a vague idea of our feelings when we finally stopped here in this city and were met by kind brothers and sisters, many of whom brought cakes, milk, and other things that for us were so much needed."[21]

Their arrival occurred at the time of the greatest crisis for Brigham Young in his entire presidency. The federal army was marching across Wyoming toward Utah, intending to remove him as governor of the territory. Simultaneously a horrific attack occurred in southern Utah at Mountain Meadows. On September 11 Mormons treacherously executed some 120 California-bound emigrants. The Mormon attackers spared only 17 children traveling with the wagon train from Arkansas—all believed to be too young to remember what happened. Young learned of the Mountain Meadows attack within a week, first from reports relayed by American Indians, including Arapeen, a Ute tribal headman, and then from John D. Lee, the man who would ultimately take the major blame and be executed for his role in the massacre.

On September 27 the official journal of the church historian noted: "Reports reached town that the companies of Cala. Emigrants south were all used up by the Indians—100 men & 1000 head of cattle,—at Mountain Meadows." Although early reports placed the blame on Paiute Indians, the act had been planned and carried out by members of the Church of Jesus Christ of Latter-day Saints. Almost certainly Brigham Young knew about it at the latest within days of the attack.

While trying to subdue reports about Mountain Meadows, Young did not wait for the advancing army to march into Utah. He now fully activated the Mormon militia (the Nauvoo Legion), which moved to interdict the federal soldiers in southwest Wyoming. After marching east out of Great Salt Lake City, the militia in late September burned Fort Bridger to render it unusable for the federal troops and prepared to take up a mostly defensive position in the canyon country leading to the city.

At the same time, on October 5, 1857, Major Lot Smith, began an offensive campaign at Simpson's Hollow, east of the Green River. He and militia members attacked and destroyed seventy-six wagons in three supply trains managed by contractors sent out to support the oncoming army. The legion also burned prairie grasses, knowing that would hinder the army's advance because the forage was essential for the federal horses and mules needed for troop movement. The Nauvoo Legion's operations were complex, "often confusing," and "not confined to a small area or, for that matter, to Utah. They ranged across plains, deserts, canyons, mountains and river valleys—a sprawling regional 'front'" that spread across Utah, Wyoming, Nebraska, Oregon, and even into California and New Mexico.[22] This alone shows how far Brigham Young's influence reached. Young considered his options for protecting the people, ultimately ordering Mormon settlers from outlying cities and towns to abandon their homes and move to Great Salt Lake City to defend the capital. He continued strengthening his ties with the Indian tribes, expecting them to join the Mormons in resisting the federal authorities and oncoming army.

Just as winter storms had descended on the 1856 handcart companies, the snow and cold again delayed trail travel in the fall of 1857 for civilians and military alike. Even so, Albert Sidney Johnston and some 1,600 troops reached the charred ruin of Fort Bridger and hunkered down for winter. There would be no attack on Salt Lake City. Lacking supplies, an army relief party later departed from Fort Bridger, heading south and east across Colorado to Fort Union, New Mexico, to obtain replacement supplies. But the goods did not reach the suffering troops at Fort Bridger until late spring of 1858.

According to some reports, during the winter Thomas L. Kane of Philadelphia, a supportive non-Mormon friend of Brigham Young, became a diplomatic liaison between the army and Young and ultimately helped broker a resolution to the conflict, even bringing newly appointed governor Alfred Cumming to Utah. But historian William MacKinnon says that the actions unfolded differently:

> Mormon characterizations of Brigham Young's meeting with Buchanan's peace commissioners as negotiating sessions, during which hard bargaining by Young extracted favorable terms from the U.S. government, missed the point of what happened. Commissioners Powell and McCulloch controlled these discussions in unyielding fashion and extended Buchanan's pardon on a federally dictated take-it-or-leave-it basis. What took place amidst Mormon bluster and bravado during the second week of June 1858 (and thereafter) was, in effect, Brigham Young's humiliating acceptance of terms drafted by James Buchanan in Washington and reprinted on an army field press in Kansas.[23]

Along with newly appointed and installed governor Alfred Cumming, the army came to Utah to stay. It built Camp Floyd, named for the secretary of war, fifty miles south of Great Salt Lake City. The Mormons may not have liked the new military post, but they had no choice in accepting it.

As tensions eased, thousands of Mormons who had fled south in April 1858 from Salt Lake City and the northern settlements filtered back. The so-called Mormon Rebellion or Utah War was declared over. The effects of the attack at Mountain Meadows would linger even to the present. Ultimately one of the Mormon perpetrators, John D. Lee, was tried, convicted, and executed for his role in the events. Often called the worst loss of life on the overland trails, it eclipsed the numbers of people who died with the Donner Party in 1846. But the 120 victims were fewer than half the number of travelers who had perished on the trail as they dragged their handcarts west with Captains Willie and Martin in 1856.

CHAPTER 13

THE EIGHTH COMPANY
Resuming the Migration, 1859

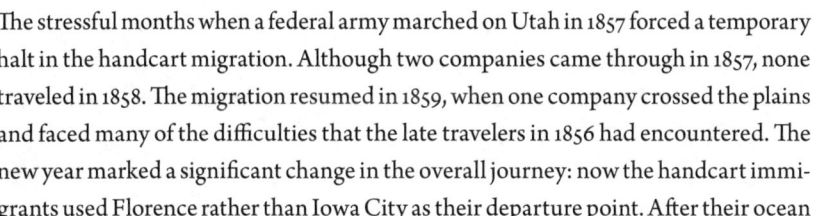

The stressful months when a federal army marched on Utah in 1857 forced a temporary halt in the handcart migration. Although two companies came through in 1857, none traveled in 1858. The migration resumed in 1859, when one company crossed the plains and faced many of the difficulties that the late travelers in 1856 had encountered. The new year marked a significant change in the overall journey: now the handcart immigrants used Florence rather than Iowa City as their departure point. After their ocean journeys the travelers crossed the eastern half of the United States on a combination of conveyances that included trains and steamboats. Once at Florence they would pick up their handcarts. The change was important, because it cut some 300 miles from the distance that they had to walk and shortened the overland trek by some three weeks.

The handcart immigrants of 1859 were new, but their backgrounds and personal lives were similar to those of the immigrants who had come before. Nineteen-year-old Sarah Hancock married Ebenezer E. Beesley, also age nineteen, in March 1859. A month later they set sail for America as members of the Eighth Handcart Company, led by Captain George Rowley. "Don't ask me anything about that," Sarah would later say. "You should go and talk to Mrs. [Hannah] Lapish. She can tell you all about it. Oh, she is full of life and very enthusiastic about it but I am not. Those are dreadful stories and I don't see why we shouldn't try to forget them. I say 'Bury them with the dead who died on the plains.' My children have often tried to get me to write my handcart story but I will not."[1]

Hunger again haunted the travelers. Twenty-three-year-old Henry Hobbs traveled with his twenty-five-year-old wife, Jane, in 1859. Although he pushed and pulled a handcart all day and took a regular turn on night guard duty, he still found time to keep a detailed journal of the trip. Henry's account clearly represents his deep faith, but he also shows that the company lacked adequate provisions and had to supplement the food allowance by living off the land. He wrote of catching fish in the Platte River and various creeks, killing rabbits, and picking gooseberries and currants. Even so, this natural bounty was wholly inadequate to sustain the immigrants.

Hobbs wrote of gathering strawberries in preparing for the journey on June 9 and said Mormon elder George Q. Cannon "addressed us & Said the Angels Should go before us & be round about us if we would be obedient to those over us."[2] Despite this prophecy, the members of the Eighth Company would face serious challenges as they pulled their carts across the plains.

Young Ebenezer Beesley carried a violin with him. At night the pioneers would "gather round the fire" to sing the Handcart Song, "For some must push and some must pull," and listen to the music. Early in the trip Frank Pitman enjoyed singing the anthem of the handcart pioneers and "would sing it for any one who would ask him," William Atkin would later recollect. When the company pulled away from Florence and traveled four miles that first day beyond the Missouri River, he "asked our little Frank, as he was by far the smallest man in the company, to sing the Hand Cart song, which he did, and [quite] a number joined in the chorus." High spirits notwithstanding, the traveling was difficult and people soon felt the effects of the journey. "Most of us were tired when we camped at night, and some were already getting foot-sore," he recalled. "Again we asked our little brother Frank to sing the Hand Cart song, but he very reluctantly complied, and I think this was the last time he ever sang it, and there were less who joined in the chorus than before."[3]

Such celebration grew more difficult. "Of course after awhile we all got so hungry that we couldn't have good times any more," said Sarah Beesley. "We didn't have nearly enough to eat and oh, the suffering!" The company had eight tents. She tried to sleep in one of them once or twice but found the experience "dreadful." With more than a dozen people in each tent, "everyone was in everyone else's way," she remembered. "We didn't like that a bit so we used to just sleep on the ground. We would draw our handcarts up in a circle and someone would guard us all night. If it rained we would sometimes sleep under the handcarts."[4]

Henry and Jane Hobbs slept beneath their handcart throughout their journey. "I engaged in prayer & then laid me down to Sleep under the H. C.," Henry recorded on June 9. The following day the captains distributed some provisions for the first week: two pounds of bacon and one pound of sugar for each person. Two days later Hobbs got additional provisions: seven pounds of flour and "a can of beens." One day later the leaders distributed tea among the company.[5]

They steadily moved west, but their mode of travel was difficult. As Beesley recalled, even going downhill was a challenge when the cart wheels were sometimes in sand "up to the hubs."[6] Henry Hobbs said that as they neared the Elkhorn River they "Should have Camped on top of the Hill," but a party of 200 soldiers en route to California already had bivouacked there and "as we did not like their Society we made a deep descent & camped near the river." The Mormons soon found that the soldiers had a good reason for camping on the high ground. "Muscatoes were very numerous," Hobbs noted, "& Scarcly a Soul Slept & all were bit very Severeley. Some of their Eyes were closed up."[7]

The summer sun beat down on them in Nebraska, leaving "the saints panting for Breath," Hobbs said. Some were overcome by the heat and exertion and "laid in the dusty road Like so many bisen and Sheep." Tempers flared. "John Smith Struck Henry Hartly [Hartley] for insulting Him & Turning his mother oute of the wagon," Hobbs wrote. "Hartly Said if he Struck him again he would put a Ball through him; in the name of the Lord."[8]

Crossing the Platte River the first time posed another challenge. They forded "in water above our waist and the current was strong," Sarah Beesley recalled. "We couldn't cross it single file. Ten or twelve of us would have to lock arms in order to get across." It was important that the flour supply not get wet, which required the men to carry the bags of flour on their shoulders as they forded rivers and streams. Once across, the people had no change of clothing so they wore their wet garments until they finally dried. "It was very disagreeable and of course impaired our health," Sarah said.[9]

Twenty-five-year-old Squire Thornton, who crossed the ocean on the *William Tapscott* and was a member of the Eighth Handcart Company, later recalled the early part of the overland journey was started "with pleasure." Before long, however, provisions ran out and "we began to feel the sting of hunger very sensibly and a great deal of suffering was experienced."[10]

At a prayer meeting in Genoa, Nebraska, Captain Rowley reprimanded the travelers because "there was much Stubbourness Manifeested with Some parties when they were Called to go on Guard." He told the saints: "Unless we were united we never Should get to the valley." At the conclusion of the meeting the captain took a collection in order to pay the fees to cross Loup Fork River on the ferry. The following day, June 21, the wagons and handcarts crossed using the ferry, but when the ferry rope broke "lots of the Boys went in naked & fixed it again."[11]

On June 24 "flower & Backon was given oute to last for 10 days" along with some salt and sugar. Even so, the next day "the Strength of the Saints was Exhausted with but a few exceptions." To aid the handcart travelers, teamsters traveling with James Lemmon's Mormon freight train, who were also crossing the plains that summer, hitched some of the handcarts to the wagons.[12] Traveling through the hot days of summer, this party "didn't suffer with cold but we did with heat," Sarah Beesley said. "The sun was so hot that sometimes it seemed as if we could stand it no longer. Or sometimes the wind would blow the sand and dirt all over us."[13]

Seeking relief from the wind and sun, Henry Hobbs took a bath in a creek on June 27. "It revived me much more than food," he said. Later that day, camped on Wood River, he caught some fish. That evening he attended a camp meeting where Captain Rowley gave instructions "about getting to the valley & working on our winter provisions. [He also] Spoke about going on gaurd, the importance of Keeping a Sharp look oute for the indians; to speak Kind to Each other & not Tread on Each others corns so much."[14] As the days passed, Hobbs fished whenever possible, using crickets for bait.

The handcart travelers of 1859 were not alone on the road. Gold was first noted in 1850 and officially discovered at today's Denver in 1858. Many "adventurers were rushing for the mines," William Atkin recalled. One group, well equipped with guns and horses, passed the handcart company and killed a buffalo along the trail. "They took one quarter of it and covered up the three quarters carefully with the hide and put up a notice that read 'This is for the hand-carts,'" Atkin said. "We found it in a very good condition and it was divided out, giving us from one to two pounds each. Although we were in the midst of buffalo, this was the only good mess of fresh meat of this kind that we had obtained."[15] The travelers had no horses and no other means to pursue and kill the big animals. They also had few guns, which they had not owned in their home countries and could not afford in America.

Henry Hobbs also recorded the discovery of this meat: "Wile Traveling today we came across the Best part of a Buffalo killed by the Pikes Peakers the day before. Some portions of it Stunk being Exposed to the Sun. but many got a good Supper out of it. I enjoyed mine well." They cooked their newfound provisions in their camp beside the Platte River, opposite from Fort Kearny. "We Saw the Soldiers camp at Fort Carnie on the opposite Side of the river. a poor place for wood."[16]

If wood was scarce, snakes were not. One day William Atkin saw a flock of ducks on a small lake. Taking his old gun, he set off to see if he could bag one or more. "Just as I was ready to crack away at the ducks, a huge rattle snake bobbed up right in front of me ready to spring on me. This was not an envious position, and in order to save myself I shot the snake instead of the ducks. The report of the gun scared the ducks away, and that ended my duck shooting." Hungry as he may have been, he apparently did not take the snake that he had killed for the cook pot. Indeed when he returned to camp he found it a huge commotion due to rattlesnakes. "We found the whole country alive with them." Camping in such a place was unthinkable, so the members of Rowley's Company hurried on after filling their containers with water.[17]

As food supplies dwindled, the people were placed on rations—just a pint of flour daily for every two people and "a very small amount of bacon." They may not have eaten any rattlesnakes, but these foreign converts welcomed trying another bounteous offering of the prairie: prickly pear. "We tried many ways to cook them," William Atkin said. "Some took the last morsel of bacon they had, peeled the prickly pears and fried them, others peeled and boiled them, while others placed in the fire and roasted them, but all to no purpose. Some did eat a very little of them, but it was a failure in general."[18]

This Eighth Company had several encounters with Indians, some quite beneficial. On July 3, west of Fort Kearny, Henry Hobbs said, they "Met with a band of Indians who were well armed & plent of Horses. They were called Sues [Sioux] & were expecting the Pawnees to Battle with them." He added that "they were quite friendly & Shook Hands with us & went & Killed a Buffalo for us & Brought the meet [meat] Several miles on their Horses & distributed it among the people. I & my wife had Several pounds which was excellent." That evening four Indians "came in to our camp, danced & yelled & made a fearful noise," Hobbs wrote. "Some of the Bretherin & Sisters were most Terribly Scared & thought the indians where upon them. others were calm & Sereene. This was only a little of their frollick. They would have Liked to have taken 2 or 3 of our Sisters for wives."[19]

The Indians took no offense when the Mormon women failed to go with them. The following day, July 4, the Indians who were "loath to Leave us" rode their horses in the wake of the handcarts for some distance before giving the "Saints the ropes round their Horses necks & helped to draw the carts." With this assistance the Mormons traveled twenty-five miles that day, but that was not the end of the aid. That evening they camped "with a company of pikes peakers. they gave us Some milk & cetera." As had been the case with the Indians, the following day the Mormons learned that the men in the "pikes peak camp ... wanted 2 of our girls."[20]

While relations between overland travelers and American Indians were sometimes tense (to the point of violence in the case of the attacks on the Almon Babbitt party in 1856), more often than not travelers encountered Indians who wanted to trade and provided geographic and other travel information, particularly in the first two decades of trail travel from 1841 to 1860. The Mormon encounters were no exception, The Indians may actually have been intrigued by the fact that the people were pulling their own carts.[21]

West of Fort Kearny, a region that Stephen Long had called the Great Desert in 1820, morale grew worse and so did the terrain. As Rowley's company trudged westward, the sun beat down. They had to pull their carts through deep, sandy soil. In places the trail veered away from the Platte River, which meant they did not always have easy access to water. These challenges led to so much grumbling that the captain "would not Let us go on any further Till a meeting was Called & things put rite." That evening at a monster camp meeting the leaders of the handcart company addressed the immigrants about the complaints. One said fathers "Snaped at their wives & children all day & in the morning as Soon as they awoke they where at it again." Another addressed concerns about lack of sugar. There had also been grumbling "that the Teamsters had as much as they Liked to Eat & others had not." The saints were told to "Expect to meet with a few Trials & have to Sacrifice a few Luxerys on Such a Journey[;] if they did not they would Shurly be disappointed." When it was noted that some travelers "had Threttened to Examine the wagons," presumably looking for food, Henry Hobbs said that Rowley told them "if they attempted that game he would Horse whip them & cut them off & they Should not Travel in our camp & those who murmered & upset the peace of the camp Should be cut off[;] he said if the murmering was not put a stop to there would be a muteny; He spoke of persons Stealing Cakes from the carts from poor woomen[;] he Said they where [were] not Mormons but Hypocrits."[22]

Their trail was well traveled. Early in the journey Rowley's Company often camped near wagon train parties headed to the Pikes Peak gold region in Colorado. The gold seekers often had more provisions and, fortuitously for the Mormons, were willing to share. On July 9 the Eighth Company "Camped near to a Company of pikes peakers on the Edge of the river plat for Several Hours," Hobbs noted. "Our new acqauaintancies Seemed much pleased with us & gave us Lots of Milk." Although many of his journal entries dealt with the day-to-day challenges of crossing the plains with a handcart, on occasion he reflected and added details: "Some of the Boyes are fishing & Some are Enjoying their rest[;] all around us Looks charming. the Broad majestic river with Some Lovely Hills & Trees in the distance is really charming."

At other times, however, he could be sarcastic, as when he noted on July 10 that they "passed Through 2 Creeks had Lots of fun[;] we also Traveled Through Some Sand." He could also turn critical, as he did when the company encountered Mormon apostates. "Met a Train of apostates[;] they where filled with [an] Evil Spirrit & Looked develish[;] One of the nincompoops Said Some thing aboute whipping our Captain[;] it was a good job for him that he closed up his mouth or he would have got what Paddy gave the drum after dinner" (a beating).

Rowley's Company also "met . . . a Large Band of Indians" that day:

> some on fine Horses. Some on foot they had a large company of the rising jeneration with them[.] They Let us have a number of maugasons [moccasins] for old Handkerchiefs[,] flower & cetera[;] quite a number of them Both men & woomen Helped us Along Through the Sand[;] they Shook Hands very Heartely with us & Seemed delighted to See us[;] they where the Sues [Sioux] they Showed us the Shallowest part to cross over the water & they did not forget to have a laugh at our women up to their knees in water.

Despite the Indians' aid and welcome at the river crossing, the Mormons took no chances. Hobbs noted that "we had as much as 60 men on watch to night to prevent our Cattle from being Stolen."

Not all the apostates they met were disagreeable. Meeting another train on July 15 that had departed Zion and was headed east, the westbound immigrants found that these people were "very civel with us." One of the men who had left Utah advised Hobbs that his company "shall find the roads & mountains much more difficult to assend than the Sand Hills have been & that there was means Enough in the PEF to Take us through comfortable withoute Breaking our Constitution[;] he Spok well of S. Lake & of the athoritys."

Ann Brown Rowley gave Hobbs some potatoes on July 16. Although there had been no prior reference to the Mormons having fowl with them, Hobbs said they "picked a Little fat Hen & Boiled it for dinner" that day. This may have been a prairie chicken killed during the day, but whatever its origin "it was quite a change for the System after having so much dry food." More Indians visited the camp that day. A California-bound wagon train also passed the handcart travelers, leaving behind a poor cow, which the saints killed and butchered. "Some where [sic] displeased. Capt Rooly wanted the Skin for the oxens feet," according to Hobbs, indicating that the oxen pulling the wagons accompanying the handcarts were growing footsore. The poor cow served another purpose, but not for all, for "in the morning the meet was devided among the Saints But it was Scarcley fit to Eat[.] The Scandinavians would not have any."

As they entered what is now Wyoming, complaints escalated, most relating to the shortage of food. This precipitated another camp meeting on July 28. "Br Rooly Said he was asshamed of the grumbling in camp." Hobbs reported. Rowley told them that "Some Said he had a pan full of bacon at Every meal But he Said he had not eat a pound on the Journey; Some Said that the Teamsters went to the bacon whenever they felt disposed: Cap Rooly Said there was only 4 weaks provisions & a few days on hand & we where barly halfway through." To alleviate some of the complaints, Rowley told the travelers that he would divide the remaining supplies.

If keeping the company together had been difficult in Nebraska, it was an even greater challenge now as the ground became more rugged and the hills steeper. Those who could not keep up fell behind and sometimes took a wrong trail, requiring others in the company to search for them. Some days people straggled into camp long after the vanguard. As Hobbs put it on August 8, "Many of the Saints where foot sore & came into camp very late[.] Some did not get in Till Morning." Such delays threatened the entire migration. Although Captain Rowley sent four men back in search of a Scandinavian who had missed the road on August 10, he said that he was losing patience and would "send back for no more that Stayed by the way."

When the handcart brigade reached the final crossing of the North Platte River, it found an Indian village. Hobbs reported on August 11: "nearly all the Indians came to See us cross the water with our H. Carts." The company put up its own camp after fording the river, waiting several hours for Rowley to arrive and finding out that "these indians here learnt the heart [art] of pilfering[;] biscuits here are 40 cents per pound." After an extremely demanding day, Hobbs noted that "we pursued our Journey with vigour Till we reached the Sweet Water 7 miles from Devils Gate[;] we had the Moon to guide us & got in camp at 11 o clock[.] We had much Sand to Travel Through & made upwards of 21 Miles[.] Some few did not reach Camp till morning."

Near the place where the Martin Company had been so devastated in 1856, Rowley's company held a dance on August 14. But all was not congenial in the camp. Henry Hobbs woke up to hear "Mark Lindsey abusing W. Adams for taking flower oute of Sister Jiekes bagg & Sister Cooks[.] Lindsey thretened to thrach him & Turn him oute of the Camp, But the evidence was not clear to our Captain & hence he did not leave the Camp." Some of the women were the source of other discord. "[As] soon as our Sisters came across any Jentiles [Gentiles] they would trim up & enter into conversation with them no matter how obseen their Language was," Hobbs observed. "Cap Rooly Said the cause of so much bickering & backbiting was because the Captains indulged in these things." A few women strayed from the faith. "Today Sarah Jones of birmingham Stayed behind & got married to a Store keeper," Hobbs noted, and "Br. Moors Wife left him to go to a Store 4 miles from devils gate." The next day Elizabeth Watson, who had been missing for several days, returned to the camp, coming in with an Indian who had "preserved" her life. But Henry Fox Strugnell had already had enough. He "Left the camp & turned back."

As it had been for travelers in previous years, the food supply for Rowley's Company was simply inadequate. Before long children were crying for bread, and parents had no way to supply any. But sometimes good luck befell them. William Atkin killed a sage hen, which he said provided "several good meals." If so, it had to have been cooked into a soup or in other manner to stretch the amount of meat. While at Devil's Gate, William encountered men he had known in England, who had set out for California a year earlier. But the men had not reached their destination and now were working in the area, operating a station to serve travelers. They shared a small amount of food, which William took to his wife and children. He returned to the men's camp to find "a loaf of bread about two inches thick and 14 or 15 inches across, baked in round campers bake oven and a good sized frying pan full of fresh fried Buffalo meat."[23]

The Eighth Handcart Company remained in camp near Devil's Gate for the next three days. Atkin and his family continued to receive food from his friends. As he later said, "while we were there our company were starving and I and my family were feasting, and some of our company said I was eating with the Gentiles and going to the Devil." When the people with Rowley picked up their carts and again began walking west, William's friends gave him additional provisions. "Our company [was] in a starving condition," he said, "and we divided most of what we had with them."[24]

The traveling conditions affected the animals as well. "When we started, we had eighteen team of oxen and not one of them reached the Valley," Sarah Beesley recalled. "They didn't seem to be able to stand the trip as well as we did. When they were worn out and about ready to die, the men would kill them and we would sit up all night watching for a little piece of meat." Even so, the food ran out by the time the party reached western Wyoming. "Before we got to Green River we were all literally on the verge of dying of starvation," Sarah wrote.

> Some of the people could go no further and we were in the heights of despair when we met some rough mountaineers. They felt very sorry for us and told us if we would come over to their camp they would give us some breakfast. I never tasted anything better in my life and it was cooked by squaws too. They seemed to be living there with those men. The first thing they gave us was milk and whiskey and we had to drink it out of gourds. Yes, I remember that so well. Then they gave us a sort of bread or cake that they cooked in kettles over the fire. Oh, it was all so good and there was plenty of it.[25]

The six or eight men at the mountain man cabins at Big Sandy in western Wyoming had "more whiskey in them than good sound sense." When the handcarts drew up, two of the men said they were looking for wives. "To our great surprise two of our young women stepped out and said they would marry them," William Atkin recalled. "Their starving condition seemed to drive all natural feelings away from them, and all the persuasion we could bring to bear on the subject could not change their minds and [make them] go on with us to the Valleys, so there were two weddings celebrated."[26]

Not all lives were saved, however. Jane Jarvis of Manchester, England, died on August 23 and was interred in a shallow grave. That day the travelers "broke up into 3 companys," Henry Hobbs said. His wife faltered, leaving him to draw their cart alone, and soon he was exhausted. Paul Henri Morel, whom he identified as "a frenchman from Italy," gave Hobbs "a warm cup of coffee & Some Sugar in it. It invigorated my whole system and enabled me to pursue my Journey."[27]

A day that began glumly ended on a better note when an Irishman arrived in camp and offered the weary, hungry travelers a supply of flour. This "Jentile" (non-Mormon) "offered to let us have 5 hundred pounds either for money or we could return it in flower by October. he also profered to kill an ox if our cap wished it," Hobbs wrote. "This was the best friend we had met with on the Journey. he gave us a loaf & 2 bottles of whiskey to some that were hungry & invited Some [of the people] to his tent to Breakfast." The meal included ham, boiled beef, bread and butter, milk, and coffee with sugar: "this was the best meal I had eat for many a day he also gave us milk, Whiskey & Sugar."[28] As they finished the repast, wagons sent by Brigham Young arrived in camp with additional supplies, including flour, bacon, and crackers or hard tack. These relief supplies from Salt Lake City "saved our lives and gave us courage to come on," Sarah Beesley said.[29]

A musical band met Rowley's Company in Emigration Canyon, escorting the handcart travelers into the city on September 4. "The first tune I recognized," Henry Hobbs wrote, was "O ye Mountains high where the Clear blue sky arches over the vales of the free." At the end of their journey, most of the handcart saints slept on the ground once again before moving in with friends, family, and strangers who welcomed them to the valley, distributing bread, butter, eggs, milk, coffee, tea, sugar, boiled beef, roast beef, mutton, pork, potatoes, cabbage, carrots, onions, cucumbers, tomatoes, squash, plus melons, peas, beans, and tarts. These travelers, who had believed that they might perish from lack of nourishment, relished the food.[30]

"The next day we carted what little baggage and luggage we had into some woman's house and dumped them on the floor," recalled Sarah Beesley. "After we got here I wrote to my mother and told her what a dreadful time we had had and that she must wait until some other means was devised." Her mother responded that "they would come [if] they only had knapsacks. They came by ox team a few years later, and mother was carried into my little home. She only lived eight weeks. The journey was too much for her." Sarah may not have wanted to recall her handcart crossing, but she had a reminder of it every day: a wild rose bush in her garden near the gate. She planted it after arrival in Salt Lake:

> You know there wasn't anything growing along the whole way that we could put in our mouths until we discovered these wild rose berries. When we would come to a bush we would pick just as many as we could and then eat them. Many a time they saved my life I know. They are rather soft and fluffy inside and didn't taste very good but we could chew on them for a long time. They were shaped like a pear only ever so much smaller, you know.[31]

Dominico Ballo's Brass Band followed by Dimick Huntington's Martial Band (Huntington was the drum major) preceded the Eighth Handcart Company into Salt Lake City on September 4, 1859.[32] Like most of the handcart pioneers who preceded them, the members of the Eighth Company received food and other welcoming gifts, but they slept on the ground in the public square that night. Their handcarts were taken away, the luggage and their possessions unloaded for the last time. Perhaps five people had died during the journey. The survivors would soon disperse to stay with families in the city until they could find the means to have homes of their own.[33]

CHAPTER 14

THE FINAL COMPANIES

1860

Having worked for the Church of Jesus Christ of Latter-day Saints in England for years, Mark Forscutt finally took his chance to immigrate to America in 1860, the last time handcarts were used to cross the plains. Four years earlier he had been attracted to fellow Englishwoman Sarah Moulton, but she had married soon after arriving in Utah with the Willie Handcart Company of 1856. So, before setting sail, Forscutt "Went to Bolton, Saw Elizabeth Unsworth and attained her consent and her mothers' to marry me and go to America With me." As he had done throughout much of his work as a missionary for the church, Forscutt regularly wrote in his journal. The seas were calm as they set off for America on April 16, 1860. The men spent time on deck, there was dancing, and in the afternoon they buried a five-month-old baby in the sea. Two days later a young man married a woman twenty years his senior. "An aged Swiss woman who had been in a decline for a long time" was buried. The sailors claimed that the eighty-four-year-old Swiss man who died the following day was a "Jonah" because the calm conditions that had kept them from making much forward progress changed to a "favorable wind" shortly after they committed his body to the ocean.[1]

By early June Forscutt and the Ninth Handcart Company led by Daniel Robison were in Florence, Nebraska, where rations were distributed, including ham and bacon. They held one meeting and prayer session in the Bowery, but on June 2 the company met in the warehouse at Florence for final instructions and preparations.[2] Robison's Company included 233 people, 43 carts and 10 tents, and 33 oxen, which gave them a larger contingent of wagons than in earlier handcart companies.[3]

It took Hannah Lapish three years to reach Florence, Nebraska, in 1860 where her handcart journey would begin. She and her husband, Joseph, had sailed from Liverpool on May 30, 1857, on the *Tuscarora*. They reached Philadelphia on July 3, 1857. With the economy unsettled, however, Joseph set off with some companions for Richmond, Virginia, to seek employment. Hannah and her three-month-old baby, Laura Jane, remained in Philadelphia. She took in sewing from a knitting factory for a three-month period until she could join Joseph in Richmond.

While the Lapishes lived in Richmond, the raid that spurred the American Civil War occurred at Harper's Ferry. Soon afterward Mormon elder George Q. Cannon encouraged them to leave for the West "as war in the East seemed inevitable. . . . We were told to leave by hook or by crook and I have always claimed that we left by the latter," Hannah would later say.[4]

Mary Ann Stucki was only six when her Swiss family sailed from England on the ship *William Tapscott* on May 11, 1860. It took just over a month to cross the Atlantic and dock in New York on June 16. In their company were 731 Mormons, including 312 from Scandinavia and 85 from Switzerland.[5] Crossing overland by rail and on rivers from New York to Florence, Nebraska, the family was often hungry. Samuel Stucki, a thirty-six-year-old Swiss, spoke German but no English, making it difficult for the family to obtain necessary supplies. Magdalena Stettler Stucki (thirty-seven) carried the infant Christian. She also cared for three-year-old Rosina, six-year-old Mary Ann, and nine-year-old John.

Hanna Lapish and her daughters Laura Jane, who was not yet three, and six-month-old Emily Virginia also set off for Zion. "Try to imagine if you can a mother with a babe at her breast undertaking a journey of hundreds of miles on foot," Hannah later said. "But even that babe seemed to understand something of the life going on about her. Why, do you know that if she were in the middle of enjoying her dinner and she heard that bugle blow, she would stop, for she knew she must be put into the cart. I couldn't carry her—indeed no, and she certainly knew it."[6]

Thirty-eight-year-old Oscar Orlando Stoddard, a native New Yorker, who had only been baptized into the church in 1856, managed the Tenth Handcart company, a group of 126 people. The members of this final company set off from Florence, Nebraska, on July 6, 1860, with 22 handcarts and 6 wagons, a month behind Robison's company. Stoddard had spent the latter half of 1859 and the first half of 1860 in Michigan on a short-term mission for the church. After leaving Salt Lake City on May 7, 1859, he had reached Kalamazoo, Michigan, on August 18, 1859. He remained in Kalamazoo perhaps a week before roaming through Michigan to baptize converts for the church. By late spring 1860 he relocated to Florence, Nebraska, where he organized the carts, supplies, and other resources that would be needed by the final group of handcart travelers.[7]

Upon reaching Florence the members of the Stucki family discovered that they would travel to Utah by walking and pushing and pulling a handcart. "So instead of better times ahead of us our hardships increased as my parents had three small children to haul in the handcart," John said.

There was no room for much except a very little clothing and bedding and as there were no team and wagon outfits, except to haul about half enough provisions for the large handcart company, we were told that they could not take those large boxes that my parents had filled with their good clothing and bedding. They could not be put in the small handcart with the three little children in it so father went to see if he could find someone who could talk German as he wished to find someone that could interpret for him and then try to sell those boxes filled with good clothing for a little something. He could not find anyone to interpret and we had to leave them there without getting a cent for them.[8]

Not far into the journey Magdalena Stucki's feet were so sore that she could barely walk. "Sometimes when we camped she was so far behind the Company we would not see anything of her for quite a while," John recalled, "so that I was afraid she might not be able to get to the Camp." Besides fatigue, the family suffered from poor nutrition, as rations were cut in half. Because Magdalena was nursing the baby and was weak, Samuel gave a portion of his food to her, but this ultimately affected his own endurance. "This shortage of food together with having the three children with everything else we had in the handcart, made it too heavy for [father] to pull alone," John recalled. "In this hungry and nearly worn-out condition, I have never forgotten how when I, a nine year old boy, would be so tired that I would wish I could sit down for just a few minutes [knowing] how much good it would do to me, but instead of that my dear, nearly worn-out father would ask me if I could not push a little more on the Handcart," John remembered. "I will never forget how hungry I was all the time."

Early in the journey Samuel Stucki bought a cow that would provide milk for the children. He constructed a rope harness and hitched the cow to the cart to pull it along. While the cow had never worked as a draft animal, Samuel soon had her broken to pull, significantly aiding the family in the daily movement. One day, however, the handcart company met a band of Indians. John recalled:

> They had their tent poles tied in bunches with the little ends tied to the sides of the horses with great packs, back of the horses, tied on the long, dragging poles of buffalo hides with different kinds of ugly looking things which they dragged along close by the side of us. This scared the cow so badly that she jumped and tore around till she got loose from father. Then she ran away with the handcart and three little children in it for quite a long ways. Then she got the handcart turned upside down with the three little children under it and the bows were all broken off.

Samuel and Magdalena feared that "some of the children might have gotten their arms or legs broken or perhaps [been] killed, but to our great relief [they] found that none of them were seriously hurt," John remembered.

Samuel repaired the bows on the cart and made a different rope halter for the cow that he believed would provide more control. But when the handcart travelers met another large "army of Indians," the cow spooked again. "She took such an awful sidejumps that she got loose from father again and ran as fast as she could go until she turned the handcart upside down again," John wrote. As before, the three small children in the cart were uninjured, but Samuel dared not risk a third accident with the cow. So he worked out a deal with three Danish boys, allowing them to use the cow in pulling their cart in exchange for assistance from one of the boys each day.

Twenty-six-year-old Henry James Harrison also traveled with Robison's Ninth Handcart Company. The traveling was steady from June 6 until June 22, when the party "met some Breathren from the [Salt Lake] Valey," Harrison recorded in his diary. "We had a Meating in the Evening with Good enstructions by Joseph W. Young an after Meating we Had fidling an Dancing an the [people] all enjoid themselves." Two days later, on June 24, the travelers held a morning meeting with a teacher who "came around to know how Your standing was in the Church." Later that afternoon they held another "Testemoney Meating." During the evening Mark H. Forscutt led a gathering where he spoke about the "Baptisiaum for the ded." On July 6 Mary McIntyre McAllister "was confind in the night with a Girl which delaid us in this place," Harrison wrote. Late that night a "Company of Preachers" arrived in the camp. The following day they "met a Company of Mule Trains from the other side of the Valey goin East." All this makes it very clear that the road was busy with people traveling both east and west.[9]

Isabella Siddoway and Hannah Lapish remembered how difficult the traveling was, especially on their feet. Siddoway was ten when she immigrated to Utah with her father, Robert, and two small brothers, Richard (eight) and Robert (six). Her mother, also named Isabella, had died in Pennsylvania. "The journey being longer than we expected, our clothing and provisions grew very scanty long before we reached our destination," Isabella recalled in her autobiography. "Our shoes were so badly worn that, at night, after a long days walk over the rough ground I would have to bathe the pebbles from my little brother's torn and bleeding feet as well as my own."[10] "The trail was marked with blood," Hannah Lapish remembered. "When my shoes wore out I got some Indian Mocasins and they were wet through and through many times—wet not with water but with blood. We handcart people will never outlive the memory of those experiences."[11]

While on the plains, the travelers successfully killed two buffalo. The meat was divided among the members of the Tenth Company. Both Mary Ann and John Stucki later recalled that their portion was placed in the handcart and their father decided that they would wait to eat it on the Sunday following the kill. It is not clear whether they cooked the meat to preserve it before placing it in the cart. As John walked along pushing the cart from behind, "the meat smelled so good to me while pushing at the handcart, and having a little pocketknife, I could not resist, but had to cut off a piece or two each half day. Although I was afraid of getting a severe whipping after cutting a little the first few times, I could not resist taking a little each half day. I would chew it so long it got perfectly tasteless." When his father pulled the meat out for Sunday dinner, "he asked me if I had been cutting off some of the meat," John recalled. "I said 'yes,' that I was so hungry that I could not let it alone. Then instead of giving me the severe scolding and whipping he did not say a word but started to wipe the tears from his eyes."[12]

Some additional provisions were forthcoming at Fort Laramie. With little left to eat, Hannah Lapish said that she "left the rest of the company" when they reached the fort "and went to a store where I offered the proprietors my jewelry in exchange for a little flour which at that time and place was $10.00 per hundred [pounds]. I soon observed that he was not going to make the exchange and as I turned around I saw a very tall man, perhaps a trapper or miner, dressed in beaded buckskin suit standing [in] the store." When this man asked what Lapish wanted for the jewelry, she told him "700 pounds of flour, Sir." He took the jewelry and later had the flour delivered to the camp. This supply was carefully doled out as the travelers continued west. "This so greatly increased our food suply and last us until we were met by a relief party at Green River," Isabella Siddoway said. She reported only one death on the overland crossing, "that of a very small child."[13]

Perhaps this was the three-year-old son of Rachel Smith Robison who would later recall that "our little son Johnny" was taken by the "grim reaper." Robison traveled with the wagons but walked most of the trip and was an excellent observer of the handcart travelers. She said the "carts were painted beautifully[;] the tongue had a cross piece about 2½ feet long fastened to the end, and it was against this cross piece the people leaned their weight. They called this pushing instead of pulling. . . . It was a common thing to see young women between the ages of 16 and 20 with a harness over their shoulders shaped like a harness then fastened to the tongue of the cart. Some 4 or 5 pushing and pulling all day long through the hot dry sand with hardly enough food to keep life in their bodies."[14]

Some of Robison's preparations helped the company get through. "Before starting on our journey across that baron waste desert I made noodles and [dried] them, these I shared with the sick, I also made yeast cake, and light dough bread, all the way across the plains," Robison recalled. Despite of her preparation, food supplies dwindled and clothing and shoes wore out. "It became a more daily occurance to see women, as their shoes dropped from their feet, bare footed leading their barefooted children by the hand through the scorching sand." Despite these difficulties Robinson remained faithful, "When ever we camped we always had prayer and song and every body seemed happy and contented with having given up their wealth and comfort for the Gospel."[15]

Mark Forscutt, who used a form of shorthand in his journal for several weeks, but returned to writing in standard English in early July, chronicled the good and the bad, such as "good spring water boiling from the sand about 100 yards from road good grass, weeds & buffalo chips but swarming with mosquitoes the people had scarcely any sleep in consequence."[16]

Some of the travelers were more intent on chronicling the spiritual aspects of their trek. Robert Stoney (twenty-five) and his twenty-three-year-old wife Sarah Jakeman Stoney along with their infant daughter, Sarah, traveled with Robison's Company. Robert Stoney was the appointed captain of the fourth group of eight handcarts. In his journal he wrote regularly of the sacrament meetings, the prayers offered, and how "the Spirit of God rested upon us." When Indians visited the camp seeking to "trade or to beg or steal. . . . Sarah bought me a par of mcc [moccasins] for about 2 lbs of bread." The Indians also traded guns and buffalo robes to the Mormon travelers. Although none of the women wrote of the prairie flowers, Robert Stoney noted that "the prairie smells very sweet as sweet as any English Garden. [It is] covered with pretty flowers." Later he wrote of a beautiful night: "The Aurora Borealis or northerun lights were seen very Clear."[17]

Traveling across Nebraska, Robert Stoney wrote of meetings with Sioux Indians, efforts to kill a buffalo and antelope, and personal issues arising in camp. "When Bro. [Joseph] Slater and Sis. Webb who were summoned to . . . answer to the Charge of Adultery . . . proof was [found] that they had slept together. It was agreed that they be excommunicated from the Church on account of their Lies." Expelling members of the company was not altogether uncommon. Weeks later in Wyoming Demas Ashdown Saunders was forced to leave the camp for neglecting his duties. Richard Gough (thirty-one) was "suspended for one week" after he called the captain a liar. Stoney wrote that if Gough did not "ask forgiveness" he would be cut off from the church. That same day Alice Metcalf Long was suspended for insulting the captain. "She will be dealt with on the same terms," Stoney wrote. Within the week "Bro. Richard Gough & [Alice] Long came & acknowledged thier fault & asked forgiveness." At the same time Samuel Crook and John Townsend also asked forgiveness "for speaking against the Captain. Bro. Crook for threatening to shoot him."

Weeks behind the Ninth Company, the Tenth Company washed clothes as the men hauled company possessions across the North Platte River when they reached Fort Laramie. "We hitched up all rady and drove one wagon over, unladed it, came back and took in the loads of the hand-carts and then went over with them, leaving the empty carts to haul over by hand," Oscar Stoddard wrote, "I helping to haul over the first one myself, none but the men hauling (carts) over the river." He added: "The women and children were hauled over in the wagons and we were over and in camp two miles up the river at sundown."[18] As with the Ninth Company, the Tenth Company's food supplies were running low when Stoddard received a letter from church immigration agent George Q. Cannon telling him that fourteen sacks of flour would be available when the handcart company reached Three Crossings of the Sweetwater, which was indeed the case when the party arrived.

Sometimes jubilation got out of hand. One day the handcart travelers encountered some wagon travelers from Great Salt Lake, who were camped not far from their camp. During the evening "they came back and spent the evening with us, enjoying themselves as young people will, between ten and eleven o'clock, when they started for [their] camp and feeling jolly, harrahed, fired off pistols, shouted etc and the Danish Saints, having gone to bed in a tent and all asleep, being suddenly aroused, by the uproar, were frightened and some one shouted 'Indians' which created a panic and a rush was made for the tent door to get outside." As one of the Danes, a small man lying at the tent door, started to go with the rest, he was "trampled under foot till the tent was cleared when he found himself free, but with a shoulder out of joint with the knuckle below the socket. The next morning, one of the brethren by using his knee as a lever, tried to pull his arm out and pry the shoulder in place. After three or four unsuccessful attempts, he begged him to stop as he could stand the pulling no longer." Stoddard was summoned and found the man with his arm in a sling. "We managed to get him on the camp pony and let him ride along the road as the camp moved along, till we camped at night."

That night Stoddard "anointed [the man's] shoulder as well as his head with consecrated oil and . . . prayed for the muscles and sinews to relax that the joint may have room to get to its place." He told the man to "go to bed and to sleep and if you will have faith you will wake up in the morning with your shoulder in place." The following morning the man's shoulder was back in the socket.

The traveling was particularly difficult for Magdalena Stucki. As Mary Ann Stucki would later write, "She would get so discouraged and down-hearted; but father never lost courage. He would always cheer her up by telling her that we were going to Zion, that the Lord would take care of us, and that better times were coming."[19] Indeed, conditions could improve in surprising ways. Reaching the Sweetwater River, the Robison Company had the "welcome treat" of finding the river "literally full of fish and every one had all they could eat. As we had had no meat of any kind excepting salty bacon since we started our tedious journey at Florence Nebraska, these fish were indeed a most welcome treat," Rachel Robison recalled. On down the trail the company camped at the mouth of Echo Canyon, where a small town called Henefer had emerged. "Here we camped for two days Mr. Henefer donated to us five bushels of potatoes, if we would dig them. The Weber River was full of fish so [after] the potatoes were dug and the fish were caught (and cooked) every one had a feast."[20]

When the Ninth Company reached the Weber River on August 24, Daniel Robison wrote to Brigham Young saying the last of the provisions had been distributed that morning: a pound and a quarter of flour and a quarter pound of bacon for each person. "We shall not be able to reach the City before Monday, and quite a number will [be] out of provisions to night as they had to breakfast this morning out of what was served to them. If therefore you can send out some more provisions, it would be a relief and a blessing to us."[21] As they neared Big Mountain, a nearby settler "sent seven yoke of oxen down to pull the carts to the top of the mountain."[22]

The Ninth Handcart Company reached Salt Lake City on August 27, 1860, after spending nearly three months on the road and recording only one death. The Tenth Company finally rolled into Great Salt Lake City a month later, on September 24. This party led by Oscar Stoddard, which recorded no deaths, would be the last to use the "two-wheeled torture devices" to cross the plains.[23]

EPILOGUE
"A day of reckoning in the future"

At least 2,927 people traveled overland to Utah with handcarts; between 250 and 300 of them died, the majority in the disastrous crossings by the Edward Martin Company and the James Grey Willie Company in 1856. All but one company recorded deaths in the overland crossing. By most accounts the greatest contributing factor was starvation. Overland trail travelers simply could not haul enough in their small carts to support themselves. They had too few wagons to carry goods. Their resources were never adequate for people who were for the most part walking and drawing their own carts and therefore expending great energy in the daily travel. They also suffered from the weather: blistering heat, drenching rain, high wind, and for more than a third of them (literally hundreds) freezing temperatures, icy river crossings, and snowstorms.

Most handcart immigrants wrote of immense buffalo herds in Nebraska and their inability to kill the animals and harvest meat for their own use. Some were successful, but most were too frightened by the big herds to approach and hunt them. They feared any attack might set off a stampede that would trample their carts and their families. Realistically, many of them were not skilled hunters; most came from England, where hunting was a sport for the nobility, not for commoners. Little documentary evidence suggests that they even had many weapons with them to shoot and kill such big animals as bison, although they recorded the successful hunting of a few prairie chickens and antelope. Some of the travelers caught fish in the rivers they followed and the creeks they crossed.

People in all handcart groups lacked adequate supplies, clothing, and footwear. The Martin Company had six teams to haul provisions, which were loaded "to the bows" with supplies, mainly flour, Josiah Rogerson later recalled. "We lacked very much in Tea, sugar, yeast powders, Bacon, and salt; which gave out, or nearly so even before we reached the Red Buttes."[1] Rogerson reflected on how it might have been different. "Our ration of flour would have gone a great deal farther, and done our bodies much more good if–we could have had something to rise it with," he said, "and lives would have been saved, if we could have had a few ounces of Cayenne pepper, with a little warming medicine, something to arrest excessive diarrhea, and a few gallons of good brand[y] or liquor, to have revived the spirits of many who died from sheer exhaustion and Cold!"

The purely physical demands on the people also contributed to their weakness, in many cases to outright death. This was true even of able-bodied men. As Rogerson noted, "If less night guarding had been done, from Laramie to the Devil's Gate, and even from Iowa City to Florence, and from Florence to Devil's Gate, the death list, would not have been so great by several, large able bodied men, who seemed at the Commencement of the Journey, able to endure anything." He added: "After a man had pulled a hand Cart 20–25 and 30 miles in a day, to go, and tramp around on guard from sundown til midnight, every other night, and sometimes oftener, is more than mortal bone and Sinew Can stand."

Most involved with the Martin Company at the time or analyzing its disastrous crossing to Salt Lake later might agree with Rogerson. "The winter setting in at least a month earlier than usual," he said, "and the mistake of starting us a month too late from Winter Quarters, are the main causes of that calamity." There is little to support the claim by church officials, and even Rogerson, that winter was early. Most would agree, however, that the conditions that winter were extremely difficult. The first significant snowstorm that year swept across Wyoming on October 19. Even in more recent times it is not unusual, and in fact almost expected, for a major storm to hit in Wyoming by mid-October.

Writing to her family, Elizabeth Sermon, who lost her husband and had to amputate the flesh from her sons' feet after they froze, was far more critical. "One after another passed away," she said. "Fathers, mothers, sisters, brothers, families and friends, all . . . through some misguided scheme and speculations, which will, some day have to be atoned for. Many, many honest souls laid away in Mother Earth—for what!" At one point, she remembered, the captains called the people together "and stated we must lay our bodies down [die] and [asked] were we willing to do so for the Gospel's sake." Elizabeth recalled years later that the answer from "many poor, starved men" was yes, but "mothers could not say that, and so leave their children, and were quiet." She added that "food would have suited us better [than preaching] for we did not think all together about religion, but my faith was still in my Father in Heaven. I have never lost my faith in Him."[2]

Others, such as John Chislett, suspected that the blame for such misfortunes rested higher up in the church. "Whether Brigham was influenced in his desire to get the poor of Europe more rapidly to Utah by his sympathy with their condition, by his well-known love of power, his glory in numbers, or his love of wealth, which an increased amount of subservient labour would enable him to acquire, is best known to himself," he wrote bitterly, remembering his journey of 1856. "But the sad results of his Hand-Cart scheme will call for a day of reckoning in the future which he cannot evade."[3]

CODA
Legacy of the Handcarts

Thomas de Beau Soleil, a French Canadian who came west with a trapper named Dakota, ultimately took the name Tom Sun and staked a mining claim in southern Carbon County, Wyoming Territory, in 1873. Seven years later he filed a homestead claim on land along the Sweetwater River at Devil's Gate, at the site of the Martin Company disaster. Sun was one of 1.6 million people who claimed more than 270 million acres in the West under the Homestead Act, which President Abraham Lincoln signed into law in 1862. Sun completed the task of "proving up" by fulfilling all requirements for homestead land ownership within three years, swearing in his homestead affidavit that he had developed the land, dug irrigation ditches, and raised crops, including potatoes, oats, hay, alfalfa, and other vegetables.

Sun's Hub and Spoke Ranch spanned what had been the main "highway" to the west during the middle decades of the nineteenth century. More than half a million travelers had followed the Oregon, California, Mormon, and Pony Express Trails, all of which crossed the land that Sun claimed. Other homesteaders moved in along the Sweetwater River, but most were comfortably distant from Sun's headquarters.

The Sun family remained on the Sweetwater. They found relics from earlier days, including Indian artifacts and trail-era items. Tom Sun built a solid house and installed a fireplace made up of some of those reminders of earlier times: Indian manos and metates. The headquarters stood near the site of the abandoned Seminoe's Fort, within view of Devil's Gate. The Suns were, in a sense, overseers for the trails, stewards of the history, and sentinels of the graveyard at Martin's Ravine, which was located on public land adjacent to the ranch holdings.

That ravine (or cove as it is now called) was a place of refuge for the Martin Handcart Company of 1856. The sheltering rocks may have saved some of those struggling handcart pioneers, But it was also the site where others took their last breaths. As the sesquicentennial of the Mormon Trail approached in the mid-1990s, the Church of Jesus Christ of Latter-day Saints made a deal with the Sun family to purchase a large portion of the historic ranch, giving the church access to the area where so many had suffered and died. As church president Gordon B. Hinckley told a large crowd on May 3, 1997, the area was sacred ground for the Mormon people. "We [sought] to know God on that trail," Hinckley said of the "terribly tedious and tragic journey" made by the Martin and Willie Companies. "We're standing on hallowed ground," Hinckley told the gathering, "made sacred by the sacrifices of those who go before us." He encouraged those in attendance to walk the trail "in a spirit of reverence and respect and know that you are walking on hallowed ground." Recognizing that too many people could irreparably change a fragile landscape, he admonished, "stay on those paths. . . . This ground must always hold for us a feeling of great sanctity."[1]

Martin's Ravine was not part of the Sun Ranch lands. Instead it is federal property, having never been deeded to private hands under the Homestead Act. For decades it was difficult to reach the site, however, because access to the cove crossed Sun Ranch property. Although the family had long been supportive of the trails and allowed organized groups such as members of the Oregon-California Trails Association to visit the trail segments that were on their land, individuals who wanted to experience the trail setting in that area could not easily do so. The first formal highway through the area had obliterated some of the trail remnants, paving over the route used by wagon-bound and handcart-pushing travelers from 1843 to 1869. But the area across the river and along the base of the Rattlesnake Range remained much as it had been in 1856.

After purchasing the Sun Ranch headquarters, the Church of Jesus Christ of Latter-day Saints controlled access to the significant area where members of Martin's party had been delayed for those few final, brutal days in early November 1856 before they resumed their walk west. Determined to have access and control of a site so significant to its history, the church subsequently negotiated a controversial long-term lease for the property with the U.S. Bureau of Land Management, the agency charged with managing federal lands in the area.

With control of the area, the Mormons developed a visitor center near Devil's Gate, which tells the story of the handcart migration, specifically concentrating on the Willie Company and Martin Company difficulties of 1856. Trails from the Mormon visitor center (in the original Sun ranch house) follow along the Sweetwater and cross over to what is assumed to be Martin's Cove/Ravine. Archaeologists excavated the original Seminoe's Fort site after the church bought the ranch land. A replica of the fort stands nearby. Two campgrounds are heavily used throughout the summer as thousands of church members, many of them youth groups, come to push and pull their own handcarts and relive a bit of the legacy of their church and, for many of them, their ancestors.

LDS ownership also means that anyone from the general public can visit the area's trail sites. Access is associated with controversy, however. The church attempted to purchase the federal land that contains the general area of Martin's Cove, but that deal fell through following strong opposition in Congress. In 2003 Congress authorized a twenty-five-year lease agreement between the Bureau of Land Management and the church, at an annual lease fee of $16,000. Two years later the American Civil Liberties Union (ACLU) filed a lawsuit in federal court on behalf of four Wyoming residents who claimed that the deal violated constitutional rights by "endorsing religion." The suit claimed that the twenty-five-year lease on 933 acres of public land gave the church "complete and unfettered control over both an important federally owned historic site and the message that visitors to the site receive."[2]

Susan M. Wozny of Laramie, Wyoming, one of four individuals who brought the lawsuit against the church, alleged that when she went to the area Mormon guides questioned her about her religious affiliation and that she was prohibited from visiting some of the public land sections at the site. LDS members, she said, told her it was "sacred" and "hallowed ground." The lawsuit alleged that "the church has been given the go-ahead to create on federal property a Mormon shrine that incorporates the church's own historical and religious interpretation of the events that occurred in Martin's Cove."[3] The lawsuit was settled out of court in 2006 when the church and BLM agreed that they would provide separate entrance points and signage providing information that would clearly identify public land and public access.[4] There have been no further challenges.

Since 1997 the church has obtained other land farther west along the trail route and along the Sweetwater River, opening the region to further exploration of the historic places by young and old handcart trekkers, among others. The church built a visitor's center in 2013 near Sweetwater Station to tell the story of the Willie Company, their difficult days at the Sixth Crossing of the Sweetwater before the rescue parties found them, their subsequent crossing of Rocky Ridge, and the deadly day at Rock Creek. This center focuses on the story of the Thomas Moulton family.[5]

Although only about 3,000 people traveled the Mormon Trail from Iowa City and Florence to Great Salt Lake City by handcart from 1856 to 1860, the handcart story has become an icon of great faith for millions of members of the Church of Jesus Christ of Latter-day Saints.

"MY ADVANTAGES FOR WRITING ARE VERY MEAGRE"

More than 150 years after the first Mormon pioneers traveled overland to the Great Salt Lake, their journey was re-created, though not in the agonizing manner of the original handcart migration, when people suffered exposure to profound cold and excruciating heat as well as a lack of food, warm clothing, and other supplies. The people who took part in a 1996 wagon train from Nauvoo, Illinois, to Florence, Nebraska, and those who followed the trail in 1997 from Florence to Salt Lake City set off to reenact the trek along the 150-year-old Mormon Trail. For many, it was also a journey of faith and an opportunity to recognize ancestors. The sesquicentennial crossing marked Brigham Young's vanguard wagon train of 1847, but the modern journey was expanded to include recognition of all Mormon pioneers, including the handcart travelers.

In 1857 Amos Musser, who traveled with the William G. Young wagon train to Utah, wrote about keeping a record of the journey: "my advantages for writing are very meagre. A crammed portfolio for a desk, an inverted wash-tub for a seat, and surrounded by a parcel of loquacious emigrants, discussing their success, and other matters of the day, while their hands are employed in performing the varied paraphernalia of a camp life."[6]

When I traveled with the sesquicentennial wagon train and wrote about its 1997 crossing, conditions were little changed, though I had reporter's notebooks and many pens. I did most of my writing sitting in the back of Ben Kern's wagon or inside the range tent that we shared. Sometimes, when the wind was strong or the mosquitoes particularly pesky, I retreated into the back of the horse trailer, which had its own unique odors of horse manure and livestock feed. Each day as I wrote the life of camp went on around me: children running and playing or bouncing on the tongue of the wagon; women sewing; men visiting; young women and men dancing to Jonathan Dew's fiddle music. The families on the 1997 wagon train did not have to cook their meals, although some did make a breakfast of oatmeal. Food preparation and the availability of supplies were simpler (and more reliable) than 150 years before.

I filed stories daily to run in the *Casper Star-Tribune*, sending them to the newspaper using modern technology: a computer upload from a recreational vehicle provided by the Mormon organization. I wondered what would Amos Musser have thought.

Organizing a wagon train in the late twentieth century presented challenges far different from similar organization in the mid-nineteenth century. For example, a modern-day wagon train would need to negotiate cities, highways, and railroad tracks. It would need to work with private landowners, federal land management agencies, and authorities in three states to travel from Florence, Nebraska, to Salt Lake City. For the sesquicentennial of the Mormon Pioneer Trail in 1997, the church engaged the services of men experienced in managing all those challenges, foremost among them Joe Vogel of Red Cloud, Nebraska; Ben Kern of Evansville, Wyoming; and Robert Lowe of Salt Lake City, Utah. These men would serve as wagon masters in their respective states and manage the day-to-day travel of a combined wagon train and handcart company.

The wagonmasters would determine the route, all arrangements for campsites, and the infrastructure needed for a mobile camp. They anticipated and had to accommodate basic needs, including twenty portable toilets, routine pumping of those facilities, and purchase of more than 150 tons of hay to feed the horses and mules needed for pulling wagons and as mounts for outriders. Working with church authorities, they arranged for a veterinarian to travel with the wagon train, for the cooks and all the necessary food, for emergency medical technicians, and for personnel and means to deal with the media, among other tasks.

The Sesquicentennial Mormon Trail Wagon Train and Handcart Company organized itself at Cutler Park in Florence, Nebraska, in April 1997. Participants came from across the United States and from around the world. They were predominantly Mormon, but a few individuals who were not members of the church also participated, mainly due to their experience in traveling by wagon. These included wagon masters Vogel and Kern, plus Russell Ledger of Plattsmouth, Nebraska, who started a wagon train in Nebraska City, which then followed the Ox-Bow Trail to Fort Kearny, where it merged with the main group.

Governor Ben Nelson of Nebraska and Hugh Pinnock, a member of the First Quorum of Seventy and president of the North American Central Area of the Church of Jesus Christ of Latter-day Saints, addressed the Sesquicentennial Wagon Train in a dedication ceremony at the Mormon Trail Visitor Center in Florence on April 18, 1997. Pinnock spoke of the first leg of the Mormon Trail from Nauvoo, Illinois, to Winter Quarters (Florence, Nebraska) in 1846. Some of the participants in the 1997 reenactment had followed the Mormon Trail from Nauvoo to Florence a year earlier and understood the difficult trail across present-day Iowa.

"I've thought a little bit about sacrifice lately," Pinnock told the hundreds assembled at the visitor center. "To live is to sacrifice, to sacrifice is to testify to our commitment." Pinnock urged those assembled in 1997 to "never lose sight of reminding ourselves, 'Why did they do it? Why did they go on the trail? Why did they stay on the trail?'" Ultimately the answer to that question, the church leader said, is that they were "unquestioningly following the prophet." He added that not only did the wagon and handcart pioneers believe in Brigham Young but that "burned in their hearts [was belief] that the church was true."[7]

Church president Gordon B. Hinckley also addressed the people as they prepared to set off on the 1,131-mile journey across the route of the original Mormon road, reflecting on the deadly legacy of the trail itself. "Many [early Mormon travelers] died along the way. They were buried on the banks of the Mississippi and on the banks of the Missouri and hundreds died here and hundreds more . . . on the trail [to Salt Lake

City]." The church president urged the wagon train participants to "remember them for their courage, their commitment ... and for the sacrifice they made ... to found a great commonwealth in the valley of the Rocky Mountains."

As the wagon train made final preparations to leave Florence, Joe Vogel, the Nebraska wagon master, confided his concerns: "You've got a lot of people here who are going to go on a wagon train for the first time. ... I just hope there's enough people with enough experience," to help them learn the ropes of harnessing, hitching, driving, camping, and literally living on the trail. In that respect, nothing was much different than for travelers in 1856. The biggest challenge Vogel said that he faced was to make sure the handcarts and the individuals walking with them kept up with the wagons, which, pulled by mules and horses, moved along more quickly. "The biggest concern is the walkers. There's no question about that," he said. His apprehension mirrored that of wagon train and handcart company leaders in the 1850s.

As they had done in the nineteenth century, travelers came from around the world to travel overland to Utah and came for varied reasons. Bre Cornell of Salt Lake City summed up the motivation for most, "We continue pioneering the future as well as paying tribute to the past."

Eighteen-year-old Jonathan Dew of Utah crossed the trail in honor of his ancestor Andrew Anderson, who had traveled the trail in 1859. "I've just always admired the courage of people who did something new, who could stand up for their rights." This young man walked all the way from Florence to Utah, pushing and pulling a handcart. Elizabeth Pietsch of Vienna, Austria, demonstrated an attitude similar to that of some nineteenth-century European immigrants. When her seventy-two-year-old husband, Freddy, said he wanted to travel with the sesquicentennial wagon train in honor of Austrians and the church body there, she did what pioneer women had done. She followed her husband on the trail. "I want to be with him," she said in western Nebraska. "It is more than I had expected. It was hard in the beginning. So hot in the tent, so cold, so muddy, so windy," Elizabeth said. "We prayed a lot in this time to be healthy. The beautiful side is the experience. It's a great [wagon train] family, very kind people. ... We have no pioneers in our family, but we feel like pioneers."

Just as the handcart immigrants of the 1850s received aid from people along the trail, so too did the travelers in 1997. "People open their home for a shower, saying you can do your laundry in my home," Elizabeth Pietsch said. Freddy Pietsch walked with the handcart company. "He is strong in walking and strong in his faith," added Elizabeth, who also walked much of the way, occasionally taking a break to "step on the wagon."

Osamu Sekiguchi came from Tokyo, Japan, with wife, Takako, and sons Yoji (nine) and Koji (seven). They had no ancestors who traveled the overland trails to Utah, but they undertook the trip for two reasons. Osamu (called Sam by the wagon train travelers) would write about it for Japanese publications and they all would have a chance for new experiences. In Nebraska Sam began helping with the horses. "I'm really enjoying that because I have never touched a horse before," he said. Like Freddy Pietsch, Sam usually walked, while his family alternated between walking and riding on the wagons.

Initially Sam had no desire to follow the trail but instead tried to find some other Japanese representative to travel with the train. His wife, however, was interested in the journey. They had read about it: "we were so impressed and especially we were impressed with pioneer children. At that time I thought it was too difficult for my children to walk." Seeking an opportunity for the boys to "learn patient, family ties" the Sekiguchis came to America. "In Japan we have never seen this kind of landscape at all. We didn't care about the weather." While on the wagon train "we are always watching the weather. We are watching the sky. [The boys] are really getting something from nature."

Although Sam spoke English, his family was fluent only in Japanese. Overcoming the language barrier, his boys made friends and communicated with the American children on the wagon train. Just a few weeks into a three-month journey, Sam said that he had already seen many changes in his sons. "When I was in Japan, I thought they were just kids. I have learned they are small, but they are not little kids."

Brian Hill, a Mormon from Nebraska who helped organize the sesquicentennial wagon train, wanted to ensure that all those traveling felt welcome. He did this in part because "I think of my fifty ancestors who walked this route and who came through here and who had no welcome."

Crossing Nebraska, the sesquicentennial wagon train had twenty-seven wagons, ten handcarts, and about two hundred people each day. (By the time the wagon train ended some 10,000 people had participated.) In Fremont, Nebraska, one driver broke the tongue of his wagon when a railroad crossing bar came down unexpectedly; in the sand ruts near Paxton, Nebraska, another wagon tipped onto its side in a piece of rough, original trail.

Upon reaching Henry, Nebraska, on the far western side of the state, wagon master Joe Vogel was relieved that the horses and mules remained in good shape; there had been incidents but no runaways or serious wrecks on the journey to that point. The handcart company had managed to stay with the wagons as the train rolled west. As it turned out, Vogel admitted that his biggest challenge had been "putting down all the gossip" and dealing with "four or five high critics."

Heavy rain at Henry, Nebraska, turned the sesquicentennial wagon train camp into a quagmire, leaving everyone challenged to find a place to pitch tents and roll out bedrolls. But there was no dampening of spirit as Nebraska wagon master Vogel handed off to Wyoming wagon master Ben Kern. Wyoming governor James Geringer was on hand for the symbolic transfer of the wagon train (a set of reins given by Vogel to Kern), noting: "There are two types of people here tonight, those who are with the wagon train and those who wish they were." The Wyoming governor acknowledged the "vision of the people who went before us who had a faith that was unshaken" and gave Kern a bit of advice. With a nod to the way a bronc rider might prepare for a ride, he said: "Take a deep seat, a short rein, and let 'er buck."

The Mormon manager Brian Hill, like Russ Leger, remarked on the spirit of the trail itself. "We have felt the power of the trail and the power of those who have gone before." The people in the forty wagons and pulling the dozen handcarts that would cross into Wyoming "are a community, a moving community," Hill said. This sense of community had manifested itself with the nineteenth-century handcart companies as well. The people drew together for support and assistance, when carts were broken and needed repairs or when someone perished and the living consoled each other.

The modern wagons and handcarts that had traveled ten or twelve miles a day across Nebraska would now face new challenges. Not only does the trail terrain become more difficult in Wyoming, but fewer towns meant that campsites had to be spaced farther apart, which in turn meant longer drives each day. Travelers felt the abrupt change immediately. The first day in Wyoming the wagons covered thirty miles from the border town of Henry, Nebraska, to Fort Laramie. It took more than ten hours for the wagons and even longer for the handcart company to travel that distance. As so often happened in the 1850s, the handcart brigade arrived in camp long after dinner was served, so many in the handcart company went to bed hungry. The next day everyone was challenged by the trek from Fort Laramie, which followed the actual trail twenty-four miles across mostly private property to Guernsey. They arrived there nearly eleven hours later, after descending the steepest hill of the trail to that point.

The train was not only covering more ground each day but also becoming far larger. More than eight hundred people were a part of the moving company, composed of forty wagons, two buggies, sixty-one horseback riders, seventeen handcarts, and hundreds of walkers on the first day out of Fort Laramie. It would remain nearly that large until it reached Casper, when the terrain shifted from crossing mainly private land to traveling on public land.

The Bureau of Land Management had approved a special use permit for the wagon train (something historic handcart and wagon groups never had to obtain). But the permit came with restrictions: no more than thirty wagons and no more than ten handcarts. The restrictions were imposed for safety, the health of the animals, and protection of the trail as a historical resource. BLM archeologists Jude Carino of Casper and Terry Del Bene of Rock Springs would administer the permit. Their primary interest was in allowing public use of public lands while protecting the precious trail remnants. Of major concern was the impact of so many people traveling with the wagon train who moved vehicles—including motor homes, campers, pickups, and horse trailers—from camp to camp. As Del Bene put it, "You won't be able to get your vehicles in and out [of camps] without tearing the guts out of the trail." This archaeologist spent years protecting trail resources in a state that still has more miles of original trail than any other location.[8]

"EVERY SINGLE STEP"

Twenty-two-year-old Mike Dunn of Whittier, California, led the handcart company traveling with the sesquicentennial wagon train. Seventy-six people, ranging in age from four-year-old Jackie Adams to seventy-two-year-old Freddy Pietsch, were part of the handcart company for the 1997 journey from Winter Quarters to Salt Lake City. Twenty-four of them, like Jackie's mother, Nancy Adams, one of the camp emergency medical technicians who made the trip barefoot, "walked every step, every single step." Nearly five hundred more walked with the handcarts or wagons for shorter periods, maybe just a day or two. Upon reaching the end of the trail, Dunn said: "It's been fun. It's been extremely hard. It's been a physical test. It's been a spiritual growth, and it's been a friendship that will last forever."[9]

The greatest challenges came during extremely hot weather, and again when carts had to be pushed and pulled against the Wyoming wind. When the canvas covers on the carts "acted like a sail" they removed them. But every day, they carried a large American flag, the handcart company's symbol that became an inspiration for the entire wagon train.

Russell Leger, who led the Oxbow Company, was not a member of the Church of Jesus Christ of Latter-day Saints. But before entering Wyoming he said: "The Mormon Trail is the legacy of our ancestors who unselfishly pioneered this nation. Engulfed by fear, sorrow, suffering and death, these brave saints fulfilled their destiny and honored their savior." He added: "Their spirits transcend time and beckon us to trace their journey. With each footstep our hearts swell with pride."

At the dedication of the Handcart Ranch in May 1997, John Creer, manager of the Church of Jesus Christ of Latter-day Saints Farm Management Corporation, which would oversee the operations at the Sun Ranch, outlined church goals for the property: people could visit, learn about the handcart migration in a visitors' center, and then walk the trail while pushing and pulling a handcart. "We wanted people to feel it in their bones," Creer said. "To hook up that handcart and pull it up that trail and then into the cove and talk to the people who died there and then back . . . across the river and back to the visitor's center." The intent was to "pass on the legacy . . . to pass on a reverence for this place."

The handcart pioneers were "pushed by faith, pulled by desire," church president Gordon B. Hinckley said during the May 1997 dedication ceremony, leading to "a legacy of faith for all generations."

The 1997 sesquicentennial wagon train involved thousands of people who took part in the reenactment or watched it pass through Nebraska, Wyoming, and Utah. There were serious accidents, amazing rescues, blossoming romances, a birth, laughter, music, tears, and moments of pure joy. Women created a legacy quilt, children wrote accounts that would be used in education programs, and friendships formed that have endured the test of time and remain strong many years after the wagons rolled west.

The last camp on Little Mountain was beautifully situated, with a nearly perfect wagon circle. It provided a last night of quiet solitude along with the realization that the ninety-one-day, 1,131-mile journey was nearly complete. On July 22, 1997, sixty wagons, sixty horseback riders, two dozen handcarts, and eight hundred walkers descended from Little Mountain to the mouth of Emigration Canyon. An estimated twenty thousand people lined the road leading to This Is the Place State Park, where the wagon train held a final commemorative ceremony. The people lining the route held flags, shared food, and saluted the wagon and handcart company.[10]

For those of us on the wagons, the entrance to Salt Lake City eclipsed any greeting along the trail. I rode on the front seat of the Wyoming wagon owned by Ben Kern and driven by Donny Marincic. Also crowded onto the seat was Englishwoman Sue Smith, who opted to ride the last few miles, even though she had walked almost every step of the journey. As we passed the throngs, the swell of emotion grew. We drove by people all in white: men, women, and children of all ages who represented people who had died in making the crossing during the prior century. By the time we made the final circle to the monuments in the park, Donny, Sue, and I had tears rolling down our cheeks. None of us spoke. We couldn't have if we had wanted to. The emotion of the end of the journey, and of the event we had relived, was simply too powerful. The previous day I had crossed Big Mountain walking beside Elizabeth Pietsch of Austria. As we first spied the Salt Lake Valley, I already knew that this trail was more than a news story for me. As a journalist, I had made every effort to remain aloof and impartial, but I lost my objectivity along the way during the three months of travel. I was no longer covering a news story: I was part of it and reporting on an experience.

Elizabeth's emotion at seeing the valley was simply overwhelming. She had never been to America before, and I had the rare privilege of seeing a destination that was Zion to so many in the nineteenth century through the eyes of a woman who had, like those earlier travelers, left the comfort of home and country behind to follow her husband and her faith. It was a profound moment for both of us.[11]

Emily Hodgetts left England in 1856 together with her sister Maria after their mother was forcibly removed from the ship *Horizon* by their father. Maria returned to England when they reached America, while Emily joined her brother, William Ben. He became captain of a wagon train that traveled near the ill-fated Fifth Handcart Company. Although Emily rode a horse and never pulled a handcart, she shared the plight of the Martin Company as they endured the bitter cold from the last crossing of the Platte River to Salt Lake City. With a wagon for her possessions, Emily had four blue crates containing a variety of personal belongings that she had brought from England. These containers were left behind at Seminoe's Fort as the handcart and wagon companies struggled together through the cold and snow. Her brother ultimately retrieved just one of the blue chests, which contained "16 yards of the very best satin which had been bought in Paris, France, by my father to make dresses for Mother and we girls. But in taking things from the ship, it had been left for Maria and me. After Maria went home, I fell heir to this, and I feel I put it to good use. I have had that material made into almost every style from polineau to hobble skirt and have been a well-dressed woman each time. I have worn this satin in some style to the christening of each of my nine children." That chest became a symbol of endurance and fortitude for Emily Hodgetts, a memory of her English roots and the hard overland crossing in 1856. "As to the blue chest," she said, "it has been my shrine and many times I have knelt before it in humbleness and tears."[12]

"The Mormon Trail is an earthly banquet for those who hunger for meaning in their lives," twentieth-century trail traveler Russ Leger said at the end of the 1997 Mormon Trail Sesquicentennial Wagon Train. "Those who anguished here are now comforted by your presence. Listen! Can you hear it? The trail is whispering to your soul."[13]

Perhaps it is not the trail whispering, but rather the souls of those who walked this pathway in the nineteenth century. Like John Chislett, who said that "the sad sad results of [Brigham Young's] Hand-Cart scheme will call for a day of reckoning in the future." The spirits may still seek solace.[14]

COMPANY ROSTERS

All spellings come from the original lists of handcart pioneers. In some cases those lists included ages and other details about the individuals, which are retained, but such details are not available for all people. Notes in brackets were added by the author.

FIRST COMPANY
Captain: Edmund Ellsworth
Departure: June 9, 1856
Arrival: September 26, 1856
Number of Participants: 234
Company Information: The First Handcart Company had about 234 individuals, 55 handcarts, and 3 wagons when it began its journey from the outfitting post at Iowa City, Iowa.

Argyle, [Rebecca] Jane (34), Wife, born England

Argyle, Benjamin (12), born England

Argyle, Frances (5), born England

Argyle, Joseph (14), born England

Argyle, Joseph (37), Gass Meter Maker, born England

Argyle, Lorenzo (3), born England

Argyle, Mary [Jane] (10), born England

Argyle, Priscilla (1), born England

Argyle, James (unknown age)

Armstrong, Eliza Salt (63)

Armstrong, Thomas Columbus (38)

Armstrong, Thomas Columbus, Jr. (13)

Ash, Elizabeth (6 months), born England

Ash, Ellen Matilda (12 months), born England

Ash, John (36), Gun Smith, born England

Ash, Joseph (7), born England

Ash, Sarah (59), Widow, born England

Ash, Sophia (26), Wife, born England

Attley, Cristina Stewart (30)

Attley, Henry William (24)

Bailey, Alfred (17), Silver P[late] Maker, born England

Bailey, James (52), Silver Plate Maker, born England

Bailey, John (21), Cock Dresser, born England

Bailey, Lousa (12), born England

Bailey, Mary Ann (15), born England

Bailey, Thos (19), Whip Maker, born England

Bailey, Mary Ann Woodcock (51)

Baker, Emma (16), born England

Baker, Harriott (11), born England

Baker, George (14)

Baker, Job (15), Groom, born England

Baker, John (19), Groom, born England

Baker, Mary Ann Symonds (45), Widow, born England

Baker, Wilford (5), born England

Baldwin, Annie Matilda (18), Servant, born England

Bates, Mary Ann (21), Dress, born England

Beus, Anne (17)

Beus, James (15)

Beus, John (12)

Beus, Louis Phillipe (6)

Beus, Magdalena (2)

Beus, Marianne Combe (43)

Beus, Mary [or Marie] (5)

Beus, Michael (10)

Beus, Michael (45)

Beus, Paul (9)

Birch, Edward James (2), born England

Birch, Elizabeth Coleman (40), Wife, born
   England

Birch, James (28) [died of diarrhea in
   Wyoming, September 1856]

Birch, Mary Ann (26), Wife, born England

Birch, Mary Ann (6), born England

Birch, Mary Ann Hale (28)

Birch, Thos (7), born England

Birch, Wm. (68), Laborer, born England

Bond, Elizabeth (55), Wife, born England

Bond, Samuel (25), Ship Maker, born
   England

Bond, Samuel (61), Laborer, born England,
   dead

Bond, Wm. (23), Potter, born England

Bourne, James (17), Builder, born England

Bourne, John William (7), born England

Bourne, Louisa (12), born England

Bourne, Margaret (20), born England

Bourne, Margaret Evans (49), Wife, born
   England

Bourne, Mary Ann (22), born England

Bourne, Priscilla (14), born England

Bourne, Thos Bradford (59), Builder, born
   England

Bowen, David (18), Peddler, Wales

Bowers, Abraham (15), Glass Polisher, born
   England

Bowers, Isaac (14), born England

Bowers, Isiah (10), born England

Bowers, Jacob (12), born England

Bowers, James (45), Miner, born England,
   dead [died late June 1856 west of Iowa
   City of consumption]

Bowers, Marie Lay (49), Wife, born England

Bowers, Sarah (18), born England

Bowers, Shadrach (7), born England

Bradley, Sarah Jane (14)

Bridges, Charles Henry (20)

Breggis, C. M. (21), Cork Cutter, born
   England

Brough, Alice (68), Widow

Brough, Wm (30), Marine

Brown [brother], (unknown age)

Bunney, Ann Mallett (25), Wife, born
   England

Bunney, John (28), Miner, born England

Butler, Emma Harvey (22), Wife, born
   England

Butler, Wm (30), G.S.L. City, born Utah

Card, Charles Ora (16)

Card, Cyrus William (42)

Card, Matilda Frances (3)

Card, Polly Caroline (14)

Card, Sarah Angeline (1)

Card, Sarah Ann Tuttle (37)

Card, Sarah Sabin (63)

Carlisle, H. W. (unknown age)

Chapman, John (58), Laborer, born England,
   backed out

Chatelain, Henriette (29)

Chatelain, Madeline Malan (21)

Chatelain, Pierre Louis (32)

Chester, Ann (20), Dressmaker, born
   England

Clarke, Hannah (6), born England

Clarke, Charlotte (19), born England

Clarke, George (55), Laborer, born England

Clarke, Mary Ann Mitchell (53), Wife, born
   England

Clarke, William Mitchell (14), born England

Commander, James (35), Mariner, born
   England

Commander, Mary Ann Brough (25), Wife

Devereaux, John (51), Laborer, born England

Doney, Ann Temperance George (24), Wife,
   born England

Doney, John (35), Laborer, born England

Doney, Mary Jane (infant)

Eldridge, Charlotte (2), born England, backed out

Eldridge, Charlotte Kettle (24), Wife, born England, backed out

Eldridge, Thos (25), Laborer, born England, backed out

Ellsworth, Edmund (37), born America

Fisby, Absalom (21), Tin Worker, born England

Fowler, Thos (19), born England

France, Joseph (41)

Franklin, Elizabeth (59), Widow, born England

Frost, Eliza Louisa Franklin (27), Wife, born England

Frost, Edward (32), Trimer, born England

Frost, John Franklin (4), born England

Frost, Isabella (7), born England

Galloway, Andrew (29), Engineer, born Scotland

Galloway, Annie Eliza (3), born England

Galloway, Jane Croft (25), Wife, born England

Goode, Maria (25), Servant, born England

Goodworth, Fredrick (6), born England

Goodworth, Hannah Chapman (43), Widow, born England

Goodworth, Joseph (9), born England

Goodworth, Richard Brooks (10), born England

Goudin, Catterina (age unknown)

Goudin, Susannah (23)

Green, Wm. (30), Miner, born England

Ham, Ann (31), Monthly Nurse, born England

Hanson, Clara Jane (15 months), born England

Hanson, Frances Hiley Booth (25), Wife, born England

Hanson, George (25), Gun Smith, born England

Harmon, George (25)

Harmon, William (52), Miner, born Wales

Henwood, Elizabeth Tregenna (15), born England

Henwood, Elizabeth Stockdale (42), Wife

Henwood, John (46), Laborer, born England

Henwood, Richard (18), born England

Hill, Eleanor (40), born England

Hunt, Abraham (30), Gass Man, born England, backed out

Hunt, Eliza (30), Wife, born England, backed out

Ivins, Thos (71), Gardner, born England

Jeffries, Eliza (21), Silk Weaver, born England

Jones, Ann (14), born Wales, backed out

Jones, Elizabeth Ann Williams (36), Wife, born Wales, backed out

Jones, Daniel (12), born Wales, backed out

Jones, William Daniel (42), Laborer, born Wales, backed out

Jones, Esther (29), Servant, born Wales

Jones, Hannah (45), Servant, born England

Jones, James (36), Spoon Maker, born England

Jones, James (infant)

Jones, Miriam (8), born Wales, backed out

Jones, Mary Ann (19)

Jones, Rachel (14), born Wales, backed out

Jones, Richard J. (3), Wales, backed out

Jones, Sabina (36), Wife, born England

Jones, Sarah (1), born Wales, backed out

Kettle, Eliza (12), born England

Kettle, Hannah (21 months), born England

Kettle, James Ward (9), born England

Kettle, John (53), Farm Laborer, born England

Kettle, Judith Ward (43), Wife, born England

Kettle, Mary Ann (18), Servant, born England

Kettle, Robert (14), born England

Kettle, Samuel (5), born England

Lee, Chancy Charles (2), born England

Lee, Elizabeth (10), born England

Lee, Fanny (11), born England

Lee, John (34), Pott Maker, born England

Lee, Samuel (4), born England

Lee, Sarah Ann (9 months), born England

Lee, Sarah Roebuck (33), Wife, born England

Lee, William (14), born England, dead [died 7th day on the trail, west of Iowa City, of consumption; buried at Little Bear Creek]

Legaird, Catterina (16)

Legaird, Giovanni (15)

Legaird, Pietro (49)

Lewis, Jane (27), Wife, born England

Lewis, John (33), Miner, born England

Lewis, John S. (8), born England

Liddiard, George (35)

Lloyd, Benjamin (24), Shoe Maker, born
Wales

Lloyd, Elizabeth Jones (38), Wife, born
Wales, backed out

Lloyd, Jane (2), born England, backed out

Lloyd, John (10), born England, backed out

Lloyd, John (39), Shoe Maker, born Wales,
backed out

Lloyd, Martha (4 weeks), born Iowa, backed
out

Lloyd, Mary (12), born England, backed out

Lloyd, John (39), Shoe Maker, born Wales

Lloyd, Thos. (26), Shoe Maker, born Wales

Lloyd, Thos. (6), born England, backed out

Lloyd, Wm. (8), born England, backed out

Marshall, Dauean Louisa (6)

Marshall, Selina (10), born England

Marshall, George Thomas (4), born England

Marshall, Josphina [Tryphena] (8), born
England

Marshall, Lavinna (12), born England

Marshall, Louisa (6), born England

Marshall, Sarah Ann (2), born England

Marshall, Sarah Goode (35), Washing, born
England

Marshall, Tryphena (8),

Mayo, Mary (65), Widow, born England,
dead [died September 13 in western
Wyoming]

Meadows, Mary Ann (21), born England

Miller, Sarah Jane (14)

Montgomery, Thomas C. (age unknown)

Morris, Sarah Ann (53), Wife, born England,
backed out

Morris, Wm. (53), Block Maker, born
England, backed out

Moss, Henry (19), Upholitster, born England

Moyle, Alfred (9), born England

Moyle, Elizabeth (19), Tailoress, born
England

Moyle, Henry (12), Tailoress, born England

Moyle, John Rowe (5), born England

Moyle, John Rowe (48), Stone Massen, born
England

Moyle, Philipa [Philliipi] (40), Wife, born
England

Moyle, Stephen (15), born England

Murray, James (27), Machinest, born
England

Neppress, George (24), Bricklayer, born
England, dead [died September 7, 1856,
west of Deer Creek, Wyoming]

Oakley, John Degroot (36), Farmer, born
Utah

Passey, Thos (18), born England

Phillips, John A., (unknown age), Minner,
born Wales

Phillips, Jonah (24)

Powell, Hannah Susan (4), born England

Powell, David Samuel (infant), born England

Powell, Sarah Elizabeth Harris (34), Wife,
born Wales

Powell, Elizabeth (6), born England

Powell, John (42), Mason, born England

Powell, Margaret Mary (8), born England

Powell, Mary Ann (12), born England

Powell, William (14), Masson, born England

Pratt, Caroline (31), Wife, born England

Pratt, Eleanor Saline (12), born England

Pratt, Emily (1), born England

Pratt, George (9), born England

Pratt, Orson (3), born England

Pratt, Wm. (31), Gun Smith, born England

Preator, Mary Salome (5), born England

Preator, Mary Haper (31), Wife, born
England

Preator, Richard (30), Carpenter, born
England

Preator, Loran Isabella (2), born England
[died on seventh day of travel, west of
Iowa City of whooping cough, buried at
Little Bear Creek]

Price, Ann Perkins (46), Widow, born
England
Price, Eliza (16), Glover, born England
Price, Emma (20), Dressmaker, born
England
Rasdell, Elizabeth Kettle (22), Wife, born
England
Rasdell, John Joseph (24), Laborer, born
England
Rasdell, Mary Ann (infant)
Richins, Albert Franklin (18 months), born
England
Richins, Harriott (22), Wife, born England
Richins, Thos. (30), Laborer, born England
Robinson, Clara Alice (1), born England
Robinson, Eliza (26), born England
Robinson, Elizabeth (21), born England
Robinson, Emma Lucas (27), Wife, born
England
Robinson, John (46), Gun Smith, England
Robinson, John (6), born England
Robinson, Sarah Naomi Elizabeth (19), born
England
Rochon, Elizabeth J. (20)
Rochon, Giovanni Michel (47)
Rochon, Jean Pierre (11)
Rochon, Marie Marguerite (7)
Rochon, Michel [or John] (infant)
Rochon, Suzanne Robert (37)
Rosong, John Peter (46)
Sanders, James (16), Brass F[ounder], born
England
Sanders, John (13), Printer, born England
Sanders, Mary (19), Servant, born England
Sanders, Thos. (10), born England
Sanders, Walter (63), Brass Founder, born
England, dead [died September 2, 1856,
west of Deer Creek, Wyoming]
Sheen, James, Sr. (60), Quarymen, born
England
Sheen, Annie (4), born England
Sheen, Ann Eliza (6 months), born England
Sheen, Eliza Elizabeth Taylor (29), Wife,
born England

Sheen, Ellen (18), Glover, born England
Sheen, Emma (2), born England, dead [died
June 26, 1856, west of Iowa City]
Sheen, Hannah (22), Glover, born England
Sheen, James, Jr. (26), Quarymen, born
England
Sheen, Louisa Eliza (5), born England
Sheen, Mary Shields (23), Wife, born England
Sheen, Mary (8), born England
Sheen, Robert (28), Quarymen, born
England
Sheen, Sydney (6 weeks), born A[t]lantic,
dead
Shelton, Richard (19), Black Smith, born
England
Shelton, Richard (18)
Sprig, Sarah Ann (18), Servant, born England
Stalle, Bartolome Daniel (18)
Stalle, Jean Pierre (52), [died August 17 in
western Nebraska, east of Chimney Rock]
Stalle, Jeanne Marie Gaudin-Moise (45)
Stalle, Marguerite (5)
Stalle, Marie (10)
Stalle, Suzette (19)
Stevenson, Alexander (36), Carpenter, born
Scotland, backed out
Stevenson, Alexander (7), born Scotland,
backed out
Stevenson, Isabella (28), Dressmaker, born
Scotland, backed out
Stevenson, John (13), born Scotland, backed
out
Stevenson, Joseph B. (3), born Scotland,
backed out
Stevenson, Magdaline (11), born Scotland,
backed out
Stevenson, Magdaline (35), Wife, Scotland,
backed out
Stevenson, Maria (1)
Stevenson, Orson (5), born Scotland, backed
out
Stoddart, Hannah (8), born England
Stoddart, Caleb (18), Weaver, born England
Stoddart, Dinah (6), born England

Stoddart, James (14), born England

Stoddart, Jane (12), born England

Stoddart, Margaret Mariah Alpin (38), Wife, born England

Stoddart, Margaret (1), born England

Stoddart, Margaret Mariah McElvin (40), Wife, born England

Stoddart, Mary (11), born England

Stoddart, Mary (3), born England

Stoddart, Robert (16), Weaver, born England

Stoddart, Robert (51), Warper, born England, dead [died August 31 and buried at Deer Creek, Wyoming]

Stoddart, Sarah (10), born England

Stoddart, Wm (43), Marble Polisher, born England

Taylor, Elizabeth (24), Servant, born England

Vaughan, Eleanor (78), Widow, born England

Walker, Elizabeth (16), Dress Maker, born England

Walker, Elizabeth, (24), born England

Walker, Emma (21)

Walker, Henry (58), Gardner, born England, dead [died July 27 when struck by lightning west of Iowa City]

Walker, Isabella Dixon (62), Wife, born England

Walters, Archer (47), Joiner, born England

Walters, Baby, born June 30, 1856, on trail west of Iowa City

Walters, Harriet (14), born England

Walters, Harriet Cross (46), Wife, born England

Walters, Henry Archer (15), Joiner, born England

Walters, Lydia (6), born England

Walters, Martha (12), born England

Walters, Sarah Ann (17), Servant, born England

Wareing, George (18)

Warner, Ann Miller Bradley (51), Wife, born England

Warner, James Constable (63), Laborer, born England

Watts, Eliza Whale (34)

Watts, Joseph (46)

Welling, Frances Elizabeth Yeoman (25), Wife, born England

Welling, Job (19 months), born England, dead [died of inflammation of the bowels, west of Iowa City]

Welling, Job (23), Tailor, born England

Williams, George Abraham (18), Boot Closer

Yeo, William (17)

SECOND COMPANY

Captain: Daniel D. McArthur

Departure: June 11, 1856

Arrival: September 26, 1856

Number of Participants: 228

Company Information: The Second Handcart Company had about 228 individuals, 44 handcarts, and 2 wagons when it began its journey from the outfitting post at Iowa City, Iowa.

Aitken, Cecelia (14)

Aitken, Thomas (11)

Aitken, William Knox (36)

Anderson, Agnes Adamson (52)

Anderson, Archibald, Jr. (20)

Anderson, James (13)

Anderson, John (15)

Arthur, [Brother] (unknown)

Bell, James (17)

Bell, John (54)

Bell, Margaret (55)

Bell, Samuel (15)

Bermingham, Catherine Elizabeth (24)

Bermingham, Edward L. (4)

Bermingham, Jane E. (3)

Bermingham, Mary Katherine (infant)

Bermingham, Patrick Twiss (26)

Bone, Mary Ann (10)

Bowring, Ellen Mary O'Keefe (16)

Bowring, Henry Ebenezer (34)

Bowring, Wallace Crocker (3)

Branagan, Mary (21)

Burdett, Elizabeth Lock (66)

Burdett, Emma Mary (19)

Chambers, David (54)

Chambers, David, Jr. (15)

Chambers, Mary Malcolm (54)

Clotworthy, Hugh (29)

Clotworthy, Jane (2)

Clotworthy, Janet (9)

Clotworthy, Jean Maitland (37)

Clotworthy, Margaret (infant)

Clotworthy, Mary (7)

Clotworthy, Thomas (4)

Crandall, Spicer Wells (33)

Crawford, James (23)

Darroch, Elizabeth (4)

Dechman [or Dickman], James (unknown)

Didriksson, Thordur (28)

Downie, Margaret (30)

Draney, Isabella Gray (infant)

Draney, John Pentland (31)

Draney, Mary Jane Park (28)

Draney, Samuel Park (2)

Eardley, Bedson (23)

Eardley, Louisa Cooper (26)

Elliker, Barbara (24)

Elliker, Conrad (21)

Elliker, Elizabeth (22)

Elliker, Hans Henry (59)

Elliker, Heinrich (27)

Elliker, Johannes (13)

Elliker, Margarethe (18)

Elliker, Margarethe Studer (53)

Elliker, Susanna (14)

Ellis, John (28)

Ellis, Mary Ann Emmett (33)

Emmett, Ann (26)

Ferguson, James (32)

Findley, Linzy Hannah (46)

Findley, Sarah L. Ann (17)

Findley, William (49)

Frew, James (9)

Frew, Jane Clotworth (35)

Frew, Janet (7)

Frew, John (29)

Frew, Mary (1)

Frew, William John Daniel Thompson
    McCallister (infant)

Furrer, Anna Regla (30)

Gale, Mary (47)

Gallop, Agnes (36)

Gallop, Thomas (39)

Gardner, Agnes (20)

Gardner, Agnes (36)

Gardner, Alexander (15)

Gardner, Ann Knox (51)

Gardner, Elizabeth (13)

Gardner, James (17)

Gardner, Walter (8)

Granger, Alexander Fullerton (9)

Granger, Catherine (20)

Granger, Catherine Guthrie (37)

Granger, Catherine McDonald (6)

Granger, John Walker (2)

Granger, Robert (14)

Granger, Walter (5)

Granger, Walter (34)

Gray, Franklin R. (4)

Gray, Jane (21)

Gray, Jane Japp (28)

Gray, John (50)

Gray, Mary (2)

Gray, William (infant)

Griffiths, John J. (unknown)

Hall, William (29)

Hardie, Agnes (22)

Hardie, Grace (13)

Hardie, James McDonald (10)

Hardie, Janet Downie (45)

Hardie, John Francis (15)

Hardie, Phyllis (23)

Hargraves, Agnes Nobel (34)

Hargraves, Elizabeth Ann (4)

Hargraves, Enoch Trane (infant)

Hargraves, Jane O'Connor (16)

Hargraves, Janet (11)

Hargraves, John (9)

Hargraves, Margaret (2)

Hargraves, Mary (13)

Hargraves, Samuel (41)

Hay, Mary (34)

Heaton, Christopher Beilby (4)

Heaton, Esther Beilby (25)

Heaton, William (29)

Heaton, William McDonald (infant)

Hillhouse, David (11)

Hillhouse, Elizabeth (6)

Hillhouse, Jeanette (24)

Hillhouse, Jeanette (infant)

Hillhouse, John (22)

Hillhouse, Margaret (52)

Hillhouse, Mary (15)

Hillhouse, Robert (13)

Hillhouse, William (46)

Hillhouse, William (2)

Hodgetts, Hannah (18)

Ipson, Georgine Maria Keller (28)

Ipson, Neils Peter (23)

Johnston, David (7)

Johnston, Elizabeth (21)

Johnston, George (39)

Johnston, Isabella (5)

Johnston, Janet (14)

Johnston, Richard (5)

Johnston, William (3)

Johnston, William (29)

Kennington, Eliza (11)

Kennington, Mary Ann (2)

Kennington, Mary Ann Davison (46)

Kennington, Richard (51)

Kennington, Richard Davison (9)

Kennington, Sarah Jane (16)

Kennington, William Henry (13)

Lawrenson, Ann Quick (52)

Lawrenson, Jane (17)

Lawrenson, Margaret (11)

Lawrenson, William (55)

Lawson, William (29)

Leonard, Truman (35)

Logan, Mary Bathgate (59)

Logan, Mary Maude Bathgate (12)

Lucas, Ann (21)

Lucas, Anthony (58)

Lucas, Elizabeth (26)

Lucas, Martha (unknown)

Lucas, Mary (57)

Lucas, Mary (14)

Lucas, Thomas (25)

Ludert, Joseph Alphonse (6)

Ludert, Josephine de La Harpe (43)

Mathieson, Mary (21)

Maxwell, Ann (13)

Maxwell, Arthur (32)

Maxwell, Catherine (27)

Maxwell, Elizabeth (21)

Maxwell, Elizabeth Donnely (51)

Maxwell, Elizabeth McAuslin (24)

Maxwell, Margaret (unknown)

Maxwell, Ralph (19)

McArthur, Daniel Duncan (36)

McCleve, Alexander Gilmore (2)

McCleve, Eliza Roxy (7)

McCleve, Isabella Wilkins (13)

McCleve, John (48)

McCleve, John T. (11)

McCleve, Joseph Smith (8)

McCleve, Margaret (17)

McCleve, Mary Jane (15)

McCleve, Nancy Jane McFerren (41)

McDonald, Alexander (26)

McDonald, John (23)

McDougal, Joseph (26)

McGowan, Mary (29)

Meikle, Isabelle (19)

Meikle, James (17)

Meikle, Margaret Jackson (57)

Meikle, William (30)

Morehouse, Elizabeth (29)

Muir, George (23)

Muir, James Mountain (infant)

Muir, Jane Howie (infant)

Muir, Margaret Hannah (26)

Muir, Mary (3)

Park, Isabella Gray (64)

Parker, Ada (infant)

Parker, Ann Ruth Hartley (37)

Parker, Arthur Hartley (6)

Parker, Martha Alice (10)

Parker, Maximilian (12)

Parker, Robert (36)

Peacock, George Daniel (6)

Peacock, George (33)

Peacock, Mary Isabelle (12)

Ramsay, Elizabeth Burns (33)

Ramsay, Joseph Smith (1)

Ramsay, Ralph (32)

Randall, Anna M. Burdette (31)

Randall, Oscar Isaac (1)

Reed, Eliza (20)

Reid, Elizabeth (11)

Reid, Elizabeth Cumming (31)

Reid, James (6)

Reid, James (40)

Reid, John Cumming (1)

Reid, Mary (4)

Richardson, Elizabeth (33)

Richardson, Peter (24)

Richardson (infant)

Russell, Ellen (23)

Sanderson, Rebecca Wood (42)

Sanderson, Rhoda (9)

Sanderson, Sarah Ann (11)

Schies, Anna Gossauer (38)

Schies, John (39)

Shields, Elizabeth (29)

Smart, Sarah (50)

Smith, Andrew (28)

Stewart, Agnes Nancy Fergenson (50)

Stewart, Jane (18)

Stewart, Margaret (13)

Stewart, Matilda (16)

Thomas, David Griffith (57)

Tweddle, Elizabeth (21)

Wandles, Ellen (28)

Wandles, Ellen (6)

Wright, Maria Brown (24)

Wright, William Tweede (24)

THIRD COMPANY

Captain: Edward Bunker

Departure: June 23, 1856

Arrival: October 2, 1856

Number of participants: 233

Company Information: About 233 individuals were in the Third Handcart Company, which began its journey from the outfitting post at Iowa City, Iowa, with 64 handcarts. This company left Florence, Nebraska on July 30, 1856, and arrived in Salt Lake City on October 2, 1856.

Axton, Elizabeth (51)

Axton, John (11)

Axton, Thomas (80)

Barker, Barbara (50)

Barker, Margaret Freeland (77)

Barker, Robert (20)

Bridges [or Bridge], James (49)

Brooks, Emma Blinstone (46)

Brooks, Francis F. (6)

Brooks, George (10)

Brooks, Mary Elizabeth (16)

Brooks, Samuel (65)

Bunker, Edward (34)

Butler, Ann Morris (39)

Butler, Elizabeth Ann (13)
Butler, Jane (24)
Butler, John (26)
Butler, William Richard (8)
Chapple, Joseph Daniel (25)
Chapple, Margaret (1)
Chapple, Mary Williams (24)
Cozzens, John (23)
Cozzens, Martha (21)
Daniels, Ann (25)
Davies, Elizabeth (17)
Davies, Elleanor (18)
Davies, Mary (unknown)
Edmunds, Jane Jones (24)
Edmunds, John (66)
Edmunds, John Jones (1)
Edmunds, Nathaniel (28)
Evans, Abram (49)
Evans, Anne (19)
Evans, David (54)
Evans, David Lewis (37)
Evans, Eliza Perkins (27)
Evans, Elizabeth (3)
Evans, Emma (8)
Evans, Gwenllian (infant)
Evans, Hannah Morgan (71)
Evans, Hyrum (5)
Evans, Jane (17)
Evans, Jenkin Abram (24)
Evans, Joseph (1)
Evans, Letitia (20)
Evans, Louisa Rosser (19)
Evans, Mary A. Davis (43)
Evans, Mary Ann (1)
Evans, Mary Elizabeth (12)
Evans, Mary Norris (24)
Evans, Morgan (22)
Evans, Moses (20)
Evans, Priscilla Merriman (21)
Evans, Thomas (unknown)
Evans, Thomas (10)
Evans, Thomas (37)
Evans, Thomas Abram (20)
Evans, Thomas David (23)

Giles, Elizabeth (infant)
Giles, Hyrum Lorenzo (6)
Giles, Joseph (7)
Giles, Margaret Thomas (35)
Giles, Thomas Davies (35)
Grant, David (39)
Hughes, Ann (15)
Hughes, Elizabeth (62)
Hughes, Owen (18)
Hughes, William (49)
James, John (27)
James, Sarah (15)
Jarman, Ann Phillips (54)
Jarman, John (8)
Jarman, Margaret (7)
Jarman, Richard (12)
Jarman, Thomas (44)
Jenkins, Elizabeth (13)
Jenkins, Henry (35)
Jenkins, John (25)
Jenkins, Margaret (18)
Jenkins, Margaret Hopkins (48)
Jenkins, Martha John (45)
Jenkins, Thomas (32)
Jenkins, Thomas Hopkins (8)
Jenkins, William (15)
Jenkins, William (49)
Job, Hannah Daniels (27)
Job, Mary Davis (7)
Jones, Eleanor (26)
Jones, Frank Parry (infant)
Jones, James (27)
Jones, John Thomas (8)
Jones, Margaret (18)
Jones, Margaret (30)
Jones, Mary (19)
Jones, Owen (21)
Jones, Ruth Thomas (51)
Jones, Sarah Parry (25)
Jones, Thomas Lee (56)
Jones, William Thomas (12)
Jones, William X. (21)
Lane, Elizabeth (44)
Lewis, Ann (23)

Lewis, Daniel (50)

Lewis, David (30)

Lewis, Eleanor Roberts (23)

Lewis, Elias (21)

Lewis, Enoch (31)

Lewis, Jane Anne (34)

Lewis, Jane Davies (21)

Lewis, John (8)

Lewis, John (1)

Lewis, Joshua (5)

Lewis, Martha Jane (5)

Lewis, Mary Ann (2)

Lewis, William John (23)

Llewellyn, Ann (16)

Llewellyn, Ann Llewellyn (19)

Llewellyn, Edmund (22)

Llewellyn, Elizabeth (12)

Llewellyn, John (20)

Llewellyn, Mary Howells (49)

Llewellyn, Rees Rees (27)

Mathews, Alma Morris (infant)

Mathews, Elizabeth (11)

Mathews, Hopkin (32)

Mathews, Joan (4)

Mathews, Margaret (7)

Mathews, Margaret Morris (34)

Mathews, Mary (9)

Matthews, Anne (21)

McDonald, John Kilpatrick (58)

Morgan, Catherine Jarman (23)

Morgan, James (28)

Morgan, Thomas (unknown)

Morgan, William (25)

Morgan, William Samuel (27)

Morgan, [Mrs.] Thomas (unknown)

Morris, Morris Nuland (25)

Morris, Susan (27)

Motley, Elizabeth Hughes (51)

Orton, Alexander (19)

Orton, Samuel Taylor (23)

Owens, Owen (18)

Parry, Ann (21)

Parry, Edward (12)

Parry, Edward (29)

Parry, Eleanor (26)

Parry, Elizabeth Louise (6)

Parry, Elizabeth (47)

Parry, Harriet (21)

Parry, Harriet Julia Roberts (27)

Parry, John (54)

Parry, John (14)

Parry, John (38)

Parry, Winifred (18)

Perkins, Ann (70)

Phillips, Edward (48)

Phillips, Elizabeth (21)

Phillips, Elizabeth Ivins (47)

Phillips, Jacob (22)

Phillips, Margaret Ann (13)

Phillips, Mary Mariah (8)

Phillips, Sarah (16)

Rees, Alfred (14)

Rees, Ann (17)

Rees, Eleanora [or Helena] (9)

Rees, Hannah (28)

Rees, Henry D. (19)

Rees, Isaac (32)

Rees, John (unknown)

Rees, Lenora (2)

Rees, Margaret (37)

Rees, Maria (5)

Rees, Nephi John (6)

Rees, Sarah Jane (12)

Rees, [Mrs.] John (unknown)

Reese, Ann (14)

Reese, George (15)

Reese, Lotwick (11)

Reese, Margaret Jones (47)

Reese, Thomas (40)

Roberts, Ann Powell (34)

Roberts, Anne (11)

Roberts, Catherine Richards (47)

Roberts, Daniel (13)

Roberts, David (15)

Roberts, David (48)

Roberts, David Robert (42)

Roberts, Elizabeth (9)

Roberts, Elizabeth (8)

Roberts, Jacob (7)

Roberts, Jane (6)

Roberts, John R. (33)

Roberts, John Dunn (38)

Roberts, John Powell (infant)

Roberts, Margaret (3)

Roberts, Mary Jane (4)

Roberts, Mary Phillips (39)

Roberts, Mary Richards (34)

Roberts, Robert David (19)

Roberts, Robert Edward (2)

Roberts, Rosa Bell (6)

Roberts, Thomas David (15)

Roberts, William (12)

Roberts, William Daniel (4)

Thain, John Teague (26)

Thain, Margaret Roach Griffiths (23)

Thomas, Ann (77)

Thomas, Daniel (37)

Thomas, Edward (14)

Thomas, Elvira Jones (48)

Thomas, Margaret (46)

Turner, George William (32)

Turner, Hannah James (23)

Walters, Elizabeth (4)

Walters, Elizabeth Ann (13)

Walters, Hannah Bateman (26)

Walters, Maria (10)

Walters, Sarah Jane (26)

Walters, Thomas (4)

Watkins, Charlotte George (26)

Watkins, William (22)

Williams, Anne (12)

Williams, Catherine James (68)

Williams, Elizabeth (18)

Williams, Jane (9)

Williams, John (40)

Williams, John (27)

Williams, Letitia (19)

Williams, Mary Parry (43)

Williams, Richard (22)

Williams, Sarah Ann (16)

Williams, Sarah Thomas (22)

FOURTH COMPANY
Captain: James G. Willie
Departure: July 15, 1856
Arrival: November 9, 1856
Number of Participants: 503
Company Information: The Fourth Handcart Company had
503 individuals, 120 handcarts, and 5 wagons when it began its journey
from the outfitting post at Iowa City, Iowa. Approximately
66–77 members of this company died on the trail.

Ahmanson, Johan August (29)

Allen, William Wilford (36)

Andersen, Anders Nielson (8)

Andersen, Christina (22)

Andersen, Johanne Kirstine (29)

Andersen, Maria Kristine Amitzbol (54)

Andersen, Mette Hansdatter (50)

Andersen, Niels (41)

Anderson, Anna (14)

Anderson, C. (unknown)

Anderson, David Patterson (18)

Atwood, Millen (39)

Bailey, Elizabeth Haywood (51)

Bailey, John (52)

Bailey, Mary Elizabeth (17)

Bain, Margery (22)

Bain, Robert Angus (25)

Baker, Adelaide Augusta Binning (22)

Baker, David Ephraim (2)

Baker, George Wesley (18)

Baker, Jeremiah Thomas (46)

Baker, Manassah Delapole White (infant)

Baker, Mary Ann (10)

Bayliss, Hannah [sailed on the *Thornton;*
   had a stillborn child May 21]

Bird, Ann (19)

Bird, Ezra (15)

Bird, Martha Ann (13)

Bird, Mary Ann Fenn (40)

Bird, Sabina (17)

Bird, Sarah (10)

Bird, Susannah (8)

Bird, William Fredrick (5)

Bowles, Ann Bolton (54)

Bowles, Edward (49)

Bowles, Enoch (12)

Bowles, Thomas (19)

Boyington, Thomas (26)

Bravandt, Emma Emelie (19)

Brazier, George (21)

Brazier, John (19)

Britton, Mary Ann Warr (50)

Brown, Christina (26)

Bryant, Ann (69)

Burt, Alexander (19)

Caldwell, Agnes (9)

Caldwell, Elizabeth (12)

Caldwell, Margaret Ann McFall (39)

Caldwell, Robert John (17)

Caldwell, Thomas (14)

Campkin, Francisca (5)

Campkin, Harriet (4)

Campkin, Isaac James (infant)

Campkin, Martha Ann (2)

Campkin, Martha Webb (35)

Campkin, Wilford George (8)

Cantwell, Elizabeth Cotterell (infant)

Cantwell, Elizabeth Cotterell Hamer (37)

Cantwell, Ellen (7)

Cantwell, Francis Robert (15)

Cantwell, James (13)

Cantwell, James Sherlock (42)

Cantwell, Mary Ann (2)

Cantwell, William Hamer (10)

Chetwin [or Chetwynd], Maria (21)

Chislett, John (24)

Choules, Sarah (23)

Christensen, Anders (21)

Christensen, Niels Lars (27)

Cook, Minnie Ann (33)

Cooper, Adelaide (4)

Cooper, Ann Brummel (38)

Cooper, Mary Ann (5)

Cox, Theophilus (25) [died November 7, east
   of Salt Lake City]

Crook, Eliza (19)

Crook, Sophia Mason (65)

Culley, Benjamin (60) [died October 4, east
   of Platte Bridge in Wyoming]

Culley, Elizabeth (20)

Culley, Jane Dorothy (25)

Cunningham, Catherine (17)

Cunningham, Elizabeth (12)

Cunningham, Elizabeth Agnes Nicholson (48)

Cunningham, George (15)

Cunningham, James (54)

Cunningham, Margaret (10)

Curtis, George (64)

Curtis, Rachel (75) [died on ocean crossing
   on the *Thornton*]

Dalglish, Margaret (31)

Davenport, Lucinda Melissa (18)

Dorney, Hannah (25)

Dorney, Mary Davis (65)

Edwick, William (17)

Elder, Joseph Benson (21)

Empey, James (6)

Empey, Jesse (31)

Empey, Mary Ann (4)

Empey, Mary Foulks (29)

Empey, Sarah Jane (1)

Empey, William (9) [died November 7, east
   of Salt Lake City]

England, Daniel (55)

England, John (15)

England, Mary Ann Medler (48)

England, Moroni (6)

England, William (18)

Evans, Amelia (18)

Findlay, Allen McPherson (27)

Findlay, Jessie Ireland (28)

Findlay, Mary McPherson (59)

Forbes, Elizabeth Wilkie (8)

Funnell, Elizabeth (23)

Funnell, Mary Ann Rice Winter (62)

Gadd, Alfred (19)

Gadd, Daniel Chapman (1) [died October 4, east of Platte Bridge in Wyoming]

Gadd, Eliza Chapman (42)

Gadd, Isaac Chapman (1)

Gadd, Jane (17)

Gadd, Mary Ann (7)

Gadd, Samuel (10)

Gadd, Samuel (40)

Gadd, Sarah (5)

Gadd, William Chapman (13)

Gardner, Agnes Eleanor (4)

Gardner, Frederick James (3)

Gardner, Hannah Gubbins (27)

Gardner, James (26)

Gardner, John William (1)

Gardner, Mary Ann (7)

Geary, Echo Workman (infant)

Geary, John Thomas (33)

Geary, Sophia Ann (3)

Geary, Sophia Fryer (26)

Gibb, James (63)

Gibb, Mary Gordon (52)

Gillman, Chesterton John (76)

Girdlestone, Emma (21)

Girdlestone, Mary Betts (59)

Girdlestone, Thomas (63)

Godfrey, Richard (21)

Gregersen, Maren (26)

Griffiths, Catherine Mary (31)

Griffiths, Edward (25)

Griffiths, Mary Priscilla (26)

Groves, William (22)

Gurney, Charles (39)

Gurney, Charlotte Brown (37)

Gurney, Joseph (14)

Gurney, Mary Ann (14)

Hailey, Catherine Coles (66)

Hailey, William (67)

Hansen, Anna (40)

Hansen, Maren (51)

Hansen, Peter (13)

Hansen, Rasmus (16) [died November 6, east of Salt Lake City]

Hansen, Rasmus (40) [died October 19, near Sixth Crossing, Sweetwater River Valley, Wyoming]

Hansen, Rasmus Peter (16) [died]

Hanson, Anna Catherine (42)

Hanson, Nils (41)

Hardwick, Richard (63)

Henderson, James (27)

Henderson, James Mitchell (1)

Henderson, Jane Allison McGibbon (26)

Herbert, Ann (25)

Herbert, Charles Martin (3)

Herbert, Hannah (15)

Hill, Emily (20)

Hill, Julia (23)

Hodges, Janetta (55)

Hodges, Mary (20)

Hooley, Thomas (22)

Howard, Ann (33)

Humphries, Ann (16)

Humphries, Clena (7)

Humphries, Edwin (24)

Humphries, Elizabeth (12)

Humphries, George (45)

Humphries, Hannah (9)

Humphries, Harriet Harding (46)

Humphries, James (2)

Humphries, Mary (15)

Hurren, Eliza Reeder (26)

Hurren, Emma (4)

Hurren, James (29)

Hurren, Mary Reeder (7)

Hurren, Sarah (2)

Hurren, Selena (infant)

Ingra, Elizabeth Stanford (74)

Ingra, George (68)

Jacobsen, Anna Kirstine Mortensen (32)

Jacobsen, Jens Peter (3)
Jacobsen, Lucy Jepsen (55)
Jacobsen, Paul (56)
Jacobsen, Peter (28)
James, Emma (17)
James, George (7)
James, Jane Haynes (41)
James, John (61)
James, John Parley (3)
James, Martha (10)
James, Mary Ann (11)
James, Reuben (14)
James, Sarah (18)
James, William (46)
Janes, Petrina C. (unknown)
Jefferies, William (24)
Jensen, Anders (47)
Jensen, Anne Christensen (49)
Jensen, Anthonin (8)
Jensen, Johanne Marie (21)
Jensen, Michael (11)
Jensen, Petrea Caroline (25)
Jenson, Carsten (unknown)
Jenson, Catherine (19)
Jones, Ellen (6)
Jorgensen, Anders (44)
Jorgensen, Anna (6)
Jorgensen, Elizabeth Nielsen (42)
Jorgensen, Hans (12)
Jorgensen, Jorgen (3)
Jorgensen, Maren (10)
Jorgensen, Maren Sophia (8) [died
    November 7, just east of Salt Lake City]
Jorgenson, Christen (unknown)
Jorgenson, Mareann (unknown)
Jost, Andrew James (3)
Jost, Catherine Ann (12)
Jost, John Alexander (44)
Jost, Mary Ann (8)
Jost, Mary Ann Zwicker (44)
Jost, Samuel Edward (11)
Jost, Thomas William (9)
Kay [Key], Rose (50)
Keetch, Alfred Greenwood (16)

Keetch, Ann Greenwood (44)
Keetch, Ann Maria (1)
Keetch, Charles Greenwood (18)
Keetch, Elizabeth (14)
Keetch, Emma (12)
Keetch, Martha Mae (10)
Keetch, William (8)
Keetch, William Kempton (44)
Kelly, Barbara (32)
Kelly, James C. (7)
Kelly, John (31)
Kelly, John Carmichael (2)
Kelly, Mary Carmichael (30)
Kirby, Hannah Watson (36)
Kirby, Maria Watson (9)
Kirkpatrick, Alexander (6)
Kirkpatrick, Elizabeth Ramsey (35)
Kirkwood, James (11)
Kirkwood, Joseph Smith Campbell (5)
Kirkwood, Margaret Campbell (46)
Kirkwood, Robert Campbell (21)
Kirkwood, Thomas (19)
Knutsen [or Knudsen], Kirstine (60)
Kockles, John [died October 19, near Sixth
    Crossing, Sweetwater River Valley,
    Wyoming]
Laird, Edward (4)
Laird, Elizabeth (1)
Laird, James (30)
Laird, Joseph Smith (6)
Laird, Mary Renney (30)
Langman, Rebecca Cula (22)
Larsen, Anna Kirstine (37)
Larsen, Hanna Sophia (11)
Larsen, Lars Julius (infant)
Larsen, Martine (6)
Larsen, Niels Peter (13)
Larsen, Peter (43)
Lautrup [or Loutross], Maria Lovise [Louisa]
    (32)
Leason, Ruvina Jane Mount (22)
Leason, William M. (1)
Ledingham, Alexander (6)
Ledingham, Catherine McKay (32)

Ledingham, Mary M. (2)

Ledingham, Robert McKay (3)

Ledingham, William (5)

Ledingham, William Dykes (29)

Lewis, Benjamin Charles (6)

Lewis, Edward P. (2)

Lewis, Eliza Freeman (33)

Lewis, Heber Brigham (infant)

Lewis, Joseph (33)

Lewis, Joseph Jr. (9)

Lewis, Mary Ann (11)

Lewis, Thomas G. (4)

Linford, Amasa Christian (11)

Linford, George John (17)

Linford, John (47)

Linford, Joseph William (14)

Linford, Maria Bentley Christian (43)

Madsen, Andrew (5)

Madsen, Ane Jensen (37)

Madsen, Ane Marie (10)

Madsen, Johanna Marie (16)

Madsen, Mette Kristine (13)

Madsen, Mette Marie Nielsen (44)

Madsen, Ole (41)

Madsen, Peter (65) [died November 5, east of
   Salt Lake City]

Madsen, Peter (49)

Madsen, Petrea Elisabeth Malita (36)

McCullough, John (22)

McKay, Joseph (57)

McNeil, Christina (24)

McNeil, Jennet [traveled on the *Thornton*,
   may not have continued overland]

McNeil, Charles Thornton [born just before
   the *Thornton* sailed]

McPhail, Archibald (39) [died November 6,
   east of Salt Lake City]

McPhail, Donald (2)

McPhail, Henrietta (14)

McPhail, Jane (3)

McPhail, Jane McKinnon (36)

Meadows, Amelia Pendrick (40)

Meadows, Joseph (25)

Millard, Esther Young (31)

Miller, Flora (61)

Miller, Mary Ann (30)

Miller, Mercy (26)

Miller, William A. S. (5)

Mitchell, Euphemia (22)

Mortensen, Anders Jorgen (22)

Mortensen, Ane Kirstine (25)

Mortensen, Bodil (9)

Mortensen, Caroline (6)

Mortensen, Hans Jorgen (19)

Mortensen, Helena Pedersen (48)

Mortensen, Lars (13)

Mortensen, Marie (9)

Mortensen, Mette Kirstine (11)

Mortensen, Peter (50)

Moulton, Charles Alma (infant) [born May
   4, 1856, after the *Thornton* sailed]

Moulton, Charlotte (5)

Moulton, James Heber (8)

Moulton, Joseph (10)

Moulton, Mary Ann (15)

Moulton, Sarah Denton (39)

Moulton, Sarah Elizabeth (19)

Moulton, Sophia Elizabeth (2)

Moulton, Thomas (45)

Moulton, William Denton (12)

Newman, Caroline (8)

Newman, Eliza (16)

Newman, Ellen (6)

Newman, John Moroni (11)

Newman, Mary Ann (7)

Newman, Mary Ann Williams (39)

Newman, William (15)

Nielsen, Birthe (13)

Nielsen, Else Rasmussen (26)

Nielsen, Helle (22)

Nielson, Jens (36)

Nielson, Niels (5)

Nockles [or Knockles], John (61)

Norris, Cecelia (26)

Norris, Sarah (22)

Oakey, Ann (19)

Oakey, Ann Collett (44)

Oakey, Charles (19)

Oakey, Heber Thomas (15)

Oakey, Jane (17)

Oakey, Lorenzo Moroni (12)

Oakey, Reuben Hyrum (9)

Oakey, Rhoda Rebecca (11) [died November 9, the day the company reached Salt Lake City]

Oakey, Sarah Ann (3)

Oakey, Thomas (42)

Oborn, John (12)

Oborn, Joseph (45)

Oborn, Maria Stradling (45)

Oliver, Ann (23)

Oliver, James (33)

Olsen, Ane [Anne] (46)

Olsen, Anne (14)

Ore, Abraham (42)

Ore, Eliza (39)

Osborn, Ann Foulks (24)

Osborne, Daniel (30)

Osborne, Daniel (7) [died October 19, near Sixth Crossing, Sweetwater Valley]

Osborne, Martha (1)

Osborne, Sarah Ann (4)

Osborne, Susannah (32) [died November 5, east of Salt Lake City]

Osborne, Susannah (10)

Page, William (17)

Panting, Christopher (4)

Panting, Elizabeth Crook (28)

Panting, Jane (1)

Peacock, Alfred (19)

Pedersen, Ane Johannah (3)

Pedersen, Emma Sophie (5)

Pedersen, Otto August (1)

Pedersen, Peter (9)

Pedersen, Sophie Catherine Wilhelmine Clawn (31)

Perkins, Mary Ann Clark (59)

Petersen, Anders Jorgensen (22)

Petersen, Anne Marie Jensen (32)

Petersen, Caroline (5)

Petersen, Christian O. (5)

Petersen, Hans Peter (8)

Petersen, Jens Christian (1)

Petersen, Jens O. (36)

Petersen, Johanna Marie (11)

Petersen, Metta Kirstine (10)

Petersen, Mette Marie (9)

Petersen, Peter O. (4)

Peterson, Anna Kirstine (24)

Peterson, Hans Jorgen (18)

Peterson, Maria (8)

Peterson, Thomas (7)

Philpot, Eliza Hancock (36)

Philpot, Julia Matilda (14)

Philpot, Martha Eliza (11)

Philpot, William (51)

Pilgrim, Rebecca (30)

Quinn, Elizabeth (17)

Quinn, George (14)

Quinn, Harriet (19)

Quinn, Isabelle (8)

Quinn, Joseph Hyrum (7)

Quinn, Mary Ann Hosking (49)

Quinn, William R. (24)

Quinn, William W. (50)

Read, Joseph (17)

Read, Sarah Brimley (63)

Read, William M. (62) [died October 2, east of Platte Bridge in Wyoming]

Reeder, Caroline (16)

Reeder, David (54)

Reeder, Robert (19)

Reid, Elizabeth (11)

Reid, Elizabeth Cumming (31)

Reid, James (6)

Reid, James (40)

Reid, John Cumming (1)

Reid, Mary (4)

Richens, Franklin Thornton (infant)

Richins, Charlotte Priscilla Taylor (22)

Richins, Hannah Louisa (1)

Richins, John (23)

Roberts, John (41)

Roberts, Mary Bubb (44)

Rogers, Jemima Brown (53)

Rogers, Lizzie (8)

Rowley, Ann Jewell (48) [died October 19, near Sixth Crossing, Sweetwater Valley]

Rowley, Elizabeth (32)

Rowley, Elizabeth (17)

Rowley, Jane (7)

Rowley, John (15)

Rowley, Louisa (19)

Rowley, Richard (11)

Rowley, Samuel (13)

Rowley, Thomas (10)

Sandberg, Jens (37)

Savage, Levi (36)

Showell, Ellen (18)

Showell, Harriet (31)

Siler, Andrew Lafayette (31)

Smith, Alexander Joseph (6)

Smith, Andrew Young (19)

Smith, Benjamin Albert (15)

Smith, Charlotte Eagle (55)

Smith, Eliza Williams (40) [died October 19, near Sixth Crossing, Sweetwater River Valley, Wyoming]

Smith, Elizabeth [or Betsy] (13)

Smith, Emily (11)

Smith, Harriet (17)

Smith, Isaac (59)

Smith, Jane (17)

Smith, Margery May McEwan Bain (51)

Smith, Mary (15)

Smith, Milicent (17)

Smith, William (48)

Sorensen, Christian (9)

Stanley, Elizabeth Gent (39)

Steed, Sarah (19)

Stewart, Ann B. (10)

Stewart, Ann Waddell (30)

Stewart, Jane Ann (31)

Stewart, John (6)

Stewart, John (4)

Stewart, John (32)

Stewart, Margaret (45)

Stewart, Margaret Ann (infant)

Stewart, Nancy (unknown)

Stewart, Thomas (40)

Stewart, Thomas (7)

Stewart, William (13)

Stockdale, Mary A. (17)

Stone, Susannah (25)

Summers, Emma (27)

Tait, Anna F. (31) [died October 20, near Sixth Crossing, Sweetwater River Valley, Wyoming]

Tait, Elizabeth Xavier (23)

Tassell, Kitty Ann Ingra (38)

Tite, Elizabeth (25)

Toffield, Ellen (44)

Turner, Richard F. (67)

Vendin [or Vandelin], Lars (67)

Wall, Frederick (35)

Wall, Joseph Laban (18)

Wall, Mariah Wheeler (30)

Wall, Sarah Emily (16)

Ward, Lucy (23)

Waters, John (65)

Watson, Andrew (23)

West, Sarah (24)

Wheeler, Ann Wood (55)

Wheeler, Edward (52)

Wheeler, Mary Ann (26)

Whithorn, Eliza Stallard (43)

Whithorn, Joseph (9)

Wicklund, Christina (8)

Wicklund, Ella Jonsson (30)

Wicklund, Jonas (6)

Wicklund, Josephine Ephraimine (1)

Wicklund, Ola (30)

Wicklund, Sarah Jacobina (3)

Wiklund, Jacob (infant)

Wilkie, Isabella (47)

Williams, Mary (50) [died July 23 in Iowa]

Williams, Sarah Ann (22)

Willie, James Grey (41)

Witts, Samuel H. (66)

Woodward, William (23)

Young, Thomas (20)

Yergensen, Hans (12)

FIFTH COMPANY

Captain: Edward Martin
Departure: July 28, 1856
Arrival: November 30, 1856
Number of Participants: 646
Company Information: The Fifth Handcart Company contained
646 individuals, 146 handcarts, and 7 wagons when it began its journey
from the outfitting post at Iowa City, Iowa. Approximately
135–150 members of the company died on the trail.

Akers, Ann Pugh (23)
Akers, Joseph (24)
Allen, Eleanor (17)
Allen, Eliza (unknown)
Allen, Maria (22)
Allen, Mary Laysell (42)
Anderson, Ann Tipping (47)
Andrews, John J. (44)
Anglesey, Martha (22)
Ashton, Betsy (11)
Ashton, Mary (4)
Ashton, Sarah Ann (infant)
Ashton, Sarah Ann Barlow (33)
Ashton, Sarah Ellen (7)
Ashton, William (34)
Atherton, Ellen Daniels (57)
Bailey, David William (5)
Bailey, Jane Allgood (46)
Bailey, John (49)
Bailey, John (15)
Bailey, Langley Allgood (18)
Bailey, Thomas (12)
Barlow, Ann Crompton (58)
Barlow, Emma Jane (15)
Barlow, John (17)
Barlow, Joseph Smith (7)
Barnes, Deborah (8)
Barnes, Elizabeth (12)
Barnes, Esther (10)
Barnes, George (41)
Barnes, Jane Howard (41)
Barnes, Margaret (15)
Barnes, Mary Jane (infant)

Barnes, William Levi (5)
Barteleme, Bone (26)
Barton, Frances (3)
Barton, Mary Ann (14)
Barton, Mary Ann Taylor (33)
Barton, William (48)
Batchelor, Emma Louise (20)
Beecroft, John Hurst (9)
Beecroft, Joseph (45)
Beecroft, Sarah Hurst (42)
Beer, Benjamin (44)
Beer, Margaret Keefe (44)
Bennett, Harriet (53)
Beswick, Ann Burtonwood (63)
Beswick, Joseph (33)
Binder, Eliza Camp (24)
Binder, William Laurence Spicer (24)
Bird, Thomas P. (18)
Bitton, Jane (19)
Bitton, John Evington (26)
Bitton, Sarah Susannah Wintle (17)
Blackham, Martha Robinson (49)
Blackham, Samuel (21)
Blackham, Sarah (16)
Blackham, Thomas (14)
Blair, David (46)
Blair, David (infant)
Blair, Deborah Jane Rushnell (39)
Blair, Deborah Louisa (8)
Blair, Elizabeth (5)
Blakey, Caroline Garstone Williams (36)
Blakey, John Moroni (6)
Blakey, Richard Brigham (1)

Blakey, Richard John (36)

Bleak, Elizabeth Moore (27)

Bleak, James Godson (26)

Bleak, James Godson, Jr. (2)

Bleak, Mary Moore (infant)

Bleak, Richard Moore (6)

Bleak, Thomas Nelson (4)

Bowers, Elizabeth (27)

Bradshaw, Elizabeth Simpson (48)

Bradshaw, Isabella Jane (10)

Bradshaw, Richard Paul (6)

Bradshaw, Robert Hall (11)

Brice, Hannah (54)

Brice, Jane (9)

Brice, John (12)

Brice, Richard (55)

Bridges, Alfred Bloomfield (21)

Briggs, Eliza (19)

Briggs, Emma (1)

Briggs, James (11)

Briggs, John (42)

Briggs, Mary Hannah (7)

Briggs, Rachel (3)

Briggs, Ruth Butterworth (39)

Briggs, Sarah Ann (4)

Briggs, Thomas (13)

Brooks, Alice (21)

Brooks, Betty Smith (54)

Brooks, Nathan (61)

Brown, Elizabeth Eleanor (35)

Brown, Jane (25)

Burton, Eliza Cusworth (32)

Burton, Joseph Friend (6)

Burton, Martha Ann (4)

Carter, Ellen Jackson (38)

Carter, John (10)

Carter, Luke (45)

Clark, Margaretta Unwin (28)

Clegg, Alice (9)

Clegg, Ellen Walmsley (40)

Clegg, Henry (3)

Clegg, Jonathan (40)

Clegg, Margaret Ellen (infant)

Clegg, William (14)

Clifton, Ann (6)

Clifton, Mary Matilda Blanchard (45)

Clifton, Rebecca (20)

Clifton, Robert (50)

Clifton, Sophia (12)

Collings, David (4)

Collings, Emma Luella Lawrence (30)

Collings, Frederick John (6)

Collings, George (2)

Collings, Louisa (9)

Collings, Richard (37)

Collings, Samuel Willard (infant)

Cook, Jemima (23)

Crane, Ann (24)

Crossley, Ephraim Jarvis (5)

Crossley, Hannah (15)

Crossley, Joseph Smith (19)

Crossley, Mary Jarvis (45)

Crossley, Sarah (12)

Crossley, William (1)

Davies, Elizabeth Williams (44)

Davis, Edmund (32)

Dixon (unknown)

Dobson, Alice Pickup (48)

Dobson, Mary Ann (24)

Dobson, Thomas (19)

Dobson, Willard Richards (17)

Dodd, Alma (10)

Dodd, Brigham Young (infant)

Dodd, Elizabeth (2)

Dodd, Elizabeth Pearson (39)

Dodd, Joseph Smith (6)

Dodd, Thomas (8)

Dodd, Thomas (36)

Douglass, John (41)

Douglass, Mary Dyson Billingham (36)

Douglass, William (14)

Durham, Mary Morton (27)

Durham, Thomas (28)

Eccles, Alice Hardman (34)

Eccles, Martha (9)

Eccles, Mary Ann (11)

Eccles, Thomas (37)

Edmonds, Charles (56)

Edwards, Harriet (18)

Edwards, William (28)

Elliott, Eliza (20)

Foster, Sarah (25)

Franklin, Jane Buckland (34)

Franklin, Lydia (14)

Franklin, Thomas Job (34)

Franks, Sarah (24)

Furner, Robert (25)

Furner, William (21)

Gibbons, Jane (26)

Giles, Aaron Barnet (15)

Gourley, Ellison Jaap (24)

Gourley, George (5)

Gourley, Janet (8)

Gourley, Margaret Glass (infant)

Gourley, Nicholaus (11)

Gourley, Paul (43)

Gourley, Paul (2)

Green, Ann (22)

Green, Charles (26)

Green, Elizabeth (23)

Green, George [or Charles] (infant)

Greening, Mary Ann (27)

Gregory, Ann (63)

Gregory, Mary (59)

Griffiths, Elizabeth (30)

Griffiths, Herbert Lorenzo (5)

Griffiths, Jane Eleanore (8)

Griffiths, John (11)

Griffiths, John (46)

Griffiths, Margaret Ann (16)

Grundy, Sarah (41)

Haigh, Samuel (20)

Haigh, Sarah Ann (18)

Halford, John (58)

Halford, Sarah (53)

Hall, Charles (21)

Hall, Elizabeth (24)

Hall (infant)

Harper, Mary (64)

Harrison, Aaron (19)

Harrison, Alice (10)

Harrison, George (14)

Harrison, Hannah (2)

Harrison, Hannah Ellis (39)

Harrison, Mary Ann (12)

Harrison, Olivia (6)

Harrison, Sam (unknown)

Harrison, Sarah Ellen (infant)

Harrison, William (41)

Hartle, Elizabeth Williams (33)

Hartle, Ephraim (infant)

Hartle, John (70)

Hartle, John (12)

Hartle, Lydia Kniveton (71)

Hartle, Mary (36)

Hartle, Samuel (6)

Hartle, William (39)

Hartle, William (3)

Hartley, Elizabeth Gill (40)

Hartley, Farewell Harrison (7)

Hartley, Josephine Lucy (10)

Hartley, Matilda Jane (17)

Hartley, Samuel (14)

Hartley, Sarah Wells (219)

Haslam, Esther Howarth (52)

Haslam, Joseph (18)

Hawkey, Hannah (3)

Hawkey, Hannah Middleton (33)

Hawkey, James (14)

Hawkey, Margaret Ann (5)

Haydock, Elizabeth (56)

Haydock, Mary (21)

Henshall, David (41)

Herring, George (16)

Herring, Mary Cook (35)

Hicks, Ann (20)

Higgs, Lydia (45)

Hill, William (48)

Hill, William, Jr. (9)

Holt, Alice (13)

Holt, Daniel (16)

Holt, Ellen Walker (44)

Holt, James (22)

Holt, Joseph (11)

Holt, Margaret (23)

Holt, Martha (5)

Holt, Robert (42)

Hooker, Lydia Elizabeth (20)

Horrocks, Mary (19)

Housley, George Frederick (19)

Housley, Harriet Agnes Cook (44)

Howard, William (10)

Hunter, Catherine (15)

Hunter, Catherine Starkey (43)

Hunter, George (19)

Hunter, Hannah (5)

Hunter, James (23)

Hunter, James (43)

Hunter, James Edward (3)

Hunter, John James (17)

Hunter, Robert (6)

Hurst, Elizabeth Sarah Hulme (48)

Hyatt, John (36)

Jackson, Aaron (2)

Jackson, Aaron (31)

Jackson, Alice (41)

Jackson, Ann Grimshaw (50)

Jackson, Charles (60)

Jackson, Elizabeth (24)

Jackson, Elizabeth Horrocks (29)

Jackson, James (47)

Jackson, Jane (75)

Jackson, Joseph (16)

Jackson, Lydia C. (15)

Jackson, Martha (22)

Jackson, Martha Ann (7)

Jackson, Mary Elizabeth (4)

Jackson, Mary Loxam (62)

Jackson, Nephi (9)

Jackson, Samuel (40)

Jackson, Samuel (12)

Jackson, William (21)

Jaques, Alpha Loader (infant)

Jaques, Ann (42)

Jaques, Caroline (16)

Jaques, Flora Loader (1)

Jaques, John (29)

Jaques, Zilpah Loader (25)

Jervis, Agnes (7)

Jervis, Amelia Ann Thomas (35)

Jervis, Amelia Jane (12)

Jervis, Frederick (5)

Johnson, Ann (32)

Johnson, Elizabeth (57)

Jones, Albert (16)

Jones, Samuel Stephen (19)

Jones, Sarah Ann Bradshaw (55)

Jones, William Mason (73)

Jupp, Mary (35)

Kemp, Henry (25)

Kewley, Ann Karran (40)

Kewley, James (53)

Kewley, Margaret (16)

Kewley, Robert (11)

Kirkman, Hyrum (4)

Kirkman, James (2)

Kirkman, John (8)

Kirkman, Joseph (6)

Kirkman, Mary Lawson (33)

Kirkman, Peter (infant)

Kirkman, Robert (10)

Kirkman, Robert Lomax (34)

Lawley, George (55)

Leah, James H. (57)

Leah, Sarah M. Berry (59)

Lloyd, Ann (36)

Lloyd, Jane (7)

Loader, Amy Britnell (54)

Loader, James (57)

Loader, Jane (14)

Loader, Maria (19)

Loader, Patience (28)

Loader, Robert (9)

Loader, Sarah (12)

Loader, Tamar (22)

Lord, Charles (39)

Lord, James (45)

Lord, Mary Hentwistle Duckworth (36)

Loynd, Elizabeth Thompson (46)

Loynd, James (16)

Loynd, James (50)

Loynd, Joseph Smith (12)

Loynd, Richard (10)

Loynd, Thomas (15)

Maisey, Daniel (39)
Maisey, George (4)
Maisey, Rebecca (1)
Maisey, Rebecca Simmons (34)
Maisey, Silas (6)
Marchant, Caroline Amanda (26)
Marshall, Emily Montague (9)
Marshall, Marion Fleming Brown (34)
Martin, Edward (37)
Martin, Eliza Salmon (23)
Martin, George (infant)
Mattinson, Ann Shaw (44)
Mattinson, Elizabeth Ann (3)
Mattinson, George Thomas (12)
Mattinson, John (17)
Mattinson, Robert (52)
Mattinson, Robert (21)
Mayho, Ann Howarth (40)
Mayho, Mary Elizabeth (9)
Mayho, Noah (6)
Mayho, Peter (40)
Mayne, John (24)
McBride, Ether Enos (8)
McBride, Heber Robert (13)
McBride, Janetta Ann (16)
McBride, Margaret Alice (2)
McBride, Margaret Ann Howard (41)
McBride, Peter Howard (6)
McBride, Robert (52)
Mee, Betsy (14)
Mee, Charlotte (22)
Mellor, Charlotte Elizabeth (14)
Mellor, Clara Althea (3)
Mellor, Emma Marintha (3)
Mellor, James (37)
Mellor, James, Jr. (8)
Mellor, Louisa (15)
Mellor, Mary Ann (10)
Mellor, Mary Ann Payne (39)
Mellor, William Charles (5)
Middleton, Amy Parsons (42)
Middleton, John (15)
Middleton, William (39)
Mitchell, James (4)

Mitchell, Mary (32)
Moores, Elizabeth (26)
Moores, Sarah Jane (2)
Morley, Sarah Ann (29)
Morton, Eliza (20)
Moss, Alice (10)
Moss, Edward (21)
Moss, Hyrum Ralph (7)
Moss, James (12)
Moss, Joseph (49)
Moss, Joseph, Jr. (15)
Moss, Mary Brabin (45)
Moss, Peter John (18)
Munn, Edward Frederick (22)
Murdoch, Mary Murray (73)
Nightingale, Jane Archer (57)
Nightingale, Jemima (21)
Nightingale, Joseph (16)
Nightingale, Sarah Ann (31)
Normington, Daniel (1)
Normington, Ephraim Robert (4)
Normington, Hannah (6)
Normington, Lovinia (10)
Normington, Maria Jackson (36)
Normington, Mary Ellen (8)
Normington, Thomas (37)
Oldham, Jane Elizabeth (4)
Oldham, John (33)
Oldham, Louis William (infant)
Oldham, Sarah Hodgkinson (23)
Ollerton, Alice (19)
Ollerton, Alice Dandy (53)
Ollerton, Jane Ann (15)
Ollerton, John (56)
Ollerton, Sarah (5)
Openshaw, Ann Walmsley Greenhalgh (50)
Openshaw, Eleanor (14)
Openshaw, Eliza Booth (20)
Openshaw, Levi (19)
Openshaw, Mary (15)
Openshaw, Mary Ann (10)
Openshaw, Samuel (22)
Openshaw, William (60)
Openshaw, William (unknown)

Ord, Eleanor Grant (26)
Ord, Thomas (29)
Orme, Amy Kirby (52)
Orme, Rebecca (18)
Orme, Samuel Washington (23)
Orme, Sarah Ann (29)
Padley, George W. (19)
Parker, Caroline (36)
Parker, Ellen (8)
Parker, Esther Rushton (37)
Parker, Priscilla (6)
Parkes, Elizabeth Hannah (29)
Parkinson, Elizabeth Jane (11)
Parkinson, Ellen (5)
Parkinson, Ellen Smalley (37)
Parkinson, Esther (2)
Parkinson, John (7)
Parkinson, John (37)
Parkinson, Joseph (16)
Parkinson, Margaret (9)
Parkinson, Samuel (18)
Patching, Susannah (49)
Pearce, Robert (31)
Pears, Eliza (19)
Pears, John Burton (57)
Pears, Rosehannah Whitehead (55)
Peel, Anna Naomi (8)
Peel, Hannah Rhoades (42)
Peel, John (58)
Peel, Marintha Althere (5)
Peyton, Eliza (infant)
Peyton, Margaret Hodges (38)
Peyton, Nathaniel (59)
Platt, Benjamin (23)
Platt, Mary Graves (19)
Porrit, Margaret McCann (36)
Porrit, Nathaniel (15)
Porrit, Rebecca (13)
Porrit, Thomas (6)
Pucell, Ann (24)
Pucell, Eliza Schofield (25)
Pucell, Ellen (9)
Pucell, Margaret August (14)
Pucell, Margaret Perren (53)

Pucell, Robert (infant)
Pucell, Samuel (50)
Pucell, William (25)
Quinn, Elizabeth (17)
Quinn, Harriet (19)
Quinn, Mary Ann (23)
Ramsden, Esther Clough (43)
Ramsden, Samuel C. (12)
Ramsden, Samuel Lee (45)
Read, Alicia Quilley (15)
Read, Elizabeth Georgiana Quilley (52)
Read, Samuel George (49)
Read, Samuel Milford (14)
Read, Thisbe Quilley (11)
Read, Walter Pyramus (7)
Rhead, Edward Henry (5)
Rhead, Eliza Lewis (31)
Rhead, Eliza Persis (1)
Rhead, Josiah (25)
Riley, Mary Ann Malley (39)
Riley, Thomas Caton (12)
Robinson, Dorothy (32)
Robinson, Elizabeth (20)
Robinson, Elizabeth Gambles (18)
Robinson, Elizabeth Sarah Gambles (15)
Robinson, Frederic Charles (29)
Robinson, George (53)
Robinson, George (13)
Robinson, Margaret Angus (52)
Robinson, Solomon (23)
Rodwell, John (55)
Rodwell, Sara Jane Morgan (59)
Rogerson, Bridget (23)
Rogerson, James (25)
Rogerson, John Edward (9)
Rogerson, Josiah (15)
Rogerson, Mary Harrison Ferron (52)
Rogerson, Sarah Ann (12)
Rogerson, William Valentine (22)
Royal [or Ryle], Sarah (67)
Scott, Berry (54)
Sculthorpe, George John (47)
Seddon, Elizabeth (18)
Seddon, Esther (12)

Seddon, Richard (36)

Sermon, Elizabeth Whitear (37)

Sermon, Henry (7)

Sermon, John Lloyd (9)

Sermon, Joseph (54) [died and buried on the trail west of Devil's Gate, 1856]

Sermon, Marian Eliza (3)

Sermon, Robert (5)

Severn, Mary Astle (19)

Severn, William Thomas (19)

Shorten, James (14)

Somerville, Mary (32)

Southwell, John William (23)

Speakman, Hannah (19)

Squires, Catherine Harriet (5)

Squires, Clara Annie (3)

Squires, Echo Levinia (infant)

Squires, Henry Augustus (31)

Squires, Mary Emily (6)

Squires, Rosetta Agnes (1)

Squires, Sarah Augusta (8)

Squires, Sarah Minnie Catlin (29)

Steele, Elizabeth Wylie (29)

Steele, James (30)

Steele, James Ephraim (4)

Steele, William George (1)

Stimpson, Frederick (3)

Stimpson, Rebecca Lubbock (30)

Stimpson, William (35)

Stimpson, William B. (1)

Stimpson (infant)

Stinson, Samuel (unknown)

Stone, Hannah Rachel (9)

Stone, James (32)

Stone, James Erastus (3)

Stone, John Charles (5)

Stone, Jonathan (53)

Stone, Mary Mills (35)

Stone, Sarah Elizabeth (8)

Tann, Catherine (14)

Tasker, Andrew (52)

Taylor, Eliza (44)

Taylor, Elizabeth (17)

Taylor, Elizabeth Hinton (53)

Taylor, Harriet Sidwell (50)

Taylor, James (39)

Taylor, Jesse Soar (10)

Taylor, Joseph (44)

Taylor, Mary Soar (31)

Taylor, William Henry (12)

Thomas, Ann Jane (14)

Thomas, James (unknown)

Thompson, John Walthew (30)

Thompson, Mary Jane (9)

Thompson, Mary Thompson (30)

Thomson, Moses (24)

Thorne, James (56)

Thornton, Amanda Jane (5)

Thornton, Hannah Heaton (29)

Thornton, Sarah Ann (3)

Thornton, Wardman (9)

Toone, John (43)

Twelves, Ann Elizabeth Henrietta (7)

Twelves, Ann Elizabeth Henrietta Gunn (36)

Twelves, Brigham (3)

Twelves, Charles (37)

Twelves, Charles Samuel (13)

Twelves, John Robert (11)

Twelves, Mary Jane (infant)

Twelves, Orson (6)

Tyler, Daniel (39)

Upton, Mary Taylor (20)

Upton, William (21)

Venner, Richard (78)

Walker, James (28)

Walker, Sarah Rebecca Ekins (23)

Walker, William T. (43)

Wallwork, Thomas (27)

Wallwork, William (6)

Walsh, Alice Fish Bury (27)

Walsh, John (3)

Walsh, Robert (5)

Walsh, Sarah (infant)

Walsh, William (30)

Wardell, Hannah (35)

Wardle, Isaac John (21)

Watkins, Elizabeth (4)

Watkins, John (22)

Watkins, John Thomas (1)

Watkins, Margaret Ackhurst (23)

Watts, Charles O. (18)

Waugh, George Peden (68)

Webster, Amy Elizabeth (infant)

Webster, Ann Elizabeth Parsons (25)

Webster, Francis (25)

White, Alice Eleanor (1)

White, Elias (26)

White, Elizabeth E. (23)

White, George Washington (5)

White, Maria Christmas (55)

Whittaker, Robert (19)

Wignall, Grace (3)

Wignall, Grace Slater (33)

Wignall, James (7)

Wignall, Jane (5)

Wignall, Joseph Smith (11)

Wignall, Mary (9)

Wignall, Mary Ann (25)

Wignall, Sarah Jane (16)

Wignall, Sarah Parkinson (48)

Wignall, William (33)

Wignall, William Henry (infant)

Wilkinson, Charles (40)

Wilkinson, Joseph Thomas (9)

Wilkinson, Mary (4)

Wilkinson, Sarah Hughes (40)

Wilkinson, Sarah Jane (6)

Williamson, Ann Aldred (48)

Williamson, Betsy (3)

Williamson, Elizabeth Ann (19)

Williamson, Ellen (23)

Williamson, John (11)

Williamson, Mary (16)

Williamson, Sarah (20)

Williamson, William (13)

Wilson, Elizabeth Ollerton (24)

Wilson, James (26)

Winn, Jane Broughton (58)

Winn, Mary Ann (12)

Wood, Mary (59)

Wood, Peter (75)

Woodcock, Charles (52)

Woodcock, Jane (34)

Woodcock, Joseph (29)

Woodhead, John (20)

Wright, Charles (13)

Wright, Elizabeth (22)

Wright, Elizabeth Adamson (59)

Wright, Emma Maria (2)

Wright, James Brigham (11)

Wright, John (48)

Wright, Rachel Watts (46)

Wright, Sarah Ann Brett (30)

Wright, Thomas Brett (4)

Wrigley, Ann (60)

Wylie, Mary Ann George (66)

SIXTH HANDCART COMPANY

Captain: Israel Evans

Departure: May 22–23, 1857

Arrival: September 11–12, 1857

Number of Participants: 82

Company Information: The Sixth Handcart Company had
82 individuals and 28 handcarts in the company when it began
its journey from the outfitting post at Iowa City, Iowa.

Alexander, Samuel Henry (17)

Angus, John Clark (21)

Ashby, Benjamin (28)

Ball, Sarah Ann Marwick Simmons (31)

Ball, William (24)

Benthan, Jane (28)

Bonelli, Anna Maria Amman (50)
Bonelli, Elizabeth (16)
Bonelli, Hans George (59)
Bonelli, Louisa (13)
Bonelli, Susanna (19)
Brighton, Annie Stewart (16)
Brighton, Catherine Bow (28)
Brighton, Janet Hare (5)
Brighton, Robert Alexander (1)
Brighton, William Stuart (27)
Brown, Adam Cook (7)
Brown, David Cook (4)
Brown, Mary Cook (34)
Brown, Walter Cook (9)
Brown, William Melville (13)
Cockshott, Mary Alice (22)
Crane, Elias (27)
Davis [or Davies], Hugh (19)
England, Annie (19)
Evans, Israel (28)
Fishburn, Robert Lemming (22)
Gibbons, Thomas (37)
Gilbert, Athaliah Weight (34)
Gilbert, James (9)
Gilbert, Richard (36)
Griffin, Jesse (28)
Griffin, Mary Chapple (27)
Hallet, Eliza (20)
Henshaw, Mary (20)
Hutchings, Mary Robbins (27)
Hutchings, William Lawrence (27)
Jack, Henry Levi (1)
Jack, Mary Ann Dunlap (33)
Jack, Thomas Patterson (35)
Jackson, Ellen (15)
Jackson, James (31)
Jones, Hannah Pendlebury (24)
Jones, Phoebe (31)
Jones [sister] (unknown)

Kelson, Ruth (37)
King, Mary (unknown)
Lunt, Alfred (11)
Lunt, Edward (41)
Lunt, Elizabeth (8)
Lunt, Harriet Wood (34)
Lunt, Nephi (3)
Lunt, Shadrick (6)
Melverton, Susan Roper (17)
Morgan, Evan Samuel (23)
Muller [brother] (unknown)
Muller [sister] (unknown)
Muller (infant)
Neal, Charles (22)
Noble, Elizabeth Priscilla (21)
Pollard, Sarah (22)
Reader, Charlotte Honor Welch (27)
Reader, James (29) [died and buried on the trail in Nebraska]
Reader, John Henry (2)
Roberts, Griffith (23)
Roberts, Jane Parry (26)
Shaw, Elizabeth (20)
Simmons, Caroline (10)
Simmons, Catherine Davis (27)
Simmons, Catherine Sophia (6)
Simmons, Hannah (1)
Simmons, Henry (30)
Simmons, Margaret (8)
Simmons, William (unknown)
Simonson, Anna May Johnson (36)
Smith, Elizabeth (26)
Smith [sister] (unknown)
Theurer, John (19)
Walker, Elizabeth (24)
Waylett, George Dowsett (26)
Winchester, Catherine (28)
Wood, Lyman (unknown)

SEVENTH COMPANY
Captain: Christian Christiansen
Departure: June 15, 1857
Arrival: September 13, 1857
Number of Participants: 275
Company Information: The Seventh Handcart Company had
275 individuals, 68 handcarts, and 3 wagons when it began its journey
from the outfitting post at Iowa City, Iowa. This company was first
headed by James Park, David Dille, and George Thurston.

Anderson, Andrea Catherine Johanne (5)
Anderson, Charles Augustus (11)
Anderson, Christina Boletta (3)
Anderson, Gustave (37)
Anderson, Jens Christian (36)
Anderson, Josephine Brighamina (1)
Anderson, Lauritz Peter (7)
Anderson, Maren Thorstensen (36)
Anderson, Margaret Nielsen Christiansen (27)
Aragerup, N. (unknown)
Bastian, Gertrude Pedersen (22)
Bastian, Jacob Sander (22)
Brothersen, Anne (1)
Brothersen, Bohne [or Bolin] (6)
Brothersen, Christian (46)
Brothersen, Diantha (9)
Brothersen, Else Mortensen (31)
Brothersen, Hans (7)
Brothersen, Martin (4)
Christensen, Anders Christian (48)
Christensen, Andrea (1)
Christensen, Anna Margretta (20)
Christensen, Carl Christian Anthon (25)
Christensen, Caroline (3)
Christensen, Christiana Jeppedatter (23)
Christensen, Christina [or Christiana] (infant)
Christensen, Eliza Rosalia Sternhjem Harby (22)
Christensen, Kirsten Margrethe Jensen (35)
Christensen, Lars Christian (25)
Christensen, Mads (32)

Christensen, Maren Johanne Jensen (30)
Christensen, Nils (25)
Christensen, Peter Christian (18)
Christensen, Rasmus Peter (infant)
Christensen, Sophia Marie Pedersen (43)
Christiansen, Ane Margrethe (51)
Christiansen, Christian (32)
Christiansen, Christian Nielson (38)
Christiansen, Karen Marie (14)
Dorius, Carl Christian Nikolai (27)
Dorius, Ellen Gurinda Rolfson (20)
Dorius, John Frederick Ferdinand (25)
Dorius, Karen Frantzen (22)
Eggertsen, Simon Peter (31)
Erickson, Kersten (20)
Erickson, Kersten Christensen (50)
Erickson, Marcus (48)
Folkman, George Jorgen Christopher (64)
Folkman, Jens Peter (28)
Folkman, Matilda Kristina Funk (20)
Frantzen, John (20)
Frantzen, Lars (45)
Frantzen, Martha Maria Johansen (44)
Garff, Christian Nielsen (9)
Garff, Decan Westmoreland (infant)
Garff, Josephine Patrine (2)
Garff, Lauritz Nielsen (4)
Garff, Marie Jacobsen (36)
Garff, Niels Jorgensen (46)
Garff, Peter Nielsen (14)
Gibb, Hanna Eugenia (3)
Gibb, Mica Martine Cathrine Margrethe Pedersen (23)

Gottfredson, Hans James (8)
Gottfredson, Jens (47)
Gottfredson, Jens Peter (11)
Gottfredson, Joseph Smith (4)
Gottfredson, Karen Marie Meilhede
    Pedersen (28)
Gottfredson, Mette Christine (6)
Gottfredson, Platine Plattina (infant)
Green, C. Christina (unknown)
Green, William (50)
Gudmundsen, Gudmund (32)
Hakanson, Anna (18)
Hakanson, Elsa (22)
Handberg, Johanna Christina (18)
Hansen, Anne Margretha Ohlsen (37)
Hansen, Bertha Maria (34)
Hansen, Christian Hans (19)
Hansen, Embreth (37)
Hansen, Erastusina (2)
Hansen, Frederik (12)
Hansen, Hans (45)
Hansen, Hans (9)
Hansen, Jens Martin (infant)
Hansen, Maren Christina (5)
Hansen, Maria (7)
Hansen, Oliver (5)
Hansen, Peter (unknown), Tailor [died
    August 4 or 5 in western Nebraska]
Holm, Jens Neilson (39)
Holm, Margaret Christina Ipson (39)
Holm, Margaret Christine (13)
Hultberg, Anders (3)
Hultberg, Anna Catrina (7)
Hultberg, Christopher (35)
Hultberg, Karna (36)
Jacobsen, Camilla Dorothy (16)
Jacobsen, Karen (32)
Jacobsen, Lars (23)
Jacobsen, Marie Ingeborg Olsen (51)
Jacobsen, Olavus (12)
Jacobsen, Soren (26)
Jensen, Anders (53)
Jensen, Ane (8)
Jensen, Ane Marie (23)

Jensen, Annie Christine Rasmussen (47)
Jensen, Christiane (19)
Jensen, Hans (40)
Jensen, Jacob Hans (11)
Jensen, Jacob Johann Heidemann (4)
Jensen, James (16)
Jensen, Jens (27)
Jensen, Jens Martin (infant)
Jensen, Karen (13)
Jensen, Mads (35)
Jensen, Maren Jacobsen Heidemann (32)
Jensen, Maren Sophia Christensen (16)
Jensen, Maria Sophia (1)
Jensen, Mary Ann (15)
Jensen, Peter M. (6)
Jensen, Sidsie Marie Jacobsen (42)
Jensen, Sophie (1)
Jensen, Soren Peter (6)
Johnson, Caroline Cecilia (23)
Johnson, James H. (20)
Johnson, Maria Elisabeth Hendrichsen
    (54)
Just, Christian A. (11)
Just, Hyrum Pedersen (infant)
Just, Jens Pedersen (8)
Just, Joseph Petersen (3)
Just, Karen Marie Christensen (34)
Just, Nels Andersen (10)
Just, Peter Anderson (40)
Karlson, Britta Anderson (36)
Karlson, Claus Herman (7)
Karlson, Lars (43)
Larson, Andrew [or Anders] (38)
Larson, Anna M. Thompson (29)
Larson, Anna Hannah (7)
Larson, Caroline Anderson [or Caroline
    Andrews] (44)
Larson, Lauritz (23)
Larson, Lewis [or Lorens] (10)
Larson, Mary Christine (5)
Laurentzen [Lund], [Mrs.] (unknown)
Liljenquist, Ola Nilsson (31)
Lorentzen, Maria Cristina (26)
Lublin, Heinman Magnus (9)

Lublin, Hyrum (infant)

Lublin, Johanna Kirstine Christensen (37)

Lublin, Kate (15)

Lublin, Samuel (40)

Madsen, Bertha Hansen Daniel (50)

Madsen, Niels Peter (51)

Mickelson, Anna Catherine Hansen (45)

Mickelson, Jens (49)

Mickelson, Martha (13)

Mickelsen, Mary Ann (15)

Mortensen, Diedrick (51)

Mortensen, Elsie Catherine (6)

Mortensen, Jens (10)

Mortensen, Johanne (12)

Mortensen, Maren Jensen (52)

Nelson, Catherine Jensen (24)

Nelson, Nels Christian (29)

Nielsen, Mette Kirsten (72)

Olsen, Andrew (13)

Olsen, Ane Andersen (33)

Olsen, Caroline Karen Marie (11)

Olsen, Caroline Margaret (33)

Olsen, Caroline Olevia (3)

Olsen, Christine (22)

Olsen, Frederick (32)

Olsen, Ludvig Just [Livy] (infant)

Olsen, Maren Justesdatter (35)

Olsen, Nicoline (21)

Olsen, Ole (6)

Olsen, Ole Christopher (32)

Olsen, Peter (35)

Park, James Pollock (35)

Pedersen, Christiana (22)

Rasmussen, Bertha Maria (15)

Rasmussen, Elizabeth (38)

Rasmussen, Rasmina M. (16)

Rasmussen, Rasmus (9)

Rolfsen, Gertrude Maria (27)

Rolfsen, Gertrude Maria Wroldsen (58)

Rudd, Lorenzo Dow (27)

Salisbury, Oke [or O. K.] (20)

Sandersen, Johanna Marie (21)

Schow, Hans Soren Sorenson (31)

Schow, Hirum Smith (infant)

Schow, Maren Nielsen (31)

Sorensen, Anders (7)

Sorensen, Anna (30)

Sorensen, Anna Maria (3)

Sorensen, Anna Marie Andersen (33)

Sorensen, Elsie (14)

Sorensen, Julie Ane Marie (infant) [born on
    the trail in Nebraska]

Sorensen, Kirsten Pedersen (38)

Sorensen, Mary Bodil (9)

Sorensen, Morten (28)

Sorensen, Niels (34)

Sorensen, Niels (33)

Sorenson, Iowa (infant) [born on the trail
    near Wood River in Nebraska]

Thomasen, Inger Andrea (28)

Thomasen, Johanne (32)

Karen (unknown)

EIGHTH COMPANY
Captain: George Rowley
Departure: June 7, 1859
Arrival: September 4, 1859
Number of Participants: 276
Company Information: The Eighth Handcart Company had
276 individuals, 60 handcarts, and 8 wagons when it began its journey
from the outfitting post at Florence, Nebraska.

Adams, William (22)
Andersen, Hakan (33)
Andrews, Franklin Wilford (4)
Andrews, Mary Ann Ashworth (31)
Arvidson, Mathilde (35)
Atkin, Esther Ann (1)
Atkin, Rachel Thompson (24)
Atkin, William (infant)
Atkin, William (24)
Atkins, Reuben (27)
Barrett, Charles (unknown)
Barrett, Matilda (16)
Bartlett, Clara (21)
Beesley, Ebenezer (18)
Beesley, Sarah Hancock (19)
Bengtsen, Bengte (48)
Bengtson, Tufva (48)
Berthelsen, Albertine (22)
Birrell, Agnes (18)
Booth, Emma (21)
Broadbent, Joseph (22)
Broadbent, Sarah Dixon (25)
Budd, Frances Caroline (18)
Budd, George (14)
Budd, Louisa Capelin (55)
Cartwright, Ann Hardwick (22)
Cartwright, John (20)
Chapel, Caroline (unknown)
Christensen, Anne Marie (infant)
Christensen, Christiane Sophia (24)
Christensen, Lars Christian (36)
Christensen, Niels Christian (5)
Christophersen, Charles (4)
Christophersen, Christian Ludvig (8)

Christophersen, Rasmine Andersen (37)
Christopherson, Jens (37)
Coltrin [brother] (unknown)
Cook, Emma (20)
Cooper, Frederick A. (21)
Cooper, Richard A. (21)
Crockroft, William (unknown)
Davies, Franklin (8)
Davies, Mary (31)
Davis [or Davies], Catharine (47)
Davis [or Davies], James (49)
Dickinson, Maryann [or Maria] (32)
Dickinson, Thomas (41)
Dixon, Elizabeth (15)
Duffin, Abraham (48)
Fahy, Catherine (32)
Farrer, Catherine (18)
Farrer, Sarah Ann (19)
Fautin, Amazene [or Ann Marie] (infant)
Fautin, Inger Kathrina Jensen (24)
Fautin, Thomas Christian Christensen (33)
Florence, Henry (18)
Foster, Hannah (64)
Freece, Anna Margretha (19)
Freece, Peter (25)
Fry, Catherine (unknown)
Fry, Fanny (17)
Gilbert, Joseph (34)
Gledhill, Charles (21)
Gledhill, Elizabeth Bardsley (27)
Godfrey, Ann (26)
Gyde [or Lyde], Ellen (22)
Haagensen [or Hakonsen], Karen Petra (28)
Haagensen [or Hakonsen], Christian (29)

Hansen, Anna (49)

Hansen, Hans Martin (3)

Hansen, Maren Karine Olsen (32)

Hansen, Martin (32)

Hansen, Martina (1)

Hanson, Alice (21)

Hanson, Jane (16)

Hanson, Maria (33)

Harris, Adeline Pamela (13)

Harris, Andrew Edmund (16)

Harris, Charles Edwin (infant) [born July 21, near Chimney Rock, Nebraska]

Harris, James (unknown)

Harris, James (unknown)

Harris, Jane Carter (19)

Harris, Rebecca Morton (43)

Harris, William Morton (19)

Harris, William Thomas (43)

Hartley, Henry (34)

Henthorn, Mary (49)

Hibbert, Ann (26) [apparently abandoned the company to live with a man near Pacific Spring in Wyoming]

Hibbert, Benjamin (18)

Hills, Richard (unknown)

Hobbs, Henry (23)

Hobbs, James (19)

Hobbs, Jane Bellman (25)

Hobbs, William (22)

Ince, John (32)

Jarvis, Ann (13)

Jarvis, Jane Morris (46) [died August 25 in western Wyoming]

Jarvis, Thomas (22) [abandoned the Mormon company near Fort Laramie to head to the Colorado goldfields]

Jarvis, William (41)

Jensen, A. (unknown)

Jensen, Alvina Maria Elnora (infant)

Jensen, Andrew Peter (21)

Jensen, Ann (48)

Jensen, Hans (16)

Jensen, Jens (unknown)

Jensen, Karen (7)

Jensen, Mads (48)

Jensen, Maren (13)

Jensen, Maria Olsen (29)

Jensen, Niels Peter (4)

Jensen, Oluf (35)

Jenson [Yonson], Jens (unknown)

Johanson, Elna Johannesdotter (67)

Johanson, Elna Petronella (36)

Johanson, Johan Elof (infant)

Johanson, Niels Johan (3)

Johnson, Albertine Josephine (22)

Johnson, Andrew John (32)

Johanson, Anders Johan (32)

Jones, George Richard (23)

Jones, Harriet Bruckshaw (32)

Jones, Richard George (36)

Jones, Sarah Jeffcott Pearson (44) [apparently abandoned the company near Devil's Gate to marry a storekeeper]

Jonson, Jens (25)

Jonson, Johannes (25)

Jonson [or Yonson], Anders Y. (21)

Jorgensen [or Yorgensen], Peter (29)

Jorgensen [or Yorgensen], Sophia (unknown)

Kirkpatrick, Mary (unknown)

Lamb, Benjamin Charles (46)

Lamb, Eliza (45)

Larsen, Christina (12)

Larsen, Peter (49)

Larsen, Peter Lawrence (18)

Larsen, Siselia Larsen (53)

Larson, Betsy (5)

Larson, Caroline (4)

Larson, Elna Olsson Malmstrom (33)

Larson, Lehi (2)

Larson, Mons (35)

Later, Peter (24)

Lewis, Ann (20)

Ligget, Joseph (53)

Lindsey, Bithiah Savill (26)

Lindsey, Mark (27)

Magleby, Gjertrude Marie Christiansen Roe (21)

Magleby, Hans Olsen (24)
Mann, Charles William (20)
Mann, Lovinia Ann Smith (23)
Martin, Thomas (23)
Maycock, Louisa Starkey (26)
Maycock, Thomas (27)
McIntyre, Thomas (25)
McKay, Agnes (16)
McKay, Agnes Shields (51)
McKay, Ellen (28)
McKay, Esther (16)
McKay, Jane (22)
McKay, Martha Blair (59)
McKay, Mary (20)
McKay, Mary (36)
McKay, Robert (49)
McKenzie, Jane Thompson (21)
Mills, Richard Isaac (22)
Mitchell, Jane (23)
Moor, Edward (46)
Moor, Hannah (46) [abandoned her husband
    near Devil's Gate]
Moor, Hyrum (unknown)
Morel, Eliza Aubert (42)
Morel, Paul Henri (57)
Nielsen, Mathias Brock (30)
Nuns , Mary Ann (19)
Olpin, Dorcas (11)
Olpin, Ellen (22)
Olpin, Henry (54)
Olpin, Julia (8)
Olpin, Sarah Ann (15)
Olpin, Sarah White (53)
Olsen, Hanna (29)
Olsen, Jorgen (37)
Olsen, Niels (30)
Pearson, Frances Elizabeth (21)
Pearson, Sarah Ann (19)
Peterson, Andrew Henry (13)
Peterson, Anthon (17)
Peterson, Bengta Matilda Nilsson (44)
Peterson, Peter Bjoruk (18)
Peterson [Pehrson], Henrick (46)
Peterson [Pehrson], John Henry (1)

Peterson [Pehrson], Kerstina (8)
Peterson [Pehrson], Ole (11)
Petroel, Mary (unknown)
Pitman, Frank (22)
Reid [or Reed], George (19)
Richardson [brother] (unknown)
Richardson [sister] (unknown)
Robinson [or Robison], Jane (43)
Robinson [or Robison], William (45)
Roseberry, Annie Marie (3)
Roseberry, Carl Nils (33)
Roseberry, Emma Caroline (infant)
Roseberry, Helena Ericksson (36)
Roseberry, Niels Joseph (infant)
Rosenblad, Ole Olsen (35)
Rowley, Alma (7)
Rowley, Anne Brown (30)
Rowley, George (31)
Rowley, Joseph Smith (11)
Rowley, William (13)
Schofield, John (29)
Schofield, Mary Broadbent (29)
Schofield, Thomas (19)
Scoggins, William (37)
Seymour, Caroline (30)
Seymour, Woodruff (9)
Shanks, Edward (66)
Shanks, Mary Jane (53)
Shaw, Alice (10)
Shaw, Joseph (14)
Shaw, Mary (45)
Simson [or Simeon], Caroline (unknown)
Slade, Emma Caroline (18)
Smith, Alexander (2)
Smith, Frances McKay (27)
Smith, John Young (25)
Smith, Martha (infant)
Snellgrove, Mary (55)
Sorensen, Anders (38)
Sorensen, Anne Marie [or Anna Maria] (3)
Sorensen, Christen (24)
Sorensen, Christena Jensen [or Christine]
    (23)
Sorensen, Christena Patrens (infant)

Sorensen, Karen (27)
Sorensen, Karen Marie [or Karen Maria] (36)
Sorensen, Soren (41)
Sorensen, Soren Hansen (10)
Sorenson, Anna (15)
Sorenson, Jens Christian (23)
Sorenson, Karen (53)
Sorenson, Niels Christian (9)
Sorenson, Soren Christian (12)
Sorenson, Sorine Kjerstine (170
Steadman, George (28)
Stewart, Fullerton (51)
Stongberg, Anna Mansson (25)
Strugnel, Henry Fox (29) [left the company
    near Devil's Gate and returned to the
    East]
Thornley, John (25)
Thornley, Margaret (25)
Thornton, Squire (25)
Tuffley, Sarah (22)
Turnbull, James (unknown)
Vadd, Anne Katrine (1)
Vadd, Anne Marie (24)
Vadd, Soren Parley (1)
Vadd [or Wadd], Soren Madsen (33)

Watson, Elizabeth (60)
Whitehead, William (19)
Wilde, Eliza (19)
Wilde, Henry (26)
Wilde, Jane Batchelor (25)
Wilde, John Frederick (6)
Wilde, Mary (14)
Wilde, Mary Elizabeth (4)
Wilde, Sarah Elizabeth (7)
Wilde, Thomas (16)
Wilde, William (52)
Wilson, Charles (33)
Wilson, Hugh (25)
Wilson, Hyrum Lorenzo (6)
Wilson, James William (4)
Wilson, Mary Catherine Fallis (56)
Wilson, Mary Farrow (28)
Wilson, Thomas Wallice (2)
Wolstenholme, Jonathan (48)
Wood, Amelia (9)
Wood, Mary McLean (36)
Wood, Nephi McLean (7)
Wright, Ann (14)
Wright, Ann (40)
Yeates, Esther (16)

NINTH COMPANY

Captain: Daniel Robison
Departure: June 6, 1860
Arrival: August 27, 1860
Number of Participants: 258
Company Information: The Ninth Handcart Company had
258 individuals, 43 handcarts, and 6 wagons when it began its journey
from the outfitting post at Florence, Nebraska.

Baker, Jane (19)
Bell, Edwin (16)
Bell, Joseph (59)
Beverland, James (23)
Beverland, Johanna McNeil (21)
Beverland, Marian (infant)
Booth, Sarah Bedford (25)
Brownlow, Mary Ann (59)

Brownlow, William (55)
Burningham, Alfred (21)
Burningham, Sarah Elizabeth (26)
Burningham, Thomas (18)
Chadwick, Benjamin (23)
Cockin, Hannah (59)
Cook, James (46)
Corbitt, Mary E. (3)

Corbitt, William R. (unknown)

Cousens, Hugh Snape (32)

Crook, Samuel Lane (27)

Crook, Sarah Ann Haines (29)

Crook, William Joshua (3)

Curtis, Edwin Morrell (20)

Curtis, Fanny Harrison (18)

Dalrymple, A. (30)

Facer, George (25)

Facer, George Henry (1)

Facer, Mary Prior (20)

Falconbridge, William (22)

Faux, Jabez (23)

Forscutt, Elizabeth Unsworth (24)

Forscutt, Mark Hill (26)

Gardner, Augusta E. (32)

Gardner, Christopher (30)

Gibson, Anna (8)

Gibson, Jacob (11)

Gibson, John (45)

Gibson, John Blench (3)

Gibson, Mary Ann Blench (36)

Gibson, Thomas (13)

Gibson, Wheatley (15)

Gorton, Mary Ann (24)

Gough, Richard (31)

Gough, Sophia (1)

Gough, Tabitha Darkis Tonks (25)

Green, Margaret Cato (52)

Green, Mary Ann (17)

Green, Thomas (52)

Green, Thomas, Jr. (15)

Gunn, Albert (unknown)

Harrison, Henry James (26)

Heggie, Andrew Walker (35)

Hemming, Emma Elizabeth (infant)

Hemming, Emma Sanford (30)

Hemming, Fanny (7)

Hemming, William (33)

Hobbs, Annie E. (21)

Holder, Ann Pearson (61)

Holder, David (20)

Holder, Edward Pearson (22)

Holmes, Maria (17)

Hook, Alice Bryant Ashdown (48)

Hook, Ann Stevens (23)

Hook, Ellen E. (18)

Hook, Foster Thomas (24)

Hook, Lilias (20)

Hook, Lois (11)

Hook, Louis (15)

Jackson, Ann [or Hannah] (15)

Jackson, Emma (22)

Jacques, Elizabeth (27)

Jacques, Henry (32)

Jacques, Mary Jane Oley (infant)

Jacques, William Thomas (4)

James, David Jenkins (4)

James, Emily (2)

James, Sarah Jenkins (26)

James, William Bowen (30)

Jeager [or Yeager], Henry L. (28)

Jones, Ann Elizabeth (11)

Jones, Anne (13)

Jones, George (11)

Jones, Gomer Thomas (19)

Jones, James (17)

Jones, Jane (6)

Jones, Rebecca (6)

Jones, Robert (14)

Jones, Sarah Rebecca (7)

Jones, Sarah Thomas (49)

Jones, Thomas (39)

Kipling, Dorothy (38)

Kipling, Jane Ann (5)

Lapish, Emily Virginia (1)

Lapish, Hannah Settle (25)

Lapish, Joseph (50)

Lapish, Laura Jane (3)

Lavender, Elizabeth (21)

Lavender, Mary (22)

Lavender, Susan (27)

Lewis, Ann (35)

Lewis, George (10)

Lewis, John (30)

Long, Alice Metcalf (37)

Long, Henry (43)

Matthews, Mary (22)

Mawson, William Oliver (32)

McAllister, Agnes Marion (infant) [born July 6 along the trail in Nebraska]

McAllister, Christine Graham (4)

McAllister, Daniel (29)

McAllister, Mary (2)

McAllister, Mary McIntyre (29)

McCulloch, Charles (2)

McCulloch, George (5)

McCulloch, John Black (28)

McCulloch, Margaret McNeil (26)

McCulloch, Maria (infant)

McNeil, Alexander (28)

McNeil, Archibald (15)

McNeil, Charles (54)

McNeil, Ellen (10)

McNeil, Isabella (13)

McNeil, Marion (54)

McNeil, Marion (24)

Meldrum, David (8)

Meldrum, George (29)

Meldrum, George (4)

Meldrum, James Lowe (6)

Meldrum, Jean (35)

Meldrum, John Barcley (11)

Meldrum, William (1)

Miller, James (unknown)

Moffat, Alexander David (8)

Moffat, Christina M. (10)

Moffat, David (48)

Moffat, Janet (17)

Moffat, Janet Leishman (43)

Moffat, Joseph Smith (14)

Moffat, Marian (6)

Moffat, Mary Jane Holliday (infant)

Moffat, Millen Atwood (3)

Moffat, William Donaldson (12)

Nash, George (39)

Nash, Maria (42)

Nash, Mary (59)

Naylor, Levi (20)

Nichols, Henry (18)

Nichols, Sarah (37)

Ordidge, Eliza (41)

Ordidge, William (40)

Parkinson, Elizabeth Cooper (48)

Parkinson, Samuel (9)

Parkinson, Thomas (12)

Payne, Ellen (22)

Pearce, Agnes Lane (15)

Pearce, Augustus Embley (40)

Pearce, Caroline Jane Pullen (39)

Pearce, Charles Henry (11)

Pearce, Christabelle (6)

Pearce, George Franklin (3)

Pearce, Georgeanna (infant)

Pearce, Lafayette Duncan (17)

Pearce, Marietta (13)

Pearce, William Augustus (9)

Pilling, John (28)

Richards, David (46)

Richards, Jane (11)

Richards, Margaret (51)

Richards, Miriam (13)

Richards, Rees M. (4)

Richards, William (7)

Richardson, Ann (58)

Robison, Daniel (29)

Robison, Daniel Alexander (6)

Robison, David (33)

Robison, David Cannon (1)

Robison, Ephraim (16)

Robison, Franey Wagaman (18)

Robison, George Quayle Cannon (infant)

Robison, Jaben Smith (3)

Robison, Margaret Smith (25)

Robison, Mary Ann (14)

Robison, Rachel Smith (23)

Robison, William (31)

Rogers, Eliza (22)

Rogers, George (31)

Rogers, Maria (20)

Rogers, William Auchson (24)

Rothwell, Amelia (33)

Royale, Elizabeth (45)

Saunders, Demas Ashdown (26)

Saunders, Hannah Barwell (19)

Shewan, Margaret Isabel (15)

Shewan, William Walter (36)

Sibbett, Hannah Lobelle Robison (34)

Sibbett, Hans (35)

Sibbett, Hugh Greenfield (33)

Sibbett, James Lowery (7)

Sibbett, Mary Alice (1)

Sibbett, Samuel Alexander (6)

Siddoway, Isabella (10)

Siddoway, John (22)

Siddoway, Mary Jones (23)

Siddoway, Richard (8)

Siddoway, Robert (32)

Siddoway, Robert, Jr. (6)

Slater, Hannah (20)

Slater, Joseph (27)

Smith, Anna Elizabeth (5)

Smith, Conrad Alma (27)

Smith, Eliza Robison (24)

Smith, Harriet Cordelia (2)

Stevens, Ann (24)

Stonestrom, Ane Christina Rasmussen (50)

Stonestrom, Christina Sophia Rasmussen (15)

Stonestrom, Hans Peter (9)

Stonestrom, John (55)

Stoney, Robert (25)

Stoney, Sarah Ann (infant)

Stoney, Sarah Jakeman (23)

Taylor, Harriet (52)

Tempest, Betsy Clark Williams (36)

Tempest, Henry (36)

Tempest, James (12)

Tempest, John Henry (10)

Thacker, Phoebe (43)

Thacker, John Pridgen (39)

Townsend, Ann Walton (40)

Townsend, Brigham H. (10)

Townsend, Elizabeth Ann (30)

Townsend, Emma Amelia (12)

Townsend, John William (44)

Townsend, Moroni (9)

Townsend, Rebecca (6)

Wagstaff, John (19)

Walker, Elizabeth Russell (52)

Walker, Sarah (17)

Walker, William (55)

Wardle, James (18)

Wardle, John (49)

Wardle, Mary Kinston Morton (54)

Webb, Charles M. (27)

Webb, Charles Moroni (infant)

Webb, Emily (2)

Webb, Jane Walker (24)

Webb, Mary Ann (28)

Welch, Benjamin Franklin (infant)

Welch, Catherine Robison (26)

Welch, John (6)

Welch, John Joseph (36)

Welch, Susannah (7)

Whitten, Margaret (29)

Wilgus, Aaron Bert (4)

Wilgus, Jesse (51)

Wilgus, Joseph (10)

Wilgus, Mary Jane (16)

Wilgus, Sarah Ann Bishop (47)

Williams, William (12)

Wright, George (25)

Young, Mary Ann (unknown)

TENTH COMPANY
Captain: Oscar O. Stoddard
Departure: July 6, 1860
Arrival: September 24, 1860
Number of Participants: 153
Company Information: The Tenth Handcart Company had
153 individuals, 22 handcarts, and 6 wagons when it began its journey
from the outfitting post at Florence, Nebraska.

Alder, Anna Elizabeth (30)

Alder, Konrad (36)

Anderson, Ane (35)

Anderson, Annie Maria Kjelson (22)

Anderson, Carl J. (35)

Anderson, Johannes G. (40)

Anderson, Lars (32)

Anderson, Neils (25)

Ashton, Mary Bunting (40)

Ashton, Samuel (45)

Bengtsen, Bengta (36)

Bengtson, Bengt (35)

Bondesson, Anders Nilsson (15)

Bondesson, Hanna (49)

Bondesson, Niels (45)

Buhler, James (33)

Chapman, Frances Camila (3)

Chapman, George Watson (5)

Chapman, Rachel Shacklitt Watson (39)

Chapman, William (41)

Chapman, William Henry (10)

Chatelain, Marie Louise (30)

Christensen, Anders (29)

Christensen, Else Pedersen (49)

Christensen, Lauritz Ulrich (15)

Christensen, Peter (18)

Christensen, Soren (59)

Christensen [or Christiansen], Christen
 Terkelsen (37)

Dietschweiler, Joachim (66)

Fields, Anna Susane (14)

Fields, Carl Johan Ellevsen (35)

Fields, Charles Peter (8)

Fields, Heber Samuel (infant)

Fields, Josephine Emelia (10)

Fields, Maren Eline Pedersen (38)

Fischer, Hans Jacob (29)

Fisher, Andrew (2)

Fisher, Anna Barbara Schaufelberger (59)

Fisher, Barbara Wehrli (19)

Fisher, David (32)

Fisher, David (7)

Fisher, Elizabeth Sigrist (24)

Fisher, James (25)

Fisher, Joseph (5)

Fisher, Martha (10)

Fisher, Martha McKay (33)

Fjeldstead, Peter A. (38)

Forscutt, Mark (26)

Fredericksen, Ingeborg Gurena (22)

Gvesh, Lorentz (56)

Hallam, Zebedee (63)

Halvorsen, Agnette (30)

Halvorsen, Johannes Larsen (6)

Halvorsen, Lars (46)

Hess, Anna (6)

Hess, Anna Maria Dietschweiler (33)

Hess, Maria Elizabeth (9)

Hirschi, John (27)

Horn, George Henry (10)

Horn, James (4)

Horn, John (13)

Horn, Maryann (8)

Horn, Moroni (1)

Horn, Sarah Morris (38)

Horn, William Henry (38)

Howard, Margaret (24)

Jackson, Henry (45)

Jackson, Maria (43)

Jensen, Elna Anna Petersson (35)

Jensen, Gotfredine Marie (27)

Jensen, Jens (31)

Jensen, Soren (22)

Kerby, Alma (6)

Kerby, Eliza (infant)

Kerby, Francis (38)

Kerby, Harriett (5)

Kerby, Joseph (3)

Kerby, Mary (9)

Kerby, Mary LeCornu (36)

Larsen, Gunild (59)

Larsen, Lars (63)

Lorentze [sister] (unknown)

Moller, Aller (35)

Moller, Mette C. (58)

Moller, Rasmus S. (53)

Nielsen, Anna Maria (26)

Nielsen, Gustave (28)

Olds, Elizabeth Uren (30)

Olds, Mary Jane (9)

Olds, Susan (3)

Olds, Thomas (5)

Olsen, Allen (35)

Olsen, Ane C. (5)

Olsen, Banguel (33)

Olsen, Jens Peter (11)

Olsen, John (12)

Olsen, Kael (30)

Olsen, Maren Kirstine (18)

Paul, Elizabeth (8)

Paul, Harriet (12)

Paul, Harriet May (33)

Paul, Jane (10)

Paul, Joseph (4)

Paul, Mary Frances (infant)

Paul, Nicholas (37)

Paul, William (6)

Pederson, Mons (unknown)

Petersen, Anders (22)

Petersen, Ane (55)

Petersen, Dorthea (17)

Petersen, Moroni (59)

Petersen, Nella (20)

Rasmussen, Anders P. (6)

Rasmussen, Andreas Andrew (39)

Rasmussen, Bertha Karina Hendrikke
        Christophersdotter (41)

Rasmussen, Carl Hermen (8)

Rasmussen, Christian Richard (16)

Rasmussen, Johan [or Johanne] (2)

Rasmussen, Maren (39)

Rasmussen, Rasmus (29)

Rasmussen, Rasmus, Jr. (8)

Rogers [sister] (unknown)

Roston, Jean Michael (43)

Roston, Martha Avandete (30)

Sorensen, Andrew (18)

Sorensen, Ane (35)

Sorensen, Ane Chris (34)

Sorensen, Ane M. (34)

Sorensen, Anne Maria Nilsson (49)

Sorensen, Bengt (34)

Sorensen, Christian (7)

Sorensen, Johanna (20)

Sorensen, Kimball (3)

Sorensen, Kjersti (24)

Sorensen, Niels (56)

Sorensen, Peter (35)

Stoddard, Henry Cooley (36)

Stoddard, Oscar Orlando (38)

Stucki, Christian (infant)

Stucki, John Stettler (9)

Stucki, Magdalena Stettler (37)

Stucki, Mary Ann (6)

Stucki, Rosina (3)

Stucki, Samuel (36)

Taylor, Adelia Caroline Rogers (50)

Taylor, Caroline (4)

Taylor, Dora (6)

Taylor, Eliza (28)

Taylor, Elizabeth (18)

Taylor, Emily (20)

Taylor, Joseph Hyrum (10)

Taylor, Sarah Jane (15)

Taylor, Stephen King (52)

Ukermaur or Uckerman, Angette (44)

NOTES

Epigraphs: Tyler, Autobiographical Sketch, 51–52; Moulton, Notebooks, April 19, 1997; Moulton, Letter to Mark H. Forscutt, August 13, 1856; Beesley, Reminiscences.

CHAPTER 1

1. Mulder, *Homeward to Zion*, 25.

2. Ibid., 19.

3. *Doctrine and Covenants*, sec. 38, verse 35.

4. Linforth, *Route from Liverpool to Great Salt Lake Valley Illustrated*, 1.

5. Ibid., 2.

6. Moore, *Bones in the Well*.

7. Linforth, *Route from Liverpool*, 5. The following quotations from the epistle and instructions are also from this source (page numbers noted parenthetically in the text).

8. Mulder, *Homeward to Zion,* 29.

9. Ibid., 81.

10. Ibid., 139.

11. Ibid., 142.

12. Young, "Second General Epistle" (October 12, 1849), 207–8.

13. Hartley, "The Place of Mormon Handcart Companies in America's Westward Migration Story," 106.

14. Linforth, *Route from Liverpool*, 12–13.

15. Hafen and Hafen, *Handcarts to Zion*, 25.

16. *Deseret News*, October 19, 1854

17. Mulder, *Homeward to Zion*, 143.

18. Bagley, *South Pass*, 170; Mulder, *Homeward to Zion*, 144.

19. *Millennial Star*, December 22, 1855.

20. "Hand Carts for the Plains," 2.

21. *Millennial Star*, December 22, 1855, quoted in Hafen and Hafen, *Handcarts to Zion*, 30–31.

22. Ibid.

23. Ibid., 32

24. "Hand Carts for the Plains," 2. The following recommendations to Taylor and his response are all from this source.

25. Taylor, "Emigration," 2.

26. Ibid. By "ironed" Taylor meant that they had iron wagon rims.

27. Smith, "Leadership, Planning, and Management of the 1856 Mormon Handcart Emigration," 148–49.

28. "Arrival of the Hand-Carts at Great Salt Lake City," 2, quoting an article that appeared in the *Mormon* in April 1856.

29. Crouch, Autobiography.

30. Harrison, *Treasures of Pioneer History*, 106–7.

31. Moyle, "Reminiscences and Pedigree of the Alphonse Family by Henry Moyle" (used with permission).

32. Ibid.

33. Bailey, Reminiscences and Journal, 3–5, 7.

34. Hobbs, Journal, 13–65, 73–74, 89, 91–92 (quotations on 31).

35. Forscutt, Journal, November 15, 1855.

36. Ibid., February 16, 1856.

37. Brinkerhoff, *Our Family Heritage*, 2–4.

38. Cussley, Unknown Company Records, Overland Pioneer Travel; ship manifest, *Siddons* (https://mormonmigration.lib.byu.edu/mii/voyage/333). The ship sailed from Liverpool on February 27, 1855, and arrived in Philadelphia on April 20, 1855.

39. Brinkerhoff, *Our Family Heritage*, 9.

40. Forscutt, Journal, April 19, 1856. Although Forscutt does not specifically say that it was the elder Sarah Moulton who had smallpox, earlier in his journal he referred to Sarah Elizabeth simply as Sarah, an indication that he used the more formal title "Sister Moulton" to refer to her stepmother. Brinkerhoff also reported that a sister of Sarah Denton Moulton died of smallpox. This quite likely was "Aunt Ann" Denton, as reported by Brinkerhoff, *Our Family Heritage*, 9.

41. Forscutt, Journal, May 4, 1856. The following Forscutt quotations are also from this source.

CHAPTER 2

1. Southwell, Autobiography, 5–10.

2. Letter to Brigham Young, from F. D. Richards, May 21, 1856, included in Young, Journal.

3. Oborn, Autobiography, 364–66.

4. Moyle, "Reminiscences," 19.

5. Beecroft, Letter from James and Elizabeth Bleak, July 24, 1856.

6. Lowder, Reminiscences, 5.

7. Walters, "Journal of Archer Walters," 1–7.

8. Smith, "Faithful Stewards," 88–95. A few entries from William Woodward's daily journal have been included in this account. The journal recorded: "Thursday 6th May. This morning at 3 A.M. Sarah Moulton from the Irchester Branch, Bedfordshire Conference was safely delivered of a son."

9. Ibid.

10. Ibid.

11. McPhail "Archibald McPhail Comes to Zion," 61–64.

12. *Millennial Star*, May 25, 1856.

13. Beecroft, Letter from James and Elizabeth Bleak, July 24, 1856.

14. Quoted in ibid.

15. Southwell, Autobiography, 5–10 (quotation on 6).

16. Jaques, Letter, *Millennial Star*, June 28, 1856, 411–13.

17. McBride, Autobiography, 6.

18. Jaques, Letter, *Millennial Star*, June 28, 1856, 411–13.

19. Openshaw, Diary, 1–3, 10.

20. Beecroft, Letter from James and Elizabeth Bleak, July 24, 1856.

21. Jaques, Letter, *Millennial Star*, August 30, 1856, 555–57.

22. Moyle, "Reminiscences," 6–8.

23. Openshaw, Diary, 1–3, 10.

24. Ibid., 2 (June 8, 1856).

25. Beecroft, Letter from James and Elizabeth Bleak, July 24, 1856.

26. Ibid.

27. Jones, Letter to Franklin D. Richards, May 21, 1856.

28. Bermingham, Journal, June 25,1856.

29. Openshaw, Diary, 2.

30. Beecroft, Letter from James and Elizabeth Bleak, July 24, 1856.

31. Ibid.

32. Jaques, Letter, *Millennial Star*, June 28, 1856, 411–13.

33. Jaques, Life History, May 23, 1856.

34. Beecroft, Journal, June 3, 1856.

35. Linford, Diary, 1–3.

36. Woodward, Journal, May 17, 1856.

37. Jaques, Letter, *Millennial Star*, August 30, 1856, 555–57.

38. Hamilton, Journal, 3–4,6.

39. Sabin, Autobiography, 6–9, 13.

40. Oborn, Autobiography, 364–66.

41. Walters, "Journal of Archer Walters," 1–7.

42. Steward, Autobiography, 187, 189.

43. Southwell, Autobiography, 5.

44. Beecroft, Journal, May 23, 1856.

45. Jaques, Life History, May 22, 1856. Wax lights were candles.

46. Beecroft, Journal, July 24, 1856.

47. Hobbs, Journal, April 9, 1859.

48. Sabin, Autobiography, 6.

49. Beecroft, Letter from James and Elizabeth Bleak, July 24, 1856.

50. James G. Willie Emigrating Company Journal. 1–15.

51. Smith, Diaries, April 24, 1856.

52. Walters, "Journal of Archer Walters," 1–7.

53. McBride, Autobiography, 7.

54. McAllister, Journal, April 6, 1856, 103–27, 137.

55. Walters, "Journal of Archer Walters," April 13, 1856.

56. Sabin, Autobiography, 6–9, 13.

57. Southwell, Autobiography, May 23, 1856, 7.

58. Ibid.

59. Ibid.

60. Hobbs, Journal, April 24, 1856.

61. Magelby [Magleby], Reminiscences and Diary, April 25, 1857.

62. Ibid., April 25, 1859.

63. Jones, Letter to Franklin D. Richards, May 21, 1856, 427–30.

64. Ibid.

65. Walters, "Journal of Archer Walters," 1–7.

66. Southwell, Autobiography, 8.

67. Cunningham, Reminiscences, 1.

68. Openshaw, Diary, 1–3, 10.

69. Ibid.; Jaques, Letter, *Millennial Star*, August 30, 1856, 555–57.

70. Hobbs, Journal, May 1, 1859.

71. Lindsey, *The Journals of Mark Lindsey*, 412–15.

72. Freece, "The Letters of an Apostate Mormon to His Son," 21–22, 32.

73. Ibid.

74. Smith, "Faithful Stewards," 88–95.

75. Dangerfield, Family History, 2–3.

76. James G. Willie Emigrating Company, Journal, May 7, 1856.

77. Jaques, Letter, *Millennial Star*, August 30, 1856, 555–57.

78. Steward, Autobiography, 187, 189.

79. Jaques, Diary, in Bell, *Life History and Writings*, June 18, 1856.

80. Hobbs, Journal, n.d.

81. Freece, "The Letters of an Apostate Mormon to His Son," 21–22, 32.

82. Bermingham, Journal, May 2–3, 1856.

83. James G. Willie Emigrating Company, Journal, June 1, 1856.

84. Rogerson, Autobiographical Sketch, 21–23, 26 (quotation on 82).

85. Jackson, Autobiography, 2, 7.

86. Jaques, Diary, in Bell, *Life History and Writings*, June 10, 1856, 79, 83–84, 95-106.

87. James G. Willie Emigrating Company, Journal, May 20, 1856.

88. Butler, Journal, 15–17.

89. Bermingham, Journal, 1–5.

90. Simons, *An Enduring Legacy*, 185–89 (the following quotations from Fanny Fry are also from this source).

CHAPTER 3

1. Openshaw, Diary, 1–3, 10.

2. Beecroft, Letter from James and Elizabeth Bleak, July 24, 1856.

3. Jaques, Life History, June 29, 1856, BYU.

4. Openshaw, Diary, 1–3, 10.

5. Jaques, Life History, June 29, 1856.

6. Jaques, Letter, in Bell, *Life History and Writings of John Jaques*, 116–17.

7. Beecroft, Journal, June 30, 1856.

8. Jaques, Live History, June 30, 1856.

9. Lowder, Reminiscences, 5.

10. McAllister, Journal, 103–27, 137.

11. Sabin, Autobiography, no pagination.

12. Crouch, Autobiography, 1–6.

13. Smith, "Faithful Stewards," 88–95 (Saturday, June 14, 1856, for quotations).

14. Tait, Letter, 478-79.

15. Beecroft, Letter from James and Elizabeth Bleak, July 24, 1856.

16. Smith, Journal, May 12, 1856.

17. Openshaw, Diary, 1–3, 10.

18. James G. Willie Emigrating Company Journal, June 17, 1856.

19. Ibid., June 18, 1856.

20. Ibid., June 19, 1856.

21. Ibid., June 23, 1856.

22. Ibid., June 24–25, 1856.

23. Jaques, Letter in Bell, *Life History and Writings of John Jaques* 116–117. The Maine Liquor Law, passed in 1851, prohibited sale of alcohol and was an early result of the temperance movement.

24. Bailey, Reminiscences and Journal, 3–5, 7.

25. Harrison, Autobiography, 106–7.

26. Hobbs, Journal, May 19, 1859.

27. Ibid., May 21, 1859.

28. Ibid., May 25, 1859.

29. Magelby [Magleby], Reminiscences and Diary.

30. Harrison, Autobiography, 106–7.

31. Matteson and Matteson, "Mormon Influence on Scandinavian Settlement in Nebraska"; and Ahmanson, *Vor Tids Muhamed*, 24 (translated awkwardly as "two-wheeled man-tormentors" by Archer in *Secret History*, 35); Bagley, *South Pass*, 194 (second quotation).

CHAPTER 4

1. Woodward, Letter to Heber C. Kimball, June 11, 1856.

2. Galloway, Edmund Ellsworth Emigrating Company, Journal.

3. Ellsworth, Diary, 1.

4. Ellsworth, "Account of His Mission," 243.

5. Sabin, Autobiography, 10–14.

6. Ellsworth, "Account of His Mission."

7. Walters, "Journal of Archer Walters," June 21, 1856. See also Walters, "Utah Pioneer Biographies," 1:119–26.

8. Gardner, Reminiscences, 20.

9. McArthur, Reminiscences, 3–6.

10. Crandal, "Autobiography of a Noble Woman," 427.

11. Ibid.

12. Roberts, Autobiographical Sketch, Church History Library.

13. Parry, Reminiscences and Diary, 55.

14. Ibid.

15. Ellsworth, "Account of His Mission," 243.

16. Ibid.

17. Crandal, "Autobiography of a Noble Woman," 266–67.

18. Walters, "Journal of Archer Walters," June 24, 1856. The following quotations from Walters are also from this source.

19. Roberts, Reminiscences, 80. The following Roberts quotations are also from this source.

20. Bermingham, "To Utah—By Hand," August 3, 1856.

21. Ibid.

22. Evans, Reminiscences, 2–3. The following Evans quotations are also from this source.

23. Crandal, "Autobiography of a Noble Woman," 427.

24. Dedrickkson, A Brief Story of Theodore Dedrickson's Voyage from Iceland to Utah, 1855–56, 5 (quotation); McArthur Company Dedrickkson, "One of the First," in *Our Pioneer Heritage*, comp. by Carter, 7:486–87.

25. Crandal, "Autobiography of a Noble Woman," 427.

26. Bermingham, "To Utah—By Hand," August 16, 1856.

27. McArthur, Reminiscences, 3–6.

28. Crandal, "Autobiography of a Noble Woman," 427.

29. Walters, "Journal of Archer Walters," July 9, 1856.

30. Barker, Reminiscences, 8.

31. Ellsworth, Diary.

32. Walters, "Journal of Archer Walters," August 26, 1856.

33. Vest, Autobiographical Sketch, 2–3.

34. Ellsworth, Diary.

35. Sabin, Autobiography, 10.

36. Walters, "Journal of Archer Walters."

37. Ellsworth, "Account of His Mission," June 20, 1856.

38. Crandal, "Autobiography of a Noble Woman," 427.

39. Vest, Autobiographical Sketch, 2.

40. Hyde, "Autobiagraphy [sic] of Elizabeth L. Hyde," 29.

41. Sabin, Autobiography, 10–14.

42. Ellsworth, Diary.

43. Aitken, "Adventures of a Mormon," July 11, 1857. Aitken would not remain in Utah.

44. Crandal, "Autobiography of a Noble Woman," 427.

45. Treseder, "Correspondence from Great Salt Lake City," 3.

46. The Pioneer Company had arrived on July 22, 1847.

47. Treseder, "Correspondence from Great Salt Lake City." 3. Young's participation in the arrival of the first handcart companies was reported in the official journal for his office, which noted that he was accompanied by Heber Kimball, "Esq Wells," A. Carrington, and "an escort of the Company of Lancers." By 5 o'clock in the evening, Young, accompanied by the citizens and the company of handcarts, had returned to Union Square in the city.

48. Ibid.

49. Crandal, "Autobiography of a Noble Woman," 427.

50. Treseder, "Correspondence from Great Salt Lake City," 3.

51. Young, President's Office Journal, September 27, 1985, 320.

52. Roberts, Autobiographical Sketch.

53. Young, President's Office Journal, October 2, 1856, recorded the arrival of the Third Company: "Captain Bunker's Hand Cart company arrived 6 P.M."

54. Evans, Reminiscences, 3.

55. "Arrivals," *Deseret News,* October 8, 1856, 245.

CHAPTER 5

1. Lowder, Reminiscences.

2. Hicken, *Thomas Moulton History,* 5; Savage, Journal, July 14, 1856 (quotation).

3. Hicken, *Thomas Moulton History,* 8. Hicken and other Moulton family sources show that Thomas Moulton worked as a butcher in England, notwithstanding his identification as a shepherd on the manifest of the *Thornton.*

4. Ibid., 6.

5. Savage, Journal, July 19–20, July 24, and July 25–27, 1856.

6. Ibid., August 11, 1856.

7. Hicken, *Thomas Moulton History,* 6.

8. Latey, Letter to John Taylor, August 14, 1856.

9. Chislett, "Mr. Chislett's Narrative."

10. Cunningham, Reminiscences, 1–3, 4.

11. Chislett, "Mr. Chislett's Narrative."

12. Savage, Journal, August 12 and 13, 1856.

13. Ibid., August 13 and 15, 1856.

14. Moulton, Letter to Mark H. Forscutt, August 13, 1856.

15. Ibid.

16. Chislett, "Mr. Chislett's Narrative."

17. Savage, Journal, September 3, 1856.

18. "Journey from Florence to G. S. L. City," *Deseret News,* October 22, 1856, 258.

19. Savage, Journal, September 5, 1856.

20. For an account of Porter Rockwell, see Schindler, *Porter Rockwell.*

21. Savage, Journal, September 7, 1856; Hicken, *Thomas Moulton History,* 8.

22. "Journey from Florence to G. S. L. City," 258. Also with the group were Chauncey G. Webb, W. C. Dunbar, James McGaw, J. D. T. McAllister, N. H. Felt, and James Ferguson. These were the men who had arrived in Salt Lake City shortly after the Third Handcart Company and reported that more travelers were still out on the trail. Before year's end some of them would have another encounter with the members of the Fourth and Fifth Companies.

23. Chislett, "Mr. Chislett's Narrative."

24. Ibid.

25. Michno and Michno, *Forgotten Fights,* 138–39; Chislett, "Mr. Chislett's Narrative" (quotation).

26. Savage, Journal, September 13, 1856.

27. Chislett, "Mr. Chislett's Narrative."

28. Savage, Journal, September 23, 1856.

29. Chislett, "Mr. Chislett's Narrative."

30. Savage, Journal, September 29, Daniel Spencer reported in the October 22, 1856, edition of the *Deseret News* that Richards had "purchased some good buffalo robes for the P.E. Fund passengers in the rear" along with a "small recruit of mules and provisions" presumably used by their own fast-traveling party ("Journey from Florence to G. S. L. City"). The robes purchased at

Fort Laramie were later provided to the Martin Handcart Company, while those bought at the more western Reshaw's post at Platte Bridge went to members of the Willie Party. A portion of hardtack bought and left at Fort Laramie was distributed to the Willie Company.

31. Savage, Journal, October 1, 1856.

32. Ibid., October 4, 1856.

33. A portion of this flour would be given to the Smoot wagon train, while teamsters hauling the remainder turned back on the trail when they became worried about the lateness of the season and saw no sign of the Willie Company. None of the supply ever reached the people traveling with Willie.

34. Quoted in "Journey from Florence to G. S. L. City," 258.

35. Savage, Journal, October 4, 1856.

36. Brinkerhoff, *Our Family Heritage*, 13.

37. Chislett, "Mr. Chislett's Narrative."

38. Savage, Journal, October 10, 1856.

39. Ibid., October 12 and 15, 1856.

40. Oborn, Autobiography, 364–66.

41. Chislett, "Mr. Chislett's Narrative."

42. Brinkerhoff, Autobiography of Charlotte "Lottie" Moulton Carroll, in *Our Family Heritage*, 16.

43. Chislett, "Mr. Chislett's Narrative."

CHAPTER 6

1. Jacques, "Emigration by Hand-Carts," 370.

2. Ibid.

3. Bailey, Reminiscences and Journal, 3–5, 7.

4. Ibid.

5. Bond, "Handcarts West in '56."

6. Rogerson, "Tells Story of Trials of the Handcart Pioneers," 11.

7. Camm, Letter to "My Dear Children," March 16, 1892.

8. Ibid.

9. Bond, "Handcarts West in '56."

10. Bleak, Journal, September 1, 1856. Bleak would turn twenty-seven on November 15, 1856. He noted that it was his birthday but said: "I do not know the distance traveled to day."

11. Ibid., September 9, 1856.

12. Jaques, "Some Reminiscences," December 8, 1878, 1; Jensen, *Encyclopedic History of the Church of Jesus Christ of Latter-day Saints*, 284. See also Michno and Michno, *Forgotten Fights*, 138–39.

13. Jaques, "Some Reminiscences," December 8, 1878, 1.

14. Bleak, Journal, October 6, 1856.

15. Camm, Letter to "My Dear Children," March 16, 1892.

16. Ibid.

17. Bond, "Handcarts West in '56."

18. McBride, "Tounge nor Pen Can Never Tell the Sorrow: Heber McBride Describes the 1856 Martin Handcart Disaster," 3–4.

19. McBride, Autobiography, 11.

20. Jaques, "Some Reminiscences," January 12, 1879, 1.

21. Camm, Letter to "My Dear Children," March 16, 1892.

22. Jaques, "Some Reminiscences," January 12, 1879, 1.

23. Camm, Letter to "My Dear Children," March 16, 1892.

24. Kingsford, Autobiographical Sketch, 2–6.

25. Bleak, Journal.

26. Bond, "Handcarts West in '56."

27. Ibid.

28. Jones, Emigrating Company Journal, Hunt Company, December 15, 1856.

29. Chislett, "Mr. Chislett's Narrative," October 19, 1856.

30. Bleak, Journal, October 19, 1856.

31. Bond, "Handcarts West in '56."

32. Kingsford, Autobiographical Sketch. Mary Horrocks would marry and become Mary Leavitt after she reached Salt Lake City.

33. Jaques, "Some Reminiscences," December 8, 1878, 1.

34. Oborn, Autobiography, 364–66.

35. Savage, Journal, October 20, 1856.

36. McBride, Autobiography, 12.

37. Ibid., 11–12. The following McBride quotations are also from this source.

38. McBride, "Tounge nor Pen Can Never Tell the Sorrow."

39. Kingsford, Autobiographical Sketch.

40. McBride, Autobiography, 12.

41. Rogerson, "Strong Men, Brave Women and Sturdy Children Crossed the Wilderness Afoot."

42. Kingsford, Autobiographical Sketch.

43. Jaques, "Some Reminiscences," December 8, 1878, 1.

44. Kingsford, Autobiographical Sketch.

45. Fullmer, Reminiscence, 3.

46. Bleak, Journal, October 23, 1856.

47. Fullmer, Reminiscence.

48. McBride, Autobiography, 13.

49. Jaques, "Some Reminiscences," December 15, 1878, 1.

50. Bond, "Handcarts West in '56."

51. McBride, Autobiography, 10.

CHAPTER 7

1. Richards, "Discourse," 252. The following Richards quotations are also from this source.

2. Spencer, "Remarks," 252.

3. Young, "Remarks," *Deseret News*, October 5, 1856.

4. Young, President's Office Journal, October 8, 1856.

5. Ibid., October 13 and 15, 1856.

6. Burton, Journal, October 16, 1856.

7. Oborn, Autobiography, 364–66.

8. Chislett, "Mr. Chislett's Narrative."

9. Savage, Journal, October 23 and 24, 1856.

10. Oborn, Autobiography, 364–66.

11. Roberts, *Devil's Gate*, 209.

12. Long, *The Journey of the James G. Willie Handcart Company*, 67.

13. Ibid.

14. Ibid.

15. Chislett, "Mr. Chislett's Narrative."

16. Long, *The Journey of the James G. Willie Handcart Company*, 69 (quotations); Jones, *Forty Years among the Indians*.

17. Chislett, "Mr. Chislett's Narrative."

18. Ibid.

19. Savage, Journal, October 23, 1856. During the night Eliza Philpot (thirty-six) and John James (sixty-one), both from England, died.

20. Brinkerhoff, *Our Family Heritage*, 19.

21. Chislett, "Mr. Chislett's Narrative."

22. Savage, Journal, October 23, 1856

23. Chislett, "Mr. Chislett's Narrative."

24. Savage, Journal, October 23, 1856.

25. Long, *The Journey of the James G. Willie Handcart Company*.

26. Chislett, "Mr. Chislett's Narrative."

27. Ibid.

28. Ibid.; Savage, Journal, October 25, 1856.

29. Savage, Journal, October 25, 1856; Young, Journal, October 26, 1856: "A number of brethren offered their teams to go out to meet the emigrating companies." This is an indication that the rescue relief party may have organized quickly but took a while to get a lot of help out on the road.

CHAPTER 8

1. Kingsford, Autobiographical Sketch, October 27, 1856.

2. Bond, "Handcarts West in '56."

3. Roberts, *Devil's Gate*, 233. Rescuer Daniel Webster Jones, an experienced frontiersman, should not be confused with Dan Jones, who had been with the missionary group that overtook the Willie and Martin Companies earlier in the year in Nebraska and would later be involved with the Welsh handcart company.

4. Rogerson, "Strong Men, Brave Women and Sturdy Children Crossed the Wilderness Afoot"; Jones, *Forty Years among the Indians*, 46 (quotations).

5. McBride, Autobiography, 13

6. Ibid., 14.

7. Grant, "The Companies Yet on the Plains," 293. Decker had been over the trail many times because he worked as a mail carrier.

8. Grant, Letter written and dated Devil's Gate, November 2, 1856, quoted in Jaques, "Some Reminiscences," December 16, 1878, 1.

9. Young, "Remarks," November 12, 1856, 283.

10. Rea, *Devil's Gate*, 43, 46–48.

11. Ibid., 67–68.

12. McBride, "Tounge nor Pen Can Never Tell the Sorrow," 3.

13. Quoted in Jaques, "Some Reminiscences," December 15, 1878, 1.

14. Grant, "The Companies Yet on the Plains," 293.

15. Smoot, Letter to Young, October 28, 1856 (quotations); Burton, Journal, October 16, 1856, 54.

16. Quoted in Woolley, Autobiography, 15. Young's official office journal on November 3 recorded that the president arrived at his office with Heber Kimball, where they found "Bro J W. Young waiting there to see them, and gave him instruction about taking 2 yoke of oxen to go back on the road and meet Bro. Smoot. he will go as far as where Bro. Smoot left the weak part of his teams." Young, Journal, 350. For more detail about the Smoot train, see Bagley, "'One Long Funeral March.'"

17. Shoshone Mission Journal, 41–60.

18. Bagley, *South Pass*, 180.

19. Shoshone Mission Journal, October 27, 1856.

20. *Baltimore Sun*, October 31, 1856.

21. Jaques, "Some Reminiscences," December 15, 1878, 1.

22. Ibid.

23. McBride, "Tounge nor Pen Can Never Tell the Sorrow." 4. This is likely Mary Ann Taylor Barton (thirty-three), who traveled with her two daughters, Frances (three) and Mary Ann (fourteen). Her husband, William (forty-eight), had died on September 30.

24. Woodward in James G. Willie Emigrating Company Journal, November 4–9, 1856. Those who died after the teams were diverted to assist the Smoot train included Peter Madsen (sixty-five) from Copenhagen, Denmark, and Susannah Osborne (thirty-two) from Norwich, Norfolk, England, on November 5; Archibald McPhail (thirty-nine) from Greenock, Argyleshire, Scotland, and Rasmus P. Hansen (sixteen) from Denmark on November 6; Maren Sophia Jorgensen (eight) from Lango, Denmark, Theophilus Cox (twenty-five), from Bristol, Somersetshire, England, and William Empey (nine) from Eaton Bray, Bedfordshire, England, on November 7; and Rhoda R. Oakey (eleven) from Eldersfield, Worcestershire, England, on November 9 before the company reached Great Salt Lake City.

25. Young, President's Office Journal, November 7, 1856, 354.

26. McBride, Autobiography, 14–15.

27. Kingsford, Autobiographical Sketch.

28. Burton, Report to the Members of the Hand Cart Association.

29. McBride, Autobiography, 15.

30. Camm, Letter to "My Dear Children," March 16, 1892.

31. Rogerson, "Strong Men, Brave Women and Sturdy Children Crossed the Wilderness Afoot." 11.

32. Young, President's Office Journal, November 8, 1856.

33. Jones, Emigrating Company Journal, Hunt Company, in *History of the Church of Jesus Christ of Latter-day Saints*, December 15, 1856.

34. Jaques, "Some Reminiscences," December 22, 1878, 1.

35. Rogerson, "Strong Men, Brave Women and Sturdy Children Crossed the Wilderness Afoot." 11; Jones, *Forty Years among the Indians* (quotations).

36. Brinkerhoff, *Our Family Heritage*, 20.

37. The number of people who died in the Willie Company ranges from sixty-six to seventy-seven, depending on whether the count includes everyone who perished after leaving Iowa

City or just those who died as a result of the hard trail and harsh conditions in Nebraska and Wyoming. Some died after they reached Utah, due to the effects of their ordeal.

38. Writing this story makes me ask why all the Moultons survived, when so many of the men, women, and children that they traveled with had died or been seriously affected by the harsh traveling conditions. Was it truly a blessing that saved them? Had they been in better physical shape to begin the journey—in spite of the ordeal with smallpox in England? Or could it have been that Thomas Moulton, as the camp butcher, had access to more food for his family than some others traveling with them? These questions are unlikely ever to have definitive answers.

39. Young, President's Office Journal, November 9, 1856.

40. It is not known exactly when the steam engine that Smoot hauled was delivered to Great Salt Lake City, but almost certainly it was late November or mid-December when the last westbound wagons reached the city that year.

41. Chislett, "Mr. Chislett's Narrative."

42. Hanks, quoted in Kingsford, Autobiographical Sketch, 2–6.

43. Kingsford, Autobiographical Sketch.

44. The exact number of deaths in the Martin Company and where those deaths occurred are unknown, but review of the official accounts, diaries, and reminiscences places the number at nearly 150 before the group reached South Pass, maybe more.

45. McBride, Autobiography, 15.

46. Camm, Letter to "My Dear Children." March 16, 1892.

47. Ibid.

48. Jones Emigrating Company Journal, Hunt Company, November 12, 1856.

49. Camm, Letter to "My Dear Children," March 16, 1892,

50. Young, "Remarks," November 16, 1856, 298. The following Young quotations are also from this source.

51. Young, Journal, November 13, 1856, 360. There is no mention of Abel Garr meeting with Young, but he accompanied Joseph A. Young on the ride from Devil's Gate to Great Salt Lake City.

52. Jaques, "Some Reminiscences," December 22, 1878, 1. This is also reported in Young, President's Office Journal, November 14, 1856, 361.

53. Young, President's Office Journal, November 11, 1856, 338.

54. "Emigration to Utah," Mormon, November 22, 1856, 2.

55. Jones, Emigrating Company Journal, Hunt Company, December 15, 1856.

56. Young, "Remarks," December 10, 1856, 320.

57. "Latest from Utah: Death of an Eminent Mormon Saint, Hand-Cart Trains in a Wretched Condition," New York Semi-Weekly Tribune, written December 4, 1856, published February 27, 1857.

58. Brigham Young accompanied this second rescue party but only for two days before he became ill and returned to Great Salt Lake.

59. Roberts, Devil's Gate, 249.

60. "Latest from Utah: Death of an Eminent Mormon Saint."

61. Jaques, "Some Reminiscences," December 22, 1878, 1.

62. Jones, Emigrating Company Journal, Hunt Company, November 12, 1856.

63. Bond, "Handcarts West in '56."

64. Ibid.

CHAPTER 9

1. Young, "Remarks," on November 2, 1856, 283. These public remarks came a day after Young gave a "discourse in the Social Hall to the High Priests' Quorum," as reported in Young, President's Office Journal, 349.

2. Young, President's Office Journal, October 31, 1856, 348.

3. Young, "Remarks," November 2, 1856, 283.

4. Letter from F. D. Richards to Brigham Young, May 21, 1856, in Young, President's Office Journal.

5. Young, "Remarks," November 2, 1856, 283. The following Young quotations are also from this source.

6. "Emigration to Utah," 2.

7. Ibid.

8. Bagley, *South Pass*, 183.

9. Taylor, Letter to Brigham Young, February 24, 1857.

10. Chislett, "Mr. Chislett's Narrative."

11. Bagley, "'One Long Funeral March.'"

12. "Fourteenth General Epistle," 313–14.

13. Ibid.

14. Lapish, Recollection, 37–40.

15. "Fourteenth General Epistle," 313–14.

16. "Arrival of the Hand-Carts at Great Salt Lake City," 2.

17. "Emigrants Perishing on the Plains," *Zanesville (Ohio) Gazette*, February 17, 1857. 1857 Scrapbook No. 6, in Historian's Office, Historical Scrapbooks 1840–1904, Church History Library.

18. Ibid. The account from the *Zanesville Gazette* appears to be the underlying source for the Vincennes, Indiana, *Gazette* article.

19. Taylor, Letter to Franklin Richards, June 5, 1856.

20. "Arrival of the Hand-Carts at Great Salt Lake City," 2.

21. Taylor, Letter to Franklin Richards, June 5, 1856, in "Arrival of the Hand-Carts at Great Salt Lake City."

22. Published in "Arrival of the Hand-Carts at Great Salt Lake City," 2. This statement does not acknowledge that more than seventy of the relief wagons failed to make a forced march to find the stranded immigrants but instead turned around before they reached them. They reversed their direction to go back to the handcart pioneers upon receipt of a second order from Brigham Young to do so.

23. "Emigrants Perishing on the Plains—The Way They Bury Them," *Cleveland Plain Dealer*, February 4, 1857.

24. "Emigration to Utah," 2.

25. Jaques, "Some Reminiscences," January 19, 1879, 1. The following Jaques quotations are also from this source.

CHAPTER 10

1. Jones, *Forty Years among the Indians*, 48. The following Jones quotations are also from this source (with parenthetical page numbers in the text).

2. Young, President's Office Journal, November 29, 1856. Hanks had traveled east earlier, encountered the Martin Company, and returned to Great Salt Lake City, where he met with Brigham Young on November 29, 1856, and "reported that the condition of the HandCart companies was very severe. Nevertheless the power of God was displayed when they were administered to by the laying on [of] hands. . . . Nothing could exceed there joy when the brethren arrived . . . their timely rescue and took them in their teams and gave them provisions about 100 died in all through the freezing weather." Hanks was in Utah less than two weeks. On December 10, 1856, the President's Office Journal outlined Brigham Young's work in writing letters to be sent with east-bound mail and noted that they would be carried by "Bro Feramorz Little & Ephraim Hanks. who will start to morrow."

3. Jones, *Forty Years among the Indians*, 54–55. The following Jones quotations are also from this source (with parenthetical page numbers in the text).

4. Glass, *Reshaw*, 111.

5. Jones, *Forty Years among the Indians*, 65.

6. Lowder, Reminiscences, 5.

7. Jones, *Forty Years among the Indians*, 89–91.

CHAPTER 11

1. Fishburn, "Pioneer Autobiographies," 204.

2. "A Trip to the Salt Lake" by William Hartle (December 27, 1856), *Lady's Newspaper* (London), February 14, 1857, 110, cols. 1–2. The following Hartle quotations are also from this source.

3. *Christian Cabinet* (London), March 6, 1857, 1, cols. 4 and 5. This reference to the Fifth Company and Sixth Company means the groups led by Jesse Haven and Edward Martin, which were later combined into one—the Fifth Company that Martin took west in 1856.

4. Taylor, "Editorial Correspondence," June 13, 1857, 2.

5. Morgan, Diary, August 18, 1857.

6. Fishburn, "Pioneer Autobiographies," 204–36 (quotation on 204).

7. Morgan, Diary, May 1, 1857.

8. Benson, Recollections, 1–3.

9. Christensen, "By Handcart to Utah."

10. Hansen, "The Great Handcart Train from Iowa City to Salt Lake City."

11. Frantzen, Reminiscence and Journal, 1857.

12. Christensen, "By Handcart to Utah."

13. Frantzen, Reminiscence and Journal.

14. Ibid.

15. Christensen, "By Handcart to Utah."

16. Hansen, "The Great Handcart Train." The following Hansen quotations are also from this source.

17. Christensen, "By Handcart to Utah."

18. Frantzen, Reminiscence and Journal.

19. Hansen, "The Great Handcart Train."

20. Jacobsen, Journal, July 1, 1857.

21. Frantzen, Reminiscence and Journal.

22. Musser, Diaries, June 9, 1857.

23. Ibid., June 12, 1857.

24. Young, "Remarks," November 2, 1856, 283.

25. Musser, Diaries, June 13, 1857. The following Musser quotations are also from this source.

26. Frantzen, Reminiscence and Journal.

27. Musser, Diaries, July 13, 1857.

28. Jensen, Reminiscences.

29. Hansen, "The Great Handcart Train."

30. Jensen, Reminiscences.

31. Benson, Recollections, 1–3.

32. Dorius, Journal, 86–88.

33. Benson, Recollections, June 20, 1857.

34. Christensen, "By Handcart to Utah."

35. Ibid.

36. Jensen, Reminiscences.

37. Ibid.; also Christensen, "By Handcart to Utah."

38. Benson, Recollections.

39. Taylor, "Editorial Correspondence," July 18, 1857, 2.

40. Fishburn, "Pioneer Autobiographies," 206.

41. Ibid.

42. Christensen, "By Handcart to Utah." The following Christensen quotations are also from this source.

43. Morgan, Diary, July 8, 1857. 44. Fishburn, "Pioneer Autobiographies." 206.

45. Morgan, Diary, July 25, 1857.

46. Fishburn, "Pioneer Autobiographies," 206. The following Fishburn quotations are also from this source.

CHAPTER 12

1. Frantzen, Reminiscence and Journal, 39.

2. Bagley, *Blood of the Prophets*, 73. For a complete account of the political situation that led Buchanan and his cabinet ministers to order the troops to Utah, see MacKinnon, *At Sword's Point: Part 1*; and Bigler and Bagley, *The Mormon Rebellion*.

3. MacKinnon, *At Sword's Point: Part 1*, 44.

4. Tyler to Buchanan, April 27, 1857, in Bagley, *Blood of the Prophets*, 74.

5. Bagley, *Blood of the Prophets*, 77, 75.

6. Ibid., 77–78.

7. Ibid., 79.

8. Bagley, *Blood of the Prophets*, 80.

9. Roberts, Reminiscence and Diary, 19–21.

10. Christensen, "By Handcart to Utah."

11. Benson, Recollections.

12. Dorius, Journal, 86–88.

13. Frantzen, Reminiscence and Journal.

14. Dorius, Journal, 86–88.

15. Musser, Diaries, August 18, 1857. The following Musser quotations are also from this source.

16. Bigler and Bagley, *The Mormon Rebellion*, 186.

17. Christensen, "By Handcart to Utah."

18. Dorius, Journal, 86–88. It is unclear why Dorius referred to "thin ice," since his party traveled in summer unlike the Willie and Martin Companies of the previous year. But this party did have unusually cold weather when traveling through the Sweetwater valley and over South Pass, so it is plausible that at times there was thin ice. In 1993, when traveling by wagon on the Oregon Trail, I saw ice that had formed on water buckets near South Pass in mid-July.

19. Christensen, "By Handcart to Utah."

20. Dorius, Journal, 86–88.

21. Christensen, "By Handcart to Utah."

22. MacKinnon, *At Sword's Point, Part 1*, 330, 331.

23. MacKinnon, *At Sword's Point, Part 2*, 618.

CHAPTER 13

1. Beesley, Reminiscences, 28.

2. Hobbs, Journal, June 9, 1859.

3. Atkin, "Handcart Experience." See also Carter, *Heart Throbs of the West,* 380–94; and Awerkamp, *William Atkin and Rachel Thompson,* 15–31.

4. Beesley, Reminiscences, 28.

5. Hobbs, Journal, June 9 and 11, 1859.

6. Beesley, Reminiscences, 28–34.

7. Hobbs, Journal, June 12, 1859.

8. Ibid., June 13 and 15, 1859.

9. Beesley, Reminiscences, 28–34.

10. Thornton, Autobiography, 2, 4.

11. Hobbs, Journal, June 21, 1859.

12. Ibid., June 25, 1859.

13. Beesley, Reminiscences, 28–34.

14. Hobbs, Journal, June 27, 1859.

15. Atkin, "Handcart Experience."

16. Hobbs, Journal, July 1, 1859.

17. Atkin, "Handcart Experience."

18. Ibid.

19. Hobbs, Journal, July 3, 1859.

20. Ibid., July 2 and August 25, 1859 (quotation).

21. For a detailed view of emigrant and Indian relations, see Tate, *Indians and Emigrants.*

22. Hobbs, Journal, July 8, 1859. The following Hobbs quotations are also from this source.

23. Atkin, "Handcart Experience."

24. Ibid.

25. Beesley, Reminiscences, 28–34.

26. Atkin, "Handcart Experience."

27. Hobbs, Journal, August 23, 1859.

28. Ibid., August 23 and 24, 1859. The food advanced by the "Jentile" was indeed repaid by the Mormons when additional supply wagons came to the area from Salt Lake City.

29. Hobbs, Journal; Beesley, Reminiscences, 28–34.

30. Hobbs, Journal, September 4, 1859.

31. Beesley, Reminiscences.

32. "Arrival of the Hand-Cart Train," 11.

33. Hafen and Hafen, *Handcarts to Zion*, 178.

CHAPTER 14

1. Forscutt, Journal, 469, March 1 and April 16, 1860.

2. Ibid., June 2, 1860.

3. Armstrong, Autobiography, 168–71.

4. Lapish, Recollection, 37.

5. Hafen, *Recollections of a Handcart Pioneer of 1860*, 21–26.

6. Lapish, Recollection, 37.

7. Stoddard, Report, 2–7.

8. Stucki, Family History Journal, 42–46. The following Stucki quotations are also from this source.

9. Harrison, Diary, 53–59.

10. Armstrong, Autobiography, 168–71.

11. Lapish, Recollection, 37–40.

12. Stucki, Family History Journal, 42–46.

13. Lapish, Recollection, 37–40; Armstrong, Autobiography, 168–171.

14. Robison, Life Sketch, 1–2.

15. Ibid.

16. Forscutt, Journal, July 7, 1860.

17. Stoney, Reminiscences and Diary, July 4, 1860. Although the aurora borealis is most often seen in spring and fall, it can be seen in summer and may indeed have been what the immigrants observed, though he may have mistaken a thunderstorm in the north for the northern lights. The following Stoney quotations are also from this source.

18. Stoddard, Report, 2–7. The following Stoddard quotations are also from this source.

19. Hafen, *Recollections of a Handcart Pioneer of 1860*, 21–26.

20. Robison, Life Sketch, 1–2.

21. Robison, Letter to Brigham Young, August 24, 1860.

22. Hafen and Hafen, *Handcarts to Zion*, 184.

23. Bagley, *South Pass*, 194.

EPILOGUE

1. Rogerson, Reminiscence, 22–28. The following Rogerson quotations are also from this source.

2. Camm, Letter to "My Dear Children," March 16, 1892.

3. Chislett, "Mr. Chislett's Narrative."

CODA

1. Gordon B. Hinckley address at Martins Cove, May 3, 1997, as recorded by Moulton, Notebooks.

2. Weinstein, "ACLU Sues over Mormon Lease" (first quotation); Royster, "ACLU Sues to Block Martin's Cove Lease" (second quotation).

3. Weinstein, "ACLU Sues over Mormon Lease"; Royster, "ACLU Sues to Block Martin's Cove Lease."

4. Byrda, "LDS Church, BLM, ACLU Settle Martin's Cove Lawsuit."

5. Long, *The Journey of the James G. Willie Handcart Company*, 81.

6. Musser, Amos M. Letter to President Appleby, July 16, 1857, 620–22.

7. As recorded by Moulton, Notebooks. The following quotations from participants are also from this source.

8. Carino and Del Bene, both archaeologists employed by the U.S. Bureau of Land Management, were responsible for administering the wagon train permit but had worked tirelessly for years (before and after the wagon train) to protect the trail resources. They both cared deeply about the trail, its story, the people who had traveled it in history, and those who were following it in more modern times. They took care of not only the Mormon Trail ruts and remnants but also the routes of the Oregon, California, and Pony Express trails that crossed the same general corridor.

9. Moulton, Notebooks. The following quotations from participants are also from this source.

10. Van Leer and Thompson, "Wagon Train Rolls on In." This arrival date was carefully planned before the wagons even left Florence in order to coincide with the anniversary date of Brigham Young's entrance into the valley 150 years earlier.

11. Months after the 1997 wagon train ended, Elizabeth Pietsch sent me a silk scarf from Austria, which I cherish in memory of Elizabeth's first view of Salt Lake City after crossing the trail by wagon train.

12. Lowder, Reminiscences, 5.

13. Moulton, Notebooks.

14. Chislett, "Mr. Chislett's Narrative."

BIBLIOGRAPHY

PRIMARY SOURCES

ARCHIVAL PRIMARY SOURCES

Unless otherwise noted, the sources in this section are all held by the Church of Jesus Christ of Latter-day Saints Church History Library, Salt Lake City, Utah.

Armstrong, Isabella Siddoway. Autobiography. In Emma Louise Armstrong Notebook.

Bailey, Langley Allgood. Reminiscences and Journal.

Barker, Margaret Stalle. Reminiscences. In Rebecca Cardin Hickman, "History of Susanna Goudin Cardon," item 2, in Biographical Sketches of the Cardon family, 1934–60.

Beecroft, Joseph. Journal. Beecroft Family Papers, 1842-1902, MS 1915.

———. Letter from James and Elizabeth Bleak, July 24, 1856. Moore Family Papers. MS 7531.

Beesley, Sarah Hancock. Reminiscences. In Handcart Stories (database), 28–34.

Benson, Kersten Erickson. Recollections of Kersten Erickson Benson Coming to Zion in 1857. Benson Biographical File.

Bermingham, Patrick Twiss. Journal. In Church Emigration Book (1855–1861).

Bleak, James Godson. Journal (1856).

Bleak, James and Elizabeth. Letters (1856).

Bond, John, "Handcarts West in '56." Privately printed in mimeograph, 1945 (no pagination).

Burton, Robert T. Journal, October 16, 1856—November 30, 1856, MS 3005.

———. Report to the Members of the Hand Cart Association, October 1, 1907. In Handcart Veterans Association, Scrapbook, 1906–14.

Butler, William. Journal. MS 8795, reel 11, no. 3.

Camm, Elizabeth Whittear Sermon. Letter to "My Dear Children," March 16, 1892, San Francisco, California. Joel Edward Ricks, Cache Valley Historical Material, reel 4, item 98.

Crouch, Ebenezer. Autobiography. TS.

Cunningham, George. Reminiscences. MS 7322 2.

Cussley, Eliza Denton. Unknown Company Records, Overland Pioneer Travel.

Dangerfield, Mary Ann James. Family History. MS 2050, reel 4, bx. 4, fd. 10, item 1.

Dedrickkson, Theodore. A Brief Story of Theodore Dedrickson's Voyage from Iceland to Utah, 1855–56. Mormon Pioneer Overland Travel Database.

Ellsworth, Mary Ann Jones. Diary of Mary Ann Jones (Age 19) on Her Trip across the Plains.

Evans, Priscilla Merriman. Reminiscences. MS 4518.

Forscutt, Mark Hill. Journal (1855–1900). MS 17393, reel 1, item 8.

Frantzen, John. Reminiscence and Journal (1889–92).

Freece, Hans P. "The Letters of an Apostate Mormon to His Son."

Galloway, Andrew. Edmund Ellsworth Emigrating Company, Journal (June–September 1856).

Hamilton, Henry. Journal. MS 1838, fd. 2, vol. 3.

Harrison, Henry James. Diary (March–July 1860).

Hobbs, Henry. Journal (May 1859–July 1860). In Mormon Migration: "Liverpool to New York 11 Apr 1859–13 May 1859." Brigham Young University. https://mormonmigration.lib.byu .edu/mii/account/1259?query=hobbs.

Jacobsen, Soren. Journal (September 1855–January 1860).

James G. Willie Emigrating Company. Journal. MS 1477.

Jaques, John. Life History. In Mormon Migration: "Liverpool to Boston 25 May 1856–30 June, 1856." BYU. https://mormonmigration.lib.byu.edu/mii/account/548?query=jaques.

Jones, Albert. Reminiscences. MS 3380.

Jones, Dan. Emigrating Company Journal, Hunt Company (May–December 1856). MS 9395.

Lapish, Hannah. Recollection. In Handcart Stories (database).

Linford, John. Diary. MS 3984, fd. 2.

Lowder, Emily Hodgetts. Reminiscences. Trail excerpt transcribed from Pioneer History Collection available at Daughters of Utah Pioneers Museum, Salt Lake City, Utah.

Magelby [Magleby], Hans Olsen. Reminiscences and Diary (1857–1865).

McAllister, John Daniel Thompson. Journal. MS 1257, reel 1, vol. 2.

McArthur, Daniel D. Reminiscences. In *Journal History of the Church of Jesus Christ of Latter-day Saints*, September 26, 1856.

McBride, Heber Robert. Autobiography (ca. 1868). MS 810.

Moore Family Papers. MS 7531.

Morgan, Evan Samuel. Diary of Evan Samuel Morgan (1856–1891). MS 10608.

Moulton, Candy. Notebooks. Mormon Trail Sesquicentennial Wagon Train (April–July 1997). MS. Author's papers.

Moulton, Sarah. Letter to Mark H. Forscutt, August 13, 1856. In Mark H. Forscutt, Journal 5. MS 17393, April 7, 1856–October 31, 1868, reel 1, 308–10.

Moyle, Henry. "Reminiscences and Pedigree of the Alphonse Family by Henry Moyle" (January 3, 1919). Copy in collection of Alyce Goodell, Sheridan, Wyoming.

Musser, Amos. M. Diaries (1852–76). Box 1, fd. 7, 12–39, and box 1, fd. 8.

Openshaw, Samuel. Diary (May–November 1856). MS 1515.

Parry, John. Reminiscences and Diary (March 1857–September 1867).

Roberts, Griffith, Reminiscence and Diary (ca. 1865).

Roberts, Robert David, Autobiographical Sketch. Robert D. Roberts, Papers of the Roberts Family Association. M 270.1.

———. Reminiscences. In Joel Ricks, "Memories of Early Days in Cache County," In Daughters of Utah Pioneers, Scrapbooks, Salt Lake City, Utah.

Robison, Daniel. Letter to Brigham Young, August 24, 1860. Brigham Young, Office Files 1832–78, reel 38, box 27, fd. 18.

Robison, Rachel Smith. Life Sketch of Rachel Smith Robison.

Rogerson, Josiah. Autobiographical Sketch. MS 3363, no. 4.

————. Reminiscence (1879).

Sabin, Mary Powell. Autobiography (1926). Formerly in MS 2050.

Savage, Levi. Journal (1856).

Shoshone Mission Journal (May 1855–October 1857). MS 418.

Smith, Andrew. Journal. (1856). MS 1394.

Smith, Marilyn Austin. "Faithful Stewards: The Life of James Gray Willie and Elizabeth Ann Pettit." MS 9248.

Smoot, Oscar. Letter to Brigham Young, October 28, 1856. Brigham Young Collection.

Southwell, John William. Autobiography. MS 8243.

Stoddard, Oscar O. Report. In *Journal History of the Church of Jesus Christ of Latter-day Saints,* September 24, 1860.

Stoney, Robert, Reminiscences and Diary (June-August, 1860).

Stucki, John S. Family History Journal of John S. Stucki (1932).

Thornton, Squire. Autobiography. MS A 1260. Utah State Historical Society, Salt Lake City.

Tyler, Daniel. Autobiographical Sketch (ca. 1879). In Autobiographical Accounts by Beaver Residents. MS 3363.

Vest, Louisa Rosser Evans. Autobiographical Sketch (June 1921).

Walters, Archer. "Journal of Archer Walters, Enroute from England to Utah, U.S.A., March 18, 1856 to September 5, 1856."

Woodward, William. Journal (1856). MS 8306. Reel 4, no. 2e. Located in Historical resources material for Cache Valley, Utah-Idaho, 1955–56.

————. Letter to Heber C. Kimball, June 11, 1856. Brigham Young, Office Files 1832–78, reel 35, box 25, fd. 9.

Woolley, Franklin Benjamin. Autobiography (ca. 1856).

Young, Brigham. Office Files, MS 1234, 1. Box 72, folder 2. Includes President's Office Journal, 1853–56.

PUBLISHED PRIMARY SOURCES

Ahmanson, John A. *Vor Tids Muhamed* [The Muhammed of Our Times]. Omaha, Neb.: Press of the Danish Pioneer, 1876. Translated by Gleason L. Archer as *Secret History: A Translation of "Vor Tids Muhamed."* Chicago: Moody Press, 1984.

Aitken, William Knox. "Adventures of a Mormon." *London Advertiser,* August 9, 1857.

"Arrival of the Hand-Carts at Great Salt Lake City." *Mormon,* February 21, 1857.

"Arrival of the Hand-Cart Train." *Mountaineer,* September 10, 1859.

"Arrivals." *Deseret News,* October 8, 1856.

Atkin, William. "Handcart Experience." *St. George Union,* May 14, 1896–November 14, 1896.

Awerkamp, Jacqueline, comp. *William Atkin and Rachel Thompson: Journal and Genealogies.* N.p., 1976.

Bell, Stella Jaques. *Life History and Writings of John Jaques, Including a Diary of the Martin Handcart Company.* Rexburg, Idaho: Ricks College Press, 1978.

Bermingham, Patrick Twiss. "To Utah—By Hand." *American Legion Magazine* (July 1937).

Byrda, Jennifer. "LDS Church, BLM, ACLU Settle Martin's Cove Lawsuit." Associated Press, May 16, 2006.

Carter, Kate B., comp. *Our Pioneer Heritage*. 20 vols. Salt Lake City: Daughters of Utah Pioneers, 1958–77.

Chislett, John. "Mr. Chislett's Narrative [1856]." In T. B. H. Stenhouse, *The Rocky Mountain Saints*. Digital copy at https://history.lds.org/overlandtravel/sources/86169/chislett-john -narrative-in-t-b-h-stenhouse-the-rocky-mountain-saints-a-full-and-complete-history-of -the-mormons-1873-313-32.

Christensen, C. C. A., "By Handcart to Utah [in 1857]: The Account of C. C. A. Christensen." Translated by Richard L. Jensen. *Nebraska History* (Winter 1985): 337–44.

Clayton, William. *The Latter-day Saints Emigrants' Guide: Being a Table of Distances, Showing All the Springs, Creeks, Rivers, Hills, Mountains, Camping Places, and All Other Notable Places, from Council Bluffs to the Valley of the Great Salt Lake*. St. Louis: Missouri Republican, 1848. Reprint, ed. Stanley B. Kimball. Gerald, Missouri: Patrice Press, 1983.

Crandal, Mary B. "Autobiography of a Noble Woman." *Young Woman's Journal*, February, April, May, June 1895.

Dorius, Carl C. N. Journal. In Earl N. Dorius and Ruth C. Rasmussen, *The Dorius Heritage*. Salt Lake City: E. N. Dorius, 1979.

Ellsworth, Edmund. "Account of His Mission By Elder Edmund Ellsworth, and His Experience In Leading the First Hand-Cart Company" (September 28, 1856). *Deseret News*, October 8, 1856.

"Emigrants Perishing on the Plains—The Way They Bury Them." *Cleveland Plain Dealer*, February, 4, 1857.

"Emigration to Utah." *Mormon*, November 22, 1856, 2.

Fishburn, Robert Leeming, "Pioneer Autobiographies." In *Chronicles of Courage*, 2:204–36. 8 vols. Salt Lake City: Daughters of Utah Pioneers, 1990–97.

"Fourteenth General Epistle." *Deseret News*, December 10, 1856.

Fullmer, Jane Griffiths. Reminiscence. In Ella Campbell, *An Early Pioneer History and Reminiscences*. N.p., 191.

Gardner, James. Reminiscences. In "Utah Heroes Who Pulled Their All across the Plains." *Deseret Evening News*, September 1, 1906.

Grant, George D. "The Companies Yet on the Plains." *Deseret News*, November 19, 1856.

———. Letter, dated Devil's Gate, November 2, 1856. Quoted in John Jaques, "Some Reminiscences." *Salt Lake Daily Herald*, December 15, 1878.

Hafen, Mary Ann. *Recollections of a Handcart Pioneer of 1860: A Woman's Life on the Mormon Frontier*. Lincoln: University of Nebraska Press, Bison Books, 1983 (originally privately printed, 1938).

"Hand Carts for the Plains. *Mormon*, December 1, 1855, 2.

Hansen, Frederick, "The Great Handcart Train from Iowa City to Salt Lake City." *Journal of History* (October 1916).

Harrison, George. *Treasures of Pioneer History*. Compiled by Kate B. Carter. 2 vols. Salt Lake City: Daughters of Utah Pioneers, 1953.

Hyde, Elizabeth Lane. "Autobiagraphy [sic] of Elizabeth L. Hyde." *Woman's Exponent*, August 15, 1896.

Jackson, Aaron. Autobiography. In *Utah Pioneer Biographies*, 15:2–7. 44 vols. Salt Lake City: LDS Church, 1935–64.

Jaques, John. "Emigration by Hand-Carts." *Millennial Star* 18:24, June 14, 1856.

———. Letter. *Millennial Star* 18:26, June 28, 1856.

———. Letter. *Millennial Star* 18:35, August 30, 1856.

———. "Some Reminiscences." *Salt Lake Daily Herald*, December 8, 1878–January 19, 1879.

Jensen, James. Reminiscences, September 13, 1857. In *A Biographical Sketch of James Jensen* by J. M. Tanner. Salt Lake City: Deseret News, 1911.

Jones, Dan. Letter to Franklin D. Richards, May 21, 1856. *Millennial Star* 18:27, July 5, 1856.

Jones, Daniel W. *Forty Years among the Indians.* Salt Lake City: Juvenile Instructor Press, 1890; reprint, Council Press, Springville, Utah, 2004.

"Journey from Florence to G. S. L. City." *Deseret News*, October 22, 1856, 258.

Kettle, John. Diary. In *Jesse Lenard Warner: The Protecting Warrior*, book 1, 54–56, 62. Murray, Utah: n.p., 1972.

Kingsford, Elizabeth Horrocks Jackson. Autobiographical Sketch. In *Leaves from the Life of Elizabeth Horrocks Jackson Kingsford.* Ogden, Utah: privately printed, 1908.

"Latest from Utah: Death of an Eminent Mormon Saint, Hand-Cart Trains in a Wretched Condition." *New York Semi-Weekly Tribune*, February 27, 1857.

Latey, J. H. Letter to John Taylor, August 14, 1856, written in Florence, Nebraska *Millennial Star* 18:637 (1856).

Lindsey, Mark. *The Journals of Mark Lindsey: Mormon Missionary, Handcart Pioneer and Entrepreneur (1832–1900).* Ed. Donald B. Lindsey and Rosy Lindsey. Privately printed, n.d.

Lowder, Emily Hodgetts. Reminiscences. In *Our Pioneer Heritage*, comp. by Kate B. Carter. Vol. 7. Salt Lake City: Daughters of Utah Pioneers, 1964.

Matteson, Edith, and Jean Matteson, "Mormon Influence on Scandinavian Settlement in Nebraska." In *On Distant Shores: Proceedings of the Marcus Lee Hansen Immigration Conference, Aalborg, Denmark, June 29–July 1, 1992*, edited by Henning Bender, Birgit Flemming Larsen, and Karen Veien. Aalborg, Denmark: Danes Worldwide Archives and Danish Society for Emigration History, 1993.

McBride, H. R. "Tounge nor Pen Can Never Tell the Sorrow: Heber McBride Describes the 1856 Martin Handcart Disaster." *Crossroads Newsletter* (Spring 1994).

McPhail, Archibald. "Archibald McPhail Comes to Zion." In *Voices from the Past: Diaries, Journals and Autobiographies*, comp. by Campus Education Week Program. Provo, Utah: Brigham Young University, 1980.

Moorman, Donald R. and Gene A. Sessions. *Camp Floyd and the Mormons: The Utah War.* Salt Lake City: University of Utah Press, 1992.

Musser, Amos M. Letter to President Appleby, July 16, 1857. *Millennial Star,* September 26, 1857.

Oborn, John. Autobiography. In *Heart Throbs of the West* comp. Kate B. Carter, vol. 6. Salt Lake City: Daughters of Utah Pioneers, 1945.

Richards, Franklin D. "Discourse" (reported by G. D. Watt). *Deseret News*, October 15, 1856.

Rogerson, Josiah. "Martin's Handcart Company, 1856." *Salt Lake Herald,* October 13, October 20, October 27, November 3, November 10, November 17, November, 24, December 1, and December 8, 1907.

———. "Strong Men, Brave Women and Sturdy Children Crossed the Wilderness Afoot." *Salt Lake Tribune*, January 4, 1914.

———. "Tells Story of Trials of the Handcart Pioneers." *Salt Lake Tribune*, November 30, 1913.

Royster, Whitney. "ACLU Sues to Block Martin's Cove Lease." *Casper Star-Tribune*, March 10, 2005.

Simons, Fanny Fry. *An Enduring Legacy*. Vol. 6. Salt Lake City: Daughters of Utah Pioneers, 1983.

Spencer, Daniel. "Remarks" (October 5, 1856). *Deseret News*, October 15, 1856

Steward, Elizabeth White. Autobiography. In *Barnard White Family Book*, ed. Ruth Johnson and Glen F. Harding. Privately printed, 1967.

Tait, Anna F. Letter. *Millennial Star* 18:30, July 26, 1856.

Taylor, John. "Editorial Correspondence." *Mormon*, June 13, 1857 (from article dated May 30, 1857).

———. "Editorial Correspondence." *Mormon*, July 18, 1857.

———. "Emigration," *Mormon*, April 26, 1856.

———. Letter to Brigham Young, February 24, 1857. MS 1346.

Treseder, Charles M. "Correspondence from Great Salt Lake City." *Mormon*, November 29, 1856.

Turner, Lynne Slater, comp. *Emigrating Journals of the Willie and Martin Handcart Companies and the Hunt and Hodgett Wagon Trains*. Salt Lake City: privately printed, 1996.

Van Leer, Twila, and Linda Thomson. "Wagon Train Rolls on In." *Deseret News*, July 22, 1997.

Weinstein, Henry. "ACLU Sues over Mormon Lease." *Los Angeles Times*, March 5, 2005.

Young, Brigham. "Remarks." *Deseret News*, October 5, 1856.

———. "Remarks" (November 2, 1856). *Deseret News*, November 12, 1856.

———. "Remarks" (November 16, 1856). *Deseret News*, November 26, 1856 (reported by George D. Watt).

———. "Remarks." *Deseret News*, December 10, 1856, 320.

———. "Second General Epistle" (October 12, 1849). In J. A. Little, *From Kirtland to Salt Lake City*, 207–8. Salt Lake City, n.p. 1890.

SECONDARY SOURCES

Allen, James B. Ronald K. Esplin, and David J. Whittaker. *Men with a Mission, 1837–1841: The Quorum of the Twelve Apostles in the British Isles*. Salt Lake City: Deseret Book, 1992.

Bagley, Will. *Blood of the Prophets: Brigham Young and the Massacre at Mountain Meadows*. Norman: University of Oklahoma Press, 2002.

———. "'One Long Funeral March': A Revisionist's View of the Mormon Handcart Disasters." *Journal of Mormon History* 35, no. 1 (2009): 50–115.

———. *South Pass: Gateway to a Continent*. Norman: University of Oklahoma Press, 2014.

Bartholomew, Rebecca, and Leonard J. Arrington. *Rescue of the 1856 Handcart Companies*. Provo: Brigham Young University, Charles Redd Center for Western Studies, 1992; rev. ed. 1993.

Bennett, Richard E. *Mormons at the Missouri: Winter Quarters, 1846–1852*. Norman: University of Oklahoma Press, 1987.

———. *We'll Find the Place: The Mormon Exodus, 1846–1848*. Norman: University of Oklahoma Press, 2009 (originally published Salt Lake City: Deseret Book Company, 1997).

Bigler, David L. *Forgotten Kingdom: The Mormon Theocracy in the American West, 1847–1896*. Logan: University of Utah Press, 1998.

Bigler, David L., and Will Bagley. *The Mormon Rebellion: America's First Civil War*. Norman: University of Oklahoma Press, 2011.

Brinkerhoff, May, comp. *Our Family Heritage: History of Charles Alma Moulton & Rhoda Frances Duke Moulton Family.* Orem, Utah: Barney McKay Design Group, n.d.

Carter, Kate B., comp. *Heart Throbs of the West.* Vol. 6. Salt Lake City: Daughters of Utah Pioneers, 1945.

Carter, Lyndia McDowell. "Handcarts across Iowa: Trial Runs for the Willie, Haven, and Martin Handcart Companies." *Annals of Iowa* 65, nos. 2 & 3 (Spring–Summer 2006): 190–225.

Christensen, Allen C. *Before Zion: An Account of the 7th Handcart Company.* Springville, Utah: Council Press, 2004.

Doctrine and Covenants. Liverpool: n.p., 1845.

Faux, David. "Faint Footsteps of 1856–1857 Retraced: The Location of the Iowa Mormon Handcart Route." *Annals of Iowa* 65, nos. 2 & 3 (Spring–Summer 2006): 226–251.

Glass. Jefferson. *Reshaw: The Life and Times of John Baptist Richard.* Glendo, Wyo.: High Plains Press, 2014.

Hafen, Leroy R., and Ann W. Hafen. *Handcarts to Zion.* Lincoln: Bison Books, 1992 (originally published Glendale, Calif.: Arthur H. Clark Co., 1960).

———. *The Utah Expedition 1857–1858.* Glendale: Arthur H. Clark Co., 1982.

Hartley, William G. "The Place of Mormon Handcart Companies in America's Westward Migration Story." *Annals of Iowa* 65, nos. 2–3 (Spring–Summer 2006): 101–123.

Hicken, Verda. *Thomas Moulton History.* N.p.: Moulton Research Foundation, 1973.

Jensen, Andrew. *Encyclopedic History of the Church of Jesus Christ of Latter-day Saints.* Vol. 1. Salt Lake City: Genealogical Society, 1975.

Long, Gary Duane. *The Journey of the James G. Willie Handcart Company, October 1856.* Glenwood Springs, CO: privately printed, 2009.

Linforth, James, ed. *Route from Liverpool to Great Salt Lake Valley Illustrated.* With illustrations by Frederick Piercy, Liverpool: Franklin D. Richards; London: Latter-day Saints Book Depot, 1855.

Little, J. A. *From Kirtland to Salt Lake City.* Salt Lake City: n.p., 1890.

Lyman, Paul D. *The Willie Handcart Company: Their Day-by-Day Experiences, Including Trail Maps and Driving Directions.* Provo: Brigham Young University, 2006.

MacKinnon, William P. *At Sword's Point, Part 1: A Documentary History of the Utah War to 1858.* Norman: Arthur H. Clark Co., 2008.

———. *At Sword's Point, Part 2: A Documentary History of the Utah War, 1858–1859.* Norman, Okla.: Arthur H. Clark Co., 2016.

Madsen, Carol Cornwall. *Journey to Zion: Voices from the Mormon Trail.* Salt Lake City: Deseret Book Co., 1997.

Madsen, Susan Arrington. *I Walked to Zion: True Stories of Young Pioneers on the Mormon Trail.* Salt Lake City: Deseret Book Co., 1994.

———. *The Second Rescue: The Story of the Spiritual Rescue of the Willie and Martin Handcart Pioneers.* Orem, Utah: Brigham Distributing, 1998.

Michno, Gregory F., and Susan J. Michno. *Forgotten Fights: Little-Known Raids and Skirmishes on the Frontier, 1823 to 1890.* Missoula, Mont.: Mountain Press Publishing Co., 2008.

Moore, Beth S. *Bones in the Well: The Haun's Mill Massacre of 1838.* Norman: University of Oklahoma Press, 2012.

Mulder, William. *Homeward to Zion: The Mormon Migration from Scandinavia*. Minneapolis: University of Minnesota Press, 1957 (reprint 1985).

Olsen, Andrew D. *The Price We Paid: The Extraordinary Story of the Willie and Martin Handcart Pioneers*. Salt Lake City: Deseret Book Co., 2006.

Proctor, Maurine Jensen, and Scot Facer Proctor. *The Gathering: Mormon Pioneers on the Trail to Zion*. Salt Lake City: Deseret Book Co., 1996.

Rea, Tom. *Devil's Gate: Owning the Land, Owning the Story*. Norman: University of Oklahoma Press, 2006.

Roberts, David. *Devil's Gate: Brigham Young and the Great Mormon Handcart Tragedy*. New York: Simon and Schuster, 2008.

Schindler, Harold, *Porter Rockwell: Man of God/Son of Thunder*. Salt Lake City: University of Utah Press, 1993.

Slaughter, William W. and Michael Landon. *Trail of Hope: The Story of the Mormon Trail*. Salt Lake City: Shadow Mountain, 1997.

Smith, Don H. "Leadership, Planning, and Management of the 1856 Mormon Handcart Emigration." *Annals of Iowa* 65, nos. 2–3 (Spring–Summer 2006): 124–61.

Spencer, Thomas M. Ed. *The Missouri Mormon Experience*. Columbia: University of Missouri Press, 2010.

Stegner, Wallace. *The Gathering of Zion: The Story of the Mormon Trail*. Lincoln: University of Nebraska Press, 1964 (reprint, Bison Books, 1992).

Stenhouse, T. B. H. *The Rocky Mountain Saints: A Full and Complete History of Mormonism*. London: n.p., 1874.

Swinton, Heidi, and Lee Groberg. *Sweetwater Rescue: The Willie and Martin Handcart Story*. American Fork, Utah: Covenant Communications, 2006.

Tate, Michael L. *Indians and Emigrants: Encounters on the Overland Trails*. Norman: University of Oklahoma Press, 2014.

Woods, Fred E. "Iowa City Bound: Mormon Migration by Sail and Rail, 1856–1857." *Annals of Iowa* 65, nos. 2 & 3 (Spring–Summer 2006): 162–89.

INDEX

Musser, Amos, 150, 160, 161, 162, 189

Nauvoo, Ill., 3, 4, 6, 7, 18, 190
Nauvoo Legion, 159, 163
Nebraska, 11, 160; Fourth Handcart
  Company arrival in, 64, 65; Sandhills, 66
Nelson, Ben, 190
Neppress, George, 54
Newfoundland, 32
Newton, Iowa, 47
New York City, N.Y., 3, 38, 39, 40
New York Semi-Weekly Tribune, 128
New York Tribune, 129
Ninth Handcart Company, 175, 178, 180, 181,
  182
Noble, Eliza P., 154
North Platte River, 5, 79, 80, 81, 105, 112, 114,
  171, 181

Oborn, John, 19, 20, 27, 70, 80
Openshaw, Samuel, 23, 24, 31, 32, 36; railroad
  travel, 40
Oregon-California Trails Association, 187
Oregon Country, 5
Osborn, Daniel, 108, 109
overland trails, through Sweetwater valley, 118
overland travel, 44–58; children, 48; to Iowa
  City, Iowa, 41
ox-drawn wagons, 48, 162
oxen, 64, 73. *See also* cattle

Paiute Indians, 163
Park, Isabella, 52
Park, James P., 148
Parry, John, 47
passenger trains: to Iowa, 40; to New York
  City, 38; fares (New York), 39
Paxman, William, 37
permits for wagon trains, 193
Perpetual Emigrating Fund Company
  (PEF), 7, 8, 10, 13, 21, 39, 40, 138
personal possessions, discarding of, 63
physical demands, 184
Piercy, Frederick, 7, 93, *101*
Pietsch, Elizabeth, 191, 195, 196
Pietsch, Freddy, 191, 192, 194
Pikes Peakers, 168

Pinnock, Hugh, 190
Pioneer Company, 5, 6, 56
Pioneer Day, 159
plains, 105
Platte Bridge, 68
Platte River, 5, 66, 156, 167, 168, 169
political support, 158
Pollard, Sarah, 154
polygamy, 18, 158
Pony Express, 145
Poor Company, 8
Porter's Station, 161
Powell, John, 26, 27
Powell, Mary, 28, 29, 38
prairie chickens, 171
Pratt, Orson, 137
Pratt, Parley P., 3, 37, 41
prayer sessions, 77
Preator, Lora, 45
President's Office Journal (Young), 121
provisions. *See* supplies

Quincy, Ill., 42
Quorum of the Twelve Apostles, 4, 6

railroad travel, 39, 40. *See also* passenger
  trains
Rasmussen, Rasmine, 32
rations: complaints about lack of, 55, 56, 61;
  Fourth Handcart Company, 61; Third
  Handcart Company, 50. *See also* supplies
Rattlesnake Range, *103*, 120
rawhide, 70
Reader, James, 157
rebaptism, 18
Recording Angel, 82
records (church), departures from England,
  19
Red Buttes, 83, 113, 114, 115, 183
Reed, William, 67
religion, endorsement of, 188
replicas, handcarts, *104*
rescues, 108, 109, 110, 111, 114, 115, 117, 127, 128,
  134, 139. *See also* Martin Company (Fifth
  Handcart Company); Willie Company
  (Fourth Handcart Company)
resupplying, 11